STUDIES IN ANCIENT SOCIETY

Past and Present Series

GENERAL EDITOR: TREVOR ASTON

CONTRIBUTORS

E. L. Bowie
John Briscoe
P. A. Brunt
G. E. M. de Ste Croix
M. I. Finley
W. H. C. Frend

Peter Garnsey
Keith Hopkins
A. H. M. Jones
A. N. Sherwin-White
E. A. Thompson
P. R. C. Weaver

FORTHCOMING

The Intellectual Revolution of the
Seventeenth Century

edited by Charles Webster

STUDIES IN ANCIENT SOCIETY

Past and Present Series

GENERAL EDITOR: TREVOR ASTON

Edited by
M. I. FINLEY

ROUTLEDGE AND KEGAN PAUL
London and Boston

First published in 1974
by Routledge & Kegan Paul Ltd
Broadway House, 68–74 Carter Lane,
London EC4V 5EL and
9 Park Street,
Boston, Mass. 02108, U.S.A.

Printed in Great Britain by
Alden & Mowbray Ltd at the Alden Press, Oxford

ISBN 0 7100 7781 5

CONTENTS

CONTENTS

ABBREVIATIONS

AHR	*American Historical Review*
AJP	*American Journal of Philology*
CAH	*Cambridge Ancient History*
CIL	*Corpus Inscriptionum Latinarum*
CP	*Classical Philology*
CQ	*Classical Quarterly*
CR	*Classical Review*
EHR	*Economic History Review*
FGH	*Fragmente der griechischen Historiker*
GRBS	*Greek, Roman and Byzantine Studies*
HTR	*Harvard Theological Review*
IG	*Inscriptiones Graecae*
IGR	*Inscriptiones Graecae ad res Romanas pertinentes*
ILS	*Inscriptiones Latinae Selectae*
JEH	*Journal of Ecclesiastical History*
JHS	*Journal of Hellenic Studies*
JRS	*Journal of Roman Studies*
JTS	*Journal of Theological Studies*
PAPS	*Proceedings of the American Philosophical Society*
PBA	*Proceedings of the British Academy*
PCPS	*Proceedings of the Cambridge Philological Society*
RE	*Realencyclopädie der classischen Altertumswissenschaft*
REA	*Revue des Études Anciennes*
RH	*Revue Historique*
RSI	*Rivista Storica Italiana*
SEG	*Supplementum Epigraphicum Graecum*

ABBREVIATIONS

*SIG*³   *Sylloge Inscriptionum Graecarum*
TAPA *Transactions of the American Philological Association*
TAPS *Transactions of the American Philosophical Society*

INTRODUCTION

M. I. Finley

The first volume of essays from *Past and Present*, published in 1965, had a central theme, as its title indicates, *Crisis in Europe 1560–1660*. In the Introduction, the Master of Balliol, whose association with the journal goes back to its beginning, wrote that the contributors to *Crisis in Europe* 'would, I imagine, agree on few points except that it is the duty of the historian to explain, not merely to record'. And he stressed that change and movement were what especially required explanation, as was already said in the statement of aims published in the first issue.

The present volume has no single theme comparable to *Crisis in Europe*, and ranges over nearly a thousand years of Graeco-Roman history. Nevertheless, every contributor would not only accept Mr Hill's dictum but would also, I believe, accept the label 'structuralist'. By that I mean none of the different, and often incompatible, schools which have adopted that identification in recent decades, but something simpler and more elementary, namely, the view that neither institutions nor their transformations (past or present) can be understood except in their role within the social structure of their day, in the network of interrelationships that make up any complex society—and it is sometimes necessary to insist that these societies *were* complex. Few of the present contributors actually use the word 'structure', but what I have called structuralism is integral to their analyses, whether in the field of politics or law or in the study of social classes and social mobility or in the history of ideas and values.

Structuralism is not to be confused with 'vulgar sociology' or 'vulgar Marxism'. It is enough to note Mr Briscoe's carefully nuanced account of how Roman preference for oligarchies in the newly conquered territories was never allowed to override immediate political-imperial considerations; Mr de Ste Croix's conclusions that the 'main motives' behind the governmental persecutions of the Christians were 'in the long run essentially religious'; or Professor Thompson's insistence that the revolts of peasants and slaves in Gaul and Spain, extending over several centuries, 'released no new productive forces' and 'included no new mode of social existence' among their ideas. Structuralism throws up questions to be answered, often new questions about old and even well-worn topics; it does not provide the answers. Most of the articles are in fact devoted to familiar subjects—Athenian politics, the Roman conquest of the east, violence in the later Roman Republic, the Second Sophistic and the persecutions. Yet without exception the authors have produced fresh and original analyses and explanations, and some of the articles have already, in a very few years, generated important research by other ancient historians.

Because there is no central theme, it seemed best to arrange the essays in a roughly, though not pedantically, chronological order, even though this left me in the embarrassing position of opening the volume with two articles of my own. The heavy concentration on the Roman Empire becomes immediately apparent. In part this is accidental, but not entirely so: it also reflects the way British scholarship in ancient history has developed in the post-war years, in the sense that more work has been done of an explanatory, structuralist nature on the Roman Empire than on either Greece or the earlier period in Roman history. It is also striking that the studies of the Empire constantly look ahead to the end of the ancient world, as much as, and perhaps more than, they look backwards in time for complicated evolutionary explanations. (I say 'British scholarship' because, despite the welcome *Past and Present* offers to historians elsewhere, ancient historians abroad have failed to respond, preferring to publish in classical journals.)

Following the precedent set in *Crisis in Europe*, authors were asked to retain their original text, making only such corrections as were indispensable, and adding brief bibliographical supplements when desirable. Dr Dorothy Crawford of Girton College, Cambridge, was kind enough to revise the notes for the chapter 'The Roman Colonate' by the late Professor A. H. M. Jones.

I

ATHENIAN DEMAGOGUES[*][1]

M. I. Finley

When the news of their defeat in Sicily in 413 B.C. reached the Athenians, they received it with disbelief. Then came the realization of the full scale of the disaster, and the people, writes Thucydides, 'were indignant with the orators who had joined in promoting the expedition, as if they [the people] had not themselves decreed it [in assembly]'.[2] To this George Grote made the following rejoinder:[3]

> From these latter words, it would seem that Thucydides considered the Athenians, after having adopted the expedition by their votes, to have debarred themselves from the right of complaining of those speakers who had stood forward prominently to advise the step. I do not at all concur in his opinion. The adviser of any important measure always makes himself morally responsible for its justice, usefulness, and practicability; and he very properly incurs disgrace, more or less according to the case, if it turns out to present results totally contrary to those which he had predicted.

These two opposing quotations raise all the fundamental prob-

*From no. 21 (1962).
1 This is a revised text of a paper to the Hellenic Society in London on 25 March 1961, of which a shortened version was broadcast on the Third Programme of the BBC and published in the *Listener* of 5 and 12 October 1961. I am grateful to Professors A. Andrewes and A. H. M. Jones, Messrs P. A. Brunt and M. J. Cowling for advice and criticism.
2 Thuc., 8.1.1.
3 *A History of Greece*, new edn (London, 1862), v, p. 317 n. 3.

lems inherent in the Athenian democracy, the problems of policy-making and leadership, of decisions and the responsibility for them. Unfortunately Thucydides tells us very little about the orators who successfully urged on the Assembly the decision to mount the great invasion of Sicily. In fact, he tells us nothing concrete about the meeting, other than that the people were given misinformation by a delegation from the Sicilian city of Segesta and by their own envoys just returned from Sicily, and that most of those who voted were so ignorant of the relevant facts that they did not even know the size of the island or of its population. Five days later a second Assembly was held to authorize the necessary armament. The general Nicias took the opportunity to seek a reversal of the whole programme. He was opposed by a number of speakers, Athenian and Sicilian, neither named by the historian nor described in any way, and by Alcibiades, who is given a speech which throws much light on Thucydides himself and on his judgment of Alcibiades, but scarcely any on the issues, whether the immediate ones being debated or the broader ones of democratic procedure and leadership. The result was a complete defeat for Nicias. Everyone, Thucydides admits, was now more eager than before to go ahead with the plan—the old and the young, the hoplite soldiers (who were drawn from the wealthier half of the citizenry) and the common people alike. The few who remained opposed, he concludes, refrained from voting lest they appeared unpatriotic.[4]

The wisdom of the Sicilian expedition is a very difficult matter. Thucydides himself had more than one view at different times in his life. However, he seems not to have changed his mind about the orators: they promoted the expedition for the wrong reasons and they gained the day by playing on the ignorance and emotions of the Assembly. Alcibiades, he says, pressed hardest of all, because he wished to thwart Nicias, because he was personally ambitious and hoped to gain fame and wealth from his general-ship in the campaign, and because his extravagant and licentious tastes were more expensive than he could really afford. Else-where, writing in more general terms, Thucydides says this:[5]

[Under Pericles] the government was a democracy in name

[4] Thuc., 6.1–25.
[5] Thuc., 2.65.9–11.

but in reality rule by the first citizen. His successors were more equal to each other, and each seeking to become the first man they even offered the conduct of affairs to the whims of the people. This, as was to be expected in a great state ruling an empire, produced many blunders.

In short, after the death of Pericles Athens fell into the hands of demagogues and was ruined. Thucydides does not use the word 'demagogue' in any of the passages I have been discussing. It is an uncommon word with him,[6] as it is in Greek literature generally, and that fact may come as a surprise, for there is no more familiar theme in the Athenian picture (despite the rarity of the word) than the demagogue and his adjutant, the sycophant. The demagogue is a bad thing: to 'lead the people' is to mislead— above all, to mislead by failing to lead. The demagogue is driven by self-interest, by the desire to advance himself in power, and through power, in wealth. To achieve this, he surrenders all principles, all genuine leadership, and he panders to the people in every way—in Thucydides' words, 'even offering the conduct of affairs to the whims of the people'. This picture is drawn not only directly, but also in reverse. Here, for example, is Thucydides' image of the right kind of leader:[7]

> Because of his prestige, intelligence, and known incorruptibility with respect to money, Pericles was able to lead the people as a free man should. He led them instead of being led by them. He did not have to humour them in the pursuit of power; on the contrary, his repute was such that he could contradict them and provoke their anger.

This was not everyone's judgment. Aristotle puts the break-down earlier: it was after Ephialtes took away the power of the Council of the Areopagus that the passion for demagogy set in. Pericles, he continues, first acquired political influence by prose-cuting Cimon for malfeasance in office; he energetically pursued a policy of naval power, 'which gave the lower classes the audacity to take over the leadership in politics more and more'; and he introduced pay for jury service, thus bribing the people with their own money. These were demagogic practices and they brought

---

[6] Used only in 4.21.3, and 'demagogy' in 8.65.2.
[7] Thuc., 2.65.8.

3

Pericles to power, which, Aristotle agrees, he then used well and properly.[8]

But my interest is neither in evaluating Pericles as an individual nor in examining the lexicography of demagogy. The Greek political vocabulary was normally vague and imprecise, apart from formal titles for individual offices or bodies (and often enough not even then). The word *demos* was itself ambiguous; among its meanings, however, was one which came to dominate literary usage, namely 'the common people', 'the lower classes', and that sense provided the overtones in 'demagogues'—they became leaders of the state thanks to the backing of the common people. All writers accepted the need for political leadership as axiomatic; their problem was to distinguish between good and bad types. With respect to Athens and its democracy, the word 'demagogue' understandably became the simplest way of identifying the bad type, and it does not matter in the least whether the word appears in any given text or not. I suppose it was Aristophanes who established the model in his portrayal of Cleon, yet he never directly applied the noun 'demagogue' to him or anyone else;[9] similarly with Thucydides, who surely thought that Cleophon, Hyperbolus, and some, if not all, of the orators responsible for the Sicilian disaster were demagogues, but who never attached the word to any of these men.

It is important to stress the word 'type', for the issue raised by Greek writers is one of the essential *qualities* of the leader, not (except very secondarily) his techniques or technical competence, not even (except in a very generalized way) his programme and policies. The crucial distinction is between the man who gives leadership with nothing else in mind but the good of the state, and the man whose self-interest makes his own position paramount and urges him to pander to the people. The former may make a mistake and adopt the wrong policy in any given situation; the latter may at times make sound proposals, as when Alcibiades dis-

---

[8] *Const. of Athens*, 27–28; cf. *Pol.*, 2.9.3 (1274a3–10). A. W. Gomme, *A Historical Commentary on Thucydides* (Oxford, 1956), ii p. 193, points out that 'Plutarch divided Perikles' political career sharply into two halves, the first when he did use base demagogic arts to gain power, the second when he had gained it and used it nobly'.

[9] Aristophanes uses 'demagogy' and 'demagogic' once each in the *Knights*, lines 191 and 217, respectively. Otherwise in his surviving plays there is only the verb 'to be a demagogue', also used once (*Frogs*, 419).

4

suaded the fleet at Samos from jeopardizing the naval position by rushing back to Athens in 411 B.C. to overthrow the oligarchs who had seized power there, an action to which Thucydides gave explicit approval.[10] But these are not fundamental distinctions. Nor are other traits attributed to individual demagogues: Cleon's habit of shouting when addressing the Assembly, personal dishonesty in money matters, and so on. Such things merely sharpen the picture. From Aristophanes to Aristotle, the attack on the demagogues always falls back on the one central question: in whose interest does the leader lead?

Behind this formulation of the question lay three propositions. The first is that men are unequal—both in their moral worth and capability and in their social and economic status. The second is that any community tends to divide into factions, the most fundamental of which are the rich and well-born on one side, the poor on the other, each with its own qualities, potentialities, and interests. The third proposition is that the well-ordered and well-run state is one which overrides faction and serves as an instrumentality for the good life.

Faction is the greatest evil and the most common danger. 'Faction' is a conventional English translation of the Greek *stasis*, one of the most remarkable words to be found in any language. Its root-sense is 'placing', 'setting' or 'stature', 'station'. Its range of political meanings can best be illustrated by merely stringing out the definitions to be found in the lexicon: 'party', 'party formed for seditious purposes', 'faction', 'sedition', 'discord', 'division', 'dissent', and, finally, a well-attested meaning which the lexicon incomprehensibly omits, namely, 'civil war' or 'revolution'. Unlike 'demagogue', *stasis* is a very common word in the literature, and its connotation is regularly pejorative. Oddly enough, it is also the most neglected concept in modern study of Greek history. It has not been observed often enough or sharply enough, I believe, that there must be deep significance in the fact that a word which has the original sense of 'station' or 'position', and which, in abstract logic, could have an equally neutral sense when used in a political context, in practice does nothing of the kind, but immediately takes on the nastiest overtones. A political position, a partisan position—that is the inescapable implication—is a bad

[10] Thuc., 8.86.

thing, leading to sedition, civil war, and the disruption of the social fabric.[11] And this same tendency is repeated throughout the language. There is no eternal law, after all, why 'demagogue', a 'leader of the people', must become 'mis-leader of the people'. Or why *hetairia*, an old Greek word which meant, among other things, 'club' or 'society', should in fifth-century Athens have come simultaneously to mean 'conspiracy', 'seditious organization'. Whatever the explanation, it lies not in philology but in Greek society itself.

No one who has read the Greek political writers can have failed to notice the unanimity of approach in this respect. Whatever the disagreements among them, they all insist that the state must stand outside class or other factional interests. Its aims and objectives are moral ones, timeless and universal, and they can be achieved— more correctly, approached or approximated—only by education, moral conduct (especially on the part of those in authority), morally correct legislation, and the choice of the right governors. The existence of classes and interests as an empirical fact is, of course, not denied. What is denied is that the choice of political goals can legitimately be linked with these classes and interests, or that the good of the state can be advanced except by ignoring (if not suppressing) private interests.

It was Plato, of course, who pursued this line of its reasoning to its most radical solutions. In the *Gorgias* he had argued that not even the great Athenian political figures of the past—Miltiades, Themistocles, Cimon and Pericles—were true statesmen. They had merely been more accomplished than their successors in gratifying the desires of the *demos* with ships and walls and dockyards. They had failed to make the citizens better men, and to call them 'statesmen' was therefore to confuse the pastrycook with the doctor.[12] Then, in the *Republic*, Plato proposed to concentrate all power in the hands of a small, select, appropriately educated class, who were to be freed from all special interests by the most radical measures, by the abolition insofar as they were concerned of both private property and the family. Only under those conditions

---

[11] The only systematic analysis known to me, and that a brief one, is the inaugural lecture of D. Loenen, *Stasis* (Amsterdam, 1953). He saw, contrary to the view most common among modern writers, that 'illegality is precisely not the *constant* element in *stasis*' (p. 5).

[12] *Gorgias*, 502E–519D.

would they behave as perfect moral agents, leading the state to its proper goals without the possibility that any self-interest might intrude. Plato, to be sure, was the most untypical of men. One does not safely generalize from Plato; not only not to all Greeks, but not even to any other single Greek. Who else shared his passionate conviction that qualified experts—philosophers—could make (and should therefore be empowered to enforce) universally correct and authoritative decisions about the good life, the life of virtue, which was the sole end of the state?[13] Yet on the one point with which I am immediately concerned—private interests and the state—Plato stood on common ground with many Greek writers (much as they disagreed with him on the answers). In the great final scene of Aeschylus' *Eumenides* the chorus expresses the doctrine explicitly: the welfare of the state can rest only on harmony and freedom from faction. Thucydides implies this more than once.[14] And it underlies the theory of the mixed constitution as we find it in Aristotle's *Politics*.

The most empirical of Greek philosophers, Aristotle collected vast quantities of data about the actual workings of Greek states, including facts about *stasis*. The *Politics* includes an elaborate taxonomy of *stasis*, and even advice on how *stasis* can be avoided under a variety of conditions. But Aristotle's canons and goals were ethical, his work a branch of moral philosophy. He viewed political behaviour teleologically, according to the moral ends which are man's by his nature; and those ends are subverted if the governors make their decisions out of personal or class interest. That is the test by which he distinguished between the three 'right' forms of government ('according to absolute justice') and their degenerate forms: monarchy becomes tyranny when an individual rules in his own interest rather than in the interest of the whole state, aristocracy similarly becomes oligarchy, and polity becomes democracy (or, in the language of Polybius, democracy becomes mob-rule).[15] Among democracies, furthermore, those in rural communities will be superior because farmers are too occupied to bother with meetings, whereas urban craftsmen and shop-

---

[13] See R. Bambrough, 'Plato's political analogies', in *Philosophy, Politics and Society*, ed. Peter Laslett (Oxford, 1956), pp. 98–115.

[14] It is developed most fully in his long account (3.69–85) of the *stasis* in Corcyra in 427 B.C.

[15] Arist., *Pol.*, 3.4–5 (1278b–79b), 4.6–7 (1293b–94b); Polyb., 6.3–9.

keepers find it easy to attend, and such people 'are generally a bad lot'.[16]

On this matter of special interest and general interest, of faction and concord, the available exceptions to the line of thinking I have summarized are strikingly few and unrewarding. One deserves particular mention, and that, ironically enough, is the pamphlet on the Athenian state by an anonymous writer of the later half of the fifth century B.C. who now generally goes under the too amiable label of the Old Oligarch. This work is a diatribe against the democracy, hammering at the theme that the system is a bad one because all its actions are determined by the interests of the poorer (inferior) sections of the citizenry. The argument is familiar enough; what gives the pamphlet its unusual interest is this conclusion:[17]

As for the Athenian system of government, I do not like it. However, since they decided to become a democracy, it seems to me that they are preserving the democracy well by the methods I have described.

In other words, the strength of the Athenian government comes precisely from that which many merely criticize, namely, the fact that it is government by a faction acting unashamedly to its own advantage.

The great difference between political analysis and moral judgment could not be better exemplified. Do not be misled, says the Old Oligarch in effect: I and some of you dislike democracy, but a reasoned consideration of the facts shows that what we condemn on moral grounds is very strong as a practical force, and its strength lies in its immorality. This is a very promising line of investigation, but it was not pursued in antiquity. Instead, those thinkers whose orientation was anti-democratic persisted in their concentration on political philosophy. And those who sided with the democracy? A. H. M. Jones has recently tried to formulate the democratic theory from the fragmentary evidence available in the surviving literature, most of it from the fourth century.[18] Still more recently, Eric Havelock made a massive attempt to discover what he calls the 'liberal temper' in fifth-century Athenian politics,

[16] Arist., *Pol.*, 6.2.7–8 (1319a); cf. Xen., *Hell.*, 5.2.5–7.
[17] Pseudo-Xenophon, *Const. of Athens*, 3.1; see A. Fuks, 'The "Old Oligarch"', *Scripta Hierosolymitana*, i (1954), pp. 21–35.
[18] *Athenian Democracy* (Oxford, 1957), ch. iii.

chiefly from the fragments of the pre-Socratic philosophers. In reviewing his book, Momigliano suggested that the effort was foredoomed because 'it is not absolutely certain that a well-articulated democratic idea existed in the fifth century'.[19] I go further: I do not believe that an articulated democratic theory ever existed in Athens. There were notions, maxims, generalities—which Jones has assembled—but they do not add up to a systematic theory. And why indeed should they? It is a curious fallacy to suppose that every social or governmental system in history must necessarily have been accompanied by an elaborate theoretical system. Where that does occur it is often the work of lawyers, and Athens had no jurists in the proper sense. Or it may be the work of philosophers, but the systematic philosophers of this period had a set of concepts and values incompatible with democracy. The committed democrats met the attack by ignoring it, by going about the business of conducting their political affairs according to their own notions, but without writing treatises on what they were about. None of this, however, is a reason why we should not attempt to make the analysis the Athenians failed to make for themselves.

No account of the Athenian democracy can have any validity if it overlooks four points, each obvious in itself, yet all four taken together, I venture to say, are rarely given sufficient weight in modern accounts. The first is that this was a direct democracy, and however much such a system may have in common with representative democracy, the two differ in certain fundamental respects, and particularly on the very issues with which I am here concerned. The second point is what Ehrenberg calls the 'narrowness of space' of the Greek city-state, an appreciation of which, he has rightly stressed, is crucial to an understanding of its political life.[20] The implications were summed up by Aristotle in a famous passage:[21]

> A state composed of too many . . . will not be a true state, for the simple reason that it can hardly have a true constitution. Who can be the general of a mass so excessively large? And who can be herald, except Stentor?

[19] E. A. Havelock, *The Liberal Temper in Greek Politics* (London, 1957), reviewed by A. Momigliano in *RSI*, lxxii (1960), pp. 534–41.
[20] *Aspects of the Ancient World* (Oxford, 1946), pp. 40–5.
[21] *Pol.*, 7.4.7 (1326b3–7).

The third point is that the Assembly was the crown of the system, possessing the right and the power to make all the policy decisions, in actual practice with few limitations, whether of precedent or scope. (Strictly speaking there was appeal from the Assembly to the popular courts with their large lay membership. Nevertheless, I ignore the courts in much, though not all, of what follows, because I believe, as the Athenians did themselves, that, though they complicated the practical mechanism of politics, the courts were an expression, not a reduction, of the absolute power of the people functioning directly: and because I believe that the operational analysis I am trying to make would not be significantly altered and would perhaps be obscured if in this brief compass I did not concentrate on the Assembly.) The Assembly, finally, was nothing other than an open-air mass meeting on the hill called the Pnyx, and the fourth point therefore is that we are dealing with problems of crowd behaviour; its psychology, its laws of behaviour, could not have been identical with those of the small group, or even of the larger kind of body of which a modern parliament is an example (though, it must be admitted, we can do little more today than acknowledge their existence).

Who were the Assembly? That is a question we cannot answer satisfactorily. Every male citizen automatically became eligible to attend when he reached his eighteenth birthday, and he retained that privilege to his death (except for the very small number who lost their civic rights for one reason or another). In Pericles' time the number eligible was of the order of 45,000. Women were excluded; so were the fairly numerous non-citizens who were free men, nearly all of them Greeks, but outsiders in the political sphere; and so were the far more numerous slaves. All figures are a guess, but it would not be wildly inaccurate to suggest that the adult male citizens comprised about one sixth of the total population (taking town and countryside together). But the critical question to be determined is which four or five or six thousand of the 45,000 actually went to meetings. It is reasonable to imagine that under normal conditions the attendance came chiefly from the urban residents. Fewer peasants would often have taken the journey in order to attend a meeting of the Assembly.[22] Therefore one large section of the eligible population was, with respect to direct

[22] That Aristotle drew very important conclusions from this state of affairs has already been indicated, at note 16.

participation, excluded. That is something to know, but it does not get us far enough. We can guess, for example, with the aid of a few hints in the sources, that the composition was normally weighted on the side of the more aged and the more well-to-do men—but that is only a guess, and the degree of weighting is beyond even guessing.

Still, one important fact can be fixed, namely, that each meeting of the Assembly was unique in its composition. There was no membership in the Assembly as such, only membership in a given Assembly on a given day. Perhaps the shifts were not significant from meeting to meeting in quiet, peaceful times when no vital issues were being debated. Yet even then an important element of predictability was lacking. When he entered the Assembly, no policy-maker could be quite sure that a change in the composition of the audience had not occurred, whether through accident or through more or less organized mobilization of some particular sector of the population, which could tip the balance of the votes against a decision made at a previous meeting. And times were often neither peaceful nor normal. In the final decade of the Peloponnesian War, to take an extreme example, the whole rural population was compelled to abandon the countryside and live within the city walls. It is beyond reasonable belief that during this period there was not a larger proportion of countrymen at meetings than was normal. A similar situation prevailed for briefer periods at other times, when an enemy army was operating in Attica. We need not interpret Aristophanes literally when he opens the *Acharnians* with a soliloquy by a farmer who is sitting in the Pnyx waiting for the Assembly to begin and saying to himself how he hates the city and everyone in it and how he intends to shout down any speaker who proposes anything except peace. But Cleon could not have afforded the luxury of ignoring this strange element seated on the hillside before him. They might upset a policy line which he had been able to carry while the Assembly was filled only with city-dwellers.

The one clearcut instance came in the year 411. Then the Assembly was terrorized into voting the democracy out of existence, and it was surely no accident that this occurred at a time when the fleet was fully mobilized and stationed on the island of Samos. The citizens who served in the navy were drawn from the poor and they were known to be the staunchest supporters of the democratic system in its late fifth-century form. Being in Samos, they could not be in Athens, thus enabling the oligarchs to win the day through a majority in the Assembly which was not only a minority of the eligible members but an untypical minority. Our sources do not permit us to study the history of Athenian policy systematically with such knowledge at our disposal, but surely the men who led Athens were acutely aware of the possibility of a change in the composition of the Assembly, and included it in their tactical calculations.

Each meeting, furthermore, was complete in itself. Granted that much preparatory work was done by the Council (*boule*), that informal canvassing took place, and that there were certain devices to control and check frivolous or irresponsible motions, it is nevertheless true that the normal procedure was for a proposal to be introduced, debated, and either passed (with or without amendment) or rejected in a single continuous sitting. We must reckon, therefore, not only with narrowness of space but also with narrowness of time, and with the pressures that generated, especially on leaders (and would-be leaders). I have already mentioned the case of the Sicilian expedition, which was decided in principle on one day and then planned, so to speak, five days later when the scale and cost were discussed and voted. Another kind of case is that of the well-known Mytilene debate. Early in the Peloponnesian War the city of Mytilene revolted from the Athenian Empire. The rebellion was crushed and the Athenian Assembly decided to make an example of the Mytileneans by putting the entire male population to death. Revulsion of feeling set in at once, the issue was reopened at another meeting the very next day, and the decision was reversed.[23] Cleon, at that time the most important political figure in Athens, advocated the policy of frightfulness. The second Assembly was a personal defeat for him —he had participated in the debates on both days—though he seems not to have lost his status even temporarily as a result (as he well might have). But how does one measure the psychological effect on him of such a twenty-four hour reversal? How does one estimate not only its impact, but also his awareness all through his career as a leader that such a possibility was a constant factor in Athenian politics? I cannot answer such questions concretely, but I submit that the weight could have been no light one. Cleon

[23] Thuc., 3.27–50.

surely appreciated, as we cannot, what it promised for men like himself that in the second year of the Peloponnesian War, when morale was temporarily shattered by the plague, the people turned on Pericles, fined him heavily, and deposed him for a brief period from the office of general.[24] If this could happen to Pericles, who was immune?

In the Mytilene case Thucydides' account suggests that Cleon's was a lost cause the second day, that he tried to persuade the Assembly to abandon a course of action which they intended to pursue from the moment the session opened, and that he failed. But the story of the meeting in 411, as Thucydides tells it, is a different one. Peisander began the day with the feeling against his proposal that the introduction of an oligarchical form of government should be considered, and he ended it with a victory. The actual debate had swung enough votes to give him a majority.[25]

Debate designed to win votes among an outdoor audience numbering several thousands means oratory, in the strict sense of the word. It was therefore perfectly precise language to call political leaders 'orators', as a synonym and not merely, as we might do, as a mark of the particular skill of a particular political figure. Under Athenian conditions, however, much more is implied. The picture of the Assembly I have been trying to draw suggests not only oratory, but also a 'spontaneity' of debate and decision which parliamentary democracy lacks, at least in our day.[26] Everyone, speakers and audience alike, knew that before night fell the issue must be decided, that each man present would vote 'freely' (without fear of whips or other party controls) and purposefully, and therefore that every speech, every argument must seek to persuade the audience on the spot, that it was all a serious performance, as a whole and in each of its parts.

I place the word 'freely' in inverted commas, for the last thing I wish to imply is the activity of a free, disembodied rational faculty, that favourite illusion of so much political theory since the Enlightenment. Members of the Assembly were free from the controls which bind the members of a parliament: they held no office, they were not elected, and therefore they could neither be

[24] Thuc., 2.65.1–4.
[25] Thuc., 8.53–54.
[26] See the valuable article by O. Reverdin, 'Remarques sur la vie politique d'Athènes au Ve siècle', *Museum Helveticum*, ii (1945), pp. 201–12.

punished nor rewarded for their voting records. But they were not free from the human condition, from habit and tradition, from the influences of family and friends, of class and status, of personal experiences, resentments, prejudices, values, aspirations, and fears, much of it in the subconscious. These they took with them when they went up on the Pnyx, and with these they listened to the debates and made up their minds, under conditions very different from the voting practices of our day. There is a vast difference between voting on infrequent occasions for a man or a party on the one hand, and on the other hand voting every few days directly on the issues themselves. In Aristotle's time the Assembly met at least four times in each thirty-six day period. Whether this was also the rule in the fifth century is not known, but there were occasions, as during the Peloponnesian War, when meetings took place even more frequently. Then there were the two other factors I have already mentioned, the smallness of the Athenian world, in which every member of the Assembly knew personally many others sitting on the Pnyx, and the mass-meeting background of the voting—a situation virtually unrelated to the impersonal act of marking a voting paper in physical isolation from every other voter; an act we perform, furthermore, with the knowledge that millions of other men and women are simultaneously doing the same thing in many places, some of them hundreds of miles distant. When, for example, Alcibiades and Nicias rose in the Assembly in 415, the one to propose the expedition against Sicily, the other to argue against it, each knew that, should the motion be carried, one or both would be asked to command in the field. And in the audience there were many who were being asked to vote on whether they, personally, were to march out in a few days, as officers, soldiers, or members of the fleet. Such examples can be duplicated in a number of other, scarcely less vital areas: taxation, food supply, pay for jury duty, extension of the franchise, laws of citizenship, and so on.

To be sure, much of the activity of the Assembly was in a lower key, largely occupied with technical measures (such as cult regulations) or ceremonial acts (such as honorary decrees for a great variety of individuals). It would be a mistake to imagine Athens as a city in which week in and week out great issues dividing the population were being debated and decided. But on the other hand, there were very few single years (and certainly no ten-year periods) in which some great issue did not arise: the two Persian invasions, the long series of measures which completed the process of democratization, the Empire, the Peloponnesian War (which occupied twenty-seven years) and its two oligarchic interludes, the endless diplomatic manoeuvres and wars of the fourth century, with their attendant fiscal crises, all culminating in the decades of Philip and Alexander. It did not often happen, as it did to Cleon in the dispute over Mytilene, that a politician was faced with a repeat performance the following day; but the Assembly did meet constantly, without long periods of holiday or recess. The week-by-week conduct of a war, for example, had to go before the Assembly week by week; as if Winston Churchill were to have been compelled to take a referendum before each move in World War II, and then to face another vote after the move was made, in the Assembly or the law-courts, to determine not merely what the next step should be but also whether he was to be dismissed and his plans abandoned, or even whether he was to be held criminally culpable, subject to a fine or exile or, conceivably, the death penalty either for the proposal itself or for the way the previous move had been carried out. It was part of the Athenian governmental system that, in addition to the endless challenge in the Assembly, a politician was faced, equally without respite, with the threat of politically inspired lawsuits.[27]

If I insist on the psychological aspect, it is not to ignore the considerable political experience of many men who voted in the Assembly—gained in the Council, the law-courts, the demes, and the Assembly itself—nor is it merely to counter what I have called the disembodied-rationalism conception. I want to stress something very positive, namely, the intense degree of involvement which attendance at the Athenian Assembly entailed. And this intensity was equally (or even more strongly) the case among the orators, for each vote judged them as well as the issue to be decided on. If I had to choose one word which best characterized the condition of being a political leader in Athens, that word would

---

[27] P. Cloché, 'Les hommes politiques et la justice populaire dans l'Athènes du IVe siècle', *Historia*, ix (1960), pp. 80–95, has recently argued that this threat is exaggerated by modern historians, at least for the fourth century. Useful as his assembling of the evidence is, he lays too much stress on the argument from silence, whereas the sources are far from full enough to bear such statistical weight.

be 'tension'. In some measure that is true of all politicians who are subject to a vote. 'The desperateness of politics and government' is R. B. McCallum's telling phrase, which he then developed in this way:[28]

> Certainly a note of cynicism and weariness with the manoeuvres and posturings of party politicians is natural and to an extent proper to discerning dons and civil servants, who can reflect independently and at leisure on the doings of their harried masters in government. But this seems to arise from a deliberate rejection . . . of the aims and ideals of party statesmen and their followers and the continual responsibility for the security and well-being in the state. For one thing party leaders are in some sense apostles, although all may not be Gladstones; there are policies to which they dedicate themselves and policies which alarm and terrify them.

I believe this to be a fair description of Athenian leaders, too, despite the absence of political parties, equally applicable to Themistocles as to Aristides, to Pericles as to Cimon, to Cleon as to Nicias; for, it should be obvious, this kind of judgment is independent of any judgment about the merits or weaknesses of a particular programme or policy. More accurately, I should have said that this understates the case for the Athenians. Their leaders had *no* respite. Because their influence had to be earned and exerted directly and immediately—this was a necessary consequence of a direct, as distinct from a representative, democracy—they had to lead in person, and they had also to bear, in person, the brunt of the opposition's attacks. More than that, they walked alone. They had their lieutenants, of course, and politicians made alliances with each other. But these were fundamentally personal links, shifting frequently, useful in helping to carry through a particular measure or even a group of measures, but lacking that quality of support, that buttressing or cushioning effect, which is provided by a bureaucracy and political party, in another way by an institutionalized Establishment like the Roman Senate, or in still another way by large-scale patronage as in the Roman clientage system. The critical point is that there was no 'government' in the modern sense. There were posts and offices, but none had any standing in the Assembly. A man was a leader solely as a function

[28] A review in the *Listener* (2 February 1961), p. 233.

of his personal, and in the literal sense, unofficial status within the Assembly itself. The test of whether or not he held that status was simply whether the Assembly did or did not vote as he wished, and therefore the test was repeated with each proposal.

These were the conditions which faced all leaders in Athens, not merely those whom Thucydides and Plato dismissed as 'demagogues', not merely those whom some modern historians miscall 'radical democrats', but everyone, aristocrat or commoner, altruist or self-seeker, able or incompetent, who, in George Grote's phrase, 'stood forward prominently to advise' the Athenians. No doubt the motives which moved men to stand forward varied greatly. But that does not matter in this context, for each one of them without exception, *chose* to aspire to, and actively to work and contest for, leadership, knowing just what that entailed, including the risks. Within narrow limits, they all had to use the same techniques, too. Cleon's platform manner may have been inelegant and boisterous, but how serious is Aristotle's remark that he was the first man to 'shout and rail'?[29] Are we to imagine that Thucydides the son of Melesias (and kinsman of the historian) and Nicias whispered when they addressed the Assembly in opposition to Pericles and Cleon, respectively? Thucydides, who brought his upper-class backers into the Assembly and seated them to form a claque?[30]

This is obviously a frivolous approach, nothing more than the expression of class prejudice and snobbishness. As Aristotle noted, the death of Pericles marked a turning-point in the social history of Athenian leadership. Until then they seem to have been drawn from the old aristocratic landed families, including the men who were responsible for carrying out the reforms which completed the democracy. After Pericles a new class of leaders emerged.[31] Despite the familiar prejudicial references to Cleon the tanner or Cleophon the lyre-maker, these were in fact not poor men, not craftsmen and labourers turned politician, but men of means who differed from their predecessors in their ancestry and their outlook, and who provoked resentment and hostility for their

[29] Arist., *Const.*, 28.3.
[30] Plut., *Pericles*, 11.2. It was against such tactics that the restored democracy in 410 required members of the Council to swear to take their seats by lot: Philochorus 328 F 140 (in *FHG*, ed. F. Jacoby).
[31] Arist., *Const.*, 28.1.

presumption in breaking the old monopoly of leadership. When such attitudes are under discussion, one can always turn to Xenophon to find the lowest level of explanation (which is not therefore necessarily the wrong one). One of the most important of the new leaders was a man called Anytus, who, like Cleon before him, drew his wealth from a slave tannery. Anytus had a long and distinguished career, but he was also the chief actor in the prosecution of Socrates. What is Xenophon's explanation? Simply that Socrates had publicly berated Anytus for bringing up his son to follow in his trade instead of educating him as a proper gentleman, and that Anytus, in revenge for this personal insult, had Socrates tried and executed.[32]

None of this is to deny that there were very fundamental issues behind the thick façade of prejudice and abuse. Throughout the fifth century there were the twin issues of democracy (or oligarchy) and empire, brought to a climax in the Peloponnesian War. Defeat in the war ended the empire and it soon also ended the debate about the kind of government Athens was to have. Oligarchy ceased to be a serious issue in practical politics. It is only the persistence of the philosophers which creates an illusion about it; they continued to argue fifth-century issues in the fourth century, but politically in a vacuum. Down to the middle of the fourth century, the actual policy questions were perhaps less dramatic than before, though not necessarily less vital to the participants—such matters as navy finance, foreign relations both with Persia and with other Greek states, and the ever-present problem of corn supply. Then came the final great conflict, over the rising power of Macedon. That debate went on for some three decades, and it ended only in the year following the death of Alexander the Great when the Macedonian army put an end to democracy itself in Athens.

All these were questions about which men could legitimately disagree, and disagree with passion. On the issues, the arguments of (say) Plato require earnest consideration—but only insofar as he addressed himself to the issues. The injection of the charge of demagogy into the polemic amounts to a resort to the very same unacceptable debating tricks for which the so-called demagogues are condemned. Suppose, for example, that Thucydides was right in attributing Alcibiades' advocacy of the Sicilian expedition to his

[32] Xen., *Apology*, 30–2. See generally Georges Méautis, *L'aristocratie athénienne* (Paris, 1927).

personal extravagance and to various discreditable private motives. What relevance has that to the merits of the proposal itself? Would the Sicilian expedition, as a war measure, have been a better idea if Alcibiades had been an angelic youth? To ask the question is to dismiss it, and all other such arguments with it. One must dismiss as summarily the objections to oratory: by definition, to wish to lead Athens implies the burden of trying to persuade Athens, and an essential part of that effort consisted in public oratory.

One can draw distinctions, of course. I should concede the label 'demagogue' in its most pejorative sense, for example, if a campaign were built around promises which a clique of orators neither intended to honour nor were capable of honouring. But, significantly enough, this accusation is rarely levelled against the so-called demagogues, and the one definite instance we know comes from the other camp. The oligarchy of 411 was sold to the Athenians on the appeal that this was now the only way to obtain Persian support and thus to win the otherwise lost war. Even on the most favourable view, as Thucydides makes quite clear, Peisander and some of his associates may have meant this originally, but they quickly abandoned all pretence of trying to win the war while they concentrated on preserving the newly won oligarchy on as narrow a base as possible.[33] That is what I should call 'demagogy', if the word is to merit its pejorative flavour. That is 'misleading the people' in the literal sense.

But what then of the interest question, of the supposed clash between the interests of the whole state and the interests of a section or faction within the state? Is that not a valid distinction? It is a pity that we have no direct evidence (and no indirect evidence of any value) about the way the long debate was conducted between 508 B.C., when Cleisthenes established the democracy in its primitive form, and the later years of Pericles' dominance. Those were the years when class interests would most likely have been expounded openly and bluntly. Actual speeches survive only from the end of the fifth century on, and they reveal what anyone could have guessed who had not been blinded by Plato and others, namely, that the appeal was customarily a national one, not a factional one. There is little open pandering to the poor against the rich, to the farmers against the town or to the town against the

[33] Thuc., 8.68–91.

farmers. Why indeed should there have been? Politicians regularly say that what they are advocating is in the best interests of the nation, and, what is much more important, they believe it. Often, too, they charge their opponents with sacrificing the national interest for special interests, and they believe that. I know of no evidence which warrants the view that Athenian politicians were somehow peculiar in this respect; nor do I know any reason to hold that the argument is an essentially different (or better) one because it is put forth not by a politician but by Aristophanes or Thucydides or Plato.

At the same time a politician cannot ignore class or sectional interests or the conflicts among them, whether in a constituency today or in the Assembly in ancient Athens. The evidence for Athens suggests that on many issues—the Empire and the Peloponnesian War, for example, or relations with Philip of Macedon—the divisions over policy did not closely follow class or sectional lines. But other questions, such as the opening of the archonship and other offices to men of the lower property censuses or of pay for jury service or, in the fourth century, the financing of the fleet, or the theoric fund, were by their nature class issues. Advocates on both sides knew this and knew how and when (and when not) to make their appeals accordingly, at the same time that they each argued, and believed, that only their respective points of view would advance Athens as a whole. To plead against Ephialtes and Pericles that *eunomia*, the well-ordered state ruled by law, had the higher moral claim, was merely a plea for the status quo dressed up in fancy language.[34]

In his little book on the Athenian constitution, Aristotle wrote the following:[35]

> Pericles was the first to give pay for jury service, as a demagogic measure to counter the wealth of Cimon. The latter, who possessed the fortune of a tyrant . . . supported many of his fellow-demesmen, every one of whom was free to come daily and receive from him enough for his sustenance. Besides, none of his estates was enclosed, so that

[34] 'Eunomia . . . the ideal of the past and even of Solon . . . now meant the best constitution, based on inequality. It was now the ideal of oligarchy': Ehrenberg, *Aspects*, p. 92.

[35] Arist., *Const.*, 27.3–4.

anyone who wished could take from its fruits. Pericles'
property did not permit such largesse, and on the advice of
Damonides . . . he distributed among the people from what
was their own . . . and so he introduced pay for the jurors.

Aristotle himself, as I indicated earlier, praised Pericles' regime
and he refused responsibility for this silly explanation, but others
who repeated it, both before and after him, thought it was a telling
instance of demagogy pandering to the common people. The
obvious retort is to ask whether what Cimon did was not pandering in equal measure, or whether opposition to pay for jury
service was not pandering, too, but in that case to the men of
property. No useful analysis is possible in such terms, for they
serve only to conceal the real grounds for disagreement. If one is
opposed to full democracy as a form of government, then it is
wrong to encourage popular participation in the juries by offering
pay; but it is wrong because the objective is wrong, not because
Pericles obtained leadership status by proposing and carrying the
measure. And vice versa, if one favours a democratic system.

What emerges from all this is a very simple proposition, namely,
that demagogues—I use the word in a neutral sense—were a
structural element in the Athenian political system. By this I mean,
first, that the system could not function at all without them;
second, that the term is equally applicable to all leaders, regardless
of class or point of view; and third, that within rather broad limits
they are to be judged individually not by their manners or their
methods, but by their performance. (And that, I need hardly add,
is precisely how they *were* judged in life, if not in books.) Up to a
point one can easily parallel the Athenian demagogue with the
modern politician, but there soon comes a point when distinctions
must be drawn, not merely because the work of government has
become so much more complex, but more basically because of the
differences between a direct and a representative democracy. I
need not repeat what I have already said about the mass-meeting
(with its uncertain composition), about the lack of a bureaucracy
and a party system, and, as a result, the continuous state of tension
in which an Athenian demagogue lived and worked. But there is
one consequence which needs a little examination, for these conditions make up an important part (if not the whole) of the
explanation of an apparently negative feature of Athenian politics,

and of Greek politics generally. David Hume put it this way:[36]

> To exclude faction from a free government, is very difficult,
> if not altogether impracticable; but such inveterate rage
> between the factions, and such bloody maxims are found, in
> modern times, amongst religious parties alone. In ancient
> history we may always observe, where one party prevailed,
> whether the nobles or people (for I can observe no difference
> in this respect), that they immediately butchered . . . and
> banished. . . . No form of process, no law, no trial, no pardon.
> . . . These people were extremely fond of liberty, but seem
> not to have understood it very well.

The remarkable thing about Athens is how near she came to
being the complete exception to this correct observation of
Hume's, to being free, in other words, from *stasis* in its ultimate
meaning. The democracy was established in 508 B.C. following a
brief civil war. Thereafter, in its history of nearly two centuries,
armed terror, butchery without process or law, was employed on
only two occasions, in 411 and 404, both times by oligarchic
factions which seized control of the state for brief periods. And
the second time, in particular, the democratic faction, when it
regained power, was generous and law-abiding in its treatment of
the oligarchs, so much so that they wrung praise even from Plato.
Writing about the restoration of 403, he said that 'no one should
be surprised that some men took savage personal revenge against
their enemies in this revolution, but in general the returning party
behaved equitably'.[37] This is not to suggest that the two centuries
were totally free from individual acts of injustice and brutality.
Hume—speaking of Greece generally and not of Athens in particular—observed 'no difference in this respect' between the
factions. We seem to have a less clear vision of Athens, at least,
blocked by the distorting mirror of men like Thucydides, Xenophon and Plato, which magnifies the exceptional incidents of
extreme democratic intolerance—such as the trial and execution of
the generals who won the battle of Arginusae and the trial and
execution of Socrates; while it minimizes and often obliterates

---

[36] 'Of the populousness of ancient nations', in *Essays*, World's Classics
edn (London, 1903), pp. 405–6. Cf. Jacob Burckhardt, *Griechische
Kulturgeschichte* (reprint Darmstadt, 1956), i, pp. 80–1.

[37] *Epist.*, VII 325B; cf. Xen., *Hell.*, 2.4.43; Arist., *Const.*, 40.

altogether the even worse behaviour on the other side, for example, the political assassination of Ephialtes in 462 or 461 and of Androcles in 411, each in his time the most influential of the popular leaders.

If Athens largely escaped the extreme forms of *stasis* so common elsewhere, she could not escape its lesser manifestations. Athenian politics had an all-or-nothing quality. The objective on each side was not merely to defeat the opposition but to crush it, to behead it by destroying its leaders. And often enough this game was played within the sides, as a number of men manoeuvred for leadership. The chief technique was the political trial, and the chief instrumentalities were the dining-clubs and the sycophants. These, too, I would argue, were structurally a part of the system, not an accidental or avoidable excrescence. Ostracism, the so-called *graphe paranomon*, and the formal popular scrutiny of archons, generals and other officials, were all deliberately intro-duced as safety devices, either against excessive individual power (and potential tyranny) or against corruption and malfeasance or against unthinking haste and passion in the Assembly itself.[38] Abstractly it may be easy enough to demonstrate that, however praiseworthy in intention, these devices inevitably invited abuse. The trouble is that they were the only kind of device available, again because the democracy was a direct one, lacking a party machinery and so forth. Leaders and would-be leaders had no alternative but to make use of them, and to seek out still other ways of harassing and breaking competitors and opponents.

Hard as this all-out warfare no doubt was on the participants, unfair and vicious on occasion, it does not follow that it was altogether an evil for the community as a whole. Substantial inequalities, serious conflicts of interest, and legitimate divergences of opinion were real and intense. Under such conditions, conflict is not only inevitable, it is a virtue in democratic politics, for it is conflict combined with consent, and not consent alone, which preserves democracy from eroding into oligarchy. On the consti-tutional issue which dominated so much of the fifth century it was the advocates of popular democracy who triumphed, and they did so precisely because they fought for it and fought hard. They

---

[38] The fourth-century legislative procedure by means of *nomothetai* could properly be added to this list; see A. R. W. Harrison, 'Law-making at Athens at the end of the fifth century B.C.', *JHS*, lxxv (1955), pp. 26–35.

fought a partisan fight, and the Old Oligarch made the correct diagnosis in attributing Athenian strength to just that. Of course, his insight, or perhaps his honesty, did not extend so far as to note the fact that in his day the democracy's leaders were still men of substance, and often of aristocratic background: not only Pericles, but Cleon and Cleophon, and then Thrasybulus and Anytus. The two latter led the democratic faction in overthrowing the Thirty Tyrants in 403, and in following their victory with the amnesty which even Plato praised. The partisan fight was not a straight class fight; it also drew support from among the rich and the well-born. Nor was it a fight without rules or legitimacy. The democratic counter-slogan to *eunomia* was *isonomia*, and, as Vlastos has said, the Athenians pursued 'the goal of political equality . . . not in defiance, but in support of the rule of law'. The Athenian poor, he noted, did not once raise the standard Greek revolutionary demand—redistribution of the land—throughout the fifth and fourth centuries.[39]

In those two centuries Athens was, by all pragmatic tests, much the greatest Greek state, with a powerful feeling of community, with a toughness and resilience tempered, even granted its imperial ambitions, by a humanity and sense of equity and responsibility quite extraordinary for its day (and for many another day as well). Lord Acton, paradoxically enough, was one of the few historians to have grasped the historic significance of the amnesty of 403. 'The hostile parties', he wrote, 'were reconciled, and proclaimed an amnesty, the first in history'.[40] *The first in history,*

[39] G. Vlastos, 'Isonomia', *AJP*, lxxiv (1953), pp. 337–66. Cf. Jones, *Democracy*, p. 52: 'In general . . . democrats tended like Aristotle to regard the laws as a code laid down once for all by a wise legislator . . . which, immutable in principle, might occasionally require to be clarified or supplemented'. The 'rule of law' is a complicated subject on its own, but it is not the subject of this paper. Nor is the evaluation of individual demagogues, e.g. Cleon, on whom see most recently A. G. Woodhead, 'Thucydides' portrait of Cleon', *Mnemosyne*, 4th ser., xiii (1960), pp. 289–317; A. Andrewes, 'The Mytilene debate', *Phoenix*, xvi (1962), pp. 64–85.

[40] 'The history of freedom in antiquity', in *Essays on Freedom and Power*, ed. G. Himmelfarb (London, 1956), p. 64. The paradox can be extended: in reviewing Grote, John Stuart Mill wrote about the years leading up to the oligarchic coups of 411 and 404: 'The Athenian Many, of whose democratic irritability and suspicion we hear so much, are rather to be accused of too easy and good-natured a confidence, when we reflect that

despite all the familiar weaknesses, despite the crowd psychology, the slaves, the personal ambition of many leaders, the impatience of the majority with opposition. Nor was this the only Athenian innovation: the structure and mechanism of the democracy were all their own invention, as they groped for something without precedent, having nothing to go on but their own notion of freedom, their community solidarity, their willingness to inquire (or at least to accept the consequences of inquiry), and their widely shared political experience.

Much of the credit for the Athenian achievement must go to the political leadership of the state. That, it seems to me, is beyond dispute. It certainly would not have been disputed by the average Athenian. Despite all the tensions and uncertainties, the occasional snap judgment and unreasonable shift in opinion, the people supported Pericles for more than two decades, as they supported a very different kind of man, Demosthenes, under very different conditions a century later. These men, and others like them (less well known now), were able to carry through a more or less consistent and successful programme over long stretches of time. It is altogether perverse to ignore this fact, or to ignore the structure of political life by which Athens became what she was, while one follows the lead of Aristophanes or Plato and looks only at the personalities of the politicians, or at the crooks and failures among them, or at some ethical norms of an ideal existence.

In the end Athens lost her freedom and independence, brought down by a superior external power. She went down fighting, with an understanding of what was at stake clearer than that possessed by many critics in later ages. That final struggle was led by Demosthenes, a demagogue. We cannot have it both ways: we cannot praise and admire the achievement of two centuries, and at the same time dismiss the demagogues who were the architects of the political framework and the makers of policy, or the Assembly in and through which they did their work.[41]

they had living in the midst of them the very men who, on the first show of an opportunity, were ready to compass the subversion of the democracy . . . .': *Dissertations and Discussions*, ii (London, 1859), p. 540.

[41] See most recently W. R. Connor, *The New Politicians of Fifth-Century Athens* (Princeton, 1971). and my *Democracy Ancient and Modern* (London, 1973).

II

ARISTOTLE AND ECONOMIC ANALYSIS*†

M. I. Finley

For the argument of this paper it is essential to distinguish, no matter how crudely, between economic analysis and the observation or description of specific economic activities, and between both and a concept of 'the economy' (with which only the final section will be concerned). By 'economic analysis', wrote Joseph Schumpeter, 'I mean . . . the intellectual efforts that men have made in order to *understand* economic phenomena or, which comes to the same thing, . . . the analytic or scientific aspects of economic thought'. And later, drawing on a suggestion of Gerhard Colm's, he added: 'economic analysis deals with the questions how people behave at any time and what the economic effects are they produce by so behaving; economic sociology deals with the question how they came to behave as they do'.[1]

Whether one is wholly satisfied with Schumpeter's definitions or not,[2] they will serve our present purposes. To illustrate the difference between analysis and observation, I quote the most

* From no. 47 (1970).

† This essay was prepared for the *Festschrift* for Professor E. C. Welskopf on her seventieth birthday, and has appeared in German translation in the *Jahrbuch für Wirtschaftsgeschichte* (1971), ii, pp. 87–105. An earlier draft was presented to the Social History Group in Oxford on 3 December 1969. I have benefited from the advice of a number of friends, A. Andrewes, F. H. Hahn, R. M. Hartwell, G. E. R. Lloyd, G. E. M. de Ste Croix.

[1] J. Schumpeter, *History of Economic Analysis*, ed. E. B. Schumpeter (New York, 1954), pp. 1, 21.

[2] See the review by I. M. D. Little in *EHR*, 2nd ser., vii (1955–6), pp. 91–8.

familiar ancient text on the division of labour, written by Xenophon before the middle of the fourth century B.C. The context—
and this should not be ignored—is the superiority of the meals
provided in the Persian palace with its staff of kitchen specialists.[3]

> That this should be the case [Xenophon explains] is not
> remarkable. For just as the various trades are most highly
> developed in the large cities, in the same way the food at the
> palace is prepared in a far superior manner. In small towns
> the same man makes couches, doors, ploughs and tables, and
> often he even builds houses, and still he is thankful if only
> he can find enough work to support himself. And it is
> impossible for a man of many trades to do all of them well.
> In large cities, however, because many make demands on
> each trade, one alone is enough to support a man, and often
> less than one: for instance, one man makes shoes for men,
> another for women, there are places even where one man
> earns a living just by mending shoes, another by cutting them
> out, another just by sewing the uppers together, while there
> is another who performs none of these operations but
> assembles the parts. Of necessity he who pursues a very
> specialized task will do it best.

This text contains important evidence for the economic historian—but not on division of labour for which it is so often cited.
In the first place, Xenophon is interested in specialization of crafts
rather than in division of labour. In the second place, the virtues of
both are, in his mind, improvement of quality, not increase in
productivity. He says this explicitly and it is anyway implicit in
the context, the meals served at the Persian court. Nor is Xenophon untypical: division of labour is not often discussed by
ancient writers, but when it is, the interest is regularly in crafts-
manship, in quality.[4] One need only glance at the model of the pin
factory at the beginning of Adam Smith's *Wealth of Nations* to
appreciate the leap taken by the latter, from observation to
genuine economic analysis.

Even as observation, furthermore, Xenophon's remarks do not
merit the accolades they have received. As Schumpeter pointed

---

[3] *Cyropaedia*, viii.2.5.
[4] See Eric Roll, *A History of Economic Thought*, 3rd edn (London, 1954),
pp. 27–8.

out, economics 'constitutes a particularly difficult case' in any study of the origins of a 'science' because[5]

> common-sense knowledge goes in this field much farther relatively to such scientific knowledge as we have been able to achieve, than does common-sense knowledge in almost any other field. The layman's knowledge that rich harvests are associated with low prices of foodstuffs or that division of labour increases the efficiency of the productive process are obviously prescientific and it is absurd to point to such statements in old writings as if they embodied discoveries.

The key for antiquity rests not with Xenophon or Plato but with Aristotle. It is agreed on all sides that only Aristotle offered the rudiments of analysis; hence histories of economic doctrine regularly feature him at the beginning. 'The essential difference' between Plato and Aristotle in this respect, writes Schumpeter, 'is that an analytic *intention*, which may be said (in a sense) to have been absent from Plato's mind, was the prime mover of Aristotle's. This is clear from the logical structure of his arguments'.[6]

Aristotle then becomes doubly troublesome. In the first place, his supposed efforts at economic analysis were fragmentary, wholly out of scale with his monumental contributions to physics, metaphysics, logic, meteorology, biology, political science, rhetoric, aesthetics and ethics. Second, and still more puzzling, his efforts produced nothing better than 'decorous, pedestrian, slightly mediocre, and more than slightly pompous common sense'. This judgement of Schumpeter's,[7] shared by many, is so wide of the universal judgement of Aristotle's other work, that it demands a serious explanation.

---

[5] *Op. cit.*, p. 9. Even if one grants Xenophon the insight that division of labour is a consequence of greater demand, the observation led to no analysis. To quote Schumpeter again: 'Classical scholars as well as economists . . . are prone to fall into the error of hailing as a discovery everything that suggests later developments, and of forgetting that, in economics as elsewhere, most statements of fundamental facts acquire importance only by the superstructures they are made to bear and are commonplace in the absence of such superstructures' (p. 54).

[6] *Ibid.*, p. 57. Cf. e.g. Roll, *op. cit.*, pp. 31-5.

[7] *Op. cit.*, p. 57.

I

There are only two sections in the whole Aristotelian corpus that permit systematic consideration, one in Book v of the *Nicomachean Ethics*, the other in Book I of the *Politics*.[8] In both, the 'economic analysis' is only a sub-section within an inquiry into other, more essential subject-matters. Insufficient attention to the contexts has been responsible for much misconception of what Aristotle is talking about.

The subject of the fifth book of the *Ethics* is justice. Aristotle first differentiates universal from particular justice, and then proceeds to a systematic analysis of the latter. It, too, is of two kinds: distributive and corrective.

Distributive (*dianemetikos*) justice is a concern when honours, goods, or other 'possessions' of the community are to be distributed. Here justice is the same as 'equality', but equality understood as a geometrical proportion (we say 'progression'), not as an arithmetical one.[9] The distribution of equal shares among unequal persons, or of unequal shares among equal persons, would be unjust. The principle of distributive justice is therefore to balance the share with the worth of the person. All are agreed on this, Aristotle adds, although all do not agree on the standard of value (*axia*) to be employed where the *polis* itself is concerned. 'For democrats it is the status of freedom, for some oligarchs wealth, for others good birth, for aristocrats it is excellence (*arete*)'.[10] That Aristotle himself favoured the last-named is not important for us, and indeed he does not himself make the point in this particular

---

[8] The first part of Book II of the pseudo-Aristotelian *Oeconomica* is without value on any issue relevant to the present discussion, as I have indicated briefly in a review of the Budé edition in *CR*, new ser., xx (1970), pp. 315–19. (See also note 51.)

[9] This difficult idea of a mathematical formulation of equality and justice was Pythagorean, probably first introduced by Archytas of Tarentum at the beginning of the fourth century B.C., and then popularized by Plato (first in *Gorgias*, 508A). See F. D. Harvey, 'Two kinds of equality', *Classica et Mediaevalia*, xxvi (1965), pp. 101–46, with corrigenda in xxvii (1966), pp. 99–100, who rightly stresses the point that the mathematical formulation is employed solely to argue against democracy. (My translations from the *Ethics* are based on H. Rackham's in the Loeb Classical Library, 1926.)

[10] *Ethics*, 1131a24–29.

context, which is concerned only to explain and defend the principle of geometric proportion.[11]

In corrective justice (*diorthotikos*, literally 'straightening out'), however, the issue is not one of distribution from a pool, but of direct, private relations between individuals in which it may be necessary to 'straighten out' a situation, to rectify an injustice by removing the (unjust) gain and restoring the loss. Here the relative nature and worth of the persons is irrelevant, 'for it makes no difference whether a good man has defrauded a bad man or a bad one a good one, nor whether it is a good or bad man that has committed adultery; the law looks only at the nature of the damage, treating the parties as equal. . . .'[12]

Corrective justice also has two subdivisions, depending on whether the 'transactions' (*synallagmata*) are voluntary or involuntary. Among the former Aristotle lists sales, loans, pledges, deposits and leases; among the latter, theft, adultery, poisoning, procuring, assault, robbery, murder.[13] There is a fundamental difficulty for us here in trying to comprehend Aristotle's categories—and no translation of *synallagmata* by a single English word eases it—but I need not enter into the controversy except to make one point relevant to some of the discussion that will follow. Under what conditions did Aristotle envisage an injustice, an unjust gain, in a voluntary transaction, especially in a sale? The answer is, I think, beyond dispute that he had in mind fraud or breach of contract, but not an 'unjust' price. An agreement over the price was part of the agreement or 'transaction' itself, and there could be no subsequent claim by the buyer of unjust gain merely because of the price. As Joachim says, 'the law gives the better bargainer *adeia* (security)'.[14] It is necessary to insist on this

[11] It is probable that for Aristotle distributive justice is also operative in a variety of private associations, permanent or temporary: see H. H. Joachim's commentary (Oxford, 1951), pp. 138–40, though I see neither necessity nor warrant for his attempt to link distributive justice with the private law suit known as *diadikasia*.

[12] *Ethics*, 1131b32–32a6.

[13] *Ethics*, 1131a3–9.

[14] *Op. cit.*, p. 137, with specific reference to 1132b11–16. I agree with A. R. W. Harrison, 'Aristotle's Nicomachean Ethics, Book v, and the law of Athens', *JHS*, lxxvii (1957), pp. 42–7, against Joachim (see also note 11), that 'Aristotle's treatment of justice in the *Ethics* shows only a very general, one might perhaps say an academic, interest in the actual legal institutions of the Athens of his day'.

(leaving aside the unfortunate injection of bargaining) because efforts have been made to drag this section of the *Ethics* into the argument about economic analysis, for example by Soudek, who offers as an illustration of corrective justice the hypothetical case of a house-buyer who brought suit on a claim that he had been overcharged and who was awarded a refund equal to half the difference between the seller's price and his own proposed 'just price'.[15] Nothing in this or any other text of Aristotle warrants this, nor does anything we know about Greek legal practice. Both argue decisively the other way. Commenting on the famous passage in the *Iliad*, 'But then Zeus son of Cronus took from Glaucus his wits, in that he exchanged golden armour with Diomedes son of Tydeus for one of bronze, the worth of a hundred oxen for the worth of nine oxen', Aristotle says tersely, 'one who gives away what is his own cannot be said to suffer injustice'.[16] We shall meet 'what is his own' again in a surprising context.

Having completed his analysis of the two kinds of particular justice, Aristotle abruptly launches into a digression,[17] introducing it polemically: 'The view is held by some that justice is reciprocity (*antipeponthos*) without any qualification, by the Pythagoreans for example'. *Antipeponthos* is a term that has a technical mathematical sense, but it also has a general sense which, in this context, amounts to the *lex talionis*, an eye for an eye.[18] On the contrary, replies Aristotle, 'in many cases reciprocity is at variance with justice', since it '*does not coincide either with distributive or with corrective justice*'. However, in the 'interchange of services' the Pythagorean definition of justice is appropriate, provided the reciprocity '*is on the basis of proportion, not on the basis of equality*'.

'Interchange of services' is Rackham's inadequate translation of Aristotle's ἐν ταῖς κοινωνίαις ταῖς ἀλλακτικαῖς, losing the force of the word *koinonia*, and I am compelled to digress. *Koinonia* is a central concept in Aristotle's *Ethics* and *Politics*. Its range of meanings extends from the *polis* itself, the highest form of *koinonia*,

---

[15] J. Soudek, 'Aristotle's theory of exchange: an inquiry into the origin of economic analysis', *PAPS*, xcvi (1952), pp. 45–75, at pp. 51–2.

[16] *Iliad*, 6.234–6; *Ethics*, 1136b9–13.

[17] *Ethics*, 1132b21–33b29.

[18] Cf. *Magna Mor.*, 1194a29 ff.; see Joachim, *op. cit.*, pp. 147–8, and the commentary by R. A. Gauthier and J. Y. Jolif (the best commentary in so far as close reading of the text is concerned), ii (Louvain and Paris, 1959), pp. 372–3.

to temporary associations such as sailors on a voyage, soldiers in a campaign, or the parties in an exchange of goods. It is a 'natural' form of association—man is by nature a *zoön koinonikon* as well as a *zoön oikonomikon* (household-being) and a *zoön politikon* (*polis*-being). Several conditions are requisite if there is to be a genuine *koinonia*: (1) the members must be free men; (2) they must have a common purpose, major or minor, temporary or of long duration; (3) they must have something in common, share something, such as place, goods, cult, meals, desire for a good life, burdens, suffering; (4) there must be *philia* (conventionally but inadequately translated 'friendship'), mutuality in other words, and *to dikaion*, which for simplicity we may reduce to 'fairness' in their mutual relations. Obviously no single word will render the spectrum of *koinoniai*. At the higher levels, 'community' is usually suitable, at the lower perhaps 'association', provided the elements of fairness, mutuality and common purpose are kept in mind.

The point to my digression is to underscore the overtones of the section in the *Ethics* on exchange: *koinonia* is as integral to the analysis as the act of exchanging. Edouard Will caught the right nuance when he replaced such translations of the opening phrase as 'interchange of services' by a paraphrase, 'exchange relations within the framework of the community' (*les relations d'échange qui ont pour cadre le communauté*).[19] Lest there be any doubt, Aristotle himself promptly dispels it. Immediately following the sentences I quoted before digressing, he goes on to say that the *polis* itself depends on proportional reciprocity. If men cannot requite evil with evil, good with good, there can be no sharing. 'That is why we set up a shrine to the Charites [Graces] in a public place, to remind men to make a return. For that is integral to grace, since it is a duty not only to return a service done one, but another time to take the initiative in doing a service oneself'.[20]

And at long last we come to our problem. The example of proportional requital which follows is the exchange of a house for shoes.[21] How is that to be accomplished? There is no *koinonia* in

---

[19] E. Will, 'De l'aspect éthique des origines grecques de la monnaie', *RH*, ccxii (1954), pp. 209–31, at p. 215 note 1.

[20] *Ethics*, 1133a3–5.

[21] Aristotle shifts from example to example and I have followed him, despite the superficial inconsistency that entails.

this context between two doctors, but only between, say, a doctor and a farmer, who are not equals but who must somehow be equalized. 'As a builder is to a shoemaker, so must so many pairs of shoes be to a house'. The latter must be 'equalized somehow', by some common measure, and that is need (*chreia*),[22] now commonly expressed in money. 'There will therefore be reciprocity when (the products) have been equalized, so that as farmer is to shoemaker, so is the shoemaker's product to that of the farmer'. In that way, there will be no excess but 'each will have his own'. If one party has no need there will be no exchange, and again money comes to the rescue: it permits a delayed exchange.[23]

There follows a short repetitive section and the digression on 'this outwork of particular justice' ends.[24] Aristotle has been thinking aloud, so to speak, as he often does in his writings as they have come down to us, about a particular nuance or a tangential question that is troublesome; he is indulging in a highly abstract exercise, analogous to the passages in the *Politics* on the application of geometric proportion to public affairs; here, as often, his reflections are introduced by a polemical statement, and soon dropped as he returns to his main theme, his systematic analysis. Exchange of goods does not again appear in the *Ethics* except in two or three casual remarks.

That this is not one of Aristotle's more transparent discussions is painfully apparent, and we must look at what the most important modern commentators have made of it. Joachim, exceptionally, accepted that Aristotle really meant it when he wrote 'as a builder is to a shoemaker', and he promptly added, 'How exactly the values of the producers are to be determined, and what the ratio between them can mean, is, I must confess, in the end un-

---

22 I have refrained from the common rendition, 'demand', to avoid the subconscious injection of the modern economic concept; so also Soudek, *op. cit.*, p. 60. The semantic cluster around *chreia* in Greek writers, including Aristotle, includes 'use', 'advantage', 'service', taking us even further from 'demand'.

23 *Ethics*, 1133b6–12. In the *Politics*, 1257a31 ff., Aristotle explains that delayed exchange became necessary when needs were satisfied by imports from foreign sources, and 'all the naturally necessary things were not easily portable'. (My translations from the *Politics* are based on Ernest Barker's, Oxford, 1946.)

24 The phrase quoted is that of Harrison, *op. cit.*, p. 45.

intelligible to me'.[25] Gauthier and Jolif make an ingenious effort to get round the difficulty by asserting that the builder and shoe-maker are meant to be considered equal 'as persons' but different (only) in their products. However, I cannot believe that Aristotle went out of his way to insist on *proportional* reciprocity as neces-sary for justice in this one field, only to conclude that one pair of ratios does not in fact exist, and to make that point in the most ambiguous way possible.[26] Max Salomon achieves the same result by more ruthless methods: the mathematics, he says, is a mere 'interpolation', a 'marginal note, so to speak, for listeners in-terested in mathematics', and the whole concept of reciprocal proportion must be omitted, leaving Aristotle to say simply that goods are exchanged according to their values, and nothing more. That then leads Salomon to a series of grotesque translations in order to get out of the text what is not there.[27]

Salomon's drastic surgery was not mere wilful caprice. Eco-nomics, he writes, cannot be turned into 'a kind of wergeld system on a mercantile base'.[28] The first principle of a market economy is, of course, indifference to the *persons* of the buyer and seller: that is what troubles most commentators on Aristotle. Soudek therefore

[25] *Op. cit.*, p. 150.

[26] *Op. cit.*, p. 377. They cite in support *Magna Mor.*, 1194a7–25, but those lines are only a simplified and more confusing statement of the argument in the *Ethics*. For future reference, it should be noted that *Magna Mor.* says explicitly that 'Plato also seems to employ proportional justice in his *Republic*'. St George Stock, in the Oxford translation (1915), cites *Rep.*, 369D, but it requires clairvoyance to see the *Magna Mor.* reference there, since Plato is not discussing at all how the exchange between builder and shoemaker is to be equated, and soon goes on to introduce the trader as a middleman (significantly absent in the Aristotelian account). In general, however, his section of Book II of the *Republic* was obviously influential on Aristotle (including the stress on need and the explanation of money). For what it is worth, in reply to the commentary by Gauthier and Jolif cited above note 18, I note that Plato says (370A–B), to justify specialization of crafts, that 'no two people are born exactly alike. There are innate differences which fit them for different occupations' (Cornford's translation, Oxford, 1941).

[27] Max Salomon, *Der Begriff der Gerechtigkeit bei Aristoteles* (Leiden, 1937), in a lengthy appendix, 'Der Begriff des Tauschgeschäftes bei Aristoteles'. My quotation appears on p. 161. Salomon is not alone in dismissing the mathematics as irrelevant: see most recently W. F. R. Hardie, *Aristotle's Ethical Theory* (Oxford, 1968), pp. 198–201.

[28] *Op. cit.*, p. 146.

34

suggests that 'as a builder is to a shoemaker' must be read 'as the skill of the builder is to the skill of the shoemaker'.[29] From there it is no great step to Schumpeter's interpretation. The key passage in the *Ethics*, he writes, 'I interpret like this: "As the farmer's labour compares with the shoemaker's labour, so the product of the farmer compares with the product of the shoemaker". At least, I cannot get any other sense out of this passage. If I am right, then Aristotle was groping for some labour-cost theory of price which he was unable to state explicitly'.[30] A few pages later Schumpeter refers to the 'just price' of the artisan's 'labour', and still later he asserts that the 'relevant part' of Aquinas's 'argument on just price . . . is strictly Aristotelian and should be interpreted exactly as we have interpreted Aristotle's'.[31] However, Aristotle does not once refer to labour costs or costs of production. The medieval theologians were the first to introduce this consideration into the discussion, as the foundation for *their* doctrine of just price, and their alleged Aristotelianism in this respect rested on the ambiguity of the Latin translations of Aristotle made available to them in the middle of the thirteenth century.[32]

Anyway, none of these interpretations of what Aristotle 'really meant' answers the question, How are prices, just or otherwise, established in the market? More specifically, how are needs, on which Aristotle insists as basic, equated with the parties or their skills or their labour or their labour costs, whichever one prefers? Obviously Aristotle does not say, or at least does not say clearly, otherwise the modern efforts to discover his concealed meaning would all be unnecessary. For Karl Marx the answer is that, though Aristotle was the first to identify the central problem of exchange value, he then admits defeat 'and gives up the further analysis of

[29] Soudek, *op. cit.*, pp. 45–6, 60. The same suggestion is made by J. J. Spengler, 'Aristotle on economic imputation and related matters', *Southern Economic Journal*, xxi (1955), pp. 371–89.

[30] *Op. cit.*, p. 60 note 1.

[31] *Ibid.*, pp. 64, 93. Hardie, *op. cit.*, p. 196, simply asserts without serious discussion that 'the comparative values of producers must in Aristotle's view here mean the comparative values of their work *done in the same time*' (my italics).

[32] See Soudek, *op. cit.*, pp. 64–5; J. W. Baldwin, *The Medieval Theories of the Just Price* (*TAPS*, new ser., xlix, part 4 (1959)), pp. 62, 74–5; E. Genzmer, 'Die antiken Grundlagen der Lehre vom gerechten Preis und der laesio enormis', *Z.f. ausländisches u. internat. Privatrecht*, Sonderheft xi (1937), pp. 25–64, at pp. 27–8.

the form of value' when he concedes[33] that 'it is impossible for things so different to become commensurable *in reality*'.[34] Soudek repeats his error on corrective justice, already discussed, then grasps at the word 'bargain' which W. D. Ross falsely injects into his translation in one passage (and Rackham in several), and concludes that the price is determined, and justice satisfied, by mutual bargaining until agreement is reached.[35] That is not a very good way to describe what happens in a real market situation, and Soudek suggests that Aristotle's trouble was that 'he was pre-occupied with the isolated exchange between individuals and not with the exchange of goods by many sellers and buyers competing with each other'[36]—a strange criticism of a discussion that explicitly sets out to look at exchanges 'within the framework of the community'.

[33] *Ethics*, 1133b18–20.

[34] Marx, *Capital*, transl. S. Moore and E. Aveling, i (Chicago, 1906), p. 68. Cf. Roll, *op. cit.*, p. 35; 'What begins with the promise of being a theory of value ends up with a mere statement of the accounting function of money'.

[35] *Op. cit.*, pp. 61–4. Both Ross (Oxford, 1925) and Rackham have 'bargain' in 1133a12, Rackham also in 1164a20; 1164a30. (It is worth noting another mistranslation by Rackham, at 1133b15: 'Hence the proper thing is for all commodities to have their prices fixed'. What Aristotle actually says is 'Therefore it is necessary for everything to be expressed in money, *tetimesthai*'.) Furthermore, I cannot accept Soudek's use of passages from the beginning of Book ix, continuing the analysis of friendship, as relevant. There Aristotle's examples are drawn from promises to pay for services by musicians, doctors and teachers of philosophy, 'exchanges' in a sense perhaps, but in a sense that is different in quality from those Book v is concerned with. That should be clear from a number of passages. In the opening statement (1163b32–35), Aristotle distinguishes 'dissimilar friendships' (which he is about to discuss) from exchange relations among craftsmen, and he soon says explicitly that the value of a philosopher's services 'is not measurable in money' (1164b3–4). Protagoras, he writes, accepted whatever fee his pupils thought proper (1164a24–26), and Aristotle thinks that is on the whole the right procedure (1164b6–8), though he cannot refrain from the sneer (1164a30–32) that Sophists had better take their payment in advance. All this seems to me to belong to the spirit of gift and counter-gift, of the Charites. There must be reciprocity and proportion here, too, as in all human relations, but I see no other link to the digression on the exchange between builder and shoemaker.

[36] Soudek, *op. cit.*, p. 46.

Schumpeter takes the opposite line. Starting from the erroneous idea that Aristotle 'condemned [monopoly] as "unjust" ' he went on to reason in this way:[37]

> It is not farfetched to equate, for Aristotle's purpose, monopoly prices with prices that some individual or group of individuals have set to their own advantage. Prices that are given to the individual and with which he cannot tamper, that is to say, the *competitive* prices that emerge in free market under normal conditions, do not come within the ban. And there is nothing strange in the conjecture that Aristotle may have taken normal competitive prices as standards of commutative justice or, more precisely, that he was prepared to accept as 'just' *any* transaction between individuals that was carried out at such prices—which is in fact what the scholastic doctors were to do explicitly.

We need not discuss whether or not it is 'farfetched' to conjecture that all this was in Aristotle's mind, though not expressed in his text; it surely takes us away completely from the starting-point stated in the introduction, with its reference to Pythagorean reciprocity and its consequent mathematics.

Scumpeter further observed that the analysis was restricted to the artisan, while the 'chiefly agrarian income of the gentleman' was ignored, the free labourer, 'an anomaly in his slave economy', was 'disposed of perfunctorily', the trader, shipowner, shopkeeper and moneylender judged only in ethical and political terms, their 'gains' not submitted to 'explanatory analysis'.[38] No wonder Schumpeter dismissed the whole performance as 'decorous,

---

[37] *Op. cit.*, p. 61. Both references to monopoly which he adduces are incorrect. *Politics*, 1259a5–36, has no condemnation but rather an implied defence of *public* monopoly, whereas the *Ethics*, 1132b21–34a16, makes no mention of monopoly at all (nor does the *Ethics*, anywhere else). Schumpeter is here also repeating his error about the scholastic theologians, from whom he takes the unfortunate word 'commutative'. Soudek, *op. cit.*, p. 64, also drags in a condemnation of monopoly, on the untenable (and irrelevant) ground that 'if the seller holds a monopolistic position, then what appears on the surface as a "voluntary transaction" is distorted in spirit'. For a correct analysis of the *Politics* passage on monopoly, see M. Defourny, *Aristote, Études sur la 'Politique'* (Paris, 1932), pp. 21–7.

[38] *Op. cit.*, pp. 64–5.

pedestrian, slightly mediocre, and more than slightly pompous common sense'.[39] An analysis that focuses so exclusively on a minor sector of the economy deserves no more complimentary evaluation. Indeed, the time has come to ask whether it is, or was intended to be, *economic* analysis at all.

Before I proceed to give a negative answer, I must confess that, like Joachim, I do not understand what the ratios between the producers can mean, but I do not rule out that 'as a builder is to a shoemaker' is somehow to be taken literally. Marx believed that there was 'an important fact which prevented Aristotle from seeing that, to attribute value to commodities, is merely a mode of expressing all labour as equal human labour, and consequently as labour of equal quality. Greek society was founded upon slavery, and had, therefore, for its natural basis, the inequality of men and of their labour power'.[40] That natural inequality is fundamental to Aristotle's thinking is beyond argument: it permeates his analysis of friendship in the *Ethics* and of slavery in the *Politics*. True, his builder and shoemaker in the exchange paradigm are free men, not slaves,[41] but the concurrent existence of slave labour would still bar his way to a conception of 'equal human labour'.[42]

Schumpeter noticed, but brushed aside, what seems to me to be central in any judgement, namely, that Aristotle by his silence separates the artisan from the trader, that he is talking exclusively of an exchange between two producers without the intervention of a middleman. Aristotle knew perfectly well that this was not the way a large volume of goods circulated in his world. He also knew perfectly well that prices sometimes responded to variations in supply and demand—that is the point underlying his page in the *Politics* on monopoly. In the discussion of money in the *Ethics* he remarks that money 'is also subject to change and is not always worth the same, but tends to be relatively constant'.[43] This observation is repeated in the *Politics* in a concrete application: in the section on revolutions, Aristotle warns against rigidly fixed

---

[39] *Ibid.*, p. 57.
[40] *Op. cit.*, p. 69. On Marx's views on Aristotle, see E. C. Welskopf, *Die Produktionsverhältnisse im alten Orient und in der griechisch-römischen Antike* (Berlin, 1957), pp. 336–46.
[41] That seems certain from *Ethics*, 1163b32–35.
[42] See J.-P. Vernant, *Mythe et pensée chez les Grecs* (Paris, 1965), ch. 4.
[43] *Pol.*, 1259a5–36. *Ethics*, 1333b13–14.

assessments in states that have a property qualification for office, since one should allow for the impact on the assessment 'when there is an abundance of coin'.[44]

In short, price variations according to supply and demand were a commonplace in Greek life in the fourth century B.C.[45] Yet in the *Ethics* Aristotle does not use any of the normal Greek words for trade and trader (as he does ruthlessly in the *Politics*), but clings to the neutral word 'exchange'. That this is deliberate I cannot doubt: in the passage in the *Republic* on which much of this section of the *Ethics* is a kind of commentary, Plato concedes that the *polis* requires petty traders (*kapeloi*) who will give money for goods and goods for money because neither farmers nor artisans can count on finding someone with whom to exchange whenever they bring goods to the market. Aristotle, however, cannot introduce the *kapelos*, since justice in the exchange (which is not Plato's question) is achieved when 'each has his own', when, in other words, there is no gain from someone else's loss.[46] As part of a theory of price this is nonsense, and Aristotle knew it to be nonsense. Therefore he was not seeking a theory of market prices.[47]

The digression on exchange, I repeat, was placed at the start 'within the framework of the community'. When the digression

---

[44] *Pol.*, 1308a36–38. Nowhere does Aristotle explain why money is 'relatively constant' compared with other commodities. The general observation, it should be noted, had already been made by so shallow a thinker as Xenophon, *Ways and Means*, 4.6.

[45] I should perhaps not have bothered with these seeming platitudes, were it not that Karl Polanyi, 'Aristotle discovers the economy', in *Trade and Market in the Early Empires*, ed. K. Polanyi, C. M. Arensberg and H. W. Pearson (Chicago, 1957), pp. 64–94, makes the strange remark (p. 87) that 'the supply-demand-price mechanism escaped Aristotle. The distribution of food in the market allowed as yet but scant room to the play of that mechanism . . . . Not before the third century B.C. was the working of a supply-demand-price mechanism in international trade noticeable'. How wrong that is will be evident from Lysias' 22nd oration, *Against the Corndealers*, to be dated about 387 B.C., on which see R. Seager in *Historia*, xv (1966), pp. 172–84, or from Demosthenes xxxii.24–25 and Pseudo-Demosthenes lvi.9–10, half a century later. (Polanyi's chapter has been reprinted in the volume cited in note 68, but my references are to the original publication.)

[46] *Rep.*, 371B–C. *Ethics*, 1133a31–b6.

[47] This is also the conclusion of Polanyi, *op. cit.* Although our analyses diverge, often sharply (see note 45), I must warmly acknowledge his having introduced me to the problem nearly twenty years ago.

ends, furthermore, Aristotle resumes the main thread as follows:[48]
'We must not forget that the subject of our investigation is both
justice in the absolute sense and political justice'. The phrase
'political justice' is an excessively literal rendering of the Greek,
for Aristotle goes on to define it as 'justice among free and
(actually or proportionately) equal men, living a community life in
order to be self-sufficient [or for the purpose of self-sufficiency]'.
Monetary gain has no place in such an investigation: 'The money-
maker is someone who lives under constraint'.[49] It is in the context of self-sufficiency, not money-making, that need provides the
measuring-rod of just exchange (and that the *proper* use of money
also became necessary and therefore ethically acceptable). In the
Ethics, in sum, there is strictly speaking *no* economic analysis
rather than poor or inadequate economic analysis.

II

It will have been noticed that in the *Ethics* Aristotle does not ask
how farmers or shoemakers come to behave as they do in exchange.
In Schumpeter's terms, then, in the *Ethics* there is no economic
sociology either. For that we must turn to Book 1 of the *Politics*,
and again begin by carefully fixing the context in which exchange
is discussed. Aristotle first establishes that both the household and
the *polis* are natural forms of human association, and proceeds to
examine various implications, such as the relations of dominance
and subjection (including between masters and slaves). Then he
turns to property and 'the art of acquiring it' (*chrematistike*) and
asks whether the latter is identical with the art of household
management (*oikonomike*).[50] His choice of words is important and
has led to much confusion and error. *Oikonomike* (or *oikonomia*) in
Greek usage normally retains the primary meaning, 'the art of
household management'. Though that may involve 'economic'

[48] *Ethics*, 1134a24–26.
[49] *Ethics*, 1096a5–6. For this translation of ὁ δὲ χρηματιστὴς βίαιός τίς ἐστιν,
    see Gauthier and Jolif, *op. cit.*, pp. 33–4, whose commentary cuts
    through all the unnecessary emendation and elaborate interpretation the
    text has been subjected to.
[50] *Politics*, 1256a1–5.

activity, it is misleading, and often flatly wrong, to translate it as 'economics'.[51] But *chrematistike* is ambiguous. (Its root is the noun *chrema*, 'a thing one needs or uses', in the plural *chremata*, 'goods, property'.) We have already met *chrematistike* (and we shall soon meet it again) in the sense of 'the art of money-making', but here it has the more generic sense of acquisition, less common in ordinary Greek usage but essential to Aristotle's argument. For he soon concludes that *oikonomia* and *chrematistike* (in the money-making sense) are different though overlapping species of the genus *chrematistike*.[52]

Exchange again enters the discussion polemically. What is wealth, Aristotle asks? Is it, as Solon had said, limitless? Or is it a means to an end and therefore limited by that end?[53] The answer is categorical. Wealth is a means, necessary for the maintenance of the household and the *polis* (with self-sufficiency a principle in the background), and, like all means, it is limited by its end. Of course, he continues, there is the second, money-making sense of *chrematistike*, and that is what has led to the false opinion that there is no limit to wealth and property. This attitude to wealth indeed sees it as limitless, but it is against nature and therefore not a proper subject of ethical or political discourse, on his fundamental principle that ethics has a natural basis. ('The money-maker', we

---

[51] Occasionally the word *oikonomia* was extended to the public sphere, and even then it usually refers to administration in general, as when Dinarchus (i. 97) calls Demosthenes 'useless in the affairs (*oikonomiai*) of the city' (note the plural). The furthest extension is to be found in a brief section at the beginning of Book II of the pseudo-Aristotelian *Oeconomica* (1345b7–46a25), in which four types of 'economy' are said to exist: royal, satrapic, city-state and private. There follow six short paragraphs of excruciating banality about the sources of revenue in each of the types, and that is the end of the discussion.

[52] Beginning with the Sophists, philosophers were faced with the problem of creating the vocabulary for systematic analysis out of everyday words. One increasingly common device was to employ the suffix *-ikos*. There are some seven hundred such words in Aristotle, many first employed by him. See P. Chantraine, *La formation des noms en grec ancien* (Paris, 1933), ch. 36. Polanyi, *op. cit.*, pp. 92–3, was right to insist that failure to distinguish between the two meanings of *chrematistike* is fatal to an understanding of this section of the *Politics*; cf. Defourny, *op. cit.*, pp. 5–7; briefly Barker, Notes E and F of his translation (pp. 22 and 27), though he adds new confusion by suggesting 'domestic economy' and 'political economy' as English equivalents.

[53] *Pol.*, 1256b30–34.

remember from the *Ethics*, 'is someone who lives under constraint'.)[54]

Although Aristotle singles out the *obolostates*, the petty usurer living on small consumer loans, as the most unnatural of all practitioners of the art of money-making[55]—money 'came into existence for the sake of exchange, interest makes it increase'—, the type he selects as the exemplar is the *kapelos*, just the man we noted as missing from the analysis of exchange in the *Ethics*. Again the choice of words is significant. Greek usage was not wholly consistent in selecting among the various words for 'trader', but *kapelos* usually denoted the petty trader, the huckster, in the market-place. In the present context, however, the accent is not on the scale of his operations but on the aim, so that *kapelike*, the art of the *kapelos*, must be translated 'trade for the sake of gain' or simply 'commercial trade'.[56] Like Plato before him, Aristotle now asks the historical question, how did exchange come to take place altogether. His answer is that as the *koinonia* grew beyond the individual household, there were shortages and surpluses and these were corrected by mutual exchange, 'as many barbarian tribes do to this day . . . When used in this way, the art of exchange is not contrary to nature, nor in any way a species of the art of money-making. It simply served to satisfy the natural requirements of self-sufficiency'.[57] But then, because of the difficulties created by foreign sources of supply (a passage I have already quoted in note 23), money was introduced, and out of that there developed *kapelike*. Its end is not 'the natural requirements of self-sufficiency' but the acquisition of money without limit. Such acquisition—we should say 'profit'—is made 'not according to nature but at the

[54] *Ethics*, 1096a5–6.

[55] *Pol.*, 1258b2–8.

[56] Polanyi, *op. cit.*, pp. 91–2, was almost alone in seeing the point. However, I cannot accept his explanations, that 'no name had yet been given to "commercial trade"' (p. 83) and that Aristotle, with a kind of Shavian wit, was exposing the fact that 'commercial trade was no mystery . . . but huckstering written large' (p. 92). Polanyi did not take sufficient notice of the Platonic background.

[57] *Pol.*, 1257a24–30. It is worth noting the contrast with the 'simplest' model for 'an economic theory of the city state' put forward by John Hicks, *A Theory of Economic History* (Oxford and London, 1969), pp. 42–6. That starts with the exchange by merchants of oil for corn, 'and the trade is unlikely to get started unless, to begin with, it is a handsome profit'.

expense of others',[58] a phrase that echoes in reverse the 'each has his own' of the *Ethics* and gives the final proof that commercial exchange was not the subject in the *Ethics*.

Aristotle was so rigorous in the ethical argument that he refused to make even Plato's concession. The *kapelos* is not only unnatural, he is also 'unnecessary'.[59] That this was not meant as a 'practical' proposal is certain, but that is irrelevant in the present analysis.[60] What is relevant is that Aristotle extended his ethical judgements to embrace the highest form of *koinonia*, the *polis* itself. The state, like the householder, must sometimes concern itself with acquisition.[61] Hence, in the discussion of the ideal state, in Book VII of the *Politics*, he recommends that the *polis* be sited so as to have easy access to food supplies, timber and the like. That immediately plunges him into another current debate, whether connection with the sea is a good or bad thing, and he decides that the advantages outweigh the disadvantages.[62]

> It should be able to import those things which it does not itself produce, and to export the surplus of its own necessities. It should practise commerce for itself [Aristotle now switches from *kapelike* to the commonest word for foreign trade, *emporike or emporia*], but not for others. States which make themselves market-places for the world only do it for the sake of revenue; and since it is not proper for a *polis* to share in such gain, it ought not have such an emporium.

There will have to be merchants, of course, but 'any disadvantage which may threaten can easily be met by laws defining the persons who may, or may not, have dealings with one another'.[63]

[58] *Pol.*, 1258b1–2.

[59] *Pol.*, 1258a14–18.

[60] Soudek, *op. cit.*, pp. 71–2, sees a programmatic difference between Plato and Aristotle. Basing himself on *Laws*, 918A–920C, and forgetting both *Rep.*, 371B–C (which I quoted earlier) and *Pol.*, 1327a25–31 (quoted later in this paragraph), Soudek writes that 'the author of the *Laws* . . . had made his peace with moneymaking and plutocracy, while Aristotle never gave up his opposition to this class'. Beneath this fundamental misunderstanding lies an equally fantastic picture of a sharp class struggle in Greece between wealthy landowners and merchants.

[61] *Pol.*, 1258a19–34, 59a34–36.

[62] *Pol.*, 1327a25–31.

[63] Plato of course drafted the legislation, *Laws*, 919D–920D.

Nowhere in the *Politics* does Aristotle ever consider the rules or mechanics of commercial exchange. On the contrary, his insistence on the unnaturalness of commercial gain rules out the possibility of such a discussion, and also helps explain the heavily restricted analysis in the *Ethics*. Of economic analysis there is not a trace.

III

One could rest the argument there, perhaps adding the familiar point that Aristotle, and even more Plato before him, were in many respects resisting the social, economic, political and moral developments of fourth-century Greece. There is the famous analogy of the way Aristotle appears to ignore completely the careers of Philip and Alexander, and their consequences for the *polis*, the natural form of political association. He was therefore equally free to ignore the unnatural developments in commercial trade and money-making, despite their growth in the same period and the tensions they generated. Schumpeter was right to comment that 'preoccupation with the ethics of pricing ... is precisely one of the strongest motives a man can possibly have for analysing actual market mechanisms'.[64] It does not follow, however, that ethical preoccupations *must* lead to such an analysis, and I have tried to show that 'pricing' was actually not Aristotle's concern.

In the end, Schumpeter opted for a strictly 'intellectual' explanation. Although he wrote in his introduction that 'to a large extent, the economics of different epochs deal with different sets of facts and problems',[65] he ignored that point when he excused Aristotle for being mediocre and commonsensical.[66]

There is nothing surprising or blameworthy in this. It is by slow degrees that the physical and social facts of the empirical universe enter the range of the analytic searchlight. In the beginnings of scientific analysis, the mass of the phenomena is left undisturbed in the compound of common-sense

[64] *Op. cit.*, p. 60.
[65] *Ibid.*, p. 5.
[66] *Ibid.*, p. 65. See the general criticism by Little, *op. cit.* in note 2.

knowledge, and only chips of this mass arouse scientific curiosity and thereupon become 'problems'.

Yet Aristotle's scientific curiosity has rarely been paralleled, and the time has come to ask; the mass of what phenomena? Would an *economic* analysis have been possible had his (or anyone else's) interest not been deflected? Indeed, would even a description of 'the economy' have been possible?

Today we write books with such titles as *The Economics of Ancient Greece*, and the chapters are headed agriculture, mining and minerals, labour, industry, commerce, money and banking, public finance—Schumpeter's 'chips' of the 'mass of the phenomena'.[67] This learned activity presupposes the existence of 'the economy' as a concept, difficult as it has become to find a generally acceptable definition. The current debate about 'economic anthropology', largely stimulated by Karl Polanyi's insistence on a sharp distinction between what he called the 'substantive' and the 'formal' definitions of the economy,[68] is a debate about definitions and their implications for (historical) analysis, not about the existence of 'the economy'. As Polyani himself said, even in early societies 'only the concept of the economy, not the economy itself, is in abeyance'.[69] No one could disagree with his substantive definition; in one of his varied formulations it is 'an instituted process of interaction between man and his environment, which results in a continuous supply of want-satisfying material means';[70] his opponents merely deny that this is a sufficient operational definition. 'Modern economists make even Robinson Crusoe speculate upon the implications of choice which they regard as the essence of economy'.[71]

[67] The title and chapter headings are those of H. Michell's book, 2nd edn (Cambridge, 1957).

[68] Polanyi's theoretical essays have been conveniently assembled under the title, *Primitive, Archaic, and Modern Economies*, ed. G. Dalton (Garden City, N.Y., 1968). For a commentary on the debate, with extensive bibliography, see M. Godelier, 'Object et méthode de l'anthropologie économique', *L'Homme*, v. no. 2 (1965), pp. 32–91, reprinted in his *Rationalité et irrationalité en économie* (Paris, 1966), pp. 232–93; S. C. Humphreys, 'History, economics and anthropology: the work of Karl Polanyi', *History and Theory*, viii (1969), pp. 165–212.

[69] Polanyi, *op. cit.*, p. 86.

[70] *Ibid.*, p. 145.

[71] Roll, *op. cit.*, p. 21.

Nor were the Greeks themselves unaware that men procure their want-satisfactions by social (Polanyi's 'instituted') arrangements, or that there were things to be said about agriculture, mining, money or commerce. Aristotle refers readers who may be interested to existing books on the practical side. He mentions by name the authors of two agronomic treatises,[72] and much practical information is scattered in the surviving botanical writings of his pupil Theophrastus. Greeks who thought about the matter were also aware that their want-satisfying arrangements were technologically and socially more complex than had been the case in the past. The Homeric poems and the witness of contemporary 'barbarians' were proof enough. Greek 'historical' accounts of the development from early times were largely speculative. One should not attribute to them too much accurate knowledge of the past on such subjects; they were, for example, ignorant of the complex palace-centred organization of the late Bronze Age. The significance of the speculation lies rather in its testimony to the values of the classical era, the fifth and fourth centuries B.C. On this two points are significant for us.

The first is that growth of population, increasing specialization and technological advances, the increase in material resources were all judged positively. They were the necessary conditions for civilization, for the 'natural', that is, the highest, form of social organization, the *polis*. This was no discovery of Plato and Aristotle; it was implicit in the Prometheus myth, it became more explicit in the 'prehistory' with which Thucydides opens his *History* and in other fifth-century writers known to us only from fragments.[73] 'The ancient Greek world', writes Thucydides, 'lived like the barbarians of today.'[74] However, progress was not an unmixed blessing. It led to bitter class struggles, imperial conquest, and the ethical dangers we have already noticed. Furthermore, there is an implication that technological and material progress has come to an end. At least I am unaware of any text which suggests that continued growth in this sphere of human behaviour was either possible or desirable, and the whole tenor of

---

[72] *Pol.*, 1258b39 ff.

[73] Thuc., *History*, i.2–19. On the fragments, see T. Cole, *Democritus and the Sources of Greek Anthropology* (American Philological Association, Monograph 25, 1967).

[74] *History*, i.6.6.

the literature argues against such a notion.[75] There can and will be progress in certain cultural spheres, such as mathematics or astronomy; there can, some thought, be improvements in ethical, social and political behaviour (more often than not put in terms of a return to older virtues); there can be better (truer) understanding of life and society. But none of that adds up to the idea of progress which, in my judgement, has been in the background of all modern economic analyses at least since the late eighteenth century.[76]

For Thucydides one of the driving forces in 'prehistoric' progress was the rise and growth of maritime commerce—and that is the second point. Given his grand theme, the Athenian empire and the Peloponnesian War, he was more concerned with the corollary, the navy and the maritime empire, a polemical subject both in his day and later. But interwoven with this aspect was always the other, on which I quoted Aristotle earlier, overseas trade as an indispensable supplement to home production, for foodstuffs, timber, metals and slaves.[77] And 'in Athens facts had a way of becoming spiritual problems'.[78] That is precisely how the discussion turned. I have in mind not maritime power but the 'prob-

[75] I have examined some aspects of this theme in 'Technical innovation and economic progress in the ancient world', *EHR*, 2nd ser., xviii (1965), pp. 29–45; cf. H. W. Pleket, 'Technology and society in the Graeco-Roman world', *Acta Historiae Neerlandica*, ii (1967), pp. 1–25, originally published in Dutch in *Tijd. v. Geschiedenis*, lxxviii (1965), pp. 1–22.

[76] The faith of some Hippocratic writers, notably the author of *On Ancient Medicine* (sect. 2), that 'the rest [of medical knowledge] will be discovered eventually', is no exception, though admittedly such progress would bring 'practical' benefits to mankind. Neglect of the fundamental distinction between material and cultural progress in my view vitiates the much praised polemic by L. Edelstein, *The Idea of Progress in Classical Antiquity* (Baltimore, 1967), against the 'orthodox' view, summed up by J. B. Bury, *The Idea of Progress* (New York, 1932 edn), p. 7: '. . . the Greeks, who were so fertile in their speculations on human life, did not hit upon an idea which seems so simple and obvious to us as the idea of Progress'. On Thucydides, see J. de Romilly, 'Thucydide et l'idée de progrès', *Annali della Scuola Normale Superiore di Pisa*, xxxv (1966), pp. 143–91.

[77] On all this see A. Momigliano, 'Sea-power in Greek thought', *CR*, lviii (1944), pp. 1–7, reprinted in his *Secondo contributo alla storia degli studi classici* (Rome, 1960), pp. 57–67.

[78] *Ibid.*, p. 58.

lem' of trade and markets. Herodotus reveals its existence a century before Aristotle. When a Spartan embassy came to warn the Persian king not to harm any Greek city, he tells us, Cyrus replied: 'I have never yet feared men of this kind, who set up a place in the centre of their city where they assemble and cheat each other with oaths.' This was addressed to all Greeks, Herodotus explains, 'because they have established market-places for buying and selling', whereas the Persians have neither the practice nor the market-place. Xenophon offers partial support in his statement that the Persians exclude all hucksters and pedlars from the 'free *agora*'(here to be translated in its original sense, 'assembly-place').[79] Whatever the truth may be about Persia, the *Greek* attitude reflected by Herodotus and Xenophon is evident. Aristotle used the same terminology as Xenophon when he proposed that 'provision should be made for an *agora* of the sort called "free" in Thessaly [a district in north-central Greece]. This should be clear of all merchandise, and neither a workingman nor a farmer nor any other such person should be permitted to enter unless summoned by the magistrates'.[80] As a final example, there was Aristotle's contemporary, Aristoxenus, who thought it reasonable to claim that the half-legendary Pythagoras had 'extolled and promoted the study of numbers more than anyone, diverting it from the business of merchants'.[81]

However, neither speculation about the origins of trade nor doubts about market ethics led to the elevation of 'the economy' (which cannot be translated into Greek) to independent status as a subject of discussion or study; at least not beyond Aristotle's division of the art of acquisition into *oikonomia* and money-making, and that was a dead end. The model that survived and was imitated was Xenophon's *Oikonomikos*, a manual covering all the human relations and activities in the household (*oikos*), the relations between husband and wife, between master and slaves, between householder and his land and goods. It was not from *Hausvaterliteratur* that modern economic thinking and writing arose in the late eighteenth century, but from the radical discovery that there were 'laws' of circulation, of market exchange, of value and prices (to which the theory of ground rent was

[79] Herod, i. 152–3. Xen., *Cyropaedia*, i.2.3.
[80] *Pol.*, 1331a30–35.
[81] *Frag.* 58B2 Diels-Kranz.

linked).[82] It is at least of symbolic interest that in precisely that era David Hume made the brilliant (and still too often neglected) observation: 'I do not remember a passage in any ancient author, where the growth of a city is ascribed to the establishment of a manufacture. The commerce, which is said to flourish, is chiefly the exchange of those commodities, for which different soils and climates were suited'.[83]

I would be prepared to argue that without the concept of relevant 'laws' (or 'statistical uniformities' if one prefers) it is not possible to have a concept of 'the economy'. However, I shall be content here merely to insist that the ancients did not (rather than could not) have the concept, and to suggest where the explanation lies. One consequence of the idea of the *koinonia* was a heavy encroachment by political and status demands on the behaviour of ordinary Greeks, not just in writings of a few doctrinaire intellectuals. If we consider investment, for example, we immediately come up against a political division of the population that was unbridgeable. All Greek states, so far as we know, restricted the right of land ownership to their citizens (save for exceptional individuals who received the right as a personal privilege). They thereby, in effect, erected a wall between the land, from which the great majority of the population received their livelihood, and that very substantial proportion of the money available for investment which was in the hands of non-citizens.[84] Among the most obvious practical consequences was a narrowing of choice of investment (whether by purchase or by loan) for the potential investors on the one hand, and a tendency on the part of money-holding citizens to turn to the land from considerations of status, not of maximization of profits.[85] The absence in our sources of

---

[82] See O. Brunner, 'Das "ganze Haus" und die alteuropäische Ökonomik', in his *Neue Wege der Sozialgeschichte* (Göttingen, 1956), ch. 2, originally published in *Z.f. Nationalök.*, xiii (1950), pp. 114–39.

[83] 'Of the populousness of ancient nations', *Essays* (London, World's Classics edn, 1903), p. 415. How widely and carefully Hume had read ancient authors is demonstrated not only in this essay but also in his notebooks.

[84] The important economic rôle of the metic (the free resident 'alien'), which underlies this point, will be considered immediately below.

[85] I have discussed the evidence briefly in *Studies in Land and Credit in Ancient Athens* (New Brunswick, N.J., 1952), pp. 74–8; again in 'Land, debt, and the man of property in classical Athens', *Political Science*

any evidence of investment (including loans) for improvements on land or in manufacture is noteworthy, especially against the considerable evidence of relatively large-scale borrowing for conspicuous consumption and for expensive political obligations.[86] No doubt a modern economist could construct a sophisticated investment model to account for these Greek conditions of choice. But first the usefulness, indeed the possibility, of such a model has to be envisaged, as it was not in antiquity.[87]

Kept off the land, the non-citizens of necessity lived by manufacture, trade and moneylending. That would be of little interest were it not for the capital fact that this metic activity was not a matter of their being tolerated by the *koinonia* but of their being indispensable. They were *sought after*, precisely because the citizens could not carry on all the activities necessary for the survival of the community.[88] (Whether or not they could not 'only' because they would not is a historically meaningless 'psychological' question that seems to me to divert attention from the central issue.) Slaves were the sole labour force in all manufacturing establish-

---

Quarterly, lxviii (1953), pp. 249–68. Detailed research into the whole question of 'investments' is urgently needed.

[86] C. Mossé, *La fin de la démocratie athénienne* (Paris, 1962), pt I, ch. 1, has argued in great detail that the fourth century B.C. witnessed more fluidity than my sketch (cited in the previous note) allowed. Even so, she agrees with the point at issue here, e.g. pp. 66–7: 'Certainly such profits [from accumulation of land holdings] were rarely reinvested in production .... That is why, if there was a concentration of landholding, it did not bring about any profound transformation in the mode of agricultural production'.

[87] Political and status 'interference' was equally significant in other aspects, for example, on prices and wages whenever the state was a party, which was often the case. To enter into details would protract this discussion unnecessarily, I believe.

[88] This was openly acknowledged by an anonymous fifth-century oligarchic pamphleteer, Pseudo-Xenophon, *Const. of Athens*, 1.11–12; Plato, *Laws*, 919D–920C, made a virtue of the fact; Aristotle was troubled in the *Politics* by his inability to get round this obtrusive element in the *koinonia*, as J. Pečírka showed in a short but important article, 'A note on Aristotle's conception of citizenship and the role of foreigners in fourth-century Athens', *Eirene*, vi (1967), pp. 23–6. On metics generally in fourth-century Athens, see Mossé, *op. cit.*, pp. 167–79. Hicks, *op. cit.*, p. 48, seems to have placed the accent exactly in the wrong place when he writes of the metics, 'what is remarkable is that there should have been a phase in which their *competition* is tolerated, or even welcomed, by those already established' (my italics).

ments exceeding the immediate family circle, right to the managerial level. Without the many thousands of free non-citizens,
mostly Greeks themselves, some transient, others permanently
resident (metics), maritime commerce in the more complex
urbanized communities would have fallen below the essential
minimum for vital supplies, not to mention luxury goods. Hence
fourth-century Athens omitted one piece from its network of laws
designed to guarantee a sufficient annual import of corn—it made
no effort to restrict or specify the personnel engaged in the trade.[89]

The position is neatly symbolized by a single pamphlet, the
Ways and Means (or *Revenues*) written by Xenophon in the period
when Aristotle was worrying about *oikonomike* and *chrematistike*.
His proposals for raising the revenues of Athens are concentrated
on two groups of people. First he suggests measures to increase
the number of metics, 'one of the best sources of revenue': they
pay taxes, they are self-supporting, and they receive no pay from
the state for their services. The steps he proposes are (1) release
metics from the burdensome obligation of service in the infantry;
(2) admit them to the cavalry (an honorific service); (3) permit
them to buy land in the city on which to build residences; (4) offer
prizes to the market officials for just and speedy settlement of
disputes; (5) give reserved seats in the theatre and other forms of
hospitality to worthy foreign merchants; (6) build more lodging-
houses and hotels in the harbour and increase the number of
market-places. Hesitantly he adds the possibility that the state
should build its own merchant fleet and lease the vessels out, and
immediately turns to his second group, slaves. Starting from the
observation that large private fortunes have been made by men
who invested in slaves and let them to holders of concessions in the
Athenian silver mines, Xenophon proposes that the state embark
on this activity itself, ploughing back the profits into the purchase
of more and more slaves. After some rough calculations and
various counter-arguments against possible objections, he writes,
'I have now explained what measures should be taken by the state
in order that every Athenian may be maintained at public expense'.[90]

---

[89] To avoid misunderstanding, I will say explicitly that a count of heads
would probably show that even in Athens the citizens who did work
of some kind, including agriculture, outnumbered the others. The point
at issue is the location within the economy of the vital minority.

[90] Xen., *Ways and Means*, iv.33.

We need not waste time examining the practicality of these schemes. Many harsh things have been said about them by modern scholars—all from the wrong point of view, that of modern economic institutions and ideas. What matters is the mentality revealed in this unique document, a mentality which pushed to the extreme the notion that what we call the economy was properly the exclusive business of outsiders.[91]

[91] I have discussed the matter raised iñ this final section (and elsewhere) more fully in *The Ancient Economy* (London, 1973).

III

ROME AND THE CLASS STRUGGLE IN THE GREEK STATES 200-146 B.C.*

John Briscoe

Class divisions in the Greek world were extremely clear-cut. The distribution of wealth was very uneven, and it is possible to speak of two parties in every state, the rich and the poor, the few and the many. These descriptions are common in ancient writers.[1] There were, no doubt, those who did not fit easily into either category but the schematism is far more fruitful than many modern ones. Strife between these two classes was a continual feature of Greek history, and changes of constitution were the symptom of the victory of one or other of the classes. Oligarchy was the ascendancy of the rich, democracy of the poor.

The class struggle in the Greek states, however, was by no means a purely internal matter for the states concerned; it also affected relations between states. In the fifth century the democrats had looked principally to Athens for support, the oligarchs to Sparta.[2] In the fourth century Philip II of Macedon supported the upper classes, and this continued to be the policy of the rulers of Macedon down to Antigonus Doson. The policy was reversed by Philip V, who came to the throne of Macedon in 221 B.C. He is known to have encouraged civil strife and to have attempted to woo popular favour by wearing common dress and portraying himself as a man of the people.[3] In 200 B.C. Rome went to war

---

*From no. 36 (1967).

[1] One thinks particularly of the famous passage in Thuc., iii. 82-3. There are innumerable references in Aristotle's *Politics*.

[2] Cf. p. 72 below.

[3] Cf. Polyb., vii. 11. 10, 12. 9, 13. 6-7, 14. 2-5, x.26; Livy, xxvii. 31. 3, xxxii. 21. 23; Plut., *Aratus*, xlix. 2 ff.

with Philip, and there followed the series of wars that led to Rome's complete domination of the Mediterranean area. Rome's policy in this period towards the rival factions in the Greek states is the subject of this paper.

I

It will be convenient first to summarize the events of these years. In 200 B.C. Rome declared war on Macedon, ostensibly to force Philip to cease his attacks on other Greek states; in fact Rome had seen the growing power of Macedon and was afraid that Philip, either by himself or in conjunction with Antiochus, the king of Syria, would invade Italy and threaten Rome's domination of the peninsula. Philip was defeated by Titus Quinctius Flamininus at the battle of Cynoscephalae in 197 and forced to evacuate all his possessions outside Macedon itself. He was, however, left his kingdom and became an ally of Rome. The Roman senate issued a famous declaration, proclaiming Greece to be completely free, without garrisons or tribute—though three of Philip's chief garrison towns continued to be occupied by Roman troops until 194. In 195 Flamininus freed the city of Argos from the domination of Nabis, the tyrant of Sparta.

Meanwhile Rome had been troubled by the aggressions of Antiochus of Syria. He had advanced along the coast of Asia Minor in 197, and by 196 had crossed the Hellespont. Negotiations with him produced no solution. Before long Roman troops were back in Greece; the Aetolians were dissatisfied with the settlement made after the defeat of Philip and called in Antiochus to 'free' Greece from Roman control. Antiochus arrived inadequately prepared and was defeated in 191 at the battle of Thermopylae. He retreated to Asia and was again defeated at Magnesia in 190. The peace settlement imposed by Rome drove Antiochus back beyond the Taurus mountains, and gave large parts of Asia Minor to Rhodes and Pergamum, Rome's chief allies amongst the Greeks.

In the 180s Rome had to deal with renewed expansionist moves by Philip and with a complex series of problems in the Peloponnese. In 179 Philip died and was succeeded by his son Perseus. The latter embarked on a policy of retrenchment at home and of renewing friendly relations with other Greek states. Spurred on by reports that Perseus was making military preparations for a new war against Rome, the Romans declared war on Macedon. Perseus was defeated at Pydna in 168 and the Macedonian monarchy was dismembered. Rome was now undisputed mistress of the Mediterranean. In the next twenty years she was occupied with various disputes in different parts of the Greek world. Military intervention was avoided until the senate decided that the last remaining independent power of any size, the Achaean League, should be destroyed. Rome went to war in 147; the next year the Achaeans were defeated, the League dismembered and the city of Corinth razed to the ground.

II

Rome was governed by an oligarchy. The people as a whole chose the magistrates, but they were organized for this purpose in assemblies which gave a dominant influence to men of wealth. The important political decisions were made by the senate, a body which was composed largely of ex-magistrates, who, once they became members, remained so for life. Rome's domination of the Italian peninsula relied to a large extent on her support from the upper classes in the allied states of Italy.[4] The natural sympathies of the senatorial government could thus be expected to be on the side of the upper classes in the Greek cities. And since Philip V was courting the masses, Rome might well feel that support for the rich was a useful weapon in winning the war. Contrariwise, the upper classes in the Greek states could naturally be expected to look to Rome for support.

It was Fustel de Coulanges who first expounded the view that Rome consistently supported the upper-class elements in the Greek states. Indeed he saw the existence of the class struggle in Greece as the chief reason for Rome's eventual domination of the Greeks.[5] This view, accepted by many later scholars,[6] was chal-

[4] On the Roman constitution cf. P. A. Brunt, 'The Roman mob', pp. 76–80 below. On Italy cf. A. H. McDonald, 'Rome and the Italian Confederation (200–186 B.C.)' *JRS*, xxxiv (1944), pp. 11–33; E. Badian, *Foreign Clientelae (264–70 B.C.)* (Oxford, 1958), p. 147; P. A. Brunt, 'Italian aims at the time of the Social War', *JRS*, lv (1965), p. 92.
[5] Fustel de Coulanges, *Questions Historiques* (Paris, 1893), pp. 121–211.
[6] G. De Sanctis, *Storia dei Romani*, iv, 1 (Turin, 1923), p. 98; F. W.

lenged by Passerini who argued that Roman policy towards the Greek states could not be correlated with a predilection in favour of the upper classes.[7]

It is easy enough to find *prima facie* evidence for the theory of Fustel de Coulanges. In 197, for example, the men of Opous were divided into two factions. One called in the Aetolians 'but the richer faction shut out the Aetolians, and sending a messenger to the Roman commander, held the city until he came'.[8] Aetolia at this time was an ally of Rome, but her constitution was democratic,[9] and it was not long before she became Rome's leading opponent in Greece. In 194 Flamininus reorganized Thessaly on timocratic lines:[10]

> the states were in complete chaos and confusion and had to be brought into some reasonable method of government. . . . Flamininus chose the senate and the judges mainly on the basis of wealth and gave the greatest influence to that element in the states which found it to their advantage that everything should remain peaceful and undisturbed.

In 192, Livy tells us, the mass of the people looked to Antiochus to save them from Roman domination, while the upper classes were on the side of Rome. 'The masses were eager for change and entirely on the side of Antiochus';[11] and 'it was evident to all that

---

Walbank, *Philip V of Macedon* (Cambridge, 1940), p. 165; Badian, *Foreign Clientelae*, p. 78, and 'Rome and Antiochus the Great: a study in Cold War', *CP*, liv (1959), p. 93 (= *Studies in Greek and Roman History* (Oxford, 1964), p. 129); A. Aymard, 'L'organisation de la Macédoine en 167 et le régime représentatif dans le monde grec', *CP*, xlv (1950), p. 106 (= *Études d'historie ancienne* (Paris, 1967), p. 176); M. Holleaux, *Rome, la Grèce et les monarchies hellenistiques* (Paris, 1921), pp. 228 ff. Holleaux is rather more cautious in *CAH*, viii (Cambridge, 1930), p. 197.

[7] 'I moti politico-sociali della Grecia e i Romani', *Athenaeum*, new ser., xi (1933), pp. 309–35. Passerini's view was accepted by M. I. Rostovtzeff, *Social and Economic History of the Hellenistic World* (Oxford, 1941), pp. 611–12 and 1460 n. 14, and, apparently, by P. Meloni, *Perseo e la fine della monarchia macedone* (Cagliari, 1953), p. 254 n. 2.

[8] Livy, xxxii. 32. 2–3.

[9] Cf. n. 20 below.

[10] Livy, xxxiv. 51. 4–6.

[11] Livy, xxxv. 33. 1.

the leading men and the aristocracy were in favour of the Roman alliance and were content with the existing situation, while the multitude and those whose affairs were not all they could desire were in favour of a complete change'.[12] In 190 the Phocaeans similarly divided: 'some were trying to sway the minds of the masses in favour of Antiochus ... but the senate and the upper classes were of the opinion that they should remain loyal to Rome'.[13] The same division of opinion is found in the years preceding the war with Perseus: 'the sympathies of a large proportion of the people were on his side'[14] and 'the masses everywhere, as usually happens, were on the worse side, being inclined towards Perseus and the Macedonians'.[15] Finally one may note the actions of L. Mummius after the defeat of the Achaeans in 146: 'he dissolved democracies, and established magistrates elected on the basis of wealth'.[16]

III

This list of evidence, however, is by no means the whole story. There are a number of instances where Rome did not give her support to the right-wing elements in the Greek states, and any account of Roman policy must explain these.[17]

[12] Livy, xxxv. 34. 3.
[13] Livy, xxxvii. 9; cf. Polyb., xxi. 6.
[14] Livy, xlii. 5. 2.
[15] Livy, xlii. 30. 1.
[16] Paus., vii. 16. 9.
[17] Some of the counter-examples adduced by Passerini and others are largely based on Livy's use of the word *principes*. Passerini assumed that this always meant *optimates*, and thus, for example, when Ismenias, the leader of the anti-Roman faction in Aetolia in the 170s, is described as a *princeps* he can be assumed to have been a supporter of the upper classes (Livy, xlii. 38. 5: in 43. 9 he is called *nobilis ac potens*. Cf. Meloni, *Perseo*, p. 147 n. 1.). The assumption is unjustified. Livy uses *princeps* and *principes* in non-Roman contexts very frequently (a list will be found in Pauly-Wissowa, *RE*, *s.v. princeps*, vol. xxii, columns 2004–5) and it is clear that in most cases it means simply 'leaders', without implying that they are leaders of the upper-class party. I can find only four passages (Livy, xxxii. 38. 7, xxxv. 34. 3, xlii. 30. 1, xlii. 44. 4) where the class meaning is apparent; and the last two of these are dubious, for one must always reckon with the leaders of the people not being in complete accord with their own followers. See further n. 63 below.

I have said it was natural that the upper classes in the Greek states should look to Rome as their natural champion. It was they who particularly wanted to resist Philip's advances, and the latter had tried to gain support among their political opponents. I believe that in the 190s Rome's natural preference was for oligarchic governments—other things being equal—but she was prepared to take support from whatever source it came, and never dreamed of pressing her ideological predilections to the point where they endangered her own best interests.

The two main powers in Greece, Macedon apart, were the great confederations of the Achaean and Aetolian Leagues. In the First Macedonian War, concurrent with Rome's struggle against Hannibal, the Achaeans had been allies of Macedon, whilst the Aetolians had been Rome's principal helper.[18] The Aetolians had, however, made a separate peace with Philip in 206, and their alliance with Rome had come to an end. The two Leagues were of very different character. The Achaean League, though nominally democratic, was in fact controlled by men of means.[19] The Aetolian League had a more democratic basis, and it was its leaders Scopas and Dorimachus who were responsible for making the alliance with Rome in 212/1.[20] In 205/4 Scopas and Dorimachus were given a special commission to enact laws. They proposed the abolition of all debts, but this was successfully resisted by one Alexander Isius. Scopas and Dorimachus then left Aetolia, Scopas to serve as a mercenary in Egypt.[21] Passerini appears to argue from these events that the Aetolian League in the

---

[18] On the alliance with Rome cf. literature cited by H. H. Schmitt, *Die Staatsvertäge des Altertums*, iii (Munich, 1969), no. 536.

[19] For the Achaean League, cf. F. W. Walbank, *Commentary on Polybius*, i (Oxford, 1956), p. 222; K. von Fritz, *The Theory of the Mixed Constitution in Antiquity* (New York, 1954), pp. 4 ff. The constitution of the League is most fully discussed by A. Aymard, *Les assemblées de la confédération achaienne* (Bordeaux, 1938), J. A. O. Larsen, *Representative Government in Greek and Roman History* (Berkeley and Los Angeles, 1955), pp. 86 ff.

[20] On the Aetolian League, cf. Larsen, *Representative Government*, pp. 70–1; Walbank, *Commentary*, pp. 453–4. It is true that by the end of the third century important decisions were taken by a small 'inner cabinet', but it was not controlled by men of wealth, and it is misleading to call it an oligarchy: thus, e.g., F. W. Walbank, *Aratus of Sicyon* (Cambridge, 1933), p. 25.

[21] Polyb., xiii. 1–2. On Scopas' later activities cf. Polyb., xv. 25.16 ff., xvi. 39 ff., xviii. 53–5; Livy, xxxi. 43.

190s shifted decisively to the right, and that because the radicals had been friends of Rome, their opponents became her enemies.[22] It is true enough that the Aetolians rejected the extreme proposals of Scopas and Dorimachus, and it is also true that Alexander Isius was one of the leading Aetolian opponents of Rome in the 190s. But the Aetolians after 204 were still far more radical than the Achaeans, and it is wrong to think that Aetolia in the 190s was ruled by an exclusively upper-class government.

Aetolia came back into alliance with Rome in 199.[23] The Achaeans joined a year later. This decision encountered violent opposition within the Achaean League,[24] but this does not seem to have had any connection with differences over internal policy. The decision whether to support Rome or Philip was discussed on its own merits. Rome was glad to accept both Achaean and Aetolian support and was not at all concerned with the internal politics of the states who were willing to support her in the war with Macedon.

This is made even clearer in the case of Nabis of Sparta. Nabis took to extremes the radical policies advanced in the third century by Agis IV and Cleomenes III and had established an extreme left-wing régime in Sparta. Polybius detested Nabis and all he stood for, and has given us a very lurid picture of his character and activities:[25]

> For he utterly exterminated those of the royal houses who survived in Sparta, and banishing those citizens who were distinguished for their wealth and illustrious ancestry, gave their property and wives to the chief of his supporters and to his mercenaries, who were for the most part murderers, mutilators, highwaymen and burglars.

On the evidence of this passage Passerini argued that Nabis was simply a personal tyrant out for his own ends, and not a man with

---

[22] Passerini, 'I moti politico-sociali', pp. 319–20. It is not all that relevant that Alexander Isius was extremely rich (Polyb., xxi. 26.9).

[23] Livy, xxxi. 41.

[24] Livy, xxxii. 19 ff. For comments on the policy, cf. Polyb., xviii. 13–15; A. Aymard, 'Le fragment de Polybe "sur les traitres"', *REA*, xlii (1940), pp. 9–19 (= *Études d'histoire ancienne*, pp. 354–63).

[25] Polyb., xiii. 6, cf. xvi. 13. On Nabis cf. V. Ehrenberg, *RE*, vol. xvi, columns 1471–82; C. Mossé, *Cahiers d'histoire*, ix (1964), pp. 313–23, B. Shimron, 'Nabis of Sparta and the helots', *CP*, lxi (1966), pp. 1–7.

an advanced social programme.[26] Polybius, however, is not an unbiased witness. He detested left-wing political movements,[27] and it is not an unusual method of attacking a policy one does not like to obscure that policy and claim that its exponents are merely evil men working for their own ends. Nabis' own claims may be more significant. These occur in a speech to Flamininus in 195: they are reported by Livy, and though, no doubt, the composition of the speech is Livy's own, the source is Polybius.[28] 'My title of tyrant and my actions are laid as accusations against me, because I summon slaves to freedom, because I give land to the impoverished masses.' And he compares his policy with that of Rome: 'You choose your cavalry on the basis of wealth, and your infantry too; you desire that a few should be pre-eminently rich, and the mass of the people should be subservient to them.'

We may allow Nabis to have been a geniune, if violent social reformer. His policy towards Rome and Macedon was undoubtedly purely expedient. In 197 Philip offered Nabis the possession of Argos, on condition that if Philip defeated the Romans, Nabis would restore the city to him.[29] Nabis occupied the town, and introduced there a social revolution of the same sort that he had instituted at Sparta itself. This achieved, Nabis made a complete volte-face and offered his services to Flamininus.[30] Flamininus, despite the objections of Attalus of Pergamum, was only too glad to accept. Once the war with Philip was over, however, Roman policy changed, and in 195 Flamininus went to war to free Argos from Nabis' control. But even this was not a war undertaken to rid the Peloponnese of an unwelcome socio-political system. The object was, in part, to free Argos from Nabis in order to weaken the growing power of the Spartan leader, and, secondly, to placate the feelings of Rome's Greek allies. They were not, in the event, very much placated. The peace terms imposed on Nabis by Flamininus left the former in charge of Sparta and did not even go so far as restoring those exiled by Nabis.[31] Flamininus did not

---

[26] 'I moti politico-sociali', pp. 315–18.
[27] Cf. Polyb., vi. 43, xx. 5–7; Walbank, *Commentary*, pp. 12–13.
[28] Livy, xxxiv. 31. 11 ff. Freeing of slaves also in Polyb., xvi. 13. 1.
[29] Livy, xxxii. 38 ff.
[30] Livy, xxxii. 40.
[31] Livy, xxxiv. 34 ff.; Plut., *Flamininus*, xiii. On the exiles, cf. A. Aymard, *Les premiers rapports de Rome et de la confédération achaienne* (Bordeaux, 1938), pp. 241–4.

want to eradicate Nabis because that would have left the Achaean League in virtually complete control of the Peloponnese. His aim was a balance of power, not upper-class constitutional government, and he preferred to tolerate the continued existence of a revolutionary government in Sparta rather than allow the Achaean League excessive power in the Peloponnese.

The Achaeans and others were upset by Flamininus' refusal to eradicate Nabis.[32] They had hoped that Rome's victory would mean the end of a social system they detested and feared. Passerini, consistently with his view that Nabis' régime was simple tyranny and not genuine social revolution, held that the Achaeans were more afraid of Nabis' expansionism than of his social aims.[33] This view is scarcely born out by Livy's own words: 'As for the Achaeans, whatever joy the restoration of Argos to the League brought them, was rendered incomplete by the fact that Sparta remained enslaved and Nabis was left as a thorn in their side'.[34] Before the final surrender of Nabis the thoughts of the allies had clearly been directed to the political nature of his régime: 'his example would incite many in other states to attack the freedom of their own citizens'.[35] Foreign domination, it is true, was part of their fear, but only because the fear was of the export of revolution. Their main concern was the danger of political upheaval in their own cities.

Thus Rome was not over-concerned with the internal politics of the Greek states where there were other, and more important, issues at stake. Where this was not so, she felt able to indulge her natural preference for the upper classes. Flamininus' behaviour in Boeotia in 196 is an interesting case in point.[36] In that year he agreed that those Boeotians who had served with Philip should be permitted to return to Boeotia. Their leader Brachylles was immediately elected to the chief magistracy. The pro-Roman party, led by Zeuxippus, wanted to murder Brachylles and asked for Flamininus' permission. Flamininus replied that 'he himself would not take part in such a deed, but he was not standing in the

---

[32] Livy, xxxiv. 41. 4 ff., 48. 5–6.
[33] At *Athenaeum*, new ser., xxiii (1945), p. 118 Passerini is less inclined to press this point.
[34] Livy, xxxiv. 41. 4.
[35] Livy, xxxiv. 33. 8.
[36] Polyb., xviii. 43, Livy, xxxiii. 27–9 for all this.

way of those who wanted to do it'.[37] The murder provoked a wave of anti-Roman feeling in Boeotia and Zeuxippus fled the country. Roman soldiers in Boeotia were massacred. Flamininus imposed severe punishments on the Boeotians for this outbreak, but Zeuxippus was not recalled.

Polybius' words suggest that the pro-Roman party was upper class. They complain to Flamininus of 'the people's present hostility towards them and the general lack of gratitude shown by the masses'.[38] It looks as if in this case Flamininus felt able to encourage the intrigues of the pro-Roman upper classes. But even so, he was not willing to take this encouragement to the extent of forcing a whole people into open opposition, and it was for that reason that he did not attempt to recall Zeuxippus.[39]

In 194 the immediate problems had been settled, and Flamininus' actions shortly before his departure from Greece indicate his natural preferences. He made constitutional alterations:[40]

> he spent his time in administering justice and altering the arrangements made in the states by the arbitrary conduct of Philip or his representatives: they had increased the power of the supporters of their own faction by depriving others of liberty and justice.

Who had been suppressed and how becomes clear from Livy's further remarks. Flamininus advocated *concordia* between the various classes of society. This presumably meant that the lower classes were to accept government by the upper classes. The only place where we know the details of Flamininus' reorganization is Thessaly. There, as we have seen, 'the states were in complete chaos and confusion and had to be brought into some reasonable method of government'. Flamininus' solution was to 'choose the senate and the judges mainly on the basis of wealth, and to give the greatest influence to that element in the states which found it to their advantage that everything should remain peaceful and

---

[37] Polyb., xviii. 43. 10.

[38] Polyb., xviii. 43. 8.

[39] But in 188 he felt safe enough to attempt to recall Zeuxippus and nearly succeeded in causing a war between Boeotia and Achaea (Polyb., xxii. 4).

[40] Livy, xxxiv. 48. 2.

undisturbed'.[41] It is not completely certain whether Flamininus restricted the franchise itself to the upper classes, or merely the offices of state; or whether he introduced a timocratic assembly modelled on that of Rome, whose main principle, according to Cicero, was that the will of the majority should not prevail.[42]

IV

As we have seen, Flamininus refused to eradicate Nabis because he was afraid of the increasing power of the Achaean League. The same desire to maintain a balance of power appears to have motivated Roman policy during the long and complex dispute between Sparta and the Achaean League in the 180s. In 192 Nabis had been murdered and the Achaean leader Philopoemen took Sparta into the Achaean League. Faced with the invasion of Antiochus, Rome was in no position to object. Then, in 189, the Spartans attacked one of the Laconian coast-towns containing the Spartan exiles who, though banished by Nabis or his predecessor Machanidas, had not been restored by Philopoemen in 192. The matter was referred to the senate, who gave a reply so ambiguous that both sides interpreted it as favouring their own case. Philopoemen proceeded to force Sparta to dismantle her walls, recall the exiles and abolish the Lycurgan constitution.[43] The senate by no means welcomed this rightwards move in Sparta. In 187 some Spartans brought complaints to the senate about Philopoemen's actions, and the consul, M. Aemilius Lepidus, wrote to the Achaeans criticizing their conduct. Meanwhile Philopoemen had despatched an embassy to Rome, and this returned in 185 to report that the senate was displeased with what had happened, though they were not taking any action.[44] The senate now instructed Q. Caecilius Metellus to investigate the situation. When Metellus arrived the pro-Roman Diophanes attacked Philopoemen's handling of both

---

[41] Livy, xxxiv. 51. 4–6.
[42] Cic., *De re publica*, ii. 39. On whether or not there was a full assembly in Thessaly, cf. Aymard, *op. cit.* (n. 6), p. 105 (=*Études d'histoire ancienne*, pp. 174–5).
[43] Livy, xxxviii. 30–4; Polyb., xxi. 32c, cf. xxii. 3. 7; Plut., *Philopoemen*, xvi; Paus., viii. 51. 3.
[44] Polyb., xxii. 7. 6; Diodorus, xxix. 17.

Spartan and Messenian affairs, but Philopoemen and his supporters Archon and Lycortas defended their policy. As before, the
different factions within the Achaean League seem to have had no
relation to class-divisions.

Metellus asked for a special assembly to be convened, but was
refused on the grounds that it was illegal for the Achaeans to summon an assembly in such circumstances unless they had received
written instructions from the senate. There are reasons for thinking that Philopoemen and his friends were rather twisting the sense
of the law involved, but the senate hardly clarified matters when,
after discussing the rebuff to Metellus, it told the Achaeans to give
the same consideration to Roman envoys as Rome did to the
representatives of the Achaean League.[45]

In 184 Areus and Alcibiades, described as representatives of the
'old exiles', disputed with the Achaeans before the senate. The
'old exiles' are clearly those exiled by the tyrants and restored in
189. In the following year, however, we find the 'old exiles' divided into two groups. One section, led by Lysis, wanted complete
restitution of the exiles' property; the other, led by Areus and
Alcibiades, proposed that only a portion of the property should
be restored. They, it seems, were willing to countenance some
redistribution of wealth.[46]

The result of the mission of Areus and Alcibiades was that the
senate instructed Appius Claudius Pulcher to investigate the
situation, but before he arrived the Achaeans had condemned
Areus and Alcibiades to death for undertaking an embassy to
Rome on their own account.[47] When Appius arrived, a long debate
ensued, and Appius appears to have threatened the use of force.
Eventually the Achaeans agreed to repeal the sentence on Areus
and Alcibiades, but asked the Romans themselves to be respon-

---

[45] Polyb., xxii. 10. On the legal issues involved, cf. Aymard, *Les assemblées
de la confédération achaienne*, pp. 188–204: *Contra*, Larsen, *Representative
Government*, pp. 90–1. The law probably said that a *synkletos* was to be
called if written instructions came from the senate. It was interpreted to
mean that it could not be held if there were no such instructions. For
the senate's rebuke, cf. Polyb., xxii. 12. 10, Livy, xxxix. 33. 8.

[46] Polyb., xxii. 11–12 for the dispute before the senate in 184. On the
political position of Areus and Alcibiades, cf. B. Niese, *Geschichte der
griechischen und makedonischen Staaten seit der Schlacht bei Chaeronea*, iii
(Gotha, 1903), p. 42 n. 4, 49.

[47] Livy, xxxix. 35. 8; Paus., vii. 9. 2.

sible for any changes they wished to institute in Sparta.[48] The matter
was thus referred back to the senate, who found themselves faced
with a situation more complicated than ever. Sparta was now
represented by four different groups of ambassadors. There were
the two sections of the 'old exiles' whom I have already mentioned,
there was Serippus who wanted the existing situation to continue,
and there was Charon representing the 'democrats' who had been
exiled in 192 or 189.[49]

The senate, floundering in the confusion, appointed a commit-
tee of experts to deal with the matter: Flamininus, Metellus and
Appius Claudius.[50] Eventually an agreement was reached among
the various Spartan groups that the exiles were to return and the
city was to remain part of the Achaean League, but no agreement
was forthcoming on the question of the restitution of property—
and what this involved, the social and economic policy that Sparta
was to follow. With some difficulty the Achaean representatives
were persuaded to add their seals to this outline settlement.
Q. Marcius Philippus was sent out to administer the settlement.

About this time, it seems, some of the 'old exiles' were again
exiled.[51] When Philippus arrived both Sparta and Messene were on
the point of revolting from the Achaean League. Messene in fact
did so, and in the resulting war Philopoemen was killed.[52] Philippus appears to have done his best to embroil both Sparta and
Messene with the League; on his return to Rome, he reported to
the senate that if the Achaeans continued with their present independent and arrogant policy, it would not be surprising if Sparta
joined Messene in revolt.

Spartan ambassadors were again present in Rome, and to these
the senate replied that it did not think that their present dispute
with the Achaeans was any concern of Rome. This ambiguous
reply[53] suggested rebellion to Sparta whilst to the Achaeans it
suggested that, although Rome had no sympathy for the Achaean

[48] Polyb., xxii. 2; Livy, xxxix. 33, 35–7; Paus., vii. 9. 4.
[49] Polyb., xxiii. 4. The senate and Livy (xxxix. 48. 2–4) were at one in their
inability to unravel the confusion.
[50] Appius has to be added in Polybius.
[51] Polyb. xxiii. 5. 18, 6, 9. 1, 18. 5.
[52] For these events and Philippus' part in them cf. *JRS*, liv (1964), pp.
66–7. Death of Philopoemen: Polyb., xxiii. 12; Livy. xxxix. 48. 5 ff.;
Plut., *Philopoemen*, xviii; Justin, xxxii. 1. 4; Paus., viii. 51. 5.
[53] For other ambiguous *senatus consulta*, cf. pp. 63 above and 69 below.

case, she was not much concerned with what happened. Soon after this Sparta did secede from the League.[54]

By 182 Lycortas had recovered both Messene and Sparta,[55] and some of the exiles returned to Sparta.[56] Charon is found in Sparta shortly after this,[57] and it seems to follow that the exiles of 192 and 189 must have been recalled in accordance with the agreement made in 183, and that it is a section of the 'old exiles' who form the subject of further disputes between the Achaeans and the senate.[58] A senatorial instruction in 181 ordering their return was ignored[59] and in 180 Lycortas was still sure that the senate would not enforce its decision. Ambassadors were sent to Rome, but one of their number, Callicrates, instead of defending Achaea, told the senate that if they wanted their will respected, they must give positive support to the pro-Romans in the Greek states.[60] The senate agreed, expressed its view clearly, and the exiles returned.

The issues between Sparta and Achaea were complex, but they were very closely connected with decisions about the social and political constitution of Sparta. The senate, however, did not concern itself with these questions. Rome's policy had been to create divisions within the League and to use ambiguous replies and veiled threats to keep the Achaeans in a state of suspicion and uncertainty. And, as we can see, even the right-wing groups in Sparta could quarrel with Achaea. As in the previous decade Rome saw her main interest as being the preservation of the balance of power in the Peloponnese. The internal structure of Sparta was of little concern to her.

V

Polybius regarded the speech of Callicrates at Rome as being of the greatest importance.[61] He took the view that before 180 Rome

[54] Cf. Polyb., xxiii. 17. 1; Niese, *Geschichte der griechischen und makedonischen Staaten*, iii, p. 49 n. 3.
[55] Polyb., xxiii. 16–17.
[56] Polyb., xxiii. 18. 1–2.
[57] Polyb., xxiii. 18. 4, xxiv. 7.
[58] Cf. *SIG*[3], no. 634, where Callicrates is honoured for securing the restitution of the 'old exiles'.
[59] Polyb., xxiv. 2. Paus., vii. 9. 5–6 is quite unintelligible.
[60] Polyb., xxiv. 8. 8 ff.
[61] Polyb., xxiv. 10. Cf. Badian, *Foreign Clientelae*, p. 91.

dealt with the Achaeans on equal terms whilst after that date the senate gave active support to her toadies to get her will enforced. The judgement seems too extreme—as we have seen Rome's attitude before 180 was nowhere near as open and honest as Polybius appears to have believed. It is true, however, that Callicrates stiffened the senate's determination to enforce its will by showing that there were people in Greece who would get its wishes obeyed. And in the following years the senate did give active support to pro-Romans in the Greek states. This is seen particularly clearly in the years following the Third Macedonian War. Charops in Epirus, Lyciscus in Aetolia, Chremas in Acarnania and Mnasippus in Boeotia were all given support by Rome, and their opponents were exiled. Polybius' description of these men appears to indicate that they were proponents of the sort of tyrannical policy exercised by Nabis. It is doubtful if the same is true of Callicrates. His differences with Lycortas and Polybius seem to have been simply about the attitude to be taken towards Rome, and were not concerned with the internal policy of the Achaean League.[62] But the senate's policy after the defeat of Perseus was ruthless: one thousand suspect Achaeans, Polybius the most famous of them, were deported to Italy.

Once again the senate looked to what she now regarded as her own interest—the elimination of her political opponents in the Greek states and the vigorous championing of her friends, irrespective of their internal policies. Previously she had refused to eradicate popular régimes; now she went further and actually supported them. The nature of the régime in each state depended to a great extent on the attitudes which the various groups or parties had taken towards Perseus at the time of the Third Macedonian War. It seems that in many states the conservatives were, at least, lukewarm towards Rome and that their opponents took the opportunity to support Rome and gain political power for themselves.[63]

[62] The evidence of all this is fully set out by Passerini, 'I moti politico-sociali', pp. 327 ff. When I speak of Rome's policy I refer to that of the senatorial majority. There are reasons for thinking that a minority disapproved. Cf. *Historia*, xviii (1969), pp. 49–70.

[63] Livy (xlii. 30. 1) says that the *plebs* were generally on Perseus' side, but the *principes* were divided. But on the ambiguity of *principes*, cf. n. 17 above. The *plebs* were no doubt forced to change their attitude towards Perseus by the fact of Roman force. The demagogic leaders may have had some difficulty in convincing their natural followers.

VI

The Achaean exiles were at last permitted to return in 150.[64] There followed in a short while the Achaean war, which led to the destruction of Corinth and the dissolution of the Achaean League in its existing form. The war has appeared to several writers to have been brought about by a newly prominent group of demagogues who felt that they had to outbid the restored exiles in nationalistic and anti-Roman sentiments.[65] Examination of the details of the war does not, I think, support this interpretation.

The antecedents of the war are complex. In about 156 Athens had attacked Oropus. Oropus appealed to the senate, who asked Sicyon to act as mediator in the matter.[66] Sicyon imposed a fine of five hundred talents on Athens, and the Athenians sent the heads of the three great Athenian philosophical schools to Rome to plead their case. The senate reduced the fine to one hundred talents. What followed is obscure, but it seems that the Athenians refused to pay the fine, and installed colonists of their own in Oropus. At this point Oropus promised the Spartan Menalcidas ten talents if he would persuade the Achaeans to help her against Athens. Half of this Menalcidas in his turn promised to Callicrates.[67]

The Achaeans appear to have been successful in restoring the Oropians to their own land. Menalcidas, however, refused to pay Callicrates, who proceeded to accuse him before the Achaeans of working in Rome to separate Sparta from the Achaean League. Menalcidas gave three of his talents to the Achaean Diaeus who helped him to get acquitted on this charge.

Menalcidas now made a fresh embassy of his own accord com-

[64] Polyb., xxxv. 6 = Plut., *Cato maior*, ix. For the date, Paus., vii. 10. 12.

[65] G. Niccolini, *La confederazione acaea* (Pavia, 1914), p. 182. Cf. Fustel de Coulanges, *Questions Historiques*, pp. 201 ff.

[66] Polyb., xxxii. 11, xxxiii. 2; Paus., vii. 11. 4 ff.; *SIG*³, no. 675. The embassy of philosophers: Polyb., xxxiii. 2.; Plut., *Cato maior*, xxii; Cic., *Academica*, ii. 137=Gellius, vi. 14. 8–10. The narrative given here is that of Pausanias corrected to make it consistent with *SIG*³, no. 675. Cf. W. S. Ferguson, *Hellenistic Athens* (London, 1911), p. 327.

[67] Paus., vii. 11. 7–8 (but cf. preceeding note). For the narrative of the Achaean War, see especially G. De Sanctis, *Storia dei Romani*, iv, 3 (Florence, 1964), pp. 127 ff. Only fragments of Polybius's account survive and for most of the details we have to rely on Pausanias (vii. 10–16).

plaining about a boundary dispute.[68] The senate replied to Menalcidas that all matters except those involving capital cases were to be dealt with by the Achaean League. Diaeus, now Achaean *strategos*, was confident that Rome was not interested in Sparta and claimed that the senate had given the federal body jurisdiction in all cases. Sparta was forced by threat of war to condemn to death those whom Diaeus held to be responsible for anti-Achaean actions in Sparta, and in 148[69] Menalcidas again journeyed to Rome to present his case to the senate. Callicrates and Diaeus were sent to represent the League. The senate despatched ambassadors and instructed them to detach several important states from the League. But the actual reply that it gave in public was so ambiguous that both sides were encouraged to think that their requests had been granted,[70] and the Roman ambassadors spent such an inordinate time in reaching Greece that fighting broke out between Sparta and Achaea, as a result of which Menalcidas committed suicide.[71] When the ambassadors arrived they announced that Sparta, Corinth, Argos, Heraclea and Orchomenos were to be detached from the League. There was a riot and the ambassadors were maltreated.[72]

Despite this, Rome made strenuous efforts to avoid going to war with the Achaean League. Sex. Julius Caesar, the next Roman ambassador, was instructed to act with moderation. Polybius says that the senate's aim was to humble the Achaeans, not destroy them altogether.[73] But the senate did not rescind its decree that the League should be emasculated by the separation of so many of its important members.[74] Critolaus, the Achaean *strategos*, refused to

[68] Paus., vii. 12. 4. This probably refers to the same territory over which there had been a dispute between Sparta and Megalopolis in 164/3 (Paus., vii. 11. 1–3; cf. Polyb., xxxi. 1. 7; *SIG*³, no. 665).

[69] It may be helpful to enumerate the *strategoi* of the last years of the Achaean League: 151/0 Menalcidas, 150/49 Diaeus, 149/8 Damocritus, 148/7 Diaeus, 147/6 Critolaus, Diaeus *suffectus*.

[70] Cf. above pp. 63 and 65.

[71] Paus., vii. 13.

[72] Paus., vii. 14; cf. Polyb., xxxviii. 9. Polybius adds that they exaggerated what had happened. Dio (fr. 72) and Livy (ep. li) are probably trying to justify Rome's action in saying that the detached cities were those that had previously belonged to Philip. Other sources: Justin, xxxiv. 1–2; Eutropius, iv. 14; Florus, i. 32; Zonaras, ix. 31.

[73] Polyb., xxxviii. 9. 6.

[74] Cf. Niese, *Geschichte der griechischen und makedonischen Staaten*, iii, p. 344.

come to an agreement, and war was declared. It is noticeable that Metellus Macedonicus made considerable efforts to persuade the Achaeans not to go to war. In 148 he had asked ambassadors on their way to Asia to stop the Achaeans from fighting Sparta.[75] Two years later he himself sent four ambassadors to Achaea, but they met with nothing but abuse.[76]

The war thus took place, and the Achaean forces, though supported by Boeotia, Euboea, Locris and Phocis, were inevitably defeated.[77] Corinth was razed to the ground and the Achaean League disbanded. A large part of Greece became an appendage of the Roman province of Macedonia.[78]

These events do not support the view that the return of the exiles from Rome provoked the democratic party into violent anti-Roman feeling in an attempt to outbid rivals in nationalistic sentiment. In fact we have no information about the political position of the various personalities involved. The measures taken by Diaeus after the death of Critolaus in 146—the freeing of slaves and forced contributions from the rich[79]—cannot be used as evidence, for they were desperate measures in a time of extreme crisis. The only known former exile mentioned is Stratios, who was accused by Critolaus of secretly intriguing with one of the ambassadors sent by Metellus[80] and who later begged Diaeus to accept the terms offered by Metellus after the death of Critolaus.[81] Earlier Thearidas, the brother of Polybius, was employed as an ambassador by the Achaeans, perhaps in an attempt to placate Roman feeling.[82]

Thus while we can in general distinguish between pro- and anti-Romans, it is difficult to go much further. Callicrates is linked by Polybius with Charops and other demagogues, but their domestic

[75] Paus., vii. 13. 2.
[76] Polyb., xxxviii. 12–13.
[77] Achaean allies: Paus. vii. 14. 6, cf. ii. 1. 2; Polyb., xxxviii. 3. 8; Livy, ep. lii. For the sources on the war cf. T. R. S. Broughton, *The Magistrates of the Roman Republic* (New York, 1951), i, pp. 465, 467.
[78] For the details of the status of Greece after 146, cf. S. Accame, *Il dominio romano in Grecia dalla guerra acaica ad Augusto* (Rome, 1946), ch. i and ii.
[79] Polyb., xxxviii. 15. Also postponement of the repayment of certain debts: Polyb., xxxviii. 11; Diodorus, xxxii. 26. 3.
[80] Polyb., xxxviii. 13. 4 ff.
[81] Polyb., xxxviii. 17. 4.
[82] Polyb., xxxviii. 10. 1, 11; Paus., vii. 14. 3.

policies may have differed considerably. Again Menalcidas was a pro-Roman,[83] but that did not stop him quarrelling with Callicrates and ingratiating himself with the supposedly anti-Roman Diaeus.[84] And in 149 Callicrates and Diaeus together were meant to represent the Achaeans before the senate in opposition to Menalcidas.[85] It looks as if complex personal rivalries played a considerable part in the events that preceded the war and the principal characters cannot be fitted into neat categories. It is not the case either that Rome attacked the Achaean League because it was showing dangerous left-wing tendencies or that a new democratic element attempted to put an end to Roman domination based on support of the upper classes. The senate had decided that its interests were best served by removing the last vestiges of independent action by the Greek states. It was not overwhelmingly concerned with internal politics: it was only after the war that Mummius destroyed the democratic structure—such as it was—of the Achaean cities.[86]

VII

The picture which emerges from these fifty years is consistent. Rome did not set out with the intention of establishing oligarchic governments in Greece, and she did not have consistent support from the oligarchs and consistent opposition from the democrats. The natural preference of the senate and its representatives was for the upper classes and for forms of government in which the upper classes were dominant. Other things being equal, it was to this end that Roman policy was directed. The activities of Flamininus in Thessaly in 194 are perhaps the best example. But in this turbulent period it is only rarely that other things were equal. Rome's object was to win the wars in which she was engaged and to

[83] Cf. Polyb., xxx. 16. 2.
[84] Paus., vii. 12. 1. De Sanctis (*Storia dei Romani*, iv, 3, pp. 129, 132) argues that Diaeus' father was Diophanes, the pro-Roman opponent of Philopoemen, and that Diaeus himself was originally pro-Roman. But there is no evidence that Diaeus was Diophanes' son—all we know is that Diophanes' father was called Diaeus: and even if he was, he need not have followed the same policy as Diophanes.
[85] Paus., vii. 12. 8.
[86] Paus., vii. 16. 9.

maintain the control over Greek affairs which her military successes bestowed on her. To this end the senate was glad to accept support from those who were willing to give it to her, irrespective of their position in the internal politics of their own states. She had no scruples in using Nabis against Philip or supporting the demagogues after 167.

We have seen, too, that differences within the Greek states concerning the policy to be adopted towards Rome did not necessarily coincide with differences on domestic policy. There is nothing very surprising about this. Many upper-class politicians would have been confident that they could maintain their position without Roman protection, and preferred to govern their states in complete independence rather than under Roman control. Others would have seen that Roman domination was inevitable and preferred to be on the winning side. Others, again, were willing to use Roman support as a means of securing their success in political disputes within the upper classes.

It is interesting to compare these conclusions with those which emerge from study of the Athenian Empire in the fifth century B.C. Thucydides tells us that in the Peloponnesian War (431–404 B.C.) the democratic elements in the Greek cities sought help from Athens, their opponents from Sparta.[87] In an epoch-making article de Ste Croix has shown that one of the chief reasons for the success of the Athenian Empire was that Athens gave active support to the democratic parties in the allied states.[88] The democrats knew that it was only because of Athenian support that they were able to maintain democratic forms of government in their own cities. Athens, as a democracy, had a natural preference for democratic government and this coincided with her self-interest as head of an empire.[89]

---

[87] Thuc., iii. 82. 1.

[88] G. E. M. de Ste Croix, 'The character of the Athenian empire', *Historia*, iii (1954–5), pp. 1–40. Cf. also his 'Notes on jurisdiction in the Athenian empire', *CQ*, lv (1961), pp. 94–112, 268–80; H. W. Pleket, 'Thasos and the popularity of the Athenian empire', *Historia*, xii (1963), pp. 70–7. The objections of D. W. Bradeen, 'The popularity of the Athenian empire', *Historia*, ix (1960), pp. 257–69 and T. J. Quinn, 'Thucydides and the popularity of the Athenian empire', *Historia*, xiii (1964), pp. 257–66 do not seem to me to have invalidated de Ste Croix's case.

[89] We know of a few cases where Athens tolerated oligarchic governments: in each case the oligarchs appear to have either seceded from Athens or

Under the Roman Empire the picture is very different. There was now no question of a struggle for leadership in the Mediterranean world—Rome's mastery was unchallenged. It is not surprising that under these conditions Rome's natural preferences came to the fore, and that both in Italy and in the provinces it was the richer classes who were dominant. The old senatorial aristocracy, it is true, no longer controlled affairs and men from lower orders could rise and hold positions of influence.[90] But the lot of the mass of the people scarcely improved at all. The result of Rome's victory was indeed to stem the tide of democracy and the ultimate victory belonged to the upper classes. But it would be wrong to infer that that was Rome's object from the very beginning.[91]

murdered or oppressed their political opponents. Cf. Ps.-Xen., *Ath. Pol.*, iii. 11, Thuc., i. 115.2–3, iii. 27. 2–3.

[90] Cf. K. Hopkins, 'Élite mobility in the Roman empire', chapter v below.

[91] It may be useful to refer to the following works which have appeared since the original publication of this article. On relations between Sparta and the Achaean League there is a full discussion in R. M. Errington, *Philopoemen* (Oxford, 1969). On the Achaean War cf. A. Fuks, 'The *Bellum Achaicum* and its social aspect', *JHS*, xc (1970), 78–89. On the policy of Flamininus, cf. E. Badian, *Titus Quinctius Flamininus, Philhellenism and Realpolitik* (Cincinnati, 1970), and my own article in *Latomus*, xxxi (1972), pp. 22–53. Also relevant is I. Touloumakos, *Der Einfluss Roms auf die Staatsform der griechischen Stadtstaaten des Festlandes und der Inseln im ersten und zweiten Jhdt. v. Chr.* (Göttingen, 1967); J. Deininger, *Der politische Widerstand gegen Rom in Griechenland 217–86 v. Chr.* (Berlin and New York, 1970), and my forthcoming review in *CR*.

IV

THE ROMAN MOB[*][1]

P. A. Brunt

I

In February 56 B.C., Publius Clodius, the patrician leader of the urban proletariat at Rome, had indicted his enemy, Titus Annius Milo, on a charge of seditious violence before the popular assembly. (Milo had successfully disputed Clodius' control of the streets by hiring gladiators and other bravadoes.) Pompey had undertaken to appear for Milo at a preliminary hearing.[2]

> Pompey spoke [wrote Cicero] or intended to; in fact, as soon as he rose, the Clodian gang raised a clamour, and throughout his speech he was interrupted not only by shouting but by loud abuse and insults. When he had finished—in this he certainly showed courage; he was not frightened away, said his piece to the end, and now and again secured silence by

* From no. 35 (1966).

[1] Many statements can readily be verified in standard histories of Rome, or for the period covered, in Greenidge and Clay, *Sources for Roman History 133–70* B.C., revised by E. W. Gray (Oxford, 1960), or under the year named in T. R. S. Broughton, *Magistrates of the Roman Republic* (New York, 1951). All dates are B.C. unless otherwise stated. For all matters concerning the rural plebs and veterans mentioned see my article in *JRS*, lii (1962), pp. 70–86. Before revising this paper I could read only parts of C. Meier, *Res Publica Amissa* (Wiesbaden, 1966), esp. pp. 95–115. J. W. Heaton, *Mob Violence in the late Roman Republic* (*Illinois Studies in Social Science*, xxiii, 4, 1939) is inaccurate in details and superficial in interpretation.

[2] *Ad Quintum fratrem*, ii. 3. 2.

his authority—up got Clodius. Our people made such a clamour—we had decided to show him the same courtesy—that he could not control his mind, tongue or expression. Pompey had barely finished at noon; this went on till two o'clock; every kind of insult and the most bawdy verses were shouted at Clodius and his sister. Livid with fury, Clodius asked his followers who was starving the people to death. The gang replied: "Pompey". Who wanted to go to Alexandria? "Pompey." Whom did they want to go? "Crassus" . . . . At about three o'clock, as if at a signal, Clodius' people began to spit in unison at ours. A crescendo of anger. They began to shove our people out. We charged; the gangsters fled; Clodius was thrown off the platform, and I took to flight; there might have been an accident.

This was a relatively peaceful scene in the 50s. In 58, when Clodius was driving Cicero into temporary exile, a senator was killed in street fighting. The day after Cicero left Rome, before he had been condemned in law, his house on the Palatine was sacked and burned, and the mob marched out to treat his Tusculan villa in the same way. Later that year, Pompey kept to his house in fear for his life. In 57 the efforts of Milo and Sestius as tribunes to restore Cicero were met by violence; Sestius was left for dead in the street; Clodius brought gladiators into the senate-house. Milo and Sestius repelled force with force, until at last the gentry and bourgeoisie of all Italy came in to vote for Cicero's return. In November, an armed band drove off the workmen who were re-building his house, demolished a neighbouring portico and set fire to the mansion of his brother 'with the city looking on'. A week later, Cicero was going down the Sacra Via, the principal street in the city centre, which ran from where the Colosseum now stands to the foot of the Capitol and was lined with great houses and luxury shops, when Clodius' gang attacked: 'there were shouts, stones, clubs, swords, all without a moment's notice'. Cicero was saved by his escort. Next day Clodius tried to storm Milo's house in a fashionable residential quarter. 'Quite openly in the middle of the morning, he brought up men with shields and drawn swords and others with lighted torches'. A successful counter-attack was made and Clodius fled for his life.[3]

<hr>

[3] T. Rice Holmes, *Roman Republic* (Oxford, 1923), i, pp. 330–3; ii, pp.

Such violence reached a climax in early 52, when Milo at last succeeded in murdering Clodius outside Rome and a frenzied mob brought the body into the senate-house, tore down tribunal and benches, seized the clerk's papers and burned everything up, the senate-house itself and the adjacent Porcian basilica, in a great funeral pyre. A rather similar scene recurred in 44, when Caesar's body was burned, and the mob tore to pieces the poet, Helvius Cinna, under the misapprehension that he was a praetor who had publicly sympathized with Caesar's assassins.[4] But, though the proportions of violence were unprecedented, violence itself was not something novel in Rome; for almost a century it had been growing more frequent.

I propose here to examine the conditions which favoured or caused it (II–IV), to sketch its progress (V), and to consider the composition of the mobs and their aims (VI–VII); I shall conclude by assessing what the mob achieved (VIII).

II

The true governing organ of the Roman Republic was the senate, which acted through annual magistrates elected by the people but drawn from its own ranks. The senate itself was dominated by a few noble families whose power reposed on their wealth and on the number of their dependants, and on the prestige they derived from their past services to the state. Candidates for office seldom stood on programmes, and organized parties did not exist. Men were returned to office occasionally for personal merits (talent could carry outsiders like Cicero to the highest place), more often by reason of their munificence and lavish bribes, in general because of their family and connections. Birth and wealth usually went together. Cicero describes Lucius Domitius Ahenobarbus as a man destined for the consulship since he was born; in 49 he could

54–61; esp. Cic., *ad Att.*, iv. 3. 2–3. Sacra Via, S. B. Platner, *Topographic Dictionary of Ancient Rome*, revised by T. Ashby (Oxford, 1929), pp. 456 ff.

[4] For 52 Ascon., 32–3 (Oxford text); Appian, *Civil Wars*, ii. 20 ff.; (Cassius) Dio, xl. 48 ff.; for 44 Appian, ii. 143–8; Dio, xliv. 35–51; Plut., *Caesar*, 68; *Antony*, 14; *Brutus*, 18; 20. The people were inflamed by the reading of Caesar's will in which he left his gardens for public use and a sum of money to every citizen domiciled at Rome.

offer farms of thirty acres apiece to some thousands of soldiers. Such nobles had numerous dependants or clients who were morally expected and often economically compelled to support them.[5] They used their power to grow richer from the profits of war and empire, and to oppose every measure to relieve the poor, the provision of cheap grain, the distribution of land or the remission of debt. Here they had the backing of the upper class in general, whose spokesman, Cicero, declared that the prime duty of government was to ensure 'that every man kept his own'. And public largesses, which did not infringe property rights, could be rejected on the ground that they were more than the treasury could bear, the treasury from which senators drew handsome allowances for themselves.[6]

In theory the people at Rome possessed great power. They elected the magistrates, declared war and ratified treaties, passed laws, and until the creation of standing courts in the late second century decided the most important criminal cases; to the end of the Republic some political charges came before them. From the late second century they voted by ballot; this naturally diminished aristocratic control.

There was more than one popular assembly. Of these the *comitia centuriata* was timocratically organized. Decisions were taken by a majority not of heads, but of voting units called centuries; the well-to-do, if they were of one mind, could decide the issues; the citizens with no property at all, and who are said to have outnumbered all the rest put together by the time of Augustus, formed only a single century, which might never even be called.[7] The rural poor therefore had little influence in this body the importance of which was great, for it elected the chief magistrates; and it was men who had held the highest offices who dominated the senate itself.

This assembly was also competent to legislate, but laws were

---

[5] H. Jolowicz, *Historical Introduction to the Study of Roman Law*, 2nd edn (Cambridge, 1952), chapter ii and iv, gives an excellent introduction to the Roman constitution. For the working of the political system see L. R. Taylor, *Party Politics in the Age of Caesar* (Berkeley, 1949). Domitius: Cic., *ad Att.*, iv. 8a, 2. Caesar, *Civil War*, i. 17. Clients; see especially M. Gelzer, *Kleine Schriften*, i (Wiesbaden, 1962), pp. 68 ff.

[6] *De officiis*, ii. 72-end, cf. Brunt, *JRS*, lii (1962), pp. 69 ff.

[7] Dionysius of Halicarnassus, *Roman Antiquities*, iv. 20. 5; 21. 1 (based on personal observation, 21. 3, after 30 B.C., i. 7. 2).

more generally passed by a less cumbrous body, in which the voting units were thirty-five tribes. The tribes were local divisions of the people; thirty-one were rural and four urban, though all freedmen (except such as were substantial landowners) were registered, wherever domiciled, in the urban tribes. In the tribes, rich and poor had equal votes.[8]

At all times by far the greater number of citizens lived in the country, and it might seem that the organization of the tribal assembly ensured that the wishes of the rural majority would prevail, perhaps even to an undue extent; thirty-one to four was not the true proportion between town and country dwellers.[9] However, as Professor Toynbee has recently pointed out, the system of primary democracy, in which the citizen can exercise his voting rights only by attending the sovereign assembly in person, can only work democratically if voters have not to spend more than two nights away from home.[10] Even in the third century many citizens were a hundred miles distant from Rome, and after 80 they comprised the free population of Italy south of the Po. It was only on rare occasions that the peasants came in to vote. If the censors who held office every five years were careful to register every citizen who moved from the country into the city in an urban tribe instead of a rural, the votes of the rural tribes must have been exercised by the minority of their members who had the leisure and means to visit Rome for the purpose, the very same class of wealthy landowners who controlled the centuriate assembly.[11]

It seems, however, that the censors did not do their work thoroughly. Dionysius of Halicarnassus sharply contrasts the centuriate assembly controlled by the respectable classes and the tribal, composed of artisans with no hearths of their own.[12] He purports to be describing the early Republic, but the picture is imaginary and drawn from the conditions known to the annalists of the first century. In the Principate urban dwellers are attested

---

[8] L. R. Taylor, *Voting Districts of the Roman Republic* (Rome, 1960) is fundamental on the tribes.

[9] In 70, 910,000 adult male citizens were returned; there might have been much failure to register, but I hope to argue elsewhere that about 1,200,000 is a realistic figure; of these in the 40s about a quarter lived in Rome (III below).

[10] *Hannibal's Legacy* (Oxford, 1965), i, p. 297.

[11] Taylor, *Party Politics*, 57 ff.; cf. Brunt, *JRS*, lv (1965), pp. 103 ff.

[12] iv. 16–21; viii. 6; x. 17.

in rural tribes. One piece of evidence suggests that this was possibly as early as 133. Tiberius Gracchus, who had hitherto relied on the rural voters (one of the few known instances in which they swarmed in to vote), began to court the urban plebs, as his followers were occupied with the harvest. His action would have had little purpose, if the urban plebs had been confined to the four urban tribes. It may be indeed that even a few immigrants who had moved into Rome since the last census and had not yet been reregistered might have balanced or outvoted the wealthier members of their tribes, and that it was to such a handful of citizens that he appealed. Even so, urban dwellers were evidently influential in the rural tribes.[13] And between 70 and 28 it is not clear that any census was completed.[14] It seems probable then that normally the urban plebs had a majority in the tribal assembly.

However, the assemblies could do nothing except with the collaboration of a magistrate. They could meet only on his summons, and only vote 'Yea' or 'Nay' on his proposals; a private citizen could not even speak except on his invitation. The plebs could not obtain redress of its grievances, unless a magistrate drawn from the upper classes was prepared to take the initiative. Genuine social concern or personal ambition led nobles like the Gracchi, Caesar and Clodius to come forward as 'popular' leaders from time to time, but there was no consistent and continuous opposition, no organized and enduring popular party.[15]

Even if a magistrate submitted a popular proposal, it did not follow that it would go through. It could be obstructed on religious pretexts, or vetoed. A single tribune could veto what all his nine colleagues proposed. The tribunate had arisen in the class struggles of the early Republic for the protection of popular

[13] H. Dessau, *ILS*, 168; 176; 286; 6045 f.; 6063 f.; Appian, i. 14. Taylor, *Party Politics*, p. 53 cites Cicero, *Sest.*, 109, but the assertion here that not more than five men might vote in a tribe could refer to uncontroversial legislation. Cic., *de lege agraria*, ii. 71 treats the voting rights of city dwellers as an important privilege, though motions to redistribute freedmen among the rural tribes in 88-7, 84 (*Perioche* of Livy, lxxxiv) and 66 (cf. Clodius' plan in 52, Asconius, 52) suggest that votes in the urban tribes were not much regarded.

[14] G. Tibiletti, *Studia et Documenta Historiae et Iuris*, xxv (1959), pp. 94 ff. thinks that Sulla and Caesar as dictators revised the lists. I do not feel certain that use was not made of the incomplete revisions effected by some censors in the intervening years.

[15] C. Meier, *RE*, Supplement, x (1965), pp. 550-67.

interests, and in the second century Polybius could still say that it was the tribune's duty to do always what the people approved. To the end most of the champions of the commons acted as tribunes. None the less, Polybius' statement did not correspond to the constitutional practice that had evolved by his time. The senate could almost always find at least one tribune to act on its behalf and (as Livy put it) to use the tribunician veto to dissolve the tribunician power. Tribunes were often nobles themselves, or in Livy's words 'chattels of the nobility'. Marcus Octavius who vetoed Tiberius Gracchus' agrarian bill (see below, page 92) was, for the middle and late Republic, the more typical tribune of the two.[16]

According to Burke 'a state without the means of some change is without the means of its conservation'. At Rome there were too many checks and balances in the constitution, which operated in practice only in the interest of the ruling class. Reformers had to use force, or at least to create conditions in which the senate had reason to fear its use (see below, pages 92 ff.). This was the first factor which favoured the growth of violence at Rome.

III

In the second place, Rome was even by modern standards a populous city, in which there was no garrison and no police to control the multitude.

To the total size of the population there is no direct testimony. But the number of recipients of free grain had risen to 320,000 in the 40s.[17] Only adult males were normally eligible,[18] and we therefore have to estimate the number of women and children in this class. The grain recipients were partly free-born, partly freedmen.

[16] Polyb., vi. 16; Livy, v. 2. 14; x. 37. 8 (both texts that reflect later conditions). Cic., de legibus, iii. 24 describes the tribunate as 'temperamentum quo tenuiores cum principibus aequari se putarent'. On its role in the middle Republic see J. Bleicken, Das Volkstribunat der klass. Republik (Munich, 1955).

[17] Suet., Caesar, 41; cf. Dio, xlii. 21. 4.

[18] Trajan included some children, and Augustus made money gifts to children (Pliny, Panegyricus, 26; Suet., Aug., 41); these seem exceptional, contra D. van Berchem, Les distributions de blé et d'argent à la plèbe romaine sous l'empire (Geneva, 1939), pp. 32 ff.

Appian implies that in 133 the poor were unable to raise children.[19] Abortion and infanticide were not forbidden by the law, and many parents must have exposed their babies, some of whom might then be brought up as slaves by the finders. The infanticide of female infants must have been common even in the senatorial class, among whom in Augustus' reign men outnumbered women; if we make the reasonable assumption that it was still more prevalent with the poor, the birth-rate would also have been depressed by a scarcity of reproductive women.[20] There is some ground, however, for thinking that the urban plebs consisted preponderantly of freedmen (see below, pages 89 f.), and particularly after Clodius made grain distributions free in 58 masters were very ready to manumit slaves, who could still be required to work for them, while obtaining rations from the state.[21] Now it seems to me unlikely that there were so many female slaves or freedwomen as male slaves or freedmen. In this period slave-women were not needed to keep up the stock of slaves, most of whom were 'made' by capture in war or kidnapping. And they were employable only for household duties and to some extent in spinning, weaving and making clothes, occupations perhaps more common on country estates than in town houses.[22] Slaves might enter into a quasi-marriage, but both spouses were not necessarily freed together, and any children born in slavery, who were slaves themselves, might be manumitted only at a later date. In many thousand sepulchral inscriptions of freedmen at Rome (mainly imperial) under thirty per cent record offspring, and still fewer marriage.[23] For these reasons I doubt if we need more than double the figure of 320,000 to include both women and children of corn-recipients.

[19] Civil Wars, i. 7.
[20] T. Mommsen, Römische Strafrecht (Leipzig, 1899), pp. 617–20, 637; Dio, liv. 16. 2.
[21] Dionysius of Halicarnassus, iv. 24. 5; Dio, xxxix. 24. The services freedmen owed patrons are best discussed by C. Cosentini, Studi sui liberti (1948–50).
[22] T. Frank, Economic Survey of Ancient Rome (Baltimore, 1933–40), i, pp. 373 f.; v, pp. 199 ff.; H. J. Loane, Industry and Commerce in the City of Rome, 50 B.C.–200 A.D. (Baltimore, 1938), pp. 69 ff.; cf. ILS, 8393 (30), where assiduity in wool-making is commemorated among the virtues of a great lady in Augustus' time; Ascon., 43 (Oxford text) for weaving 'ex vetere more' in a town house.
[23] T. Frank, AHR, xxi (1915/6), pp. 689 ff.

Well-to-do residents were presumably not numerically significant. There remain the slaves. A rich man required a large staff of domestic servants, secretaries, etc; and his standing might be measured by the number of his attendants and flunkeys. There might also be women engaged in textile work. Under Nero an eminent senator had four hundred slaves in his town-house.[24] However, in the 50s the scale of manumissions should have diminished the slave population. I guess that 100,000 would be a liberal estimate. The city population might then have been more or less than 750,000. Clodius' bill probably accelerated the drift from the country, but it had been going on before, and the number of slaves and freedmen had been progressively increasing. However, no numerical estimate can be ventured for any earlier date.[25]

In the early Principate the government had at least 12,000 soldiers in Rome, not to speak of seven cohorts, which ultimately and perhaps from the first comprised 7,000 men, raised to deal with fires; they were military units and could also be used as police. Even so, it was hard to keep order. In 39 B.C., though there were troops at hand which saved him in the end, Octavian was almost lynched in a riot, and Claudius later was only rescued by soldiers from a famished mob. The narrow, winding streets and high buildings (see below, page 85) did not help in suppressing riots. In A.D. 238 the populace, armed by the senate, besieged the depleted praetorian guard in its camp; when the soldiers sallied out and pursued them into the streets,

> the people climbed up into the houses and harassed the soldiers by throwing down on them tiles, stones and pots of all kinds; the soldiers dared not go up after them, not knowing their way about the houses; but as the houses and workshops had their doors barred, they set fire to the many wooden balconies; the tenements were set close together, and large parts of the buildings were wooden; so the flames soon devastated a very great part of the city, one section after another.

[24] Tac., *Ann.*, iii. 55; xiv, 43; cf. n. 22.
[25] Brunt, *JRS*, lii (1962), pp. 69 f.; here I underestimated the opportunities of employment for free men (cf. p. 89 below), and went too far in minimizing the drift before 58. The building of the Marcian aqueduct in 144 is a notable indication of increased population.

Something of the same kind nearly occurred in 88, when Sulla marched into the city. No doubt it was such dangers that made the emperors ready to spend large sums on 'bread and circuses'. In other towns they had no such motive to care for the poor and did not do so.[26]

The aristocratic government of the Republic had no police available; the magistrates had but a few attendants. Nor were troops normally found in the city, though in 121 the consul happened to have at his disposal Cretan archers whom he used in suppressing the Gracchans.[27] How could the nobility ever hold the mob in check, when it was inflamed against the government?

The mob was generally unarmed and relied on sticks and stones. To carry arms was a capital offence,[28] and in any event the poor would possess none, except knives. Moreover, as legions were recruited in the country, not the city, the urban poor were not trained in the use of arms. The well-to-do would have their own equipment, including body-armour, and had mostly seen military service; and the senate could authorize the arming of their followers. On occasions popular leaders distributed arms illegally to the mob, but even then, man for man, their followers were probably unequal to their opponents. Though armed, the partisans of Gaius Gracchus in 121 put up but a feeble resistance. The numerous clients of the great houses in the city itself often enabled the governing class to make a stand against the mob, reciprocating or even initiating violence (see below, pages 90-1, 94-5).

Given time, the senate or magistrates or individual nobles could call up clients with military experience from the country. In 100,

---

[26] Imperial police: A. Passerini, *Le coorti pretorie* (Rome, 1939), pp. 44–66 (esp. on Dio, lv. 24. 6 and Tac., *Ann.*, iv. 5); P. K. Baillie Reynolds, *Vigiles of Imperial Rome* (Oxford, 1926); for their police duties see *Dig.*, i. 15. 3. Riots: Appian, v. 68; Tac., *Ann.*, xii. 43; Herodian, vii, 12. 5; cf. Appian i. 58. C. Meier, *Res Publica Amissa*, pp. 157 ff. is interesting on the lack of a police force in the Republic.

[27] Plut., *C. Gracchus*, 16; Orosius, v. 12. 7.

[28] W. Kunkel, *Untersuchungen zur Entwicklung des röm. Kriminalverfahrens in vorsullanischer Zeit* (Munich, 1962), pp. 64 ff. shows that Sulla's law (cf. Cic., *pro Milone*, 11) has much earlier antecedents (Plautus, *Aulularia*, 415 ff.). Arms were given to the 'mob' in 121, 100, 88, 87, 62 (Plut., *Cato Minor*, 27 f.) and of course by Clodius; by the senate in 121 to senators, *equites* and their servants (Plut., *C. Gracchus*, 14), to the plebs or 'populus' in 100 (Cic., *pro C. Rabirio*, 20; Oros., v. 17. 7), presumably only to reliable elements.

men from Picenum took part in the suppression of Saturninus. The armed followers with whom Cicero surrounded himself during the Catilinarian conspiracy of 63 included chosen young men from Reate. In 59 he was hoping to resist Clodius by force; his friends and their clients, freedmen and slaves would band together in his defence. A great concourse of substantial citizens from all over Italy ensured that he was recalled from exile in 57, although his enemy, Clodius, remained dominant over the city proletariate. In 56 Pompey summoned followers from Picenum and the Po valley for his protection. To end the uproar ensuing on Clodius' murder in 52, the senate authorized a levy all over Italy, and soldiers restored order in the city. But between 59 and 52 the senate was generally impotent, because Pompey with his veterans and Caesar with his great army in the north could marshal forces stronger than the senate could command.[29]

IV

The third factor in the turbulence of the city population may be found in the misery and squalor in which they lived, which naturally made them responsive to politicians who promised to improve their conditions and engendered hostility (if only intermittent) to the upper classes who showed little care for their interests.[30]

For lack of modern means of transport, the people were crammed into a small built-up area, not much larger than that of

[29] Cic., *pro C. Rabirio*, 22 (100); *in Cat.*, i. 11; ii. 5; iii. 5; *pro Murena*, 52; cf. Sall., *Cat.*, 26. 4; 30. 7; 50. 4 (63). Cicero was accused of using armed slaves but claims to have mobilized in December all the upper classes, and all true citizens, indeed 'omnis ingenuorum multitudo, etiam tenuissimorum' (implausible), *Phil.*, ii. 16; cf. *in Cat.*, iv. 15 f.; they took a military oath, Dio, xxxvii. 35. Rice Holmes, *Roman Republic*, ii, p. 60 (57); Cic., *ad Quintum fratrem*, i. 2. 16 (59); ii. 3. 4 (56); Holmes, ii, p. 167 (52).

[30] In this section where references are omitted, the texts are cited by J. Carcopino, *Daily Life in Ancient Rome* (London, 1941), mainly based on imperial evidence; in the Republic things were worse. Z. Yavetz, *Latomus*, xvii (1958), pp. 500 ff. gives further details for Republic (e.g. on fearful conditions created by plagues); his references and interpretation of texts are not all reliable.

modern Oxford, with a density seven or eight times as great. The streets were winding and narrow, even main thorough-fares under twenty feet wide. While the rich had their luxurious mansions on the Palatine or spacious gardens in the suburbs, most inhabitants were penned into tiny flats in tenements, which had to be built high; Augustus imposed a limit of seventy feet (which suggests that this had been exceeded), and Trajan pronounced that dangerous, reducing it to sixty. Cicero constrasts a newly planned city with Rome 'situated on hills and in valleys, lifted up and suspended in the air, with no fine streets to boast of but only narrow paths'.

The lower parts of the city were subject to periodic floods, and the collapse and conflagration of buildings were common occurrences. In the Principate it is said that not a day passed without a serious fire, yet then there were 7,000 *vigiles* to put them out; in the Republic only a small force of publicly owned slaves. Crassus had a gang of five hundred builders, and bought up houses that were afire or adjacent to a blaze at knock-down prices with a view to rebuilding on the sites.[31] These dangers were aggravated by bad methods of construction. Owners would not or could not afford to employ skilled architects or suitable materials. The local travertine cracked in fires, but it was too costly to bring better stone even fifty miles by land. A thin facing of stone might conceal a filling of soft rubble. To conserve space, party walls had to be not more than a foot and a half thick; given this limit, only baked brick was strong enough for high buildings, yet sun-dried brick was often used. Walls were sometimes of wattlework, the more dangerous as it was too expensive to bring larchwood, relatively impervious to fire, all the way from the Adriatic. In 44 Cicero reported to Atticus that two of his tenements had fallen down, and that cracks were showing in others; the tenants—and the mice—had all fled.[32]

The houses of the poor must also have been ill-lit, ill-ventilated and unwarmed; facilites for cooking were inadequate; water had to be fetched from the public fountains, and the supply cannot

[31] Catullus, 23. 9; *Dig.*, i. 15. 2; Plut., *Crassus*, 2.
[32] Vitruv., i. 3. 2; ii. 2; 7. 3 f.; 8. 7–9; 8. 16 f.; 8. 20; 9. 14–17; vi. 8. 9; x. pr. 2; Cic., *de divinatione*, ii. 99; *ad Att.*, xiv. 9. 1. Yavetz thinks that many of Vitruvius' precepts are directed against common bad practices in building.

have been abundant until the old conduits were repaired and new. aqueducts built under Augustus; further, the tenements were not connected with the public sewers. We may fairly suppose that most of the inhabitants of Rome lived in appalling slums. They offered shelter, but little more. As for furniture, Cicero speaks of the poor man as having no more than a stool and a bed where he lived, worked and slept.[33]

From such tenements men like Cicero drew as landlords a good income. Cicero's property on the Aventine and in the Argiletum, probably two lower-class districts, was in 44 bringing him in 80,000 HSS, enough to have paid 160 legionaries for a year under the rates that had obtained until recently; he appropriated it to the allowance for his undergraduate son at Athens, and was anxious to have tenants who would pay on the nail.[34] Perhaps that was not so easy to ensure. Then, as later, it is probable that the return on investment in house-property was high precisely because the risk was great.[35]

In the 40s there was a prolonged agitation about urban rents. In 48 the praetor, Marcus Caelius, who proposed a year's remission, was driven out of the city by the consul, but only after bloodshed. Caesar, however, granted the remission in the same year, and perhaps extended it in 47, after further tumults, when barricades were raised, soldiers called in and eight hundred rioters killed. It applied to rents up to 2,000 sesterces in Rome, and 500 elsewhere, an indication that the cost of living in Rome was exceptionally high.[36] (A generation earlier, Cicero gave the daily wage for an unskilled labourer as three sesterces; obviously he could not have afforded 2,000 for a year's rent. We cannot say whether wages had risen in the interim, or whether the remission was intended to benefit people at a rather higher level, such as shopkeepers.) Cicero's comment is characteristic. 'There is no equity in abolishing or suspending rents. Am I to buy and build and repair and spend, and you to have the benefit against my will? Is this not to

[33] Cic., in Cat., iv. 17.
[34] Cic., ad Att., xii. 32. 2; xv. 17. 1; 20. 4; xvi. 1. 5.
[35] Gellius, xv. 1. 3. But F. Schulz, Classical Roman Law (Oxford, 1951), pp. 542 ff. shows how the law favoured owners against tenants.
[36] Caesar, Civil Wars, iii. 20 f.; Dio, xli. 37 f.; Appian, ii. 48 (Caelius); Dio, xlii. 29–33 (riots of 47). The Fasti Ostienses under 48 record a year's remission of rents; Dio, xlii. 51 puts remission in 47; other details in Suet., Caesar, 38; 42.

take away the property of some and give to others what does not belong to them?'[37]

How did the people of Rome live? Rome was never a great industrial city; indeed there never was any large-scale industry in the ancient world of the kind familiar since the industrial revolution: the high cost of transport alone forbade the production of factory goods for a world-wide market.[38] Adjacent to Rome there were no abundant supplies of fuel or raw materials. The Tiber is not well suited to navigation, and the port of Ostia had not yet been developed; the larger ships had to discharge in an open roadstead into lighters. None the less far more use was made of the river and its affluents (for downstream traffic as well as for transport from the mouth) than we would expect from present conditions; the growth of the urban population left no alternative.[39] The supply of this population created a great demand for wholesale and retail traders, dock labour, carters and so on. So too large numbers must have been employed in the building trade: more fine public edifices were now being put up; the rich were continually erecting more luxurious town-houses and villas in the vicinity of Rome, and the increase of the population in itself required more tenements and shops, a demand augmented by the frequency of fires and collapses. Evidence from pre-industrial cities in other times may help to supply the lack of ancient statistics. In 1586 up to 6,000 workmen were engaged on public buildings at Rome, of whom 800 with 150 horses were needed to move the obelisk into the Piazza of St Peter's; at the time the total population seems to have been under 100,000. In 1791 a third of all Paris wage-earners were occupied in the building trade.[40] In addition, there were artisans and shopkeepers of all kinds, many of whom must have sold goods they made themselves, perhaps to the order of clients. Beggars, curiously, are hardly ever mentioned, perhaps because the Romans (unlike the Jews, and the Christians

---

[37] Cic., *pro Roscio comoedo*, 28; *de officiis*, ii. 83 f.

[38] See e.g. A. H. M. Jones, *Later Roman Empire* (Oxford, 1964), ii, pp. 841 ff.

[39] See R. Meiggs, *Roman Ostia* (Oxford, 1960), chapters ii, iv and viii; J. le Gall, *Le Tibre, fleuve de Rome dans l'antiquité* (Paris, 1953), *passim*; L. Casson, *JRS*, lv (1965), pp. 31 ff.

[40] J. Delumeau, *Vie économique et sociale de Rome dans la seconde moitié du XVIᵉ siècle* (Paris, 1959), i, pp. 366 f.; cf. p. 281. G. Rudé, *The Crowd in the French Revolution* (Oxford, 1959), p. 19.

after them) recognized no special obligation to relieve the poor as such; it was another matter if the great houses supported idle dependants, whose votes and strong arms they could employ; on them they conferred benefits in accordance with the usual principle of Roman morality: 'do ut des'.[41]

According to tradition king Numa had organized craftsmen into *collegia* or corporations of flautists, goldsmiths, carpenters—the word *fabri* came to mean builders in all sorts of material—dyers, shoemakers, coppersmiths and potters. If only these particular corporations were in fact ancient, they go back to a very remote time, when for instance the use of iron was still unknown; in the historic period there must have been many ironworkers, especially to make arms for the legions which were regularly enrolled and equipped just outside the city. The list also does not include bakers; according to Pliny there were none down to the middle of the second century; the women used to grind and bake at home; presumably they ceased to do so, when so many of the poor were lodged in houses without suitable ovens. In the course of time many more corporations came into existence. The fishermen who fished in the Tiber had an old festival. Fulling ceased to be a domestic craft. Plautus casually mentions a score of other trades. Cato in the second century recommended buying at Rome tunics, togas, cloaks, patchwork cloth and wooden shoes (though some of these things were also made on his estates), and in addition jars, bowls, ploughs, yokes, locks and keys and the finest baskets.[42]

As in medieval towns men of one craft tended to congregate.

---

[41] H. Bolkestein, *Wohltätigkeit und Armenspflege im vorchristlichen Altertum* (Utrecht, 1939), *passim*; for beggars, pp. 339–41; add Seneca, *de beata vita*, 25.

[42] For trades at Rome see Loane (n. 22); for *collegia* J-P. Waltzing, *Études historiques sur les corporations professionelles chez les romains*, i–iv (Louvain, 1895–1900), esp. i, pp. 62–92 (Republic); W. Liebenam, *Zur Gesch. u. Organisation des röm. Vereinswesens* (Leipzig, 1890); F. M. de Robertis, *Il Diritto Associativo Romano* (Bari, 1938). Numa, Plut., *Numa*, 17; arms factories, Livy, xxi. 57. 10; Cic., *Phil.* vii. 13; bakers, Pliny, *Nat. Hist.*, xviii. 107; fishing, Festus, 232; 274L; Horace, *Sat.*, ii. 2, 31 ff.; fulling, Pliny, xxxv. 197 (220 B.C.); Vitruv., vi. pr. 7 (no longer domestic); Cato: see his *de agricultura*, 135. Waltzing gives a list of known *collegia* at Rome; for Republican *collegia* there and in Italian towns attested in inscriptions, see A. Degrassi, *Inscriptiones Latinae liberae reipublicae* (Florence, 1963), ii, pp. 476 ff.

There was a pottery district, and streets were named after the silversmiths, grain merchants, sandal-makers, timber merchants, log-sellers, perfumers and scythemakers, probably many more.[43] *Collegia* of artisans would thus be composed of neighbours.

Many traders and artisans were not of free birth. Slaves were employed in every trade, craft and profession. Freedom was a necessary incentive to good work and seems often to have been granted fairly soon, or bought by the slave from the wage or share of the profits he was allowed. The freedman naturally worked at his old trade and was probably often still financed by his old master. Most of our evidence comes from epitaphs, which tend no doubt to give the impression that more craftsmen were free than was the case; most slaves who appear had probably been unlucky enough to die early. Of jewellers and goldsmiths at Rome, to take one instance, 35% are slaves, 58% freedmen, only 7% of free birth. The last figure is astoundingly low. But the inscriptions only fortify the evidence we have from literary sources that in the urban population as a whole, as well as in the crafts and trades, men of servile origin preponderated. The statistics may exaggerate the preponderance; the freeborn may have been less ready to indicate manual employments in which they took no pride or even to commemorate their lives at all (a freedman could be proud of having been freed); they may even have been too poor to leave a record, having been confined to unskilled and unremunerative work.[44]

Many freedmen (perhaps most in Rome) came from the east and probably brought with them new skills; with the capital their patrons provided, they thus had an advantage over native workmen.[45] Freeborn Italians, some of whom were displaced peasants, would then have had no means of employment except casual, unskilled labour. They could go out into the country for the harvest, vintage and olive-picking, just as Londoners go out today to pick the Kent hops. This is well attested, and can be explained. The Roman landowner preferred to rely on a permanent labour-

[43] Liebenam, *Zur Gesch. u. Organization*, p. 9 f.

[44] L. R. Taylor, *AJP*, lxxiii (1961), pp. 113 ff., with earlier literature; add A. M. Duff, *Freedmen in the Early Roman Empire* (Oxford, 1928) ch. vi.

[45] Also, like Jews and Quakers at other times, they were barred from many other activities and their energies were directed into economic advancement.

force of slaves, but as Cato makes clear, he did not wish to feed idle mouths. For seasonal operations, therefore, he required supplementary labour provided by free hired men.[46] On the same principle we must suppose that most dock labour and the ancillary carting of supplies was free; there was little sailing for half the year, and work must have bunched in a few months or weeks.[47] And it required no special skill. Similarly building contractors, whose business is likely to have fluctuated, would not have found it profitable to keep enough slaves throughout the year for *all* their work. The builders on Cicero's Tusculan villa went back to Rome to collect their free grain rations as citizens. It has been plausibly conjectured that the distress Tiberius Gracchus sought to alleviate had been newly aggravated by unemployment resulting from the completion of the Marcian aqueduct. The emperor Vespasian was to refuse to adopt a labour-saving device; if he did so, he asked, how could he feed his poor commons?[48]

Sallust and others tell of the drift of countryfolk into Rome; Sallust speaks of young men who had barely made a livelihood with labour in the fields and were attracted by the private and public largesses in the city, and Cicero could urge the urban plebs with some success in 63 not to forsake the advantages of life there, their votes (which could of course be sold), games, festivals and so on, for land allotments in barren or malarial places. What Sallust says of the private largesses is probably important; the great houses could afford to maintain clients, and they might even be given rent-free lodgings.[49] Sometimes magistrates, to enhance their popularity, distributed grain or oil at low prices, bearing the cost themselves.[50] Above all there were the cheap or free public

[46] Brunt (n. 1), p. 72. Toynbee, *Hannibal's Legacy*, ii, pp. 296 ff. on Cato.

[47] J. Rougé, *REA*, liv (1954), pp. 316 ff. Piracy or hope of great profits made merchants sail in winter; Claudius had to assume the risk of storm damage, to induce shipowners to bring grain to Rome in winter (Pliny, *Nat. Hist.*, ii. 125; Suet., *Claud.*, 18).

[48] Cic., *ad Att.*, xiv. 3. 1; H. C. Boren, *AJP*, lxxix (1958), pp. 140 ff; *AHR*, lxiii (1957-8), pp. 890 ff.; Suet., *Vesp.*, 18. See Loane, *Industry and Commerce*, pp. 79 ff.; builders naturally had permanent gangs of slaves too.

[49] Sall., *Cat.*, 37 (cf. Varro, *de re rustica*, ii. pr. 3; Appian, ii. 120; Suet., *Aug.*, 42); Cic., *de lege agraria*, ii. 72. Rent paid, Trebatius in *Dig.*, ix. 3. 5. 1.

[50] E.g. Cic., *in Verrem*, ii. 3. 215, *de offic.*, ii. 58; Pliny, *Nat. Hist.*, xv. 2; xviii. 16.

corn-doles instituted generally by popular leaders, partly perhaps to reduce the dependence of the plebs on noble patrons. However, the distributions were not free until 58, the liberality of the cheap distributions provided under Gaius Gracchus' law in 123 was soon reduced and not restored till 100, and distributions were in abeyance from 80 to 73 and restricted to only some 40,000 recipients from 73 to 62.[51] Moreover men could not live on bread and shows alone; there was other food, and clothes to be paid for, and rent. Augustus was to introduce a quicker method of distributing free grain which did not take the recipients away from their work so long as in the past.[52] The people of Rome had to earn much of their living, and for many of them casual employment was the only means. Gaius Gracchus must have won much support by his programme for building roads and granaries.[53]

The feeding of the city population was also a grave problem. There were large imports from Sicily, Sardinia and Africa, but the supply was precarious, liable to be interrupted by piracy and wars. Much grain must still have come from Italy, or else the population could not have survived the years 43–36, for most of which it was cut off from oversea supplies.[54] The public rations did not suffice for a family,[55] and some, if only a minority, of the recipients must have had wives and children. Some grain had to be bought on the market, even in the years when there were public distributions to most of the free population. In 57–6 it seems likely that there was

[51] Brunt, *JRS*, lii (1962), p. 70 n. 10. R. J. Rowland Jr, *Acta Antiqua*, xiii. 81 denies the restriction in 73 without explaining the evidence for it (Sallust, *Oratio Macri*, 19 with Cicero *in Verrem*, ii. 3. 72) on the ground that Sicilian surpluses in the late 70s acquired by the government sufficed for 180,000 (*in Verrem*, ii. 3. 163); but some of this grain was probably needed for large armies in Italy and Spain, and the rest sold at market prices, which fluctuated (*ibid.*, 215).

[52] Suet., *Aug.*, 42.

[53] Plut., *C. Gracchus*, 6. About 85 a praetor, Marius Gratidianus, gained great popularity by trying to eliminate debased coinage, see Broughton, *Magistrates*, ii, p. 57; this seems to imply that the masses were interested in stopping an inflationary rise in prices.

[54] M. Rostovtzeff, *RE*, vii (1910), pp. 126 ff., who like all writers (esp. Toynbee, *Hannibal's Legacy*, ii, pp. 296 ff.; pp. 585 ff.) unduly depreciates the continuance of cereal cultivation in Italy; I hope to show this elsewhere.

[55] 5 *modii* (about 41 litres) a month. Cato gave his slaves 3–4½, according to the heaviness of their work; *de agricultura*, 56.

not enough in the public granaries to honour the state's obligation; the market price was a matter of general concern and might
soar to famine rates (see below, pages 99 f.). And market prices
fluctuated sharply, soaring when the harvests were poor and
when hoarding by growers and merchants aggravated the shortage. It is an illusion that in the late Republic the urban plebs was
usually well and cheaply fed by the state. As for modern scholars
who repeat ancient gibes that the doles corrupted the urban
population, one must wonder if they would also condemn all
modern measures of social welfare; in Rome there were no
charitable foundations for the poor, and no unemployment
benefits.

V

The progress of violence may now be sketched. In 133 Tiberius
Gracchus proposed to redistribute among the poor public lands
which the rich had occupied. His colleague, Octavius, interposed a
veto; Gracchus had him deposed by vote of the assembly, an
unprecedented act which set aside the most important of the
constitutional checks. His bill was then carried. Actual violence
was not used, but the menacing attitude of the peasantry who had
flocked in to back Gracchus may explain why Octavius did not
dare to veto the motion for his own deposition. Later in the year
the senators charged Gracchus with aspiring to tyranny and
lynched him in public. The first open act of illegal political violence
came from the nobility.

In 123–2 Gaius Gracchus as tribune carried many anti-senatorial
measures. (In 123 no other tribune had the will or courage to
oppose him; he had the backing of both urban and rural plebs and
of the *equites*, rich men outside the senate, on whom he conferred
important benefits; he did not need to use force.) But eventually
he lost popular favour and office, and as a private person in 121
armed his followers to obstruct the repeal of one of his laws; he
and they were massacred by senatorial forces quite legally.[56]

56 The biased and contradictory evidence hardly enables us to decide the
extent to which *either* of the Gracchi was to blame. Amid the tumults
the true facts may never have been known.

In 103 and 100 the tribune, Saturninus, who also proposed land-distribution and revived the grain dole on the Gracchan scale, did not scruple to murder opponents and rivals; he too was suppressed by the senate. In 88 the tribune Sulpicius, promoting the interests of the newly enfranchised Italians, and also of the freedmen whom he proposed to redistribute among all the tribes, drove his opponents from the forum by force; the consul, Sulla, appealed to his army (where his ability and generosity assured him of support), marched on Rome and proscribed Sulpicius and his friends. This was the first occasion on which the army was employed to over-turn decisions made at Rome; once again, it was a noble and conservative who took the fatal step. Sulla's successor, Cinna, revived Sulpicius' proposals; the streets ran with blood in conflict between him and his colleague, Octavius. Defeated in the city, Cinna imitated Sulla in appealing to the army, and with like success. Only a great civil war concluded this phase of the revolu-tion and enabled Sulla to restore and consolidate the senate's control of the state.

So far it is not clear that the urban proletariate, even though it owed cheap grain to popular leaders, took a strong part against the senate, which in 100 and 87 is said to have had the support of the townsmen. The Gracchi and Saturninus relied chiefly on the rural poor, Cinna and perhaps Sulpicius on the new Italian citizens. Sulla, however, severely limited the powers of tribunes and put an end to corn doles. The latter measure directly injured the urban poor, and the former denied them hope of redress for their grievances.

In the 70s the prevalence of piracy began to affect the corn-supply. In 75 the price of grain was cruel, and a mob attacked the consuls proceeding along the Sacra Via and put them to flight; this riot does not seem to have been 'incited by demagogues'.[57] The senate itself re-instituted corn doles in 73, but on a miserably limited scale (see above, note 51). Pompey in 70 forced through the restoration of the tribunes' powers; he probably envisaged that tribunician legislation could be advantageous to him (as it proved); and his wishes could not be denied, as he had a large and loyal army outside the city. Three years later, the tribune Gabinius had

[57] Sall., *Hist.* fragments, iii. 45 f. Shipping had been diverted from the corn-trade, and the treasury was short of money, *Oratio Cottae*, 6 f. Cf. also *Oratio Macri*, 19.

a great command conferred on Pompey to put down the pirates. Almost all the senators opposed the bill; the mob stormed the senate-house and put them to flight. Tribunes who tried to interpose their veto were overawed by a threat of deposition. The people would not tolerate any opposition to a measure that might end the scarcity. Pompey's mere appointment resulted in fact in an immediate and abrupt fall in the price of grain, and within a few weeks he cleared the seas of pirates.[58] His prestige was such that he could not be debarred from another great command in the east. It could be foreseen that on his return with a large army he would be potentially master of the state. This was why the senate had resisted the proposal in 67 to grant him extraordinary powers.

The years from 67 to 62 (when Pompey came back) were full of violence and threats of violence. In 63 Catiline rose in arms against the government with a band of discontented peasants. The urban plebs had at first favoured him, perhaps because his proposal to cancel debts would have relieved them of some payments of rent-arrears. Cicero won them over to the government by alleging that Catiline's friends in the city intended to burn it down and deprive them of their miserable shelter and few personal belongings.[59] But his execution without trial of Catiline's accomplices violated the principle on which the humblest Roman relied for the protection of his own person. Cicero incurred the lasting hatred of the masses. When Clodius had him banished in 58, he erected a shrine to Liberty on the site of Cicero's town house; he had vindicated the freedom of citizens against arbitrary ill-treatment by magistrates.[60]

Early in 62 Marcus Cato greatly extended the scale of distribution of cheap grain. He was the staunchest champion of the senate's power. It seems paradoxical that he should be the author of this measure. But the urban masses were volatile, and it was necessary to assuage their discontents, when Catiline was still in arms and there was a proposal to bring Pompey back to deal with the crisis.[61]

[58] Cic., *de imperio Cn. Pompeii*, 31–5; 44, cf. Rice Holmes, i, pp. 167 ff.
[59] Cic., *in Cat.*, iii. 15; 21; iv. 17; Sall., *Cat.*, 48. 2.
[60] C. Wirszubski, *Libertas as a Political Idea at Rome* (Cambridge, 1950), pp. 24–7; 55–61; Rice Holmes, *Roman Republic*, i, pp. 82 f. Cicero's unpopularity, *ad Att.*, i. 16. 11; ii. 3. 4; viii. 11 D. 7; Ascon., 37 (Oxford text); in *Phil.*, vii. 4 he refers to himself as a well-known adversary of the multitude. Temple of Liberty, Plut., *Cic.*, 33.
[61] Plut., *Cato Minor*, 26–9.

The fears entertained of Pompey proved unjustified. On his return he disbanded his army. But he needed to reward his veterans with land-allotments. Senatorial obstruction threw him into alliance with Caesar, who had consistently identified himself with popular aims, and as consul in 59 Caesar carried agrarian laws by the help of the strong arms of Pompey's veterans. In return, he received the great command in Gaul. To check senatorial reaction once Caesar had left for his province, Pompey and Caesar promoted the election to the tribunate of Publius Clodius, and it was Clodius who finally made the grain distributions free. This was the prime source of the enormous popularity he enjoyed with the plebs so long as he lived. Another measure, to be considered presently, ensured that he, unlike previous demagogues, remained powerful in the city even when out of office.

VI

This sketch will have shown that violence at Rome did not proceed from any single section of the people. Before Sulla 'popular' leaders drew support mainly from citizens who came in from the country to vote and fight in the streets; in 70 it was Pompey's army (recruited in the country) that made the restoration of tribunician power irresistible; in 59 it was again his verterans who forced through Caesar's bills. On the other hand, in 67 it was the *urban* plebs which broke the opposition to Gabinius' law, and in most of the post-Sullan period it is their riots that we hear of. But the senate also, or some of its members, initiated illegal violence from time to time, or at least met force with force. They could mobilize their clients not only from other parts of Italy (see above, pages 83 f.), but within the city itself. The urban plebs was not a united body, and sometimes we are not told what section of it took this or that action.[62]

In annalistic accounts of the class-struggles in the early Republic, which are coloured in detail by the experience of the second and first centuries, we hear much of the dependants (clients) of the nobility supporting them against plebeian leaders.[63] In 133 the

[62] Meier, *Res Publica Amissa*, pp. 112 f. is too ready to assume that where the people is mentioned, the urban plebs is meant.

[63] E.g. Livy, ii. 35. 4; 56. 3; 64. 2; iii. 14. 4; 16. 4; v. 32. 8; 30. 4; vi. 18. 5; 37. 6 f.; Dionysius, vii. 18. 2; viii. 71. 3; ix. 41. 5; 44. 7 etc.

assailants of Tiberius Gracchus included, besides members of the upper classes, 'the plebs uncontaminated by pernicious schemes'.[64] The nobility drew support within the city against Saturninus in 100 and Cinna in 87; and it may be that we should think of this coming rather from their own clients than from the urban masses in general (though Saturninus' followers were countrymen, and Cinna's new citizens from Italy, and neither is known to have had much urban backing). Cicero's claims that his return in 57 was popular, if true at all, may be so only in the sense that the dependants of the nobility demonstrated in his favour.[65] Tacitus' distinction for A.D. 69 between 'the sound section of the populace, attached to the great houses' and the 'sordid plebs, habitués of the circus and theatres' may be relevant.[66] But perhaps some Republican acclamations of 'anti-popular' figures in the theatres might be explained by the hypothesis that they were crowded with clients, for whom their patrons had procured places.[67]

Sallust asserts that in 63 the whole plebs was at first on Catiline's side against the government, which he explains by saying that invariably men who have nothing are envious of the 'good'—the term is in practice indistinguishable from 'rich'; 'they hate the old order and yearn for a new; in detestation of their own lot they work for total change; to them turmoil and riots are a source not of anxiety, but of nourishment; for the destitute cannot easily suffer any loss'. Cicero too more than once says that the property and fortunes of the rich were endangered by Clodius' gangs; and the existence of class-hatred in Rome can hardly be doubted; it is significant that in 52 the mob killed anyone they met wearing gold rings or fine clothes.[68] But it was not felt or evinced by *all* the poor there; a large number depended on the upper classes.

[64] Velleius, ii. 3. 2.
[65] *ad Att.*, iv. 1. 5. His claim that all *collegia* supported his return cannot be accepted (*de domo*, 74); *some* must have done so, perhaps those with upper-class officers (for whom see *ad Quintum fratrem*, ii. 6. 2; *ILS*, 2676). Cicero also boasts of the popularity of his policy in 43 (*Phil.*, vii. 22; xiv. 16); improbable, as it was likely to result in corn-scarcity (xiv. 5); viii. 8 is significant: 'omnes idem volunt . . . cum omnis dico, eos excipio quos nemo civitate dignos putat'. Cf. *pro Milone*, 3: 'reliqua multitudo, quae quidem civium est, tota nostra est'; Ascon., 32; 37; 40; 42 shows that the masses were against Milo.
[66] *Hist.*, i. 4.
[67] E.g. Cic., *ad Att.*, ii. 19. 3.
[68] Sall., *Cat.*, 37; Cic., *Sest.*, 49; 111; *de domo*, 12 f.; *pro Plancio*, 86; *pro*

Sallust thought that the plebs was at a disadvantage against the nobility in that it was less organized. It could do nothing except with leadership from inside the ruling class.[69] It was also notoriously volatile, and could be persuaded to desert its leaders by the plausible demagogy of senatorial spokesmen, as in 122 and 63.[70] And no popular leader before Clodius sought to organize his supporters in such a way that they would effectively support him beyond the brief period for which he held office.

The Twelve Tables, the ancient code of Roman law, apparently allowed freedom of association, if there was no conflict with public law.[71] Many *collegia* of artisans as such or of persons living in the same district (*vicus*) thus arose, some at a very early date. Evidently some of them were implicated in riots in the 60s, and in 64 the senate dissolved all 'except a few named corporations required by the public interest'. At the time Catiline was standing for the consulship, and it was probably feared that they would exert themselves on his behalf. In 58 a law of Clodius restored the right of association, and he himself organized *collegia*, old and new, on a local basis in para-military units and provided a supply of arms. The proximity of Caesar's army and the backing the consuls, who also had some soldiers, gave Clodius, made it impossible for the senate to resist; and henceforth Clodius was an independent power in Rome, even when a private individual, thanks to his control of the *collegia*.[72]

Only from Cicero do we know anything of the composition of Clodius' bands. He speaks of slaves, including runaways and thugs whom Clodius had brought himself for the purpose of terrorism, criminals—'assassins freed from the jail', which Clodius

Milone, 95; cf. Appian, ii. 22 with modern parallels in G. Rudé, *The Crowd in History* (New York, 1964), pp. 224 f.

[69] *Jugurthine War*, 41. 6 as interpreted by J. Hellegouarc'h, *Vocabulaire Latin des relations et des partis* . . . (Paris, 1963), p. 101; Cic., *pro Murena*, 50.

[70] Cf. Livy, vi. 17.

[71] *Dig.*, xlvii. 22. 4.

[72] Ascon., 7; 45; 59 f.; 75 (Oxford text); Cic., *pro Murena*, 71. If the *Commentariolum Petitionis* is by Q. Cicero, or at least well-informed, the suppression must be later in 64; cf. sect. 30. Clodius' law: e.g. Ascon., 8; Cic., *Sest.*, 33 f.; 55; *de domo*, 54; *in Pisonem*, 8–11. Caesar's army, *Sest.*, 40 f.; *de domo*, 131; cf. E. Meyer, *Caesars Monarchie u. das Principat des Pompeius* (Stuttgart, 1922), 3rd edn, p. 94. Consuls' soldiers, *de domo*, 55; 119.

'emptied into the forum'—foreigners; at best they were hirelings (*operae, conducti, mercennarii*). Clodius was a rich man, and according to Cicero he acquired illicit funds to distribute; no doubt he could afford to buy or hire armed escorts. Freedmen and indeed slaves were admitted to *collegia* in large numbers (as inscriptions show), and such people, foreigners by extraction, naturally formed a substantial element in his gangs. Wherever slavery is found, there are always runaways, and in the unpoliced purlieus of Rome they could easily lurk. Rome must also have provided armed robbers with ample opportunities, though it may be noted that in Roman law imprisonment was not a penalty, and if Clodius freed prisoners, they may have been not only persons merely awaiting trial but also men seized for debt.[73] Cicero's descriptions are, however, suspect; he admits himself that it was a common rhetorical device to vilify all who attended political meetings as 'exiles, slaves, madmen', and we know of at least one occasion when he chose to speak of freedmen as slaves.[74] In his view Clodius was Catiline's heir and enjoyed the support of survivors from his movement; we may recall that Catiline had originally had the favour of the whole urban population.

Cicero writes of Clodius' followers much as contemporaries of the better classes wrote of the mobs which rioted in Paris in 1789–95 or 1848, or in English towns of the eighteenth and early nineteenth centuries; they were, it was said, banditti, desperadoes, ragamuffins, convicts and the like. Professor Rudé has shown that wherever records exist to check these descriptions they prove to be largely false. Men with criminal convictions were never more than a minority among the rioters; mostly they were men of 'fixed abode and settled occupation'; for instance all the 662 'vainqueurs de la Bastille' were small workshop masters and journeymen, retailers, artisans and labourers of all kinds.[75] In

---

[73] See e.g. *Sest.*, 6; 27; 34; 38; 53; 57; 59; 65; 75; 78; 81 f.; 84 f.; 89; 95; 106; 112; 126 f.; *de domo*, 5–7; 13; 45; 53 f.; 75; 79; 89 f.; 92; 129; *in Pisonem*, 8–11. Clodius' funds, *de haruspicum responsis*, 28. Runaways, W. Buckland, *Roman Law of Slavery* (Cambridge, 1908), pp. 257 ff. Dionysius, iv. 24. 5 attests the practice of liberating thugs; Augustus was to bar such freedmen from citizenship or from living within 100 miles of Rome. For riots ascribed to slaves, freedmen and hirelings before 58, cf. Ascon., 45; 66; Cic., *ad Att.*, i. 1. 13; 14. 5; ii. 1. 8.

[74] Cic., *Academica*, ii. 144; Ascon., 52, cf. 8. 23.

[75] Rudé *The Crowd in History*, pp. 7 ff.; pp. 195 ff.

Rome the Catilinarians tried to raise 'the *artisans* and slaves', and Cicero lets out that Clodius' following included shopkeepers; when he wished to gather a mob, he had the shops closed, a practice common with seditious tribunes.[76] We should not assume on his biased testimony that artisans and shopkeepers needed to be incited or hired on every occasion to give up their day's earnings and risk their lives and limbs in a demonstration, without real grievances to demonstrate about. In 41, when famine was raging, 'the people closed their shops and drove the magistrates from their places, thinking that they had no need of magistrates or crafts in a city suffering from want and robbery [by soldiers]'.[77] Then at least they acted without any demagogue to instigate and pay them. I suspect that when Shakespeare makes a carpenter and a cobbler typical members of the Roman mob, he was, by intuition, right, and that Clodius would have had little power over such people but that they had complaints and looked on him as their champion. But even if most of them (freedmen included) were artisans and shopkeepers, that would not have endeared them to Cicero; he had once spoken of 'artisans, shopkeepers and all the scum in cities whom it is so easy to excite'. He characterizes the Clodians as 'destitute' (*egentes*); but their plight did not evoke his compassion; the word is almost a synonym with the epithet which often accompanies it—'scoundrels' (*perditi*). He recognized that the plebs was 'wretched and half-starved', but added at once that it was 'the bloodsucker of the treasury'.[78] It was such attitudes on the part of the governing class which gave Clodius his opportunity.

VII

Violence was actuated by many different aims. The clients of the great houses used it simply in their patrons' interest, the followers of popular leaders sometimes merely from loyalty to their leaders. But they were attached to the 'demagogues' because the demagogues were active for their welfare. Country people, including

[76] Sall., *Cat.*, 50. 1; Cic., *de domo*, 13; 54; 89 f.; *Academica*, ii. 144; Ascon., 40 f.
[77] Appian, v. 18.
[78] *Pro Flacco*, 18; *ad Att.*, i. 16. 11; 19. 4; ii. 1. 8. 'Egentes' and 'perditi', e.g. *de domo*, 45.

the veterans, usually sought land distributions. The burden of rent, indignation at arbitrary punishments, proposals to redistribute freedmen among all the tribes could sometimes raise an urban mob. But in 75, 67, in the heyday of Clodius' ascendancy and again in 41 and 39 hunger seems to have been the chief motive force.[79]

When Cicero was banished, there was a scarcity; his sarcasm that the bands who pulled down his house were not going to satisfy their appetite on tiles and cement implies that they were hungry.[80] Clodius' grain law may have increased the effective demand, which certainly outran the supply. In July 57 there was a food riot. A few days later, when the senate voted for Cicero's restoration, the price of grain providentially sank. It was but a temporary improvement. For days together the senate debated the corn supply. Cicero gave three possible explanations for the shortage: exporting provinces had no surplus, or they sent it elsewhere to get higher prices, or the suppliers held grain in store in the expectation of famine rates. On the 5th September he boasted that plenty had returned with him. This was an illusion. Prices continued to oscillate (a familiar phenomenon in many ages). On the next two days they went sky-high, and the mob rose; Cicero acknowledged that there was suffering and hunger. He and others did not venture to the senate-house. But a day or two later he risked attendance; the streets were evidently quiet again. If the rioters had been merely Clodius' hirelings, out for Cicero's blood, this would be strange; if they were exasperated artisans and shopkeepers, with work to do, they could not be kept in the streets continuously. On Cicero's motion Pompey was now invested with the procurement of grain and given wide powers, probably enabling him to requisition grain from recalcitrant suppliers. Plutarch thought he secured abundance as by magic, but soon all was not well again, and now the blame could be laid on Pompey.

---

[79] The locust plague in Africa in 125 (Orosius, v. 11. 2) may also have paved the way for Gaius Gracchus; for hunger in the Gracchan period: cf. Lucilius, fragment 214 (Loeb edn). In the 40s too the rent-burden must have been the greater, as Africa was under Pompeian control and grain must have been scarce and dearer, leaving less money to pay the rent.

[80] *De domo*, 61. For what follows see *de domo*, 9–17 with Ascon., 48; Cic., *post reditum in senatu*, 34; *ad Quirites*, 18; *ad Att.*, iv. 1. 6; *ad Quintum fratrem*, ii. 5. 1; *de haruspicum responsis*, 31.

Hence, in the scene with which I opened, the mob shouted that Pompey was starving them. In April 56 there were renewed debates on the high price of grain, and Pompey was voted more money. In August Cicero deplored high costs, the infertility of the fields, the poor harvest. Persistent scarcity was the background to continual violence.

Rudé has shown that in eighteenth- and nineteenth-century France and England riots were often (not always) provoked by, or associated with scarcities, whatever their avowed aims. In October 1789, when the Paris mob went to bring the royal family from Versailles, they said that they would fetch 'the baker, the baker's wife and the little baker boy'; they thought that there would be plenty with the king in their midst.[81] If we had data for the fluctuating grain prices of Rome, it might well be that we could plot a correlation with the outbreaks of mob violence. But this must remain a speculation.

VIII

If we look beyond the ambitions and machinations of the great figures of the late Republic, the main cause of its fall must in my view be found in agrarian discontents; it was the soldiers, who were of peasant origin, whose disloyalty to the Republic was fatal. The rôle of the *urban* mob was more restricted. Still, it was their clamour that gave Pompey his extraordinary command in 67 and set in motion the events that led to his alliance with Caesar in 59. And the violence in the city from 58 to 52, which was itself one result of that alliance, produced such chaos that it finally brought Pompey and the senatorial leaders together again, and helped to sever his connection with Caesar; hence the civil wars in which the Republic foundered.

Popular leaders sometimes proclaimed the sovereignty of the people. But the people who could actually attend meetings at Rome were not truly representative and were incapable of governing an empire. The only workable alternative to the government of the few was the government of one man. The interventions of the people in affairs led on to monarchy.[82]

[81] Rudé, *The Crowd in History*, ch. 14.
[82] Wirszubski, *Libertas*, pp. 47 ff. Cf. Sallust, *Jugurthine War*, 31: 'sane fuerit regni paratio plebi sua restituere'.

To the urban proletariate this was no disadvantage. It was the aristocracy who suffered from loss of liberty. Tacitus says that Augustus won over the people with bread, and this was the greatest need.[83] They also benefited from improvements in the supply of water, from better fire-protection, better preservation of water, more splendid shows, more expenditure on buildings which gave employment. The emperors for their own security had to keep them content, and their misery was somewhat reduced. This was all they could expect in a world whose material resources remained small.[84]

[83] *Ann.*, i. 5; cf. Augustus' *Res Gestae*, 5.

[84] I have made no change in the text in this article. Since writing it, I have sought to justify the statements on population (n. 4 and pp. 80–1) in my *Italian Manpower* (Oxford, 1971), Part 1 and chapter xxi. The statement on p. 80 that only *adult* males were eligible for grain rations is wrong; cf. *Italian Manpower*, p. 382, though it would perhaps be best to amend Suet., *Aug.* 41, to mean that eligibility began not at the age of ten but at that of fourteen, the conventional age for male puberty. On free and slave labour, J. A. Crook, *Law and Life of Rome* (London, 1967), pp. 191 ff. supplies further information, and G. E. Rickman, *Roman Granaries and Store Buildings* (Cambridge, 1971) shows the great number of porters required (pp. 8–11, 79, 86); on my view they would have been mostly free. In my *Social Conflicts in the Roman Republic* (London, 1971) further examples can be found of the importance of public works (see the index *s.v.*) in the activity of popular leaders. *Italian Manpower* also contains material promised in n. 54 on the continuance of grain cultivation (index *s.v.*) in Italy. On p. 80 or 92 I should have made it plain that Octavius' veto of a tribunician bill was as bizarre constitutionally as Tiberius Gracchus' *riposte*. The text of Cicero cited in n. 32 (*Att.* xiv 9, 1) may refer to slum property at Puteoli, but conditions will have been no better at Rome.

V

ÉLITE MOBILITY IN THE ROMAN EMPIRE*†

Keith Hopkins

I

THE SYSTEM OF STRATIFICATION

Rome was throughout the empire an 'estate' society, that is, there were legal distinctions of status. The aristocratic élite was the senate, which in the first three centuries A.D. had about six hundred members. There was a general expectation that the sons of a senator would also be senators—but there was also the proviso that each member should have property worth at least one million sesterces and be elected to office. In principle election was by the senate, in effect often by the emperor, who also appointed his own nominees. The second estate was the equestrian order (*equites*), whose minimum property requirement was 400,000 sesterces. The formal method of entry was by imperial grant. A third privileged group consisted of the decurions, in general the top one hundred men of each city. Their wealth varied immensely, as did the size of cities. Below them came the urban plebs and the rural peasantry. Juridically at the bottom came the ex-slaves and the slaves themselves.

The senators and equestrians each wore distinctive dress, and between them filled most important and honorific governmental posts. It seems especially significant that both orders depended

* From no. 32 (1965).
† I should like to thank Dr M. I. Finley, Professor A. H. M. Jones and Dr A. N. Little for their help.

upon a minimum property holding and election. In the aristocracy these requirements were reinforced by the competitive demands of ostentatious expenditure. The major source of income was land; a lot of nonsense has been written about the *equites* as a merchant class. Fortunes may sometimes have had their origin in trade, but were soon converted into land which was safer than trade and gave higher prestige. Professor A. H. M. Jones has shown for the later empire that mercantile fortunes were small compared with those of noble landowners.[1]

The system of formal stratification was supplemented, even cut across, by other groupings. In the first century A.D., Roman citizens had important social privileges denied to non-citizens, though within both groups, especially among citizens, there were great differences, for example in wealth. In 212 as the climax of a long process of assimilation, Roman citizenship was granted to virtually all provincials. But already, and perhaps in its place, a new division of society, more in alignment with the formal stratification, had become established. This distinguished the *humiliores*—or lower class—from the *honestiores*, who comprised the top three privileged groups, senators, *equites* and decurions and all legionaries of whatever rank—a symptom of the army's political power.

The process of political unification which marks the empire had great consequences for social mobility. The Roman empire had been won by Romans and their Italian allies who initially monopolized all high status positions in the central government. Correspondingly wealthy provincials in the early period had been 'content' with local or provincial honours. As the government became more centralized the spheres of its control broadened, leading provincials became Roman citizens and competed for traditional Roman honours. By the end of the first century, for example, there was a Spanish Roman as emperor, by the end of the second an African, by the beginning of the third a Syrian. The crises of continuous barbarian invasions in the third century invested the armies and their professional officers with supreme power. They broke the aristocratic senate's monopoly of privilege, and in fact excluded senators from all important or powerful positions.

Under Diocletian (284–305) and Constantine (306–337), the

[1] A. H. M. Jones, *The Later Roman Empire* (Oxford, 1964), pp. 870–1.

army was doubled in size, additional taxes were raised, bureaucratic control much tightened. Under Constantine, aristocrats were readmitted to high positions, but the equestrian and senatorial orders were fused. The new expanded order (*clarissimi*), based upon the same admixture of hereditary expectation and actual tenure of office or imperial grant, was the highest estate for the whole empire. As taxes and bureaucratic interference increased, decurions could less and less opt out of the single status system; they tried to become senators—*clarissimi*. It is arguable, therefore, that the centralization of the administration and the political unification of the empire promoted mobility in the fourth century to an unprecedented degree. The spate of fourth-century laws against social mobility has traditionally been regarded as evidence of immobility.[2] But the laws were only spasmodically enforced; their repetition is evidence of their failure.[3]

II

GENERAL PROPOSITIONS

I have presumptuously compressed the developments of four centuries into two pages. The historian may rightly object that in doing so I have neglected not only numerous exceptions but also important areas of differentiation within the estates. He might also feel uncomfortable with the transition from a formal analysis of stratification which coincides with the Romans' own terminology and institutions (senate, *equites*, etc.), to an historical interpretation of the pressures which produced changes in the formal system. All these objections seem to me to be valid and germane; germane because it is exactly in these areas of objection that we shall find social mobility concentrated.

This situation arises because there are in any complex society several criteria of status; for example: wealth, birth, formal education, learnt skill, ability, achievement, style of life. The formal and dominant estate system of stratification assumes their con-

---

[2] Cf. for example, O. Seeck, *Geschichte des Untergangs der antiken Welt* (Berlin, 1901), ii, p. 301.

[3] A random collection of cases of upward mobility may be found in R. MacMullen, 'Social mobility and the Theodosian code', *JRS*, liv (1964), pp. 49–53.

gruence, that is that people who rate highly on one criterion or dimension will rate highly on others. There is a general and strong belief in the legitimacy of the hierarchy and a general and strong expectation that status will be inherited. Various institutions allow the aristocratic child, for example, privileged access to situations in which he can distinguish himself and succeed his father.

Social mobility, whether upward or downward, by its very nature confounds these expectations of inherited status and straddles the formal system of stratification. It can be usefully seen as a process of status discrepancy or dissonance, that is a situation in which people rate highly on one or more dimensions, but not on others. The upwardly mobile man, for example, rating relatively low on birth may acquire a good formal education, a highly valued professional skill, and be successful in his profession. He may still be relatively poor and not on equal terms of social friendship with born nobles. In time, he may acquire this too, and this may especially be the case if we look at mobility as a function of family, rather than of individuals. A *nouveau riche* father may have a more socially acceptable son.

This process occurred in Rome as well as in modern Britain, but there is, I think, one major difference. In a complex industrial society like Britain, occupational groups are in some ways insulated from one another; each has its own specific criteria of excellence; a good historian in Britain is content by and large to be a professor: he rejects birth or income as an overall criterion by which his standing relative to other groups should be judged. Rome, on the other hand, was dominated by its own overall estate system of stratification; it really did matter whether one was a senator or not. A man's rank (e.g. senator, *eques*, *servus*) was noted in the ancient sources in the context in which a modern writer would name his occupation. But even if this formal system was dominant, it was not the only source of status. There are numerous examples of senators or equestrians who rated high on some dimensions of status, but not on others. This is exactly the point; the more differentiated a society becomes (that is, the more professions and occupations become insulated), the more mobility is possible; and the more possible it becomes to accept or assimilate the socially mobile—men or women who rate high on some status dimensions, but low on others.

My first two general propositions are thus that:

(1) social mobility may usefully be seen as a process of status dissonance—especially in a society with a strong ideology of hereditary status;

(2) social mobility was a product of the structural differentiation of institutions (for example, bureaucracy, army, law).

The third general proposition relates to the processes at work in the political unification of the empire. Put baldly, a major element of this process was the tension or conflict primarily between the emperor and the aristocracy and secondarily between each of those two and the structurally differentiated institutions. In spite of the massive evidence of Tacitus, Suetonius, Dio Cassius and the *Scriptores Historiae Augustae*, there is a tendency among modern historians to minimize this conflict, and of course it is difficult or impossible to *prove* its importance. It was certainly not the only factor. But equally, leading ancient writers thought the conflict important, and as I shall argue certain patterns of mobility can be most easily understood in terms of it.

Lastly I shall take a brief look at elements of the structure of property and inheritance, and at high aristocratic consumption and low fertility: the combined effect of these was to reduce tension caused by upward mobility. For by downward mobility, and biological non-replacement, the aristocracy left vacant established and highly valued administrative positions.

Thus I also propose that:

(3) certain patterns of mobility may be best understood as the product of conflict between the emperor and the aristocracy, and between each of these two and the structurally differentiated institutions;

(4) resistance to upward mobility was diminished by the downward mobility of the aristocracy, and their biological non-replacement.

In the remainder of this paper I shall expand and illustrate these propositions.

III

STRUCTURAL DIFFERENTIATION AND STATUS DISSONANCE

In early Rome, say before 300 B.C., the chief magistrates were nobles in charge of military, civil, religious, judicial, legislative and executive actions. The aristocracy was the locus of most virtue. Its pride was its noble birth and ancestors; its expectations were hereditary. It had a near monopoly of power. It was protected against outsiders by institutions, but where these failed it could always rely upon a pervasive belief in superior 'nature' or 'blood'. By what other belief can an aristocracy set itself apart, when the technical thresholds of an aristocrat's duties are low? The final defence is the defence against acceptance; the *arriviste* is pinned by the hostile stereotype of the *nouveau riche*.

As Rome expanded to a huge empire with a population of some fifty millions (first century A.D.), the complexity of government and its centralization under the emperors brought about the development and separation of, for example, military, bureaucratic, legal, educational and economic institutions. One can trace the growth of a professional army, the separation of military from civil bureaucratic careers, the creation of a hierarchy of bureaucratic ranks, the codification of laws, the creation of law schools, the establishment of publicly supported education and of capitalistic market production.

The differentiation of these various activities created new professions, new careers, new criteria of status. Each profession had its own criteria of excellence, its own rules of entry and advancement. The aristocracy could not monopolize all valued skills or fill all important executive positions. To do so they would have had to sacrifice their valued leisure and metropolitan pleasures. At the same time if the aristocracy was not to become a placid backwater reflecting only a glorious past it had to keep its finger on the pulse of all the new elements of the complex society. The aristocracy was already acknowledged as the 'better part of the human race', 'the flower of the whole world'.[4] It was also ideally and often in fact the most wealthy, the most literary element in society and

---

[4] Symmachus, *Epist.*, 1. 52; *Paneg. Lat.*, iv. 35. 2.

held the highest offices and the highest military commands. Because of this, it survived as the supreme stratum; but because of
this also it opened its own ranks to *arrivistes*. So long as an aristocracy depends upon birth alone it can remain exclusive; when it
admits complementary criteria of achievement, whether money or
professional skill, it opens the way to *arrivistes*. If aristocrats want
to be literateurs, literateurs have a credit which helps to disguise
them as aristocrats. If aristocrats want to be generals, generals
who are not aristocrats have a fulcrum by which they can lever
themselves into acceptability. This is not to say that all literateurs
or military leaders were equally acceptable or accepted as equals
by aristocrats. Far from it. But at least we can see that social
mobility is a process of gradual acquisition of status on a variety of
fronts; and the process is made much easier if the aristocrats
themselves try to acquire status on a number of fronts too.

Yet the patterns of mobility, that is the patterns of acquisition
of highly valued marks of status, were by no means random.
There were a few channels of mobility which seem to have been
most often used. I shall discuss two briefly: the military and literary
spheres. Traditionally the aristocracy had seen itself as embattled
heroes competing for the conqueror's glory, of course for Rome's
benefit. Its culmination was the award of a Triumph. When the
government came under the control of a single emperor, such
pursuits of military glory through the unified command of an
army presented a threat to the emperor's position. Victory, as
Tacitus noted, was a virtue suited to an emperor. Without hope
of a Triumph a military career had only tradition to recommend it
to the senator; it was part of his normal career to hold a couple of
short-term commands of military units. The armies were, moreover, stationed on the frontiers, and it was hardly worth being an
aristocrat permanently stationed at a distance from Rome.[5] The
long-term professional officers, formally subordinates to senatorial
commanders, were never aristocrats. When the barbarians in-
vaded continuously in the third century it seems either that the
necessity and technical demands of winning excluded amateurish
aristocrats, or more likely that the professional groups of under-
officers were in a position to reject their amateurish aristocratic
commanders. Certainly they did; for from the middle of the third

[5] E. Birley, 'Senators in the Emperors' service', *PBA*, xxxix (1953), pp.
207–8.

century, aristocrats were excluded first from military and then from other important government posts.

Literary skill was part and parcel of aristocratic daily life; it was used as a secondary reinforcement of aristocratic nature. It was a mark of noble polish to write skilfully and allusively. Those who taught nobles, especially those who helped adult nobles maintain their skills, could with practice pass themselves off as aristocrats. Libanius, for example, a teacher of rhetoric in Antioch in the fourth century, was made an honorary praetorian prefect, a very high position; and there are several similar cases. A study of thirty-four teachers at Bordeaux in the fourth century shows that at least twelve were upwardly mobile, that is became professors in the capitals Constantinople or Rome, married rich or noble wives or held provincial governorships.[6] While literateurs were more attractive to aristocrats than skilful but boorish generals, they also had less power to force their way into the highest ranks.

Both literateurs and military officers were subjected to repeated public tests of competence, the one in rhetorical exhibitions, the other in battle. It is not that aristocrats were *per se* incompetent in these fields—several were clearly masters of literary style (Tacitus, Gellius). But mostly that they had no ethos of gaining professional competence. If one is superior by nature, one is good without seeming to try.

The aristocratic ethos pervaded the Roman élite. Even the now differentiated professions (for example, military, legal, literary) owed their high status partly to the fact that in the old days their best or only practitioners were aristocrats. But on occasion professionalism outweighed the aristocratic ethos. This happened in the military and bureaucratic spheres in the third century. Yet although one can point to the exclusion of the aristocracy from military and from bureaucratic office at that time and call it a victory for professionalism, the end of the story points another moral. For Constantine re-engaged aristocrats in high positions and like his predecessors rewarded *equites* (non-aristocrats) in terms of the traditional honour system. The legitimation of the emperor was too insecure, even when he was supreme general, for him to be able to ignore the social power of aristocrats or the traditional system of honour. There was no possibility of revolu-

---

[6] M. K. Hopkins, 'Social mobility in the later Roman empire: the evidence of Ausonius', *CQ*, xi (1961), pp. 246–7.

tion based upon a professional bourgeoisie. Such bourgeois as there were, were too imbued with the sense of aristocratic superiority and wanted to be rewarded by being made aristocrats. It is not surprising then that the military government of the latter part of the third century capitulated to the aristocratic system, even if it compromised partly by employing aristocrats and partly by ennobling generals. The whole society was pervaded by standards which emphasized personal attachments rather than objective professional achievements. The conflict between them can be seen in the regulations of the praetorian prefect's court, for example, which insisted upon legal knowledge as a prerequisite for enrolment, but also upon priority and privilege for sons of lawyers.[7]

Outbursts of professionalism were the exception; the rule was a victory of the aristocratic ethos, in one of two ways. Firstly aristocrats, though amateurs, headed or directed the professional institutions. They held most high government offices, commanded armies, wrote *belles lettres*, history and philosophy. Secondly they absorbed the aspiring professionals. We know very little of the ways in which aristocrats and professionals mixed; but almost certainly it was not as equals. What survives is a cruel stereotype of the social riser, and the undercurrent of an ideology that ability should be rewarded. As far as formal rank is concerned, generals, literateurs, lawyers and financiers were promoted to the senate.

IV

SOCIAL MOBILITY AS A FUNCTION OF POLITICAL CONFLICT

Just before his death, Augustus, the first emperor, discussed possible contenders for the throne. 'All those mentioned, except one, were soon struck down on one charge or another, at the instigation of Tiberius [his successor]'. Domitian, emperor A.D. 81–96, invited leading senators to dinner—they came to find each place decorated with a tombstone engraved with the guest's name, the hall decked out as a tomb; the servants were black boys,

[7] *Classical Journal*, ii. 7. 11 (460).

and the food was that traditionally given to the dead. Only the emperor's voice was to be heard and the guests were in fear for their lives.[8] Admittedly a macabre rarity, but examples of hostility between the emperor and the senatorial aristocracy are innumerable. Many emperors on their accession swore not to kill any senators, or not without proper trial. Few, if any, kept their promise.

Historians, ancient and modern, have generally concentrated on aspects of behaviour which differentiate emperors from each other, and have tried to explain the assassination or persecution of aristocrats in terms of the emperors' psychopathology. Nero, Domitian, Commodus and Elagabalus give considerable justification to such an approach. Nevertheless, at a different level of analysis, it seems appropriate to see all the emperors as autocratic, as necessarily engaged with the aristocracy in a struggle for power. Partly aristocrats' fear of disgrace or assassination prompted their rebellion, or fear of rebellion prompted the emperor to assassinate aristocrats or confiscate their property. The same conflict is visible in other spheres. For example, it was to the emperor's advantage to limit the aristocratic governors' rapacious exploitation of provincials. This can be used as a paradigm. By tradition, the emperor used aristocrats as governors, but in his own interest and that of the provincials, he limited their power.

The techniques and institutions which developed in response to this conflict involved social mobility. Firstly, since it was aristocratic exercise of power which threatened the emperor's supremacy, the emperor could and did employ non-aristocrats in positions of power. Secondly, emperors helped in the development of differentiated institutions. These gave rise to interest groups, which limited aristocratic power (for example, the professional under-officers in the army). In the same way, the differentiated institutions depended upon bureaucratic rules, for example, or legal institutions or norms (for example, a belief that laws were valid and should be obeyed), which also limited aristocratic power. These differentiated institutions, as we have seen, also provided channels of upward mobility. Thirdly, emperors were interested in the uniform or maximum exploitation of the empire—hence census-taking, for example, and bureaucratic control of tax-raising. To the emperors the privileges of Romans or Italians,

[8] Tac., *Ann.*, i. 13; Dio, lxvii. 9.

which were the original basis of the empire, became of less importance than its political and administrative unification. Because of these centralizing tendencies, access to the bureaucratic machine rather than birth-status by itself became the major source of power. One can see this process in the expansion of Roman citizenship, in the reduction of Italy to the status of an ordinary province, and in the creation of an aristocracy whose rank rested formally upon its holding bureaucratic office. It involved mobility in the assimilation of provincials into the Roman honour system. In the next three sections I shall illustrate these processes.

The employment of non-aristocrats in positions of power

In the first century A.D. some of the highest administrative positions of the empire and some of the largest personal fortunes ever amassed in Rome were in the hands of ex-slaves, the notorious imperial freedmen. In the later empire, in the fourth and fifth centuries, court eunuchs, who were ex-slaves and barbarians, were acknowledged to be at the centre of power.[9] The chief eunuch, *ex officio*, ranked after the prefects and the very highest generals. If we consider freedmen and eunuchs as groups rather than as individuals, then the continuity is too great to be explicable only in terms of emperors' characters. Powerful eunuchs, for instance, were loathed by aristocrats, often sacrificed to their baying, exiled, even burnt—only to be succeeded by other eunuchs.

Imperial freedmen and court eunuchs provide dramatic examples of upward mobility. Their elevation is most easily explicable in terms of the conflict between the emperor and the aristocracy; for the aristocracy was angered by their power, yet the emperors, who could hardly be unaware of this hatred, repeatedly used them. The conventional explanation that freedmen traditionally did such jobs in large Roman households is hardly a sufficient explanation; it certainly does not explain the transition from freedmen to *equites*.

From about the beginning of the second century, imperial freedmen in the palace administration were supervised by *equites* who

---

[9] A. M. Duff, *Freedmen in the Early Roman Empire* (Cambridge, 1958); M. K. Hopkins 'Eunuchs in politics in the later Roman empire', *PCPS*, clxxxix (1963), pp. 62 ff.

also held the chief positions in the imperial fiscal service. *Equites* were also exclusively in charge of the highly centralized government of Egypt. Indeed, no senator was ever allowed to visit Egypt without special permission. The crack troops stationed in or near the court were commanded by *equites* also, and this office, the praetorian prefecture, developed from a military command to a post almost of vice-emperor, with wide administrative, judicial and supervisory powers. But before the fourth century, when the equestrian and senatorial orders were amalgamated, this post was never held by a senator; even in the fourth century, praetorian prefects were quite often men of humble origin.

Emperors used men of lowly origin in key positions of the administration because they were not identified with aristocratic interests, because their mobility made them more dependent upon, even grateful to, the emperors, and because they might not be too easily assimilated to the aristocracy. In this respect it is easy to understand why eunuchs managed to occupy such a tactically important position among palace servants. For others, like most emperors too, were influenced by the existing honours system. They saw rewards in terms of ennoblement. Freedmen were made praetors, equestrian prefects were given the insignia of consuls.[10] Formally, even if not in their associations, they had become aristocrats. Their sons might not be of the same usefulness to the emperors as their *arriviste* fathers.

It was not only individuals who were assimilated to the aristocracy. The very channels of mobility went through the same process; the climbers climbed and drew up their ladders after them. For example, the imperial cabinet secretaries in the early fourth century were shorthand writers, who were, as their skill dictated, of humble origins. Their access to state secrets prompted the emperors to use them on private and important missions. They won prestige, and as a group gained privileges. Their job now became both possible for and attractive to aristocrats. By the end of the fourth century it was an aristocratic sinecure requiring no skill.[11] Something of this same process, the upgrading of a job because it gave access to power, occurred with the displacement of freedmen by *equites*.

10 Cf. A. Stein, *Der römische Ritterstand* (Munich, 1927), pp. 245 ff.
11 Jones, *op. cit.*, pp. 572–4.

Differentiated institutions

It is, of course, very difficult to investigate the conscious policy of the emperors. They certainly aided the development of differentiated institutions, for example by establishing professorial chairs with state funds or by employing lawyers as legislative or judicial advisers. But it would be rash to see this as exclusively dictated by a desire to control the aristocracy rather than by the complex needs of administering a large empire. We have already seen how the differentiated institutions provided new criteria of status and new careers. What concerns us here is rather to point out that laws and bureaucratic rules, as well as courts and bureaucratic practices (for example tax-gathering) also served to control aristocrats. But besides providing an extra element of power which the emperor could use in his battle against aristocrats, these institutions provided sources of power which limited him, and which he sought to control. Emperors made laws, but they could not break them too often without robbing the legal system of some of its power. They had to raise most money by taxation rather than by confiscation. They were caught by the system they had helped to create. One example of this can be seen in their ambivalence over promotion within the bureaucracy. They might have liked to promote by merit but this would have opened the way to subjective (that is nepotistic or patronal) and therefore uncontrollable estimates of talent by subordinates. By and large, therefore, emperors favoured seniority as the principle of promotion; they met the constant pressures for special treatment by the cheapening of privilege and by the creation of extra places. Positions were pre-empted by supernumeraries and even sold.[12] There was then a consistent pressure towards hereditary privilege, stability, even inertia. Spasmodically the system was attacked by energetic emperors, or beaten by the whimsical promotions of their favourites. But it is wrong to say that the system was beaten; both the tendency to inertia and the spasmodic whimsy were themselves elements of the system.

[12] *Ibid.*, pp. 602–6, especially n. 94.

The political unification of the empire

One of the primary forces which brought about the political unification of the empire was the increasing bureaucratic interference in previously autonomous cities. It was borne in upon municipal leaders that their chances of resisting the exploitation of the central bureaucracy, and their social standing with its representatives, depended upon their own place in the Roman honour system. It was no longer enough to be a leading member of the local community, with nothing but local standing.

Certainly leading provincials were gradually assimilated to the Roman aristocracy. In accord with prevailing cultural values it was easier for Latinized than for Hellenized provincials to be accepted. The figures for the known Roman senators are striking: by the end of the first century A.D. (in the time of Domitian), 23% were of provincial origin; by the middle of the second century A.D. (in the time of Antoninus Pius), the percentage had risen to 42%; by the third century it was 56%.[13] These figures give a very rough idea of the degree to which the originally Italian aristocracy was not in fact hereditary. In the fourth century, rates of mobility seem to have increased. For as bureaucratic control reached an unprecedented intensity, the positive disadvantages of remaining only a municipal decurion (the old third estate) became apparent. The decurions pushed upwards into the expanded first estate (the clarissimate) or into the expanded bureaucracy.

Only occasionally can one see traces of the conflict between aristocracy and emperor in this type of mobility. The elevation of Gauls by the emperor Claudius (41–54), and of Pannonians by Valentinian I (264–76) obviously angered the entrenched nobility, and was obviously intended as a breach of vested interests.[14] But mostly the assimilation of the provincial leaders proceeded gradually and without fuss. This assimilation forms one of the most important patterns of élite mobility in Rome, yet it is significantly different from what is generally understood by mobility.

---

[13] M. Hammond, 'Composition of the Senate A.D. 68–235', *JRS*, xlvii (1957), p. 77.

[14] Tac., *Ann.*, ii. 23; *CIL*, xii, 1668. A. Alföldi, *A Conflict of Ideas in the Later Roman Empire. The Clash between the Senate and Valentinian I* (Oxford, 1952), pp. 13 ff.

For these men were mostly 'of good family' and high standing within a local or provincial status system; they did not so much increase their fortunes as change their point of reference from their locality to the empire.

The small range of their social movement must have done much to remove aristocratic obstructions. The more dramatic examples of mobility catch the eye and are of great political significance: equestrian imperial freedmen in the first century, soldier-emperors in the third century, praetorian prefects, bureaucratic innovators like John the Cappadocian, are notable examples. But the predominant form of mobility is *a priori* likely to have been the movement of a wealthy equestrian or provincial dignitary to the lesser aristocracy, and thence perhaps to higher things. Most often it must have been the slow climb of a family over generations, not the rocketing climb of individuals. Certainly this gradual mobility existed unsupported by any major ideology of advancement. There are occasional statements which praise ability rather than birth, but the dominant ideology praised aristocratic birth, blood and nature above all else. The rapid climber gained formal status, but was warded off from assimilation by the stereotype of the *nouveau riche*.

V

DEMOGRAPHIC FACTORS

I have tried to show that there was a steady and significant stream of mobility into the Roman aristocracy. This resulted partly in its expansion; in part its effects were muted by the low fertility of Roman aristocrats.[15] Augustus offered rewards to aristocrats with three children, and later emperors re-enacted his laws. There is plenty of evidence that aristocrats regarded three children as an upper limit or as an unreachable target. This low figure was achieved mostly by abortion, much less by contraception and perhaps by infanticide. Given the high mortality then prevalent, three children born was far below the level of replacement.

[15] The detailed evidence and argument of this section is taken from M. K. Hopkins, 'The later Roman aristocracy: a demographic profile' (unpublished fellowship dissertation, King's College, Cambridge, 1963).

Therefore as aristocratic families died out, posts once held by them were available to *arrivistes*.

Nevertheless succession in the male line was highly valued, so that low aristocratic fertility needs some explanation. It might be tempting to point to the inheritance system; for it was customary in Rome to split property more or less equally among all children irrespective of sex. More than two children surviving their parents' death would therefore result in a diminution of the children's wealth. But Lorimer has suggested that neither primogeniture nor partible inheritance *per se* have any definite effect upon levels of fertility.[16] This does not mean to say that the structure of inheritance is irrelevant, but rather that it cannot by itself explain low fertility.

Several other influential factors are worth mentioning, though there is no certain way of assessing their relative importance. Firstly, Roman aristocrats were engaged in a bitter struggle of ostentatious expenditure. For some this resulted in their downfall; there are several references to impoverished patricians. The ostentation and wealth of others aroused the jealousy or fear of emperors. For yet others the demands of expenditure involved a limit on children, because children were expensive. Daughters had to be given dowries commensurate with their father's status. Spinsterhood was almost unknown before Christian times (fourth century). Sons had to be launched into public life, and the games celebrating their first high office sometimes cost the whole of an aristocrat's annual cash income or even twice that.[17] Secondly, the socially approved ways in which an aristocrat could get money were restricted to inheritance, dowry and government office. This was not an iron rule, but it was general practice. The typical tenure of government office was short. This was in the emperors' interest, because they wanted to restrict aristocratic power; and it was in accord with the aristocratic ideal of *otium cum dignitate*. Thirdly, aristocratic women had sufficient social power, for example control over their own property and rights of initiating their divorce, to be able to refuse to have children. They lived in a competitive salon culture, and did not want to spoil their figures with large numbers of children. Lastly, we, with the benefit of modern statistics and statistical concepts, can talk of rates of

[16] F. Lorimer *et al.*, *Culture and Human Fertility* (Unesco, Paris, 1954), p. 165.
[17] Olympiodorus, *frag.* 44 (*FGH*, iv).

mortality and average expectation of life at birth; such concepts were not available to the Romans. They saw death as capricious. If one had five children all might survive and the family would sink in the social scale, or be ruined. Aemilius Paullus, for example, had four sons. While they were still young he gave two away to be adopted by noble families. His own two remaining sons then died prematurely. Many nobles apparently had one son only and preferred to risk his survival, rather than have more and risk their survival and the consequent lowering of the family's wealth and status. Whatever the result in individual cases, the result for the aristocracy as a whole was the continual dwindling of their numbers.

VI

SUMMARY

A brief summary may be useful. There is little quantitative evidence of social mobility in Rome. In this paper therefore I have attempted a structural analysis of some aspects of élite mobility. The task was made simpler because Rome had an estate system of stratification, with legal distinctions between strata. In accord with this, Romans expected a high degree of status congruence. Social mobility may usefully be seen as a process of status dissonance, that is a process in which the social riser rates highly on some status dimensions but not on others. This in turn raises the problem of his acceptability to the élite. I have tried to explain the increased chances of such acceptance when differentiated or specialized social institutions replace undifferentiated ones: for example schools, the army. Traditionally, whether in myth or reality, Roman aristocrats had been good at everything that mattered. They strove to live up to this ideal and recognized achievement; they thus opened the way for the assimilation of the upwardly mobile.

Not all achievers were immediately acceptable, and some of these were used by emperors in their rivalry with the established aristocracy. Such a contest seems a function of autocracy. Objection to social risers might have been greater but for two factors. Firstly, there was a reservoir of wealthy provincials 'of good family', who became assimilated to the old nobility as the empire became more of a political unity. Secondly, the old aristocracy left vacant places partly through its own downward social mobility, but mostly through its keeping the number of children below the level of replacement.

VI

SOCIAL MOBILITY IN THE EARLY ROMAN EMPIRE: THE EVIDENCE OF THE IMPERIAL FREEDMEN AND SLAVES*

P. R. C. Weaver

Roman Imperial society, both of the early and late empire, exhibits a highly developed system of formal stratification. It was made up of a rigid hierarchy of orders or 'estates' with legal distinctions of status between them. In the early empire these estates were the senatorial and equestrian orders, the free-born plebs and rural peasantry, the slave-born freedmen (*liberti*) and those still of slave status (*servi*). However, juridical status is far from being a reliable indication of social status. A considerable degree of flexibility in the working of the system of stratification was permitted, and was indeed inescapable, if the basic structure was not to be strained and break down in social discontent and revolution. Social mobility, or social movement in the restricted sense of changes in class or status, the process by which discrepancies arose between the legal system of stratification and actual social status, and were tolerated, is important enough in the history of the Roman empire to demand more attention than it has hitherto received.[1] It cannot be measured statistically. In the absence of anything approaching complete data or statistically significant samples, or devices such as indices of association, or even an agreed list of power and occupational rankings, a different, non-

---

* From no. 37 (1967).
[1] Foremost in this field is M. K. Hopkins: 'Social mobility in the later Roman empire: the evidence of Ausonius', *CQ*, new ser., xi (1961), pp. 239–49; 'Eunuchs in politics in the later Roman empire', *PCPS*, new ser., ix (1963), pp. 62–80; 'Elite Mobility in the Roman Empire', chapter v above; cf. also Hopkins, 'Contraception in the Roman empire', *Comparative Studies in Society and History*, vii (1965), pp. 124–51.

numerical approach has to be adopted for the problem of social mobility in the Roman empire. M. K. Hopkins has recently suggested such an approach.[2] It involves tracing what he calls patterns of mobility, that is the order in which highly valued status symbols are acquired by members of a group or class to which they were not appropriate in the hierarchical society of the empire. Social mobility in Rome is thus seen as a process of status dissonance by which persons rate highly on some criteria of status, such as ability, achievement, wealth, but low on others, such as birth or legal condition.

Taking Hopkins's article as a starting point, I propose to consider to what extent the evidence from the *Familia Caesaris* (the slaves and freedmen of the Imperial household) supports or illustrates the propositions that:

(1) social mobility can usefully be seen as a process of status dissonance;

(2) social mobility was a product of the structural differentiation of institutions (including an investigation of the importance of bureaucracy as a differential source of mobility for the lower ranks of society);

(3) certain patterns of mobility may be best understood as the product of conflict between the emperor and the aristocracy, and between these two and the structurally differentiated institutions.

First, what is meant by 'structurally differentiated' institutions? The greater the size, complexity and centralization in the administrative apparatus of the empire, the greater the tendency for (for example) the military, bureaucratic, legal, and educational institutions to separate from one another. These required specialized training and acquired an increasingly professional status, as shown in the recorded military and bureaucratic careers. The bureaucracy in particular rapidly became a 'structurally differentiated' institution. In effect these changes proceeded to the point where considerable differentiation, both administrative and social/legal, developed not only within the bureaucracy itself (*equites*, freedmen, slaves), but also within the *Familia Caesaris* (domestic—administrative; sub-clerical—clerical—procuratorial).

[2] See chapter v, above.

I

STATUS DISSONANCE IN THE FAMILIA CAESARIS

Some of the most spectacular examples of social mobility in the early empire are Imperial freedmen. Many rose from humble slave status in a junior post in the emperor's service, to freed status with a responsible position in the bureaucracy; and some, because of their ability, which was usually financial, and their legal and often personal relationship to the emperor, reached senior posts from which they exercised great and, in a few cases, undue influence in the Imperial power structure. The cases of Licinus under Augustus, Pallas and Narcissus under Claudius, Epaphroditus and Helius under Nero, the father of Claudius Etruscus and Hormus under Vespasian, and Parthenius under Domitian illustrate the continuity of this phenomenon throughout the first century. Nor did it stop there, as I will show later. However, it is not the individual examples, significant as they are, that are important here; it is the *Familia Caesaris* as a whole, as a status-group whose members can be readily identified and which is of sufficient size and importance to be of general significance in Roman society of the early empire. As a group the *Familia Caesaris* constitutes one of the most notably 'unstable' elements in Imperial society.[3] An examination of the causes of their social 'instability' may, among other things, throw light on the process of social mobility in general.

The *Familia Caesaris*, the slaves and freedmen of the emperor's household, were the élite status-group in the slave-freedman section of Roman Imperial society. This was partly due to the pre-eminent status of their master or patron, the emperor himself. But even more important was the nature of their duties. As assistants to the emperor in the performance of many of his manifold magisterial duties they had access to positions of power in the state which were totally inaccessible to other slaves and freedmen outside the *Familia*, except in the case of the *servi publici* (public slaves) (much less significant under the empire than the republic both in prestige and numbers) who in many aspects serve as forerunners of the *servi Caesaris* (Imperial slaves) as an élite group. These occupational functions gave the *Familia Caesaris* status in

[3] Cf. D. V. Glass, *Social Mobility in Britain* (London, 1954), p. 286.

Roman society as a whole and not only within the slave and freedman classes. From the legal point of view the slave-born orders (*servi, liberti*) were inferior to free-born society (plebs, *equites*, senators). However, from the social point of view many *liberti* enjoyed higher status than many of the plebs. In the *Familia Caesaris*, most *servi* and *liberti* were higher in status than most of the plebs and indeed some had status equal to that of some equestrians. They thus serve as a clear example of status dissonance, rating highly on some status criteria, such as acquired skills, ability and possibly intelligence, power ranking, and to a considerable extent, wealth and style of life, but low on others, such as birth or legal status.

Within the *Familia Caesaris* the distinction between the *familia urbana* (the urban household) and the *familia rustica* (the rural household) which is normal in the large household of any wealthy Roman did not apply. The basic criterion for membership of the Imperial *familia* is use of the Imperial status-indication: *Aug(usti) lib(ertus)* for freedmen and *Caes(aris) ser(vus)* or *Aug(usti) vern(a)* for slaves. But this status-indication, with some exceptions largely confined to the African inscriptions, tended not to be used by women or children or by low status agricultural workers. It came to indicate not birth from Imperial slave parents or actual or former ownership by the emperor, but rather the holding of a post in the emperor's service. This could be either in the domestic service, properly so called, of the emperor's household concerned with the upkeep of the Imperial establishments and gardens on the Palatine and elsewhere in Rome or in the Imperial villas throughout Italy. The duties ranged from the menial (porters, gardeners, ushers) to the managerial (*procuratores* [supervisors] of individual villas, including the *procurator castrensis* [head of the Palatine domestic service]) up to the highly influential *a cubiculo* [supervisor of the emperor's bed-chamber]). But, apart from the unofficial influence of the last-named, the power of this section of the *Familia Caesaris* was small compared with that of the bureaucratic section.

The administrative service itself had a wide range in the status of the posts which were included in it. Corresponding to the low status domestic staff were the sub-clerical administrative staff, such as *tabellarii* (postmen), *pedisequi* (ushers, attendants), *custodes* (watchmen) and so on. They rarely rose to the posts which can properly be regarded as forming part of the slave-freedman administrative *cursus* or 'career'.[4] These ranged from the junior posts of *adiutor* (assistant) held at the age of twenty to thirty, to the intermediate slave and freedman posts, *dispensator* (paymaster), *a commentariis* (record officer), *tabularius* (accountant), held roughly between the ages of thirty and forty, and the senior grades of *proximus* (deputy-head), *procurator*, and the secretaries of the Palatine bureaux, *a rationibus* (the financial secretary), *ab epistulis* (the secretary in charge of correspondence), etc., not normally appointed before the age of forty or later. Those who were fortunate enough to gain entry to the administrative *cursus* did so normally as slaves by the age of twenty, after preliminary attendance at one of the Imperial administrative training establishments.[5] They were selected at a comparatively early age for a professional administrative career, and thus were the most favoured section of the *Familia Caesaris*.

In the case of the *Caesaris servi*, the basic cause of mobility is the dissonance or discrepancy between their high occupational prestige and power and their low legal status and birth. One of the clearest indicators of social mobility is change in the marriage pattern of the group concerned. The legal and social status of one marriage partner is important for the status of the other. A change in the pattern involves upward mobility for one partner and downward mobility for the other, unless there is a compensating factor according to some other status criterion, such as power-ranking or wealth. Marriage is rarely the initiating factor in social mobility, but as a secondary characteristic it is relatively easy to identify. In Imperial society there were legal restrictions on the freedom of intermarriage between members of some classes. Under the *Lex Iulia* of 18 B.C. (part of the Augustan social legislation) freedmen were forbidden to marry women of senatorial families;[6] and under the *Senatus consultum Claudianum* of A.D. 52, legal penalties were imposed on freeborn women who cohabited with slaves, with or without the consent of the master: a free-born woman (*ingenua*)

---

[4] See P. R. C. Weaver, 'The slave and freedman *cursus* in the imperial administration', *PCPS*, new ser., x (1964), pp. 74 ff.

[5] See S. L. Mohler, 'Slave education in the Roman empire', *TAPA*, lxxi (1940), pp. 262 ff., esp. on the Imperial *paedagogium ad Caput Africae* on the Caelian, pp. 271 ff.

[6] *Dig.*, xxiii. 2. 44.

was reduced to the status of either *serva* or *liberta*, and the children also became slaves. These restraints were mostly rigidly enforced: it was rare even for an Imperial freedman to marry the daughter of a senatorial family. In the well-known case of Claudius Etruscus' father, there is no direct evidence that Etrusca, his wife, was of senatorial birth despite the fact that her brother was of consular status (he is usually identified with L. Tettius Iulianus, consul A.D. 83). Adoption of the brother from an equestrian into a senatorial family is just as likely as (or even more likely than) the marriage of his sister to a freedman, if she were of senatorial birth.[7] Even amidst the magnificent successes of Antonius Felix, the brother of Pallas, who married two princesses and one queen, we must assume that those wives whom he married before his elevation to equestrian status were all non-citizens and not of senatorial rank.[8]

As for marriage between partners of slave and freeborn status, this too was comparatively rare. Beryl Rawson[9] has found little evidence of such a marriage pattern among the sepulchral inscriptions from Rome in which the names of children and both parents occur. In an analysis of 700 slave or freedman marriages from Rome, outside the *Familia Caesaris*, where the slave or ex-slave status of at least one of the partners is certain, I found that for *liberti* in this group a maximum of only 15 per cent of wives may have been *ingenuae*, and for *servi* a maximum of only 10 per cent. In fact the actual proportion is likely to be even lower, perhaps considerably lower. This is the normal slave or freedman marriage pattern: to an overwhelming extent they married partners of their own status and origin, as is to be expected, given the provisions of the Claudian *Senatus consultum*. Thus, for slaves and freedmen not belonging to the emperor's *familia*, there is little, if any, evidence of significant mobility through marriage.

By contrast, the upward mobility of the *Caesaris servi* in respect of the status of their wives is very marked, if not astonishing.

---

[7] See P. R. C. Weaver, 'The father of Claudius Etruscus', *CQ*, new ser., xv (1965), pp. 150 ff.

[8] Antonius Felix: *Prosopographia Imperii Romani*, 2nd edn (Berlin, 1933), A 828; Suet., *Claud.*, 28.

[9] B. Rawson, 'Family life among the lower classes at Rome in the first two centuries of the empire', *CP*, lxi (1966), pp. 71 ff.; cf. her Bryn Mawr dissertation, 'The names of children in Roman imperial epitaphs' (1961).

From a detailed analysis of the *nomina* (family names) of all wives in this group, it can be clearly shown that for the Julian period (Augustus to Gaius) the marriage pattern of members of the *Familia Caesaris* conforms fairly closely with that of other slaves and freedmen, that is a *Iulius Augusti libertus* is usually found married to a *Iulia Augusti liberta*; but from the Claudian period (Claudius and Nero) right through to the end of the Aurelian period (M. Aurelius to Severus Alexander) the pattern is quite reversed. The proportion of *Caesaris servi* who marry *ingenuae* is at least 66 per cent, and more likely 75 per cent or even more.[10]

The only other group of slave status with a comparable marriage pattern are the *servi publici*, especially under the late Republic. It is certain that *servi publici* frequently married *ingenuae*.[11] The reasons are the same as for the *Caesaris servi*: high social status resulting from their holding official positions and hence exercising some degree of power. The *Caesaris servi*, at least in their lower and middle ranks, were the successors of the *servi publici*, but in their higher echelons the functions and responsibilities of the *Augusti liberti* were greatly extended, up to and overlapping with the equestrian procuratorial level.[12] Their power ranking and social status were correspondingly higher. Hence it is to be expected that the members of the *Familia Caesaris*, and certainly those in the administrative service and favoured posts in the domestic service, would increasingly marry freeborn women once the tradition and status of these services had been firmly established. It would, indeed, be surprising if this were not the case. It is not possible here to discuss the detailed breakdown, period by period, of the *nomina* of wives in the *Familia Caesaris*, but one feature to be noted is the higher proportion of non-imperial *nomina* belonging to wives of *Augusti*

[10] Note that as the average age at marriage for slaves was some ten to fifteen years earlier than their average age at manumission—normally not before the age of thirty, according to the *Lex Aelia Sentia* of A.D. 4 —the marriage pattern of *liberti* does not differ greatly from that of *servi*; it merely represents the same set of social facts at a later stage. A great number of the sepulchral inscriptions owe their existence to the fact of manumission of one or other of those named on them; a greater number, of course, owe their existence to an even later fact—death.

[11] T. Mommsen, *Römisches Staatsrecht*, 3rd edn (Leipzig, 1887), i, p. 324; L. Halkin, *Les Esclaves publics chez les Romains* (Brussels, 1897), pp. 118 ff.

[12] For other privileges of the *servi publici*, with regard to salary, *peculium* and will: Frontinus, *de Aqu.*, 100; Pliny, *Epist.*, x. 31; *Dig.*, xvi. 2. 19; Ulpian, *Frag.*, 20. 16; *CIL*, vi. 2354.

liberti and *Caesaris servi* in the higher status career-groups. Because of the names and status of the children (apart from the intrinsic improbability of such a pattern), these wives can scarcely have been, at the time of their marriage, slaves or (even less likely, because of the age factor) freedwomen of masters/patrons unconnected with the Imperial family. If the freeborn status of the wives is also taken as a criterion of their husbands' occupational status within the *Familia Caesaris*, it appears (what might also have been confidently surmised) that by and large the administrative service enjoyed higher prestige than the rest of the *Familia Caesaris*, and that posts in Rome, within a given service, were of higher status than those in the provincial centres. In fact, the family data of these officials becomes one fruitful method of approaching the relationship of the government in Rome to the administrative organization in the provinces, the question of the centre and the periphery, and the degree of bureaucratization in the early empire.

More surprising, however, is the Claudian *Senatus consultum*, both in its timing, A.D. 52, and in the manner of its passing. By the middle of the first century A.D., in the early Claudian period, the definitive marriage pattern in the *Familia Caesaris* discussed above had become firmly established. By penalizing the unions of freeborn women with slaves, the *Senatus consultum* brought precisely the marriages in the *Familia Caesaris* itself within its scope.[13] Moreover, the inspiration for the measure, according to its proposer Claudius, the *dominus* (master) of the *Familia Caesaris*, came from Pallas, who was himself an *Augusti libertus*, however little his actual power corresponded with his legal status. His name is placed prominently and ironically by Tacitus at the beginning of the sentence in *Annals*, xii. 53, following the account

---

[13] Strictly speaking, it is not possible to speak of slave marriage at all, but only of *contubernium* or concubinage. This applied when either one or both parties were of slave status: e.g. Ulpian 5. 5, 'cum servis nullum est conubium'; *Sent. Pauli*, ii. 19. 6, 'inter servos et liberos matrimonium contrahi non potest'. But the terminology of legal marriage (*iustum matrimonium* between partners with *conubium*), e.g. *uxor, maritus, filius*, etc., is so constantly used of *contubernium* in the inscriptions, and even in the legal texts themselves (cf. W. Buckland, *Roman Law of Slavery* (Cambridge, 1908), p. 76, n. 15), that it is convenient to speak normally of slave marriage and to use terms such as *contubernium* and *matrimonium* only when the distinction is relevant to the argument.

of the *Senatus consultum*: 'Pallas was named by the emperor as the author of this proposal'. There are complications about the precise provisions and subsequent changes in the law, entered in Gaius i. 84 ff., which need not be discussed here;[14] but it seems to me clear that at least one, and probably the main, purpose of the Claudian *Senatus consultum* was to regulate in the interests of the *fiscus* (imperial Treasury) the rights of inheritance accruing from the wives and children of members of the *Familia Caesaris* which might otherwise have been lost to it if the *Caesaris servi* had been allowed to continue marrying women of freeborn status. The practical effect of the measure on the real marriage pattern was nil, as the marriages with *ingenuae* continued unabated; but as such *ingenuae* and their children henceforth became technically *servae* (or *libertae*) and *servi*, the *fiscus*, of which Pallas was the head, did not suffer financially. The need for the measure is in effect a tribute to the social mobility of the *Caesaris servi* as expressed in their marriages.

Not unconnected with their marriage-pattern is the economic status of members of the Imperial *Familia*. The discordance here between their high level of wealth and their low legal status is most marked; it is also well known and need only be briefly mentioned. The sources of this wealth can only be a matter for speculation: regular salary cannot fully account for the fortunes which were frequently made; financial opportunities and acumen as well as corruption on the usual scale also played a significant part. Certainly their official position gave them a strong economic advantage and was the basis of their power. Economically, not only the Imperial freedmen but the younger Imperial slaves as well were a favoured section in Roman society. It has been speculated that the colossal fortunes of Pallas and Narcissus were greater than those of anyone else, bond or freeborn, in the empire with the exception of the emperor. Even humbler officials than these, notably *dispensatores*, were very wealthy; for example, Rotundus Drusillianus in Hither Spain, who, according to Pliny, had a special factory built to fabricate silver plate—one weighed 500 lbs. and eight others 250 lbs. each;[15] there was also Musicus Scur-

---

[14] For references and literature, see *CR*, new ser., xiv (1964), p. 138, n. 1; *CQ*, new ser., xv (1965), p. 324, n. 4. See most recently J. Crook, *CR*, new ser., xvii (1967), pp. 7 ff.
[15] Pliny, *Nat. Hist.*, xxxiii. 145.

ranus,[16] and several who offered large sums for manumission or promotion.[17]

In addition to the status relationship between the *Familia Caesaris* and slave-born society on the one hand, and free-born society on the other, a further question is whether there is status dissonance *within* the *Familia Caesaris* itself: that is, do the categories of juridical and occupational status coincide within the *Familia* as a whole and even within the élite of the administrative service itself? Thus, do freedmen regularly hold posts of higher status than slaves? In terms of the slave-freedman *cursus* or career grades in the administration, is promotion to the intermediate clerical grades dependent on manumission?

Firstly, it would be foolish to underestimate the rôle of patronage in determining advancement in the sub-equestrian careers as much as in the equestrian and senatorial careers. For the slave-freedman services this might be dispensed, in varying degrees of effectiveness, by the emperor, by senators, *equites* or Imperial freedmen and sometimes slaves themselves, in the latter cases often with financial implications. An amusing example of the emperor (typically, Vespasian) getting the better of one of his own slaves in this rôle is in Suetonius, *Vespasian*, 23 (which should be compared with Suetonius, *Otho*, 5):

> When one of his favourite slaves was asking for a financial post for someone he pretended was his brother, Vespasian put him off and summoned the applicant in person; and after extracting from him the sum which he had contracted to pay his sponsor, the emperor appointed him without delay.

The system of official patronage and promotion for freedmen is illustrated by Pliny's testimonial for Maximus, Trajan's freedman and assistant procurator of Virdius Gemellinus in Pontus et Bithynia;[18] and by Fronto's to M. Caesar on behalf of the latter's freedman Aridelus.[19] The career of Vespasian himself is said to have been helped in the reign of Claudius by the patronage of the

[16] See below n. 29.
[17] Pliny, *Nat. Hist.*, vii. 129; Suet., *Otho*, 5; *Vesp.*, 23.
[18] Pliny, *Epist.*, x. 85; cf. A. N. Sherwin-White, *The Letters of Pliny* (Oxford, 1966), pp. 681 f.
[19] Fronto, *ad Marcum Caesarem*, v. 37 (ed. Nab, p. 87). Cf. H. G. Pflaum, *Les Procurateurs équestres sous le Haut-empire Romain* (Paris, 1950), pp. 198 f.

freedman Narcissus, in his appointment as legionary commander (*legatus legionis*) in Upper Germany.[20]

However, patronage, at least in the administrative service of the *Familia Caesaris*, is exercised mostly within the framework of a set of bureaucratic rules. There was a regular system of annual promotion, probably in November.[21] The principle of seniority was favoured over that of unrestricted patronage, both in the early and later empire.[22] The clearest evidence that this was regular in the career administrative service of the *Familia Caesaris* is to be found in the age-at-death figures. In the many cases where an official died in office and his age at death was recorded on his tombstone, there is a high degree of correspondence between the grade of post held and the age recorded. Thus, the senior grades are not held by slaves or even by freedmen under forty to forty-five years—the youngest *procurator* whose age at death is known died aged fifty-five years—and for the intermediate grades of *tabularius, dispensator, a commentariis* the regular age range is thirty to forty, with very few, if any, under the age of thirty.[23] The conclusion is that, generally speaking, the age and promotion structure corresponded, and that just as it was rare for a *Caesaris servus* to gain early manumission before the age of thirty, so also was it rare for promotion from a junior to an intermediate grade and thence to a senior grade to occur before the ages of thirty and forty years respectively. This can be seen to apply to such successful careers as those of Pallas and the father of Claudius Etruscus. Thus, most freedmen were of higher status than most slaves in the *Familia* purely because of the application of the *Lex Aelia Sentia* of A.D. 4 which limited formal manumission to slaves aged thirty and over, unless one of the valid grounds for manumission (*iustae causae manumissionis*) could be upheld before the council (*consilium*) as provided for by the law. With the *Caesaris servi* the acknowledged *iustae causae*, such as blood relationship to the

---

[20] Suet., *Vesp.*, 4. 1. Cf. also the senatorial Vespasian's contemptuous rebuff by the slave/freedman official of Nero's *officium admissionis*: *ibid.*, 14.

[21] See Pflaum and Sherwin-White, *loc. cit.* (notes 18 and 19 above).

[22] Cf. Hopkins, p. 115 above; A. H. M. Jones, *The Later Roman Empire* (Oxford, 1964), pp. 602–6.

[23] On the age-at-death figures and for references see Weaver, *PCPS*, new ser., x (1964), pp. 76 f. On the father of Claudius Etruscus, see also *CQ*, new ser., xv (1965), pp. 146 f.

manumittor and intention to marry, could scarcely apply. In fact, the law was quite strictly observed in their case, no doubt in the interests of the *fiscus peculiorum* (treasury for the receipt of manumission taxes) whither went the proceeds of manumission purchased by Imperial slaves at the regular age.

But some slaves were of higher status than some freedmen. Despite the rules of manumission and promotion, there are two notable exceptions which constitute clear cases of status dissonance of this kind within the core of the administrative service. Among the most powerful and wealthy officials of intermediate grade were the *dispensatores*. Their responsibilities were exclusively financial—they had personal supervision over cash transactions, payments, etc. in each provincial *fiscus* and in many of the smaller departments in Rome.

The *dispensatores* were all of slave status.[24] The reason lies in their responsibilities, the desire to avoid peculation and in the closer degree of control over them by the emperor which their slave status afforded. The manipulation of the financial strings of administration was always of vital concern to the emperor. For slaves in this grade manumission was normally delayed for ten to fifteen years, till the age of forty to forty-five, after which time they were manumitted and moved directly into the senior grades. Thereafter their ascent was rapid. They were in fact a favoured section of the slave-freedman élite.

The other group in which status dissonance is found are the *vicarii*, the assistants or deputies of the *dispensatores*. Their functions were also financial and as they were directly responsible to their *dispensator* in each case, who was in turn responsible to the emperor; the *vicarius*, who had the legal status of slave of his *dispensator*, stood also in the same legal relationship to the *dispensator* as the latter did to the emperor. Hence the anomaly of the lowest legal status, that of slave of a slave (*vicarius*), attaching to officials who, although junior, were of considerable influence in the financial administration, and who were mostly destined to become *dispensatores* in their turn on the retirement or promotion of their master.[25]

On the other hand, there are also the occasional examples of

[24] *Cod. Iust.*, xi. 37. 1.
[25] For further details see P. R. C. Weaver, 'Vicarius and vicarianus in the Familia Caesaris', *JRS*, liv (1964), pp. 117 ff.

holders of junior posts, such as *adiutores* (normally held by slaves), who have been manumitted at the normal age but not promoted to a post of intermediate rank.

In the domestic service of the Imperial household, of course, because of the much closer degree of personal contact with the emperor, and greater flexibility in the promotion structure, the scope for personal influence was much enlarged. Hence the unscrupulous, and often unworthy slave-born palace officials, usually *cubicularii*, who won their way to irregular and unofficial, but none the less real, positions of power.[26]

II

STRUCTURAL DIFFERENTIATION WITHIN THE BUREAUCRACY

Tacitus, by a natural reflex action, was always inclined to see vice, corruption and disgrace whenever the Imperial freedmen and slaves are mentioned. For him, as for any Roman *nobilis*, they represented one of the most hateful and degrading aspects of the Principate. Where freedmen flourish in high places, there liberty is extinguished. This feeling is nowhere more explicitly expressed than in *Germania* 25, where he contrasts the natural situation under primitive but more honourable conditions:[27]

Freedmen are not of much higher status than slaves, they seldom have much influence in the household, and never in the state, with the exception of course of those peoples who are under a monarchical form of government. In these cases freedmen rise above both those of free and those of aristocratic birth. But amongst other peoples, the lower status of freedmen is a sure sign of freedom.

This passage illustrates clearly the tension under the Principate between emperor and nobility. The more autocratic the régime the less dependent was the emperor on the traditional Roman institutions of government. Even under the 'best' emperors, the Senate was of much less significance as a source of legislation or

[26] See E. Fairon, 'L'Organisation du palais impériale à Rome', *Musée Belge*, iv (1900), pp. 5 ff.; and for the later empire, Jones, *op. cit.*, pp. 566 ff., and Hopkins, *PCPS*, new ser., ix (1963), pp. 62 ff.

[27] Cf. *Ann.*, xiv. 39.

for the performance of any constitutional function than as the chief repository of ability and experience in military and civil administration in the empire. The commanders of legions, the governors of provinces, consular or praetorian, armed or unarmed, the members of the Imperial *consilium* (council), were all, with few exceptions, drawn from the higher echelons of the senatorial order. But while *nobiles* monopolized most of the honorific positions in the state, and *novi homines*—the first of consular standing in their families—occupied more than their share of the top executive posts, especially in the provinces, even together they did not by any means have a monopoloy of power in the administration. The emperor from the beginning was at great pains to create institutions of his own devising and under his own control as a bulwark for his own position, a source of power to counterbalance that of the senate, and as a channel for the reservoir of talent and energy in all parts of the empire and in all sections of society to be usefully employed in administering and defending the empire. Augustus was the creator of the equestrian order in its vastly changed Imperial form; he was also the creator of the Imperial civil service, which from the beginning of the Principate employed not only equestrians in responsible positions but also freedmen and slaves. Highly significant (and notorious) is C. Iulius Licinus, the slave and freedman of Caesar, employed by Augustus as his procurator in Gaul. Licinus' avarice and abuse of his position led to his recall, but not before he had laid the basis of a fortune that was to be a by-word in Imperial literature of the first century. The power of Licinus was real and an object of envy to the noble aristocrats who observed its effects.[28] At a lower level of responsibility the Imperial freedmen and slaves in the administration exercised power and continued to accumulate wealth, though less spectacularly, under every emperor from Augustus on. For example, Musicus, the slave of Tiberius, chief *dispensator* in the treasury at Lugdunum, came to Rome (where he died) accompanied by no fewer than sixteen personal slaves of his own, who stayed to dedicate a monument to him.[29]

[28] Licinus: Dio, 54. 21; Suet., *Aug.*, 67. Cf. *Prosopographia Imperii Romani*, 1st edn (Berlin, 1897), L 193; Stein, Pauly-Wissowa, *RE*, xiii, cols 501 ff.; V. Gardthausen, *Augustus und seine Zeit* (Leipzig, 1896), i, pp. 616 f., ii, p. 336.
[29] *CIL*, vi, 5197.

The creation and extension of the slave-freedman service in the bureaucracy demands an explanation at the general institutional level, and not as a more or less whimsical or accidental by-product of the personalities of particular emperors. The hey-day of the freedmen in the middle of the first century was no doubt partly due to the laxity of Imperial control by Claudius and Nero, but Claudius did not call into being a monster which he could not control. The bureaucracy was deliberately established by Augustus. It kept expanding under Tiberius, Claudius, Nero and Vespasian, and the slave-freedman share of it, if anything, increased proportionally. The cohesion of the bureaucracy survived unimpaired the upheaval of civil war in A.D. 68–69.[30] Vespasian not only appointed a former slave of Tiberius to control the financial bureau which Pallas had notoriously controlled under Claudius, but he also elevated this official to full equestrian status, the kind of practical reward that even Claudius and Nero were chary of dispensing. The slave-freedman bureaucracy persisted with undiminished numbers, status, and to a large extent power, into the second century, and in the course of the second century, in the period after Hadrian, the number of posts available, including senior posts, even expanded considerably. The permanent place which the slaves and freedmen filled in the administration cannot be explained on the assumption that this was simply an extension of the kind of employment slaves and freedmen could be expected to have in the household of any wealthy Roman magnate. This has as much validity as a belief in the continued existence of the 'restored republic' after it had served the ends of Augustus in the decade before 19 B.C. The bureaucracy in its financial and managerial aspects was staffed by freedmen and slaves as well as by equestrians as a matter of policy.

An instructive example of how this policy could be applied is found in Tacitus, *Annals*, xiv. 39, already quoted.[31] In A.D. 61 Nero's freedman Polyclitus was sent by the emperor on a mission to Britain to resolve the differences between the Imperial legate, Suetonius Paulinus, and the Imperial procurator Iulius Classicianus. The four main institutional elements in the power situation and the tensions between them are here represented: the emperor, the senatorial aristocracy, the equestrian hierarchy and

[30] Cf. Statius, *Silvae*, iii. 3. 83–4.
[31] Above, note 27.

the freedman administration in the bureaucracy: 'An imperial freedman Polyclitus was sent, by whose authority Nero fervently hoped . . . that harmony could be restored between the legate and the procurators'. The other three are, with varying degrees of patronage, all appointees of the emperor.

This policy was common to all emperors till after the Severan period. The motives behind it are clear enough as regards the equestrians. By reorganizing a second order within the upper class, dependent on himself for professional advancement and patronage, the emperor was creating a source of power on which he could rely in the institutional tug-of-war between himself and the senatorial aristocracy. The equestrian bureaucracy was a differentiated institution which also served the ends of social mobility. It provided the main channel of social advancement for members of the second order into the aristocracy under Imperial patronage. Such diversification, with a separate hierarchy in the senatorial career as well as in the equestrian career, also tended to produce a greater stability in the higher ranks of the army, and to provide regular channels of promotion from the junior through to the senior officer grades.[32]

However, the interesting thing about the bureaucracy of the early empire is not its differentiation from the aristocracy but the degree of differentiation within its own ranks. This was of a much more fundamental nature. The legal distinctions between those of slave and freedman status who made up the lower and middle grades of the bureaucracy (as well as some of the higher grades at least for a time) and those of equestrian status in the upper grades of the bureaucracy were much greater than those between the equestrian bureaucracy and the senatorial aristocracy. Upward mobility between the equestrian and senatorial orders was regular and common, indeed inevitable; that between the equestrian order and the Imperial freedmen, for all the high status of the latter relative both to all other slaves and freedmen and to the eques-

[32] In the language of S. N. Eisenstadt, *The Political Systems of Empires* (New York, Free Press, 1963), pp. 273 ff., the equestrian bureaucracy was moderately service-orientated both to the ruler and to the aristocratic elements in society but more especially to the former. The bureaucracy's goals were some degree of autonomy from the ruler and also service goals partly in common with the aristocracy to whom they tended to assimilate themselves through formal elevation in status, intermarriage, and access to positions of equal power.

trians themselves, was the merest trickle. Emperors of all periods, and endowed with whatever degree of historical approbation, declined to endanger their support in the upper ranks of society by massive promotion of freedmen to equestrian dignity.[33]

Examples of freedmen in financial posts rising to equestrian status, such as the father of Claudius Etruscus, are very rare.[34] Most of the cases of such elevation to equestrian rank are to be explained as due to personal influence with the emperor (for example Antonius Felix, Icelus Marcianus, L. Aurelius Nicomedes, tutor of L. Verus), often through the post of a cubiculo (for example Cleander, Theocritus).

Nor was occupational differentiation between the two sections of the bureaucracy any less rigidly observed than the social and legal differentiation. The flow of freedmen to posts carrying equestrian responsibilities and hence greater power, without the appropriate rise in legal status, was also very slight. The idea that has recently been canvassed,[35] that the majority of civilian posts open to equestrians could also be held by freedmen and that there was no type of procuratorial post from which the freedmen were rigidly excluded, could scarcely be further from the truth. Roman Imperial society was extremely status-conscious, and if freedmen in the upper ranks of the administrative hierarchy had full parity of occupational rank with their equestrian counterparts, this remarkable state of affairs could scarcely have escaped the notice of the rather sensitive literary authorities of the first and second centuries. In fact, the whole relationship between the equestrian and slave-freedman sections of the bureaucracy as it developed in the first and second centuries A.D. needs reappraisal, paying close attention to the massive epigraphic evidence along strictly chronological lines.[36]

---

[33] A. Stein, *Das römische Ritterstand* (Munich, 1927), pp. 107 ff.

[34] Stein, *op. cit.*, p. 112, assumes equestrian status for Licinus, but this is very doubtful. Cf. O. Hirschfeld, *Die Kaiserlichen Verwaltungsbeamten bis auf Diocletian*, 3rd edn (Berlin, 1963), pp. 377, n. 7, 468, n. 1.

[35] By F. Millar, *Historia*, xiii (1964), p. 187, and *JRS*, liii (1963), p. 196.

[36] The starting point, and often the finishing point, of many enquiries into the development of the Imperial administration in this period is bound to be the *Historia Augusta*, Hadrian, 22. 8: '[Hadrian] was the first to appoint equestrians as secretaries in charge of the correspondence (*ab epistulis*) and petitions (*a libellis*) bureaux'. That the *Historia Augusta* in general and in many particulars is about as thoroughly discredited a

Attention has naturally centred on the equestrian hierarchy, the élite of the professional administrators, the prefects and the procurators. Such scholars as Last, Rostovtzeff and Hirschfeld have to a large extent consecrated the view that the key phenomenon in the development of the administrative hierarchy is 'the ousting of the freedmen by *equites*' (Last).[37] The secret of the administration's success is revealed as a kind of class struggle: the true Roman equestrians against the upstart oriental freedmen, with virtue and superior breeding, but not necessarily superior intellect or education, inevitably winning the day.

This alleged second-century A.D. conflict of the orders—between the equestrian procurators on the one hand, and the Palatine freedmen officials on the other—is, for this period at least, under the five 'good' emperors Nerva to M. Aurelius when the decisive equestrian victory is alleged to have occurred, a misinterpretation of the evidence. It arises from the traumatic experience of the senatorial historians and other writers in the first century under such notorious and arrogant upstarts as Pallas, Narcissus and Callistus under Claudius, Phaon, Epaphroditus and Helius under

literary source as can well be for the serious historian of the second and third centuries A.D. is no obstacle. There are always to hand persuasive arguments to show why any particular passage, phrase, or even word should be singled out for respectful treatment, like a pearl in a pig-trough, by referring it back to its original, and usually hypothetical, author. The words quoted above enshrine Hadrian's well-known 'reform' of the Roman administration—his replacing of freedmen by equestrians in all the important departments of the Palatine secretariate. In the first place, *Historia Augusta Hadrian*, 22. 8 is factually wrong. The first equestrian *ab epistulis* was Cn. Octavius Capito, the friend of Pliny the Younger; he held the post from the reign of Domitian till early in the reign of Trajan: H. G. Pflaum, *Les carrières procuratoriennes équestres sous le haut-empire romain* (Paris, 1960), no. 60. The first equestrian *a libellis* was Sex. Caesius Propertianus who was appointed by Vitellius in A.D. 69: *ibid.*, no. 37. In the second place, among the Palatine secretaries who were equestrian by the time of Hadrian, no mention is made of the most important of them all, the secretary *a rationibus*. And appropriately enough, because Trajan regularly employed *equites* in the post, and even as early as Vespasian the first equestrian *a rationibus* is to be found in the person of the father of Claudius Etruscus, raised to equestrian status in A.D. 72–73.

[37] E.g. H. Last, in *CAH*, xi, pp. 430 f.; Hirschfeld, *Die Kaiserlichen Verwaltungsbeamten*, pp. 429, 459; M. Rostovtzeff, *Dizionario Epigrafico* (Rome, 1895–), iii. 137.

Nero, and Parthenius and other *cubicularii* under Domitian. But for the second century A.D., much the most important evidence is not literary but documentary—the hundreds of inscriptions recording the careers of officials at all levels in the administration. This evidence has the advantage of being for the most part emotionally restrained or even neutral.

Formerly the freedmen in charge of the Palatine bureaux (*officia Palatina*) were notorious partly because of their arrogance and corruption, but also partly, and even mainly, because they had remained at the head of the largest departments, in positions of the greatest power, long after the importance and size of these had warranted their inclusion in the equestrian *cursus*. Equestrians, if differentiation within the bureaucracy was to mean anything at all, had to have a monopoly of the posts carrying the highest official status. In general it can be said that equestrian procurators moved from one post to the next with greater frequency than their freedmen subordinates. These latter, by their less frequent occupational mobility, often filled the rôle of permanent secretary and thus exercised an effective power. But from the point of view of official status-ranking, the equestrian and freedman careers could not be mixed. The differentiation became, if anything, more marked as the second century progressed. Hadrian was not the first to employ *equites* as secretaries *ab epistulis* or even *a libellis*, despite what is said in the *Historia Augusta*. Yet there are plentiful signs that the *Augusti liberti* continued in honourable and indeed senior employment in the administrative service throughout the second century. The new freedmen *proximi* and the new freedmen *procuratores provinciae* illustrate this both for the central departments in Rome, the *officia Palatina*, and for the provincial administration throughout the empire, both in Imperial and in senatorial provinces.[38]

The purpose of these new senior freedman posts was to provide a full senior career for the *Augusti liberti* distinct from the equestrian *cursus* in terms of official titles and duties. The talent of the freedmen officials was not wasted or discarded. It was fruitfully assimilated until the middle of the third century, when chaos and disaster appear in the administrative as well as the military sphere.

[38] These changes belong substantively to the early period of M. Aurelius' reign, as I have argued in *PCPS*, new ser., x (1964), pp. 85 ff., and in *Historia*, xiv (1965), pp. 460 ff.

This exercise in structural differentiation within the bureaucracy was not merely to provide a counter-check, firmly under the emperor's control, against the potential movement of the equestrian bureaucracy towards greater autonomy or independence from the emperor. Nor does it appear to have been precipitated by any significant weakening in the power of the senatorial aristocracy. The freedman bureaucracy not only kept a watchful eye on their equestrian counterparts, but also provided deputies or temporary replacements for all important posts in all important departments. They thus also served the interests of efficiency and administrative continuity.

VII

LEGAL PRIVILEGE IN THE ROMAN EMPIRE*†

Peter Garnsey

I

INTRODUCTION

For the equality aimed at by the many (*sc. arithmetical equality*) is the greatest of all injustices, and God has removed it out of the world as being unattainable; but he protects and maintains the distribution of things according to merit, determining it geometrically, that is, in accordance with proportion and law.

Thus a speaker in Plutarch's *Dinner-Table Discussions* tried to interpret Plato's statement (authentic or apochryphal) that 'God is always busy with geometry'.[1] Whatever may be thought of his ingenious explanation, it does not misrepresent Plato's views on the subject of equality. Both Plato and Aristotle held that the equal distribution of things to persons of unequal merit was unequal.[2] The Roman governing classes showed by their administration of the law that they shared this conviction. So much can be deduced from the operation in Rome, Italy and the pro-

---

* From no. 41 (1968).
† I wish to thank Mr G. E. M. de Ste Croix for his valuable advice and criticism.
1 Plut., *Mor.*, § 719. b–c, quoted B. Farrington, *Science and Politics in the Ancient World* (London, 1939), pp. 29–30.
2 Plato, *Laws*, §757. a. ff.; cf. § 744. b–c. See also Arist., *Nic. Eth.*, § 1131. a. 15 ff.

vinces of a thorough-going system of legal discrimination to the advantage of certain privileged classes.

The legal system of any state may be biased in at least three main ways. The law may favour certain parties in a relationship— for example, creditors over debtors or landlords over tenants, the poor being usually on the losing side in such relationships. Secondly, inequality may result from the incapacity of some through their social or economic position to enjoy the full bene- fits of the law even where these are not officially denied them— thus the rich can afford bail, while the poor must generally go to prison. Finally, the law as written or the law as administered may deny equal benefits and protection to different sections of the population, again in accordance with differing social and eco- nomic situations—thus a commoner might be whipped and an aristocrat fined for the like offences.[3] Only examples of the second and third varieties of inequality, *de facto* and *de iure* inequality, are explored in any detail in this paper. For the period that is examined, developments in procedure and in the administration of the law are of special interest.

For practical reasons, this investigation has been limited to the period from about the beginning of the Empire to about the end of the Severan dynasty, that is, from 27 B.C. to A.D. 235. These years, following the civil wars of the first century B.C., saw the emergence of a disguised monarchy which claimed to be the restored Republic. The political revolution brought in its train institutional changes in the sphere of law. New procedures grew up alongside the old ones (which, like the old political structures, were not destroyed, but allowed to wither away), and were characterized by new types of discrimination. One aim of this paper is to describe and contrast the different patterns of dis- crimination associated with Republican and Imperial procedures in civil and criminal law.

Three excerpts from literary sources are quoted first to indicate the kinds of people who gained preferential treatment in the law courts and to give an idea of the privileges they enjoyed. The details of the system of privilege are then assembled, and an analy- sis attempted of aspects of the Roman civil suit and criminal trial.

[3] This scheme of classification is used in J. E. Carlin, J. Howard and S. Messinger, 'Civil justice and the poor: issues for sociological research', *Law and Society Review*, i (1966), pp. 9–90.

Next, problems connected with the growth of the system and its basis in law are considered. Finally, the relationship between the upper-class/lower-class distinction (the so-called *honestiores/humiliores* distinction)[4] and the citizen/alien distinction is discussed.

<h2 style="text-align:center">II</h2>

THREE ILLUSTRATIONS

(1) L. Calpurnius Piso caused the Emperor Tiberius considerable embarrassment because of his independent attitudes and free speech. Once, according to Tacitus, Piso threatened to retire from politics in protest against the prevalence of judicial corruption and other abuses. Tiberius was able to mollify him temporarily:[5]

> The same Piso before long gave just as vivid proof of his free and passionate spirit by summoning to court Urgulania, whose friendship with Augusta had lifted her beyond the reach of the laws. Urgulania did not obey the summons, but, scorning Piso, rode in a carriage to the Emperor's house. But Piso held his ground, despite Augusta's complaints that her majesty was being dragged in the dust. Tiberius, thinking he should so far gratify his mother as to say that he would go to the praetor's tribunal and support Urgulania, set out from the Palatium. His soldiers had orders to follow at a distance. The mob rushed up to look, as Tiberius, his face composed, and pausing every now and then for conversation, made his leisurely way, until, Piso's relations being unable to restrain Piso, Augusta issued orders for the payment of the money he was claiming. This ended an affair from which Piso emerged with glory and Caesar with an enhanced reputation.

Tacitus told this story for the moral it conveyed about the way in which senators should stand up to emperors. Our present interest is less in Piso's boldness and the way the case was resolved

---

[4] The *honestiores/humiliores* formula is only one of several that occur in the legal sources. It is in fact confined to the 'Sentences of Paulus', a late third-century compilation, which uses hardly any other terms. An earlier juristic writer once employs *honestior/humilioris loci*, a close approximation. See *Dig.*, xlviii. 5. 39. 8.

[5] Tac., *Ann.*, ii. 34; cf. iv. 21 ff.

than in the attitudes of Urgulania and Livia and, in particular, in a structural weakness of the Roman civil-law procedure which the incident reveals. It was for a plaintiff, and not the authorities of the state, to see that the defendant appeared before the praetor at the start of a judicial action. However, the would-be plaintiff might find himself in difficulties if his opponent were stronger than he (or had strong supporters) and resisted or ignored the summons. Similarly, execution of sentence lay with the individual rather than the state.

Later we will ask how far the upper classes made use of the biased nature of the system of self-help as outlined here.[6] It is doubtful whether Urgulania's behaviour was typical of that of members of the privileged classes when they were faced with legal actions brought against them by their social inferiors. It might be claimed that there was no need for an upper-class defendant to flout the law—and it might be prudent of him not to do so—as there was a good chance that the natural prejudices of the judge, who invariably came from the same social milieu, might operate in his favour.

(2) A letter of Pliny the Younger gives some force to this last suggestion. The setting of the letter is provincial rather than Roman, which serves as a reminder that preferential treatment in the law courts was given not only to officials of the central administration (senators and equestrians) but also to the provincial and Italian aristocracy, the 'curial' class.[7] Pliny was writing to Calestrius Tiro, who was on the point of taking up office as governor of Baetica in Spain (in succession to another governorship). As governor, Tiro would be personally responsible for the administration of justice in his province. The letter runs:[8]

> You have done splendidly—and I hope you will not rest on your laurels—in commending your administration of justice to the provincials by your exercise of tact. This you have shown particularly in maintaining consideration for the best men,[9] but, in doing so, winning the respect of the lower

[6] See pp. 147–8 below.

[7] The legal sources do not give a complete list of those who benefited from legal privilege; but these included senators, equestrians, decurions, veterans and soldiers (and their families).

[8] Pliny, *Epist.*, ix. 5.

[9] *Honestissimum quemque.* The adjective is ambiguous, implying both high

classes while holding the affection of their superiors. Many men, in their anxiety to avoid seeming to show excessive favour to men of influence, succeed only in gaining a reputation for perversity and malice. I know there is no chance of your falling prey to that vice, but in praising you for the way you tread the middle-course, I cannot help sounding as if I were offering you advice: that you maintain the distinctions between ranks and degrees of dignity. Nothing could be more unequal than that equality which results when those distinctions are confused or broken down.

Tiro had achieved what might seem to us the remarkable feat of paying due respect to *dignitas* (social position) while avoiding *gratia* (excessive favour).[10] Tiberius was less successful in observing this precarious distinction in his supervision of judicial affairs in Rome. This at any rate was Tacitus' judgement:[11]

> The investigations in the Senate were not enough for Tiberius. He sat in the courts, at the side of the tribunal, so as not to drive the praetor from his chair. In his presence, many judgments were reached which disregarded the bribes and pressure of the powerful. But in his concern for truth, Tiberius undermined liberty.

(3) In his treatise on criminal investigations, Callistratus, a jurist of the Severan age (A.D. 193–235), dealt with the question of the trustworthiness of witnesses:[12]

> It is especially important to examine the status of each man, to see whether he is a decurion or a commoner; to ask whether his life is virtuous or marred by vice, whether he is rich or poor (for poverty might imply that he is out for gain), and whether he is personally hostile to the man against whom

---

moral character and social and political ascendance. See Cicero, *Brutus*, 282, and n. 21 below.

[10] On *gratia*, see J. N. L. Myres, 'Pelagius and the end of Roman rule in Britain', *JRS*, 1 (1960), pp. 24 ff.

[11] Tac., *Ann.*, i. 75.

[12] *Dig.*, xxii. 5. 3. preface (decurions were the members of the councils of cities in Italy and the provinces). The key word is *fides*, trustworthiness. Cf. Gellius, *Noctes Atticae*, xiv, 2. 10, where the claimant is said to be well-endowed with *fides* ('fidei . . . plenum'). See p. 149 below.

he is witnessing or friendly to the man whose cause he is
advocating. . . .

The questions range widely, covering not only the witness's
interest in the trial, but also his character and social and economic
condition. By contrast, in a modern court of law in a democratic
society it would be thought relevant (in theory at any rate) to
establish only a witness's impartiality—unless a previous conviction for perjury should bring his character into consideration.[13]

III

THE CIVIL SUIT

In Rome the private claims of possession, breach of contract,
damage, fraud or injury (to mention only the most important)
were settled by the civil law according to the 'formulary' procedure. The civil suit (or *actio*) consisted of two stages, *actio in iure*
before the praetor, and *actio apud iudicem* before a private judge.
The praetor was responsible for appointing the judge, with the
agreement of both parties, and for passing on to him a *formula*, or
a list of instructions setting out the factual and legal grounds on
which the case was to be decided.[14]

A man who sought a civil action, therefore, approached the
praetor. The praetor, however, was not obliged to grant him an
action, and indeed was expected to withhold from a man of low
rank (*humilis*) an action for fraud against his social superior.[15] The
authority for this is Labeo, the Augustan jurist, whose commentary on the praetor's edict, in which a statement to this effect
appears, was intended as a guide to magistrates and legal practitioners. The commentary probably contained little original
material, for the statements of jurists were commonly based upon

[13] Callistratus goes on to refer to Hadrianic rescripts: see p. 149 below. A
rescript was a reply by the Emperor to the consultation of a governor
or another official. It was meant as an order, and taken as such, probably
from the early Empire.

[14] See F. Schulz, *Classical Roman Law* (Oxford, 1951), pp. 19 ff.

[15] *Dig.*, iv. 3. 11. 1. The praetor's permission was needed for the issuing of
any summons against parents, patrons, magistrates, priests, etc.: see
ibid., 11. 4. 2 and 4. The recurrence of the word *reverentia* in *ibid.*, 13 and
Dig., xlviii. 19. 28. 4 is suggestive.

or were explanatory of tendencies or norms already present in the legal system. It is probable that the same rule which existed in relation to the action for fraud applied in respect of other actions which carried *infamia*, or loss of status.

The most dangerous of these actions for the higher orders in the Roman state was the action for debt. The consequences of this action, which was in effect a bankruptcy suit, included sale of property, loss of status, and political extinction. The ruling classes appear to have relied on the aristocratic prejudices of the praetor to ward off from themselves this disastrous action until the time of Julius Caesar, when a law was passed permitting impoverished aristocrats to cede part of their land to their creditors without loss of status. Moreover, under the early Empire, a milder alternative to the *venditio bonorum* (sale of property) which was the lot of the ordinary debtor was set up or confirmed by senatorial decree. This was *distractio bonorum* (division of property). By this procedure, a part of the property was sold by a special agent, again without loss of status on the part of the former owner. *Distractio bonorum* was available to men of high status (*clarae personae*), especially members of the senatorial class.[16]

The plaintiff surmounted one barrier if the praetor granted him an action; the next obstacle was provided not so much by the magistrate who administered the civil law as by the civil law itself. The formulary procedure operated on the assumption that any plaintiff could get his opponent to court. It is true that some resistance on the part of defendants was bargained for, but the measures which were intended to cope with this eventuality (praetorian interdicts and the order for the seizure of the defendant's property preparatory to sale) did not include the use of physical force by the organs of the state. It is not difficult to imagine situations where a defendant, relying on his greater strength or influence, might defy the would-be plaintiff: it will be recalled that Urgulania refused to go to court and sought sanctuary in the palace, in the knowledge that Livia would protect her.[17]

---

[16] For the background and context of Caesar's law *de bonis cedendis*, see M. W. Frederiksen, *JRS*, lvi (1966), pp. 128 ff. For the (first-century) decree, *Dig.*, xxvii. 10. 5.

[17] The problem discussed in this paragraph is posed forcefully by J. M. Kelly, in *Roman Litigation* (Oxford, 1966), ch. 1; reviewed by J. Crook and R. Stone, *CR*, xvii (1967), pp. 83 ff.

On the other side it must be acknowledged that the plaintiff of low status was not necessarily on his own in his efforts to get his opponent to justice. He might have a patron of greater influence and more substantial physical resources than himself who could perhaps bring pressure to bear on his opponent. In the case of Urgulania it was the defendant who possessed a powerful patron. Livia's friendship raised Urgulania 'above the laws'. If the defendant still failed to respond, the plaintiff could look for assistance from a different quarter: with the aid of the local auctioneer, who had a financial interest in the matter, he might enforce a seizure of the defendant's property.[18] A third ally of the plaintiff was the Roman social conscience. Romans in general considered it important to maintain their good name in the community and their standing with the magistrates. Probably few men were prepared to flout convention and the law by refusing to obey a summons. But there were exceptions: why else did the Julian law on violence cover the case of those who resisted a court-summons with the aid of a gang of thugs?[19]

Even if the plaintiff of low rank had been granted an action, and had secured the appearance of his opponent before the praetor, he could not have had much confidence in the outcome of the action. For a man of influence would stand a good chance of winning his case, even without corruption or the threat of force. Judges and juries (where there were juries)[20] were easily impressed by qualities such as social prominence, wealth and good character,[21] and this

18 The latter could be rich (Cic., *pro Caecina*, 10) and strong (*ibid.*, 27).
19 *Dig.*, xlviii. 7. 4 (Julian law on violence—? of Julius Caesar). Later it became a criminal offence to disobey the injunctions of magistrates: see *ibid.*, xlviii. 19. 5. preface.
20 The juries for the public criminal courts of the Republic were drawn from the upper classes. The advisers who assisted a judge or magistrate in reaching a decision in an *extra ordinem* court characteristic of the Empire were similarly drawn from the higher orders.
21 For the Romans, good character was in part a matter of birth and social position. It is significant that a word with a primarily moral meaning, *honestus*, should have been chosen to describe men of distinguished social position, *honestiores*. (Note that moral words such as *boni* and *optimates* were used to describe political groups under the Republic.) Quintilian, *Instit.*, v. 10. 24, noted that there is sometimes a causal connection between birth (*genus*) and manner of life: '... et nonnumquam ad *honeste* turpiterque vivendum inde causae fluunt'. Cf. *Dig.*, xlvii. 2. 52. 21, where *honestus vir* is synonymous with *vir locuples* ('rich man').

was thought perfectly proper. When Aulus Gellius judged a money-claim, he could not bring himself to decide against a plaintiff who was upright and trustworthy in favour of a defendant who was in his eyes a rascal, and 'not possessed of good fortune' (*non bonae rei*), even though the former's case was quite unconvincing. He took the problem to the philosopher Favorinus. Favorinus quoted words of Marcus Cato to the effect that, if a cause was evenly balanced, the judge should decide which of the two parties was 'better' (*melior*), a term ambiguous as between character and property, and should come down for him. Cato added that this was not a private opinion of his own, but a traditional Roman attitude. But Gellius could not declare for the claimant, and backed out of the case, pleading youth and lack of merit.[22]

Cato had held that the outcome should depend on the character of the parties only if witnesses were lacking. Gellius' plaintiff could produce 'neither documents nor witnesses'. The excerpt from Callistratus quoted above[23] shows that, where witnesses were called, the judge reckoned their social position and character as relevant as the quality of their evidence. Nor was this merely Callistratus' private judgment. He went on to cite a series of rescripts of Hadrian (A.D. 117–138) in support of his statement. The burden of the rescripts is that a witness with *dignitas*, *existimatio* and *auctoritas* was especially acceptable. These are three upper-class virtues: social standing, good reputation, and prestige.

To sum up, as long as plaintiffs could have recourse only to the praetor and a private judge, both of whom shared the feelings and prejudices of the upper classes, and as long as private summons and private execution were the rule, actions by commoners against members of the upper classes were not likely to be frequent.[24] The end of the Republic saw an improvement in the lot of the humble plaintiff in several respects. A clause on violence from the Lex Iulia, already referred to in another connection, shows that

[22] Gellius, *Noctes Atticae*, xiv. 2.
[23] Above pp. 145–6.
[24] Kelly, *op. cit.*, pp. 62 ff. On private execution and its difficulties, *ibid.*, pp. 12 ff. In addition, many matters would have been settled out of court. Cicero often brought pressure to bear on judges on behalf of clients, who as a result were sometimes able to avoid court-cases. See e.g. *ad familiares*, xiii. 54. Cf. the Piso/Urgulania affair: as far as we can tell this never reached the courts.

forcible resistance to a summons was viewed as a crime in the early Empire.[25] Crimes were punishable by the state, so that neither summons nor execution was the responsibility of the individual. Further, it became possible under the Empire for a plaintiff to approach the city prefect and to seek the settlement of a claim outside the formulary procedure.[26] Again, summons and execution fell to the state—and the plaintiff might gain a fairer hearing.

Before concluding this section on the civil law, we may return once more to the role of the praetor. The praetor was in a position to discriminate against the weaker party both as the controller of the sanctions behind the judicial summons and execution, and as the granter or withholder of actions. In addition, during the first stages of some suits, notably suits for injury, he fixed the amount of compensation payable in the event of the court's deciding against the defendant. Now, according to Labeo, the *persona* of the injured party might, presumably by the praetor's decision, convert an action for injury into an action for 'grave' injury, with higher penalties.[27] The word *persona* has a broad connotation, as is shown by statements of later jurists which expand Labeo's sentence. We read, for instance, in the 'Sentences of Paulus', a late-third-century compilation, the following:[28]

> Injury is regarded as grave . . . with respect to person, whenever the injured party is a senator or equestrian or decurion, or someone else of conspicuous prestige: for example, if a plebeian or a man of low birth has injured a senator or equestrian, or if a decurion or magistrate or aedile or judge has suffered at the hands of a plebeian.

Other passages show that injury by a child against a parent or by a freedman against a patron were also automatically 'grave'. If all the texts dealing with this matter are put together, it can be seen that in Roman society, some persons were given special protection because and in so far as they performed certain social, political or judicial rôles (as parents, magistrates, and judges, respectively), and others because of personal status.

[25] See n. 19 above.
[26] See e.g. *Dig.*, i. 12. 2: the intrusion of the prefect's court into the sphere of pecuniary cases, at least from Hadrian's time.
[27] *Dig.*, xlvii. 10. 7. 8.
[28] *Sent. Pauli*, v. 4. 10; cf. Gaius, *Instit*, iii. 225; *Instit. Just.*, iv. 4. 9.

IV

THE CRIMINAL TRIAL

In the late Republic, laws were passed which defined as 'public', and therefore 'criminal', offences such as extortion, treason, homicide, forgery, peculation, electoral bribery and violence, and which set up permanent jury-courts to try them. The jury-courts (or *quaestiones*) survived into the Empire, and indeed Augustus himself was behind the legislation which established a court for adultery. However, the form of criminal proceeding most characteristic of the Empire was the *cognitio* or *extra ordinem* procedure, which placed the whole trial, including the passing of sentence, in the hands of the judge. (The praetor in charge of a jury-court merely chaired the proceedings and was bound by the verdict of the jury.) The jury-court system proved less durable than the formulary system in civil law, although both were Republican in origin. As late as the Severan period, those seeking redress for private injury or loss could still turn to the formulary system as a viable alternative to *cognitio*. By contrast, there is no evidence that 'public' offences were ever investigated by a jury-court after about the turn of the first century A.D.[29]

The civil action by the formulary process and the criminal trial by the *cognitio* procedure were very different in structure, and this difference is reflected in the patterns of discrimination which were characteristic of each. But two qualifications should be kept in mind. It is probable that criminal judges, especially provincial governors, used their discretion in granting and withholding trials, as praetors did when administering the civil law. Again, the influences to which a private judge was subjected in the course of a trial were felt equally by a criminal judge. On the other hand, discrimination in the apportionment of cases to courts was a distinctive feature of the Imperial criminal law. In addition, there was much more scope in a criminal trial by *cognitio* for the variation of penalty according to the social class of the defendant. The Republican system of criminal law knew neither of these methods of discrimination. Only one set of courts was provided for the

[29] See *JRS*, lvii (1967), pp. 56–60.

trial of all defendants, and no penalties were inflicted other than those fixed by the laws which set up the courts.[30]

Under the Empire, however, several courts were capable of hearing most criminal cases, and the choice of court was sometimes of consequence for the defendant. The senatorial court was notoriously 'soft' on senatorial defendants. Charges against equestrian officials were heard by the Emperor, to whom these officials were personally responsible, and he might be expected to have their interests at heart.[31] Again, by the late-second century, governors were not allowed to execute a sentence of deportation or capital exile. In practice this meant that capital cases involving members of the provincial élite were automatically referred to the Emperor.[32] Other courts in Rome, the jury-courts, for as long as they existed, and the court of the urban prefect, must have dealt principally, though not exclusively,[33] with lower-class offenders.

The *cognitio* procedure was notable for the degree of freedom it left to the judge. Not only the examination of the parties and their

[30] Defendants before jury-courts might be favoured (and it is commonly assumed were favoured, if of senatorial if not equestrian rank) in two principal ways. Either the court could bring in a verdict of not guilty when an acquittal was not justified (this form of favouritism was not, of course, peculiar to a jury-court); or the magistrates could permit a defendant to go into voluntary exile and so avoid the necessity of having him executed (in capital cases).

[31] *Senators*: see Pliny, *Epist.*, ix. 13. 21. Pliny claims to have caused the indignation of 'the other orders' to subside. The indignation arose from the fact that 'the Senate was harsh to others and lenient only to senators, as if by mutual connivance'.

    Equestrians: for an early example of the trial of an equestrian by the Emperor (Claudius), see Dio, lx. 33. 6. In a later incident (Pliny, *Epist.*, vi. 31. 7 ff.), Trajan angrily rejected the imputation that an Emperor was likely to be lenient to his own officials. In this case the defendant was a freedman-procurator (it is unclear whether the co-defendant, an equestrian, was an Imperial official or not). But another 'good' Emperor, Augustus, had shown favouritism to Licinus, a freedman-procurator (Dio, liv. 21). (A procurator was a financial agent responsible especially for tax-collection.)

[32] *Dig.*, xlviii. 22. 6. 1.

[33] See Tac., *Ann.*, xiv. 40–41, for both prefect and jury-courts. The defendants, who included senators, might have been tried either by the prefect or by the jury-court for *falsum* (forgery)—their crime was testamentary forgery. The prefect also had the right to deport, the *ius deportandi*: see *Dig.*, i. 12. 1. 3; xxxii. 1. 4; xlviii. 22. 6. 1; etc. Deportation became an upper-class penalty (see p. 153 below).

witnesses and advocates, but also the choice of penalty was in his hands. The laws which set up jury-courts had both defined certain crimes and prescribed fixed penalties for anyone convicted of them in those courts. The *cognitio* judge was not restricted in this way. 'Today', wrote Ulpian early in the third century, 'he who sits in judgment in a criminal case *extra ordinem* may issue the sentence which pleases him, be it relatively severe or relatively mild, so long as he stays within the limits defined by reason.'[34]

There is a further point. The judge, in choosing a penalty, could go beyond those few which had gained recognition in the law, the straight death penalty, interdiction from fire and water (a form of exile), and the monetary fine. He could apply sanctions which had been used under the Republic mainly as administrative measures against free aliens or slaves.

The 'dual-penalty system', familiar to jurists of the age of the Severans, recognized the distinction between 'legal' and 'non-legal' penalties. In practice, each group of penalties was aligned with a broad social category, such that members of the upper classes, or *honestiores*, suffered only penalties drawn from the first group, and members of the lower classes only penalties from the second group.[35] 'Deportation' and 'relegation', two forms of exile, were standard penalties in the first group.[36] The former deprived the condemned of citizenship but not freedom, and the latter of neither. Execution, which was rare for *honestiores*, was by decapitation. The money-fine, once the only penalty in civil law, was used as a common minor sanction. Expulsion from the senate (in the case of a senator) and from a local council (in the case of a decurion), and prohibition from office-holding, were also known. The most serious 'lower-class penalty' is called by the jurists *summum supplicium* ('the highest punishment'). The term stood for aggravated forms of the death penalty, including exposure to wild

---

[34] *Dig.*, xlviii. 19. 3. The judge's freedom in choosing penalties was to a certain extent restricted by Imperial rescripts, at least from the turn of the first century. See F. M. de Robertis, *Zeitschrift Savigny-Stiftung*, lix (1939), pp. 219–60.

[35] Most of the penalties listed below are mentioned and graded in an edict ('upper-class penalties', *Dig.*, xlix. 19. 28. 13) and a rescript ('lower-class penalties', *ibid.*, 28. 14) of Hadrian.

[36] *Relegatio* became the 'legal' penalty for adultery under Augustus. See *Collatio*, ii. 26. 14. *Deportatio*, strictly speaking, was not a 'legal' penalty, but was similar to, if it did not succeed, interdiction.

beasts, crucifixion, and death by fire. Next, condemnation to hard labour in the mines was for life, and the condemned was reduced to a status akin to slavery. Condemnation to live and fight as a gladiator was just as degrading and carried a greater risk of death. A less severe penalty of the same type was labour on public works. Corporal punishment was also reserved for *humiliores*. Torture was, by tradition, applied only to slaves. But legal texts which forbid the use of torture for certain classes of free men indicate both that free men were not immune from torture in the middle- and late-second century, and that only well-connected free men were considered worthy of protection against it.[37] As for the treatment of accused men before trial, *honestiores* could generally avoid imprisonment. They might be entrusted to guarantors, or soldiers, or 'to themselves', though not if the charge was serious.[38]

V

LEGAL PRIVILEGE: EVOLUTION AND BASIS IN LAW

Much of our knowledge of legal privilege in Rome is derived from the writings of the Severan jurists. But legal privilege was not a phenomenon peculiar to the Severan age. The system which the jurists describe evolved in my view gradually in the course of the first century, and was well-established in legal practice in the second. This was true as much of the 'dual-penalty system' as of other forms of discrimination.

In an important article[39] published in 1950, G. Cardascia expressed a rather different opinion on the development of one

---

[37] See espec. *Cod. Just.*, ix. 41. 11; *Dig.*, xlviii. 18. 15. preface; l. 2. 14; cf. xlviii. 18. 9. 2. All texts but the second rule out torture for various privileged groups; the second implies that a freeman can be tortured if his statements as a witness are inconsistent. It is unlikely that lower-class defendants generally suffered judicial or inquisitorial torture (as distinct from 'third-degree' torture, torture as a punitive measure) in the first century and early second (see e.g. Pliny, *Epist.*, x. 96. 8 (slave women were tortured, but not those prisoners who were free). But the Christians at Lyons in A.D. 177(?) were certainly tortured: Euseb., *Eccl. Hist.*, v. 1.

[38] *Dig.*, xlviii. 3. 1 and 3.

[39] 'L'apparition dans le droit des classes d' "honestiores" et d' "humiliores", *Revue historique du droit français et étranger*, xxvii (1950), pp. 305–37, 461–85.

aspect of the system of privilege, differential punishment. He granted that variation of penalty was a reality in legal practice as early as the reign of Augustus (27 B.C.–A.D. 14), but claimed that a judge was under no obligation to make concessions to rank until the time of Pius (A.D. 138–160), when, according to him, distinctions began 'to pass into the law'. Subsequently variation in penalty became frequent in 'legislation', until under the Severans it took on 'a general character'.[40]

By 'the law' and 'legislation' are apparently meant Imperial constitutions, the rescripts and edicts of Emperors. It is not clear whether Cardascia holds that the rescripts of Pius and later Emperors 'established' the system of privilege in a newer, more highly-developed form; or whether the rescripts are supposed to have given a system which was already complete a new validity, by the fact that they refer to it and thereby indirectly sanction it. Both ideas deserve investigation.

Those rescripts issued by Pius and his successors which are at all relevant to the question of differential punishments can be divided into three groups. The first group comprises two rescripts, both of Pius, which set forth how two crimes were to be punished, the murder of an adulterer by the aggrieved husband, and thefts from imperial mines.[41] The second group consists of four rescripts banning the use of certain penalties against children or descendants of certain privileged groups.[42] Finally, four rescripts directly concern decurions or soldiers.[43]

It can be seen that the rescripts fail to cover the whole field of penalties, crimes and privileged categories. Instead of a general edict launching the dual-penalty system, there are two judicial decisions in which a differential penalty-scale is employed. Again, the fact that veterans, for example, are favoured has to be inferred from the sentencing of their sons to exile rather than forced labour of any kind.[44] Further, it is nowhere explicitly stated by an Emperor that decurions were not to be condemned to the mines. But the Emperor Severus Alexander (A.D. 222–235) informed

---

[40] *Ibid.*, p. 471.
[41] *Dig.*, xlviii. 5. 39. 8; cf. xlviii. 9. 1. 5; xlviii. 13. 8.
[42] *Cod. Just.*, ix. 41. 11. preface (includes torture); ix. 47. 5; 9; 12. We might add ix. 41. 8, preface; but the reference to soldiers is primary, so it is included in the third group.
[43] See notes 47–50 below.
[44] *Cod. Just.*, ix. 47. 5.

Demetrianus that, as his mother was the daughter of a decurion, she was not to suffer that fate.[45]

There is a second, related, difficulty. The rescripts, far from establishing a system of privilege, were apparently designed to preserve one which already existed. For example, all the rescripts in the third group reaffirm known regulations, or simply make reference to them.[46] The first of the Severan Emperors, Septimius Severus (A.D. 193–211), in a reply to the petition of Ambrosius, cited the rule (*prohibitum est*) that decurions were not to be beaten.[47] His son and successor Caracalla (A.D. 197–217) wrote to Geminius that decurions patently (*manifestum est*) should not be sentenced to forced labour.[48] There was plenty of precedent for Diocletian's protection of soldiers from torture and 'plebeian' penalties.[49] Finally, Marcus and Verus (A.D. 161–9), when consulted by a governor on the proper penalty for a certain Priscus, wrote that decurions ought to be relegated or deported for capital crimes.[50] Nor was this a novelty: a ruling of Hadrian which prohibited execution and prescribed exile for decurions who were murderers (except for parricides) had implied as much.[51]

The first relevant 'legislation', indeed, was issued not by Pius, but by Hadrian. In addition to the ruling just mentioned, there is record of a judicial decision of A.D. 119—of the same type as the rescripts of Pius in the first group referred to above—in which Hadrian stated that exile (*relegatio*) was the proper penalty for *splendidiores personae* (which stands for *honestiores*), and two years' labour on public works (*opus publicum*) and a beating for *alii* ('the rest', equivalent to *humiliores*), for the offence of moving boundary-stones.[52] We must therefore ask whether either or both of Hadrian's rescripts[53] were innovatory.

---

[45] *Cod. Just.*, ix.47.9.

[46] In the second group, only the edict of Marcus (*Cod. Just.*, ix. 41. 11. preface) might have added to the ranks of the privileged class (in a very small way)—unless the edict was intended to re-state an accepted rule which had been disregarded, or to make explicit an exemption which had until then been only implicit.

[47] *Cod. Just.*, ii. 11. 5.

[48] *Ibid.*, ix. 47. 3.

[49] *Ibid.*, ix. 41. 8. preface; cf. *Dig.*, xlix. 18. 1 and 3.

[50] *Dig.*, xlviii. 22. 6. 2.

[51] *Ibid.*, xlviii. 19. 15.

[52] *Ibid.*, xlvii. 21. 2; cf. *Collatio*, xiii. 3. 1–2. For Cardascia's discussion of the text, see *art. cit.*, pp. 468–9.

[53] *Dig.*, xlvii. 21. 2, and xlvii. 19. 15.

The rescript over boundary-stones, if it was the first of its kind, may have actually 'set up' the penalty differential. The grounds for asserting this are purely and simply that no earlier rescript is recorded in the *Digest* and other legal compilations.[54] But chance played an important part in the selection and preservation of such texts as have survived. Another band of compilers, working in A.D. 530-3 (when the *Digest* was compiled) or at another time, might have come up with a different set of rescripts, including some from an earlier period. It is obvious that neither the classical jurists from whose works excerpts were drawn, nor the Justinianic compilers, had the intention of describing the evolution of class discrimination in the law.[55]

As for the second rescript, it was genuinely innovatory if it elevated decurions as a class. But it must be said that it does not *look* like an edict which deliberately conferred a new status and a new set of privileges, and it was very limited in application since it concerned only murder cases.[56] It cannot therefore be seen as, for instance, one of a series of edicts exempting decurions from specific penalties. Nor is there any indication that it announced or constituted a departure from previous policy. Pliny's letter to Calestrius Tiro, quoted in full above,[57] belongs to the previous reign (it was perhaps written in 107-8), and is important evidence for the care with which the Roman administration distinguished between the local aristocracy and the rest of the provincial population. Nor was this a new attitude, originating in Trajan's reign (A.D. 97-117) and voiced first by his officials. The wealth, social status and political usefulness of the provincial gentry had long been evident.[58] These were the qualities which made it inevitable

[54] It is held by d'Ors in *Les empereurs romains d'Espagne* (Paris, 1965), pp. 147 ff. and Gaudemet in *Festschrift E. Rabel* (Tübingen, 1954), ii, pp. 169 ff. that Hadrian's rescripts were the first 'true' rescripts, 'des rescrits proprement dit'. This doctrine rests on one text, *Vita Macrini*, 13. 1, which shows that Trajan was averse to sending rescripts in reply to the petitions of private individuals (*libelli*), but not that he was unwilling to send rescripts (of the Hadrianic type) to functionaries. There are in fact numerous examples of the second type of rescript from the pre-Hadrianic era.

[55] For the aims of the latter, see *Const. Tanta*, 10.

[56] This is an inference from the references in the text (*Dig.*, xlviii. 19. 15) to the 'poena legis Corneliae (*sc.*, de sicariis)', and to parricide.

[57] Above, pp. 144-5.

[58] On class division in Greek cities under the Republic and the Roman attitude to it, see J. Briscoe, 'Rome and the class struggle 200-146 B.C.' chapter III above.

that their most conspicuous representatives would gain the citizenship and advance into the higher orders. The actions and attitudes of courts had long respected these same qualities. It was expected of judges that they would discriminate in favour of upper-class provincials.

Thus, Hadrian may have been not so much raising decurions, or leading provincial notables, to a new status, as confirming them in one they already possessed. This would have been an appropriate measure at a time when penalties were becoming more severe, and the newer, degrading sanctions were coming into wider use—and when governors were no less inclined to arbitrary behaviour than their predecessors had been. The Emperor's biographer reports that Hadrian, in his travels throughout the Empire, made it his business to correct abuses where he found them. Governors, amongst others, were punished.[59] Their misdemeanors may have included acts implying an unwillingness to make any distinction between decurions on the one hand, and the rest of the free population in the provinces on the other.[60]

The 'dual-penalty system', then, does not seem to have been set up by formal enactments, or, if it was (and this must be counted unlikely), those enactments are lost to us. Nor, for that matter, does a law survive which gave senators the prerogative of trial by their peers or which maintained that privilege. Further, to my knowledge, the inequitable aspects of the formulary system, referred to above,[61] were not set up or sanctioned by any edict.

It remains for us to consider briefly the more modest suggestion that the rescripts gave the system of discrimination a new validity in law. This theory has unsatisfactory implications. Our informa-

---

[59] *Vita Hadriani*, xiii. 10. Hadrian was a notorious 'busybody': see Dio, lxix. 5. 1.

[60] Here is a summary of the evidence for the dual-penalty system in the time of Hadrian: the arrangement of penalties 'legal' and 'non-legal' into two distinct groups is not attested before Hadrian: see *Dig.*, xlviii. 19. 28. 13–14. Hadrian further recognized a correspondence between a category of penalties and a social class: see xlvii. 21. 2. *Dig.*, xlviii. 19. 15, indeed, implies the existence of a whole system of differential punishments. The fact that Hadrian's successors made few additions to the system indirectly confirms that the system was well-established under Hadrian. *Dig.*, xlvii. 14. 1. preface and xlviii. 8. 4. 2 show, at the most, that the dual-penalty scale was not yet applied universally, in the punishment of every crime (cf. *ibid.*, xlvii. 9. 4. 1, for Pius).

[61] Above, III, The Civil Suit.

tion on the system of differential penalties comes to us through both Imperial rescripts and juristic generalizations. But, as we have seen, no Imperial pronouncements are preserved which so much as mention the bulk of upper-class privileges. It would seem to follow that only a few of these privileges were well-based in law. The difficulty can be resolved if it is asked what was in the mind of a jurist when he cited an Imperial rescript, and also what was the Emperor's motive in issuing the rescript. Callistratus did not cite Hadrian's rescripts on witnesses, referred to above,[62] because they authorized judges in a new and superior way to favour upper-class witnesses; nor was that either the purpose, or the effect of the rescripts. Again, Hadrian's rescript on boundaries (quoted by Callistratus) shows that he believed in the principle that criminals of different social status should be punished differently; but he did not intend, by issuing the rescript, to give that principal a legal standing which it did not have before, nor was that an indirect result of the publication of the rescript. The rescript set up new penalties for an old crime, penalties which still held good in Callistratus' day.[63] In short, differential punishment was already a feature of the judicial system, and had been tacitly if not overtly approved and sanctioned by judges, jurists and Emperors.

VI

THE ROMAN CITIZENSHIP

The Romans recognized in their society distinctions other than that between the upper class and lower class (*honestiores* and *humiliores*); for example that between freemen and slaves, and between citizens and aliens. The relationship of these to that between *honestiores* and *humiliores* will now be considered.

For writers of juristic handbooks, the distinction between the freeman and the slave was 'the basic division in the law of persons'.[64] But it is evidently not assimilable to that between the *honestiores* and the *humiliores*. *Humiliores*, the lower classes, included

---

[62] Above, p. 149.

[63] *Dig.*, xxii. 5. 3. 1 ff. (witnesses); xlvii. 21. 2 (boundaries).

[64] Gaius, *Instit.*, i. 9. For a reflection of the division in penal law, *Dig.*, xlviii. 19. 28. 16.

slaves, freedmen, and also any men of free birth who lacked the criteria for legal privilege, that is, the dignity and prestige associated with good birth and character and the possession of wealth and office.

The distinction between citizen and alien requires closer analysis. It has been suggested that it was replaced by that between *honestiores* and *humiliores*, which is said to have arisen in the late first or early second century.[65] Citizens held several important advantages over aliens. They could seek the help of a tribune, or exercise their right of appeal, against the arbitrary actions of magistrates. Aliens, strictly speaking, had no standing within the civil law, and hence lacked these rights. In Jerusalem in the reign of Nero (A.D. 54–68), St Paul staved off a beating and struck fear into a tribune with the words: 'Is it lawful for you to scourge a Roman citizen, uncondemned?'[66] St Paul had previously embarrassed the magistrates of the colony of Philippi by disclosing his citizen-status *after* he and his companions had been beaten and cast into prison.[67] Considerably later, peasants on an Imperial estate in Africa protested to the Emperor Commodus (A.D. 180–193) that, even though some of them were Roman citizens, they had been beaten by a procurator and various overseers of the estate.[68] This incident indicates that appeal was not a dead letter in the Antonine period. About a generation later, Ulpian cited the section of the Julian law on public violence which dealt with appeal in his treatise on the duties of a proconsul,[69] and several sections of the *Digest* are devoted to appeal.[70]

Further, a citizen might expect to gain a less severe sentence than an alien if both were defendants on the same charge. In A.D. 17, the Senate took firm measures to stamp out astrology: among the astrologers, citizens were exiled while foreigners were put to death.[71] In A.D. 177(?), Christians arrested at Lyons were either

[65] A. N. Sherwin-White, *Roman Society and Roman Law in the New Testament* (Oxford, 1963), p. 174. See also A. H. M. Jones, *Studies in Roman Government and Law* (Oxford, 1960), pp. 64–5.

[66] Acts 22:24.

[67] *Ibid.*, 16:37.

[68] Riccobono, *Fontes Iuris Romani Antejust.*, 2nd edn, i, n. 103, p. 496, ll. 10 ff.

[69] *Dig.*, xlviii. 6. 7.

[70] On appeal, see *JRS*, lvi (1966), pp. 167 ff.

[71] *Collatio*, xv. 2. 1; cf. Dio, lvii. 15. 8, and Tac., *Ann.*, ii. 32. 5.

beheaded or sent to the beasts, depending on whether they were citizens or aliens.[72]

The preferential treatment of citizens as opposed to aliens was therefore a long-standing form of legal discrimination, which persisted in the first two centuries of the Empire. It was based on the exclusion of aliens from the civil law (*ius civile*), but was practised also in other spheres of the law; for example in the criminal law, which under the Empire was subject to the *cognitio* of magistrates, and which covered both citizens and non-citizens.

The dividing line between the *honestiores* and *humiliores* was not identical with that between citizens and aliens, for there were citizens (and non-citizens) on both sides of it.

First, those with legal privilege included non-citizens, because decurions were a privileged group, and not all decurions were citizens. Decurions of cities of 'Roman' status had citizenship. In 'Latin' cities,[73] however, citizenship was won by performance of a magistracy rather than by mere membership of a city-council. From the time of Hadrian or Pius it was possible for a 'Latin' city to obtain a higher grade of Latinity, *Latium maius*, and so gain citizenship for all its decurions.[74] But the epigraphic evidence suggests that this had to be sued for; apparently *Latium maius* was not conferred on all 'Latin' cities by an act of the central administration. Moreover, while *Latium maius* undoubtedly reduced the numbers of decurions who lacked citizenship in the West, it made no impact on the Eastern half of the Empire. Cities in the Greek East had never been anxious for either 'Roman' or 'Latin' status; there, citizenship was possessed by individuals and families rather than by whole city-populations or ruling castes.[75]

Secondly, the sources imply that citizenship did not exclude the humble from cruel and humiliating penalties. The African peasants were, after all, beaten, and though this may have been strictly

[72] Euseb., *Eccl. Hist.*, v. 1. 47. But Attalus, a citizen (§ 44), was sent to the beasts. Decapitation was the least unpleasant and least degrading form of the death penalty.

[73] 'Latinity' in the late Republic and early Empire was a half-way stage between the position of an alien and full Roman citizenship.

[74] Gaius, *Instit.*, i. 96; *ILS*, 6780 (Gigthis, N. Africa).

[75] See A. N. Sherwin-White, *Roman Citizenship* (Oxford, 1939), pp. 194–257 esp. pp. 236 ff. It should be added that in no source is it stated or implied that only those decurions who were citizens were entitled to milder punishments.

illegal, it could have been expected. The peasants call themselves 'ordinary men of the countryside' (*homines rustici tenues*), a description which finds an echo in Callistratus:[76]

> It is not normal for everybody to be beaten, but only free men whose standing is relatively low (*hi . . . qui liberi sunt et quidem tenuiores homines*). Members of the upper classes (*honestiores*) are exempt, and this is emphasized in Imperial rescripts.

Callistratus may have had in mind a rescript of Septimius Severus which pointed out that decurions were not to be beaten.[77] This was no new development. Severus was citing an established rule (*prohibitum est*), and long before, in A.D. 119, Hadrian had ruled that the offence of moving boundary-stones was to be punished in part by beating, except when the culprits were *splendidiores personae* or *honestiores*.[78]

Citizens were in theory protected not only against beating, but also against the execution of a death sentence in the face of an appeal. But decurions, and other members of the privileged classes, were in the more enviable position of knowing that the highest punishment to which they were liable was exile, unless they were guilty of parricide or treason.

In general, an explanation is required for the failure of the jurists to mention citizenship in those passages in which they dealt with the criteria on the basis of which the privileged class was to be identified. The omission may be due to systematic re-writing of the classical legal texts by later jurists and especially the sixth-century compilers, for whom citizenship held little significance. But perhaps the classical jurists themselves considered that the distinction between humble citizens and free aliens was unimportant compared with the distinction between senators, equestrians or decurions on the one hand, and members of the lower classes, whether citizens or aliens, on the other. If this was the case, and the evidence already adduced seems to point that way, then Justinian's men would have had no cause to make substantial alterations in the relevant texts.

[76] *Dig.*, xlviii. 19. 28. 2.
[77] *Cod. Just.*, ii. 11. 5 (A.D. 198).
[78] *Dig.*, xlvii. 21. 2.

The distinction between *honestiores* and *humiliores*, then, cuts across that between citizens and aliens. It is, of course, a further step to say that the former replaced the latter. That would seem to imply that the former distinction was not important in the pre-Hadrianic period; and, conversely, that the latter was once (perhaps in the first century) as fundamental as the former became (perhaps in the course of the second century).

There may be a close association between the 'replacement' theory and the idea that the differential-penalty system began to emerge in the reigns of Hadrian and Pius. If so, it should be stated that there is good reason for believing that the differential-penalty system existed in its essentials by the reign of Hadrian;[79] and that discrimination in favour of the upper classes involved more than the assigning of milder penalties.

To reinforce the second point, it may be helpful to pick out some forms of upper-class discrimination which were practised in the course of the first century A.D.[80] The formulary procedure was in its hey-day in the late Republic and early Empire. It will be recalled that it was administered by praetors and private judges with wide discretionary powers, which they used to the advantage of men of wealth and social position. Again, senators appear to have had the right to a senatorial trial in the first century, while equestrians went before the tribunal of the Emperor or the Senate, and the public courts and the urban prefect dealt mainly with lower-class criminals at Rome. Thirdly, in the matter of punishments, variation of penalty was practised as soon as *extra ordinem* courts began to operate, and it appears that while citizens were favoured above aliens, citizens of low rank lost in comparison with upper-class citizens.[81] This last statement is neces-

---

[79] See n. 60 above.

[80] The 'honestiores'/'humiliores' formula will not be found in first-century sources. This is doubtless partly due to the fact that those sources are largely non-legal: they are concerned with individual events, affecting individuals, and do not generalize (except about politics). It should also be emphasized that even the classical jurists fail to use the formula (see n. 4 above). There is a perfectly good equivalent in an excerpt from the Augustan jurist Labeo, in *Dig.*, iv. 3. 11. 1: it is unnecessary to hold that the words are Ulpian's and not Labeo's. Nor is it likely that for Labeo the phrase 'qui dignitate excellet' applied only to ex-consuls.

[81] *Citizens/aliens*: See n. 71, above; Pliny, *Epist.*, x. 96. 4.

Equestrians/others: *ibid.*, ii. 11. 8: an equestrian is exiled, his friends (*sc.*, of lower status) are executed: another equestrian is strangled after

sarily cautious, given the nature of the evidence. The *Digest* is preoccupied with the post-Trajanic period, and, with few exceptions, the historical and biographical authors are Rome-based and caught up in the political struggle between Emperor and Senate. Hence information is lacking about the way in which penalties were normally applied to lesser men, including citizens of low station, and to provincials of all ranks.[82]

The conclusion is not that citizenship was worth nothing. There is some evidence that the Emperor was interested in the welfare of citizens in the provinces,[83] although this does not mean that he was not prepared to come to the assistance of free aliens.[84] The rights of citizens were respected by some officials at least, and the authors describe with disapproval occasions when they were

the application of servile sanctions—but Marius Priscus apparently demands a higher sum for this.

Senators/others: Suet., *Aug.*, v: a patrician (*sc.*, a senator) asks the senate for a milder penalty because of his age and birth; Pliny, *Epist.*, iv. 11. 10 ff.: an equestrian is beaten to death, an ex-praetor allowed to take much of his property into exile (on the latter's complicity, see A. N. Sherwin-White, *Commentary* (Oxford, 1966), on iv. 11. 11); *ibid.*, ix. 13. 21 (see n. 31 above).

Foreign prince/citizen: Tac., *Ann.*, vi. 40: even Tigranes cannot escape 'supplicia civium' (citizen-punishments).

[82] Penalties *abnormally* applied to equestrians or to men of rank (grade unspecified): Suet., *Tiber.*, li (treadmill); *Gaius*, xxvii. 3–4 (mutilation, exposure to beasts; condemnation to mines and road-building); Jos., *Bell. Iud.*, ii. 308 (Gessius Florus, Nero; flogging and crucifixion); Pliny, *Epist.*, ii. 11. 8 (n. 81 above). *Epist.*, x. 58 is more problematic: Flavius Archippus was sent to the mines for forgery; there is no hint of irregularity; he was a citizen, but otherwise nothing is known about his status at the time of the trial—his later prosperity may be solely due to Domitian's favour. Suet., *Galba*, ix is also difficult: a citizen is crucified, again for a genuine, serious crime. Was this atypical? Florus' crucifixions (above) undoubtedly were. Suetonius implies the penalty was harsh, and the man pleads his citizen-status, as if expecting a milder punishment.

[83] Cyzicus lost its freedom once (perhaps twice) and Rhodes once for violence against Romans or for putting them to death: Dio, liv. 7. 6; lvii. 24. 6; Tac., *Ann.*, iv. 36. 2–3; cf. Suet., *Tiber.*, xxxvii. 3.

[84] See e.g. Riccobono, *op. cit.*, ii, n. 185, p. 582 (Cnidus; Augustus assists free aliens). Only some of the African peasants who petitioned Commodus (see n. 68 above) were citizens. *Dig.*, xlviii. 6. 6 may or may not be relevant: Pius instructs a proconsul to investigate a savage attack on a youth, whose name indicates he was a citizen; yet Pius describes him simply as *ingenuus* ('free-born').

ignored.[85] The relevant references are concentrated within a period of about 175 years, from the 70s B.C. to the reign of Trajan. This suggests that the value of citizenship may have declined in the second century, perhaps because of the increase in the numbers of citizens.[86] Alternatively, the imbalance in the evidence may be due to mere chance. Citizenship was still sought after in the second century,[87] and the verdict at Lyons in A.D. 177(?) already referred to[88] suggests that the reasons were not entirely sentimental. But the fact remains that the distinction between citizens and aliens was at all times only one of several which the Romans recognized, and it skated over the realities of Roman politics and social life. The Romans rejected juridical equality, the equality of all citizens before the law, as easily as they rejected political equality. Cicero viewed as unequal that kind of equality which 'does not recognize grades of dignity'.[89] This attitude must have been universal among those who dominated politics and the administration of justice in both Republican and Imperial Rome.[90]

[85] *Respected*: Acts, 22: 24; cf. 25: 9 ff. (and see *JRS*, lvi (1966), p. 167); Pliny, *Epist.*, x. 96. 4; Euseb., *Eccl. Hist.*, v. 1. 47.
   Ignored: Cic., *ad familiares*, x. 32. 2 (Balbus); *2 in Verrem*, v. 162 ff. (Verres); Suet., *Galba*, ix (Galba); Dio, lxiv. 2. 3 (Capito).
[86] If Tacitus was any judge, the 'snob-value' of citizenship had declined anyway by the late first century. See *Ann.*, iii. 40. 2: the citizenship was once 'rare, and given solely as a reward for virtue'. This is a conservative, upper-class-Roman view.
[87] Sherwin-White, *Roman Citizenship*, chapters ix–x. The citizen/alien distinction lost most of its meaning when Caracalla made virtually the whole free population of the Empire Roman citizens in A.D. 212(?).
[88] Above, pp. 160–1.
[89] Cic., *de re publica*, i. 43: '. . . tamen ipsa aequabilitas est iniqua, cum habet nullos gradus dignitatis'.
[90] The matters discussed in this paper are treated more fully in *Social Status and Legal Privilege in the Roman Empire* (Oxford, 1970). On increasing severity of penalties, see Garnsey, 'Why penalties became harsher: the Roman case, late republic to fourth-century empire', *Natural Law Forum*, no. 13 (1968), pp. 141 ff.

VIII

GREEKS AND THEIR PAST IN THE
SECOND SOPHISTIC*†

E. L. Bowie

INTRODUCTION

This paper attempts to gather together and interpret the principal
manifestations of archaism in the Greek world of the late first, the
second and the early third centuries A.D., a period known to
literary historians by Philostratus's name 'the second sophistic'.
The archaism has been observed by historians of society and
literature alike, but the most recent work on the sophists does little
more than allude to it, while literary historians have seen it
primarily in terms of linguistic *Atticism*, that imitation of fifth-
and fourth-century Attic prose writers which was already the
subject of controversy in the first century B.C. and which affected
all Greek writers of the imperial period to a greater or lesser
extent. This linguistic Atticism has been exhaustively documented
by Wilhelm Schmid in his great work *Der Atticismus*. But Schmid
sees the development of Atticizing fashions almost entirely as a
movement *within* literature.[1] This paper tries to show that the

* From no. 46 (1970).
† An earlier draft of this paper was read to the Oxford Philological
Society on 1 December 1967. I am very grateful to its members and to
the editorial board of *Past and Present* for their helpful criticism.
[1] G. W. Bowersock, *Greek Sophists in the Roman Empire* (Oxford, 1969),
pp. 15–16 touches on the matter of archaism, but although he excludes
the explanations that 'the sophists were eaten up by nostalgia for the
old times' and that they were 'affirming the independent greatness of
the Greeks against the Romans' he offers no positive elucidation of the
phenomenon. For the linguistic aspects W. Schmid, *Der Atticismus*,
4 vols (Stuttgart, 1887–96), remains fundamental. Literary archaism is

archaism of language and style known as Atticism is only part of a wider tendency, a tendency that prevails in literature not only in style but also in choice of theme and treatment, and that equally affects other areas of cultural activity.

If archaism affects the cultural activity of upper-class Greeks over a wide range, a purely literary explanation should not be sufficient. After presenting the evidence for archaism in the sophists, in the historians and related literary practitioners, and in other aspects of life, this paper offers an explanation in wider terms, relating the Greeks' preoccupation with their past to their dissatisfaction with the political situation of the present. This is not to deny that other factors, such as the classicizing emphasis of Greek education or the personal tastes of influential individuals like Hadrian, contributed to the ultimate amalgam. In particular it is clear that the archaism of the second century A.D. is not *solely* a function of the Greeks' relation to their present from the fact that archaism is evident in the Latin as well as in the Greek world. Although the Latin and the Greek archaism must have influenced each other—their exponents were often the same and bilingual, like Hadrian or Fronto, and they belonged to a world of Greco-Roman upper-class culture that was essentially a unity— both chronology and Greek archaism's puristic rejection of Latin exclude the possibility that Latin archaism can be a sufficient explanation of the growth of Greek archaism. It can only have helped it on its way. Accordingly this paper does not take account of archaism in Latin writers, although it is worth observing that there too there were political overtones that correspond *mutatis mutandis* to those suggested for Greek archaism, a hankering for the *libertas* of the *respublica*. It should also be said that although the theme here discussed is an important aspect of Greek attitudes to

described and its extension beyond literature noted, but not fully explained, by B. A. van Groningen, 'General literary tendencies in the second century A.D.', *Mnemosyne*, xviii (1965), pp. 41 ff. F. Millar, 'P. Herennius Dexippus: the Greek world and the third-century invasions', *JRS*, lix (1969), pp. 12–29, appeared when this paper was already in proof. Millar's contention that constant allusion to the past acted as a 'frame of reference or a channel of communication' is illuminating, but does not exclude the question 'why *this* frame of reference?' and the answer (which he seems to regard as an *alternative*, not a further, explanation) that it was 'a means of flight from an oppressive and inglorious present' (p. 12). See also below, nn. 110, 111.

the contemporary Roman world, it is only *one* aspect: the range of attitudes within the Greek upper classes is wide and complex, and this paper is intended to explore only one constituent of the amalgam.

SOPHISTS

The most characteristic and influential figures of the age, not least in their own eyes, were the sophists. Oratory had always been important in Greek society, before even it had been developed as an art to help the individual to survive or succeed in the fifth-century democracies of Sicily and Athens. Training in rhetoric became a major part of Greek higher education and was for many synonymous with it, contesting the rôle of educator with philosophy. Hence rhetoric continued to dominate education after the opportunities of achieving Periclean or Demosthenic greatness by successful oratory had been considerably restricted by the over-shadowing of the city states by Hellenistic monarchies. It is to the time of this change in the centres of political power that we can trace the earliest attested declamation on a fictitious theme, attributed to Demetrius of Phaleron.[2] It is doubtless no coincidence that the practice seems to have been instituted at a time when Alexander's conquests had made it clear that the era of city state politics was coming to an end.

By the time Octavian's victory at Actium guaranteed the absorption of the last great Hellenistic monarchy, Ptolemaic Egypt, into the Roman empire, declamations on fictitious topics, both judicial and historical, had long been a standard element in Greek rhetorical education, though it is only in the elder Seneca's records of declaimers under Augustus and Tiberius that we first get any substantial information on their content and treatment.[3] It is not clear at what point such declamations became more than simply a part of rhetorical training and joined panegyric and commemorative speeches in the rôle of public entertainment: certainly by the second half of the first century A.D. declamation seems to have moved into the first rank of cultural activities and acquired an unprecedented and almost unintelligible popularity. Its practi-

[2] Quintilian, *Institutio Oratoria*, ii. 4. 41.
[3] See H. Bornecque, *Les déclamations et les déclamateurs d'après Sénèque le père* (Lille, 1902).

tioners were often from the wealthiest and most influential families in their city's aristocracy, and they displayed their skill to enraptured or critical audiences, not only in their native places, but throughout the Greek world, in the great cities that vied with each other in honouring or acquiring as residents the most brilliant exponents—Athens, Ephesus, Smyrna and even Rome. The name of *rhetor* (initially 'orator', but by now connoting a teacher and exponent of epideictic rhetoric) was sufficiently grand to appear on sepulchral or honorific inscriptions, but even greater was the name sophist (σοφιστής). The fifth-century sophists had taught rhetoric as well as conducting more serious enquiries, and it was from them, as we learn from Philostratus, their biographer, that the 'sophists' of the second sophistic derived their tradition of epideictic oratory. The term 'sophist' appears to be contained within the term *rhetor* and to apply particularly to those teachers of rhetoric (*rhetors*) whose attainment was of such a level as to give public performances. Its link with the use of the term 'sophist' in the fifth century B.C. will hardly stand close examination, but the claim of classical precedent on however slender a basis is itself symptomatic of the times.[4]

The world in which sophistic oratory moved was not *purely* artificial. The place of rhetoric in the Hellenistic and Roman worlds can be distorted if it is forgotten that members of the city aristocracies were still faced by many occasions on which real speeches were required and could be influential. Embassies to monarchs or to other cities, seeking privilege or offering honour; debates in the council (*boule*), still important within city politics even when (as in the Roman period) the assembly (*ecclesia*) had lost all powers; exhortatory addresses to the citizen body at crises of riot or famine (such as we find among the speeches of Dio of Prusa); and, requiring not persuasion but dignity and brilliance, ceremonial speeches at the dedication of public buildings, festivals or the welcome of visiting potentates. All these—quite apart from

[4] See Bowersock, *Greek Sophists in the Roman Empire*, pp. 12–14. That *public performance* marked the difference between sophist and rhetor seems clear from Galen's phrase (of Hadrianus in his early career) ὁ ῥήτωρ οὔπω σοφιστεύων (14. 627 Kühn)—the use of the verb σοφιστεύων, denoting an activity rather than simply claim to a status, is significant. σοφιστεύων does not, of course, mean 'giving public performances', but refers to the pursuit of a career involving these: cf. the context of ἐν Γαλατίᾳ σοφιστεύων in Plut., *Mor.*, 131A.

law-court oratory, usually looked upon with contempt by sophists
—offered a valid ground for the acquisition and practice of the art
of public speaking by ambitious members of the Greek city
aristocracies. What is surprising is that they were not enough, and
that the same men who were sent on embassies to the emperor
would sweat out their intellectual talents on perfecting declamations set in a fictitious classical context for audiences who were
more interested in tricks of style and delivery than in content.[5]

The choice of these themes may have something to do with the
causes of the rise of this fashion as a whole among the Greek city
aristocracies (though these are outside the scope of this paper). It
would be intelligible that Greeks of the first and second century,
denied that aspect of public oratory which had acquired power and
immortality for a Pericles or Demosthenes in the classical period,
speeches of persuasion to sovereign assemblies in autonomous
cities, should choose to display their intellectual superiority to
their fellow citizens and enjoy the rhetorician's control of his
audience's emotions in treating themes that precisely substituted
for the occasions that were lacking. What is certain, at least, is that
the favoured themes of the sophists harked back constantly to the
classical period. The classicism of theme is as much evident in
those orators whose rhythms have been labelled 'Asian' (as
opposed to 'Attic').[6]

The most prominent themes derive from the history of Athens,
the greatest of the classical Greek cities, or Alexander, the greatest
individual Greek. Alexander figures in two of the orations of Dio
of Prusa, written in the first decade of the second century: in one
(the second) he converses with his father Philip, in the other (the
fourth) with the cynic Diogenes. Dio also wrote eight books *On
the virtues of Alexander*, now lost.[7] Plutarch, slightly his junior and

---

[5] For the strain of declaiming cf. Polemo's comparison with the situation
of a gladiator and use of the verb ἀγωνιᾶν 'be in agony' in Philostratus,
Lives of the Sophists, 1. 25, p. 541 (the last figure here and subsequently
refers to the Olearius pagination which alone offers any precision of
reference to the editions both of C. L. Kayser, *Flavii Philostrati Opera*,
vol. ii (Leipzig 1871, repr. Hildesheim, 1964) and of W. C. Wright,
Philostratus and Eunapius (Loeb Classical Library, 1921).

[6] On the 'Asian' style in Greek oratory see especially U. von Wilamowitz,
'Asianismus und Attizismus', *Hermes*, xxxv (1900), pp. 1 ff.

[7] For the lost work περὶ τῶν Ἀλεξάνδρου ἀρετῶν see the Suda lexicon
s.v. Δίων (n. 1240 Adler).

unlikely ever to have been a practising sophist (he has several criticisms of sophistic rhetoric) was nevertheless the author of some declamatory works, two of which (purporting to be delivered on successive days) deal with Alexander's debt to Fortune.[8] Another, discussing whether the Athenians were more famous for their intellectual or military achievements, draws its examples of Athenian glory exclusively from the classical period.

The same applies to the sophists known to us from Philostratus, none of whose themes, as has been observed, post-dates the year 326 B.C.[9] Scopelianus of Clazomenae, in real life a successful envoy to Domitian, was particularly admired for his treatment of themes set in the Persian wars and involving Darius and Xerxes.[10] Under Hadrian the masterpieces of Dionysius of Miletus included a *Dirge for Chaeronea*, the symbolic end of Greek freedom and a favourite sophistic topic, attested also for Polemon of Laodicea and mentioned in later rhetoricians, and *The Arcadians on trial for serving as mercenaries* (that is against Greeks).[11] His coeval, the Ephesian Lollianus, delivered a speech *Against Leptines* (the situation envisaged might have come about—though it did not—after Demosthenes' speech against Leptines of 355 B.C.) and in another assumed a situation in which the Athenians were planning to sell Delos.[12]

Polemon of Laodicea (*c.* A.D. 87–143) is one of the few of Philostratus' sophists of whom complete works survive—in his case, a pair of declamations ostensibly delivered by the fathers of Callimachus and Cynegirus, contestants for the (posthumous) award for valour at the battle of Marathon. Three declamations he delivered in the presence of Herodes Atticus all had classical

---

[8] The two speeches *On the fortune or the virtue of Alexander* (περὶ τῆς Ἀλεξάνδρου τύχης ἢ ἀρετῆς) are rightly characterized as 'epideictic display-pieces' in their most recent treatment, that of J. R. Hamilton in his commentary on Plutarch, *Alexander* (Oxford, 1969), pp. xxiii ff. They and the declamation on Athens (πότερον Ἀθηναῖοι κατὰ πόλεμον ἢ κατὰ σοφίαν ἐνδοξότεροι) are most easily accessible in the Loeb edition of Plutarch's *Moralia*, vol. iv, ed. F. C. Babbitt (1936).

[9] Most recently Hamilton, *op. cit.*, p. xxii, n. 1.

[10] Philostratus, *Lives of the Sophists*, 1. 21, p. 519.

[11] *Ibid.*, 1. 22, p. 522; 1. 25, p. 542.

[12] *Ibid.*, 1. 23, p. 527. The Persian wars were already a favourite with Nicetes of Smyrna, the earliest of Philostratus' sophists and already active under Nero: see *Lives of the Sophists*, 1. 20, p. 513. For Chaeronea cf. Syrianus, ii. 165; Apsines, ix. 471. For Leptines cf. Apsines, ix. 496.

themes:[13] Demosthenes swears that he did not take the bribe of fifty talents (the charge brought against him by Demades); an argument that the trophies erected by the Greeks be taken down at the end of the Peloponnesian war; and an exhortation to the Athenians to return to their demes after the battle of Aegospotami. Other of his declamations included the arguments of Xenophon refusing to survive Socrates; Solon demanding that his legislation be annulled after Pisistratus had obtained a bodyguard; and three further Demosthenic pieces. No wonder that one of his witticisms, when he encountered a sophist buying sausages and sprats, was to remark 'My dear chap, you can't give a good representation of the arrogance of Darius and Xerxes if you live on that'.[14]

Athens was not the only favourite. Plutarch's *Moralia* show as much interest in ancient Sparta as his *Lives*, and his coeval Isaeus from Syria (or, as the archaizing sophists liked to say, Assyria) debated the hackneyed topic of whether the Lacedaemonians should fortify Sparta with walls.[15] Marcus of Byzantium, a decade or two later, argued that the Spartans should not take back the hoplites who had surrendered themselves and their weapons at Sphacteria.[16] Sometimes the theme was Homeric, as in Dio of Prusa's *Trojan Speech* (arguing that Troy was never captured by the Greeks), Aristides' *Speech for an embassy to Achilles* (from *Iliad*, Book 9), or Philostratus' own *Heroic Tale*.[17]

A very high proportion of the themes mentioned in the *Lives* by Philostratus derives from Greek history, and all these from the period before 326 B.C. That this fairly reflects sophistic behaviour and is not simply the consequence of deliberate selection by the archaizing Philostratus is guaranteed by a comparison with the extant corpus of Aristides' works. Aristides (chiefly active under Pius and Marcus) sets *all* his purely declamatory works (as opposed to speeches for real and contemporary occasions) in the

[13] Philostratus, *op. cit.*, 1. 25, p. 538.

[14] *Ibid.*, 1. 25, p. 541.

[15] *Ibid.*, 1. 20, p. 514; cf. also Aristides, *ibid.*, 2.9, p. 584.

[16] *Ibid.*, 1. 24, p. 528.

[17] Dio's Τρωικὸς λόγος (*Or.*, 11 in the traditional order) is in the first volume of the Loeb's edition of J. W. Cohoon (1932). For Aristides' πρεσβευτικὸς πρὸς Αχιλλέα, Dindorf's edition (Leipzig, 1829), *Or.*, 52; and Philostratus's Ηρωικὸς, C. L. Kayser's edition, vol. ii (see n. 5), on which see below, p. 197.

classical period. We are not in a position to judge how different this choice of material was from that of Greek rhetoricians of earlier periods. Seneca the elder is some help: historical themes from the classical period are well represented, but far from universal, in the selection he gives in his *suasoriae* (deliberations by historical figures at moments of crisis), whereas there are only a few—about half a dozen—in the *controversiae* (fictitious court arguments). It would seem that in the early first century A.D. historical themes were less popular, but Seneca's testimony is not sufficiently comprehensive for us to judge how much so.[18]

What is clear, however, is that in our period the tendency was at its height. Some of its practitioners might ridicule it, as did Lucian, who asked why one should imitate Aeschines in a time of peace when there was no Philip attacking and no Alexander issuing orders. But Lucian too betrays himself as a child of his time, not only by his Atticizing idiom but by the setting of his dialogues. They often take themes from earlier writers and are set in Athens, sometimes classical Athens with antiquarian details carefully sketched in. When he turns to satirical dialogue it is Plato and Old Comedy that he proclaims as his principal models. It would not have been hard to guess, if Lucian had not told us, that he started his literary career as a practising sophist and commanded high fees.[19]

The same phenomenon appears in some of the minor genres which the sophists, self-appointed experts in all branches of literary activity, did not hesitate to cultivate. In epistolography, for example, Alciphron's letters are set in Athens of the fourth century B.C., made amply clear by choice of names and local descriptions. The erotic novel is less helpful, for its stereotyped plot demanded fantastic adventures little conducive to a precise historical setting ancient or modern. Chariton, however, writing in the first or second century A.D., set his romance explicitly in the fifth century B.C. Longus's *Daphnis and Chloe* (? late second century A.D.) shows the same hankering for the primitive and

[18] For classical figures in Seneca's *controversiae* cf. 3. 8 the Olynthians; 6. 5 Iphicrates; 8. 2 Phidias; 9. 1 Miltiades; 10. 5 Parrhasius.

[19] Lucian on imitating Aeschines καὶ ταῦτα ἐν εἰρήνῃ μήτε Φιλίππου ἐπιόντος μήτε Ἀλεξάνδρου ἐπιτάττοντος, *Rhetorum praeceptor*, 10. For his relation to classical Athens, J. Bompaire, *Lucien écrivain* (Paris, 1958) and J. Delz, *Lukians Kenntnis der Athenischen Antiquitäten* (Basel diss., 1947; Fribourg, 1950); Plato and comedy as models Lucian, *Bis accusatus*, 32.

'unspoilt' life of the Greek countryside (now considerably affected by imperial estates) that we find in Dio of Prusa's *Euboean Tale* and in Herodes Atticus's cultivation of the rustic Agathion.[20]

The most illuminating genre, however, is that of historiography, likewise attempted by sophists, but reaching greater heights in other hands. To this I shall now turn.

HISTORIANS

A valuable commentary on the mentality of an age is usually to be found in the sort of history it chooses to write and read and the manner in which the chosen themes are treated. In attempting to apply this criterion to the Greek world of the second sophistic we are fortunate in possessing substantial proportions of Arrian and Appian from the second century and of Cassius Dio and Herodian from the early third century. We have also a wealth of historical biography in Plutarch and a representative of antiquarian literature in Pausanias. But the material that has been preserved is only a small proportion of what was written. Little value could attach to analysis of it alone, and some attempt must be made to assess such tendencies as can be detected in the mass of lost historiography. On much of it our only information is late (often the tenth-century Suda lexicon) and sometimes adds imprecision to dubious reliability. Accordingly any reconstruction of the general pattern of historiography is precarious. It must be checked against the behaviour of the better documented writers who have survived. I shall therefore follow a general and in many ways superficial conspectus with a closer examination of one writer, Arrian, who will be found to exemplify several of the proclivities observable elsewhere. At the same time I shall try to guarantee the soundness of the general conspectus by working as far as possible from those writers of whom there are considerable remains.

[20] See below, p. 197. For Alciphron see the Loeb edition of *Alciphron, Aelian and Philostratus' Letters* (1949), ed. A. R. Benner and F. H. Forbes (with a discussion of the vexed question of date). Dio's Εὐβοικὸs (*Or.* 7) is in the Loeb volume cited n. 17 above. For the novelists see B. E. Perry, *The Ancient Romances* (California, 1967).

Universal Histories

I shall first consider the writing of 'universal' histories, that is histories covering several nations or empires over a considerable span of time.[21] The consolidation of a world empire by Rome in the first century B.C. had called forth world histories. Nicolaus of Damascus and Diodorus from Agyrion in Sicily had written the first such since Ephorus: Nicolaus had naturally brought it down to his own time; Diodorus put considerable emphasis on the archaic period, but there is no hint that it might have been conceivable to stop there. The historical work of Strabo, although not starting till the Hellenistic period, had the character of a world history and predictably came down to his own time. For Strabo, the contemporary Greek world was vital and interesting, as we can judge from the wealth of biographic notices on his coevals and immediate seniors that he gives us in his geography. Moreover, his positive attitude to the uses of history, that it should be 'of political and public utility',[22] required a knowledge and assumed an interest in the affairs of the recent past. When a writer like Dionysius of Halicarnassus did devote himself exclusively to the past as in the *Roman Antiquities* (they terminated with the first Punic War), it was to the past of the great world power of his time and not to the past of Greece.

Thereafter, for more than a century, the Greek world seems not to have produced histories covering a great span. When they reappear, they are notably different. The difference does not, of course, extend to chronography, for it might be argued that the work of chronographers must, by necessity of the genre, come down to their own time. That had been the course adopted by Apollodorus of Athens and Castor of Rhodes at a time when Greek contemporary history still had vestiges of life, and seems to

---

[21] For categories of Greek historical writing cf. F. Jacoby, 'Über die Entwicklung der griechischen Historiographie', *Klio*, ix (1909), pp. 80–123 (repr. in F. Jacoby, *Abhandlungen zur griechischen Geschichtschreibung*, ed. H. Bloch (Leiden, 1956). Jacoby's collection of the fragments of the Greek historians, *FGH* (Berlin, 1923–) is fundamental to any study of this sort. For Greek historiography in the second and third centuries A.D., see now F. Millar, *op. cit.* (n. 1 above), pp. 14 ff.

[22] Strabo, *Geography*, i. 1. 22–3: πολιτικὸν καὶ δημωφελές. For Strabo's history, Jacoby, *FGH*, no. 91. For Nicolaus *ibid.*, no. 90.

have been followed by the shadowy chronographer Thallos, if chronographer he was (our evidence is not sufficient to be certain that he was not simply an epitomator).[23] It was maintained by Hadrian's freedman Phlegon of Tralles who brought his chronicle entitled *Olympiades* up to the 229th Olympiad (A.D. 137–140). Ominously, however, it has been inferred that the period from Tiberius to Trajan must have been treated very briefly.[24]

The chronographers apart, world history when it reappears in the middle of the second century seems to divide into two categories, each predictable by inference from the times.

One form of treatment metamorphoses world history into Roman history. Thus Appian, handling Hellenistic history from the point of view of Rome's acquisition of provinces.[25] The process has been carried further in the *Roman History* of Cassius Dio of Nicaea and the *Thousand Years* (χιλιετηρίς) of Asinius Quadratus. In the latter case the way in which Roman history is taking over the rôle of world history is particularly clear: Quadratus seems to have equated the first Olympiad (the traditional starting point for Greek historians) with the date of the foundation of Rome (usually set later).[26] Chryseros, a freedman of Marcus Aurelius, seems already to have followed the same technique of centring world around Roman history in his work which came down from the foundation of Rome to his own time.[27] These men were realists, themselves part of the government and contemporary history. Appian of Alexandria held a high position in his native Alexandria, pleaded in the courts at Rome and eventually obtained a procuratorial post under Pius. Cassius Dio's senatorial career carried him to high administrative office and a second consulate under Alexander Severus in 229. They identify with the empire and see Rome as the natural focal point of history.[28]

---

[23] Apollodorus, Jacoby, *FGH*, no. 244. See now R. Pfeiffer, *History of Classical Scholarship* (Oxford, 1968). For Castor, Jacoby, *FGH*, no. 250; Thallos, *ibid.*, no. 256.

[24] Jacoby, *FGH*, no. 257 with his commentary p. 838. Phlegon does, however, seem to have done justice to his own times in his work *On long lives* (περὶ μακροβίων): cf. Schmid-Stählin, *Geschichte der griechischen Literatur*, 6th edn (Munich, 1924), ii. 2, p. 762.

[25] See below, p. 179.

[26] Jacoby, *FGH*, no. 97 commentary, p. 301 (on T 1).

[27] *Ibid.*, no. 96 commentary, p. 300.

[28] Appian's career, culminating only in his old age in some procuratorial

The other approach betrays a different preoccupation of the era. Cephalion, dated by the Suda to the reign of Hadrian, is thus the first Greek known to us to have written a world history since Nicolaus. Significantly, he chooses to end his *Histories* with Alexander of Macedon. They started with Ninus and Semiramis, and their treatment seems to have shared the archaism of the subject: nine books named after the Muses, written in the Ionic dialect, the model being Herodotus. Neither this nor the neglect of the period after Alexander should surprise us in the reign of Hadrian. We know little of the person Cephalion, but the Suda's description of him as *rhetor* and historian and its attribution of rhetorical compositions indicate that we are dealing with a sophist whose attitude to the past will have been predisposed to archaism. Discontent with the present might well have been augmented by the fact that he was writing in exile in Sicily, a datum there is no good reason to doubt.[29]

The work of Jason of Argos, treating Greek history from the earliest times to the fall of Athens in 322 B.C., should also be set in our period. The notice of the Suda has been suspected of running together two different persons, but although there may be a case for suspecting some confusion, the middle of the second century, indicated by the label 'junior to Plutarch of Chaeronea', is precisely the time we should expect such a terminus to be chosen for a Greek history, and the man's very name fits well into contemporary fashion.[30] There is certainly nothing to suggest that Jason was writing in the late fourth or early third century B.C., the only other time when a stopping point of 322 would be natural, so

post, is referred to in his preface: *Appiani Historia Romana*, ed. Viereck-Roos-Gabba (Leipzig, 1962), vol. i, c. 62. Cf. Fronto's request to Pius that Appian should be given such a post: Fronto, ed. C. R. Haines (Loeb Classical Library, 1919), i, p. 262. Appian's identification with the establishment is very clear in his savage attack on philosophers who criticize rulers: *Mithridateius*, 28. 110–11. For Dio's career and attitudes see F. Millar, *A Study of Cassius Dio* (Oxford, 1964), esp. pp. 174–92.

29 For Cephalion see Photius, *Bibliotheca*, 34 a 16, ed. R. Henry (Paris, 1959); Jacoby, *FGH*, no. 93. There is no difficulty in accepting the exile of a *rhetor* by a literary emperor like Hadrian (*pace* Jacoby, *op. cit.*, commentary p. 296): for parallels in Hadrian's behaviour, Bowersock, *op. cit.*, pp. 51 ff.

30 See below, p. 199.

failing positive arguments against it his ascription to the middle of the second century A.D. should stand.[31]

There may be an exception to the tendency to turn world history into Roman history or to stop with Alexander in the consul Aulus Claudius Charax of Pergamum (identification as consul in 147 having now solved the problem of his date).[32] But the title of his work is uncertain (*Greek and Roman History*, or *Greek and Italian History*, seems more likely for his forty books than simply *Greek History*), and although it is clear that there was much material on the early period, its preponderance in our fragments might merely reflect the interests of our excerptors. We have no basis for assessment of his approach to the Hellenistic period, and although his membership of the Roman governing class and his treatment of Augustus and Nero would suggest that he too centred more recent history around Rome, it remains possible that his was a largely Greek history descending nearer to his time than those of the other Greeks we have mentioned. But the uncertainty should keep him out of the reckoning.[33]

Special Periods

When we turn to historians of shorter spans we find a similar neglect of the era after Alexander that is in striking contrast to the interest in Alexander himself. Alexander continued to fascinate throughout the Hellenistic period, while from the early empire we know of works by the *rhetor* Potamon of Mytilene and Apion of Alexandria: the latter, if not the former, will have been a rhetorical rather than historical composition, comparable with those of Plutarch and Dio of Prusa mentioned above.[34] Fragments of a work of more historical nature have been preserved on an Oxyrhynchus papyrus; it must precede the second and may well

[31] Cf. Jacoby, *FGH*, no. 94.

[32] For the new evidence on Charax, C. Habicht, *Istanbuler Mitteilungen*, ix/x (1959/60), pp. 109 ff.

[33] Jacoby, *FGH*, no. 103; Suda *s.v.* Χάραξ (note especially the epigram with its allusions to the early connections of Pergamum with Achilles and Telephus); Schmid-Stählin, *op. cit.*, p. 762.

[34] Above, p. 170. For Potamon, Jacoby, *FGH*, no. 147; Apion, *ibid.*, no. 616.

have been written in the first century A.D.[35]

In the second century Arrian's work on Alexander, the *Anabasis*, stands out for historical and stylistic merit,[36] but it was not alone. We know from Photius's *Bibliotheca* 97a9 f. (Codex 131) of an Alexander-history by one Amyntianus addressed to Marcus Aurelius. It is only a guess that another scrap of material on Alexander, the *fragmentum Sabbaiticum*, belongs to this work—it might equally well be evidence for another. There was also a composition *On the empire of the Macedonians* by the prolific Criton of Pieria, but this man's ascription to the second century A.D., though probable, is not secure.[37]

Interest in the Hellenistic period, on the other hand, is extremely limited after Timagenes of Alexandria, the historian of the Hellenistic monarchies who quarrelled with Augustus and seems to have infused his material with a general hostility to Rome. Plutarch's biographies of Greeks do not, indeed, stop with his *Alexander*, but by far the greater part is drawn from the classical period. Arrian's interest in Alexander led him to follow up the history of the Successors, but for him the work on Alexander was the more significant and had been his constant goal.[38] Appian preserves valuable material on the Hellenistic kingdoms, especially Syria, and an even richer store is likely to have been contained in his lost books on Egypt. But his approach to the history of these monarchies is deliberately Romano-centric (see notably his outline of his method in his preface to the whole history).[39] There is little in all that has been mentioned to suggest a deep interest in the Hellenistic period for its own sake. Only at the beginning of the

---

[35] No. 1798, on which see Jacoby, *FGH*, no. 148.

[36] See below, pp. 191 ff.

[37] Photius is almost our only evidence for Amyntianus' existence. See Jacoby, *FGH*, no. 150. Date, and some details of phraseology in Photius' report, might suggest conscious rivalry with Arrian for which I shall argue elsewhere. The *fragmentum Sabbaiticum* appears as Jacoby, *FGH*, no. 151. Our only evidence for Criton is the Suda article *s.v.*: cf. Jacoby, *FGH*, no. 277.

[38] See below, p. 193.

[39] Timagenes, Jacoby, *FGH*, no. 88: cf. H. Fuchs, *Der geistige Widerstand gegen Rom in der antiken Welt* (1938, repr. Berlin, 1964), pp. 14 ff. On Appian's method see his preface, esp. cc. 58 ff. On the value of the *Syriaca*, E. Gabba, 'Sul libro Siriaco di Appiano', *Rendiconti dell'accademia dei Lincei, Classe Scienze Morali*, 8th ser., xii (1957), pp. 339–51; R. A. Hadley, *Historia*, xviii (1969), pp. 142 ff.

third century with Athenaeus of Naucratis' work *On the kings of Syria* do we return to the theme that attracted Timagenes (the contribution of Syria to the imperial family might be conjectured to be relevant to the renewed interest) and we can guess that it was treated very differently by the dilettante whose antiquarianism produced the *Deipnosophistae* (*Dons at Dinner*).[40]

The attraction for Greeks towards the contemporary history of the mediterranean world seems not to have been much greater. They prefer monographs on particular wars or biographies of emperors. The Roman civil wars were written about until the end of the Augustan period; thereafter it is as likely that interest simply waned as that the subject was felt to be exhausted or perilous. The first century A.D. has left no contemporary history by a Greek until Plutarch's imperial biographies, although the existence of works on the civil wars of 69 is attested by Josephus (whom I exclude as a Jewish writer outside the main Greek tradition).[41] In the second century Trajan's wars produced a *Getica* (*Getic Wars*) by his doctor Statilius Crito—here the element of biography will have been important too—and later Arrian's *Parthica* (*Parthian Wars*), certainly dealing with Trajan's campaign although probably deriving their immediate inspiration from the wars of Verus in the 160s. The Eastern frontier also provided matter for Arrian's *Order of Battle against the Alans*, but this seems to have been nearer to the genre of *commentarii* than to history proper.[42] The same seems likely to have been true of at least some of the men stimulated by Verus's wars, whose approach and methods, if not their real names, are presented with satire and criticism in Lucian's essay *On the writing of history*. Polyaenus, we

[40] Athenaeus refers to his work on Syrian kings in his *Deipnosophistae*, v. 47, p. 211 A–D (see Jacoby, *FGH*, no. 166).

[41] Plutarch wrote biographies of the emperors from Augustus to Vitellius (*Galba* and *Otho* alone survive). Josephus's attack on Greek historians of the Jewish War (*de bello Iudaico*, Book i, preface, esp. cc. 13 ff.) is particularly interesting as blaming the Greeks for belittling a contemporary upheaval of historical significance while preferring to rehash histories of the Medes and Persians. Josephus *contrasts* his work with contemporary Greek trends, although it can be fairly said that his approach and arguments fall squarely within the Greek tradition that goes back to Thucydides, and in excluding him I do not wish to deny that in this sense he does fall in the main Greek tradition. For his references to works on the civil wars, *de bello Iudaico*, iv. 496.

[42] See also below, p. 192.

know, intended to write on the Parthian wars, but the work was never written. The same category of military history should claim Ariston of Pella's book on the Jewish War under Hadrian.[43]

The other genre that showed life was imperial biography. Plutarch's are the only ones to survive, but the philhellenic Hadrian, admirable subject for a Greek writer, provoked much biography or encomium. Philo of Byblos's work *On the reign of Hadrian* was presumably in the former class, as (if it ever existed) the work attributed to Phlegon of Tralles by the author of the *Historia Augusta*; encomia of Hadrian are attested for Aspasius of Byblos and Zenobius. Later Amyntianus, historian of Alexander, wrote parallel lives of Alexander's father Philip and Augustus, and of the Sicilian tyrant Dionysius and Domitian, and the sophist Aelius Antipater wrote a biography of Severus.[44]

But military history and biography are no substitute for contemporary history proper. Such was, of course, contained in the later books of Appian and Cassius Dio, but only with Herodian do we encounter a political history that did not plunge into the past and assume the character of a world history. His span was the sixty years from the death of Marcus in 180 to the accession of Gordian III in 238, his treatment distressingly rhetorical. Like Appian and Dio he saw government service and was writing from a Romano-centric point of view. No Greek seems to have been tempted to write a recent history of the Greek world (as a whole) and *only* the Greek world, nor even a treatment of the empire from the sole point of view of the Greek provinces. Appian's treatment does to a certain extent betray his Eastern and provincial origin,[45] but not so far as to make his work in any sense a history of the *Greek*

---

[43] For T. Statilius Crito see Jacoby, *FGH*, no. 200 and *SEG*, xv. 700. Arrian's *Parthica*, Jacoby, no. 156, frag. 112 ff. and Arrianus, *Opera*, vol. ii, *scripta minova*, ed. Roos-Wirth (Leipzig, 1968). Polyaenus refers in his *Stratagems*, Book viii, preface (dedicated to Marcus and Verus in A.D. 162) to a planned work on the Parthian wars. For Ariston of Pella see Jacoby, *FGH*, no. 201.

[44] Plut., see n. 41; Philo of Byblos, Jacoby, *FGH*, no. 790; Phlegon's work on Hadrian, *Scriptores Historiae Augustae*, *Vita Hadriani*, 16. 1; cf. R. Syme, *Ammianus and the Historia Augusta* (Oxford, 1968), p. 60. On Zenobius and Aspasius, the Suda *s.vv.* Ζηνόβιος and Ἀσπάσιος and Schmid-Stählin, *op. cit.*, pp. 694 and 698. On Amyntianus, above n. 37. On Antipater, Philostratus, *op. cit.*, 2. 24, p. 607.

[45] Cf. above, note 39.

world. There is even less in Cassius Dio to suggest that his treatment is very different from what it would have been had he been of Western origin and writing in Latin.

There is, of course, a simple explanation for this, but it does not dispense us from asking what follows from the situation as regards Greek attitudes to the contemporary world. The explanation is that a history of the Greek provinces such as one might write today—administrative, economic and social—would not have commended itself to a Greek. History, different from antiquarianism, had to deal with politically independent units—cities, kingdoms and empires. The pattern had been established in the fifth century by Herodotus and Thucydides in an age when autonomous powers were thick on the ground. By this criterion, there was no contemporary history of the Greek world to be written. The nearest approach that could be made was treatment of material where the exercise of power and Greek activity coincided: biographies of philhellenic emperors like Hadrian (there would be many benefactions to Greek cities and individuals to record) or the conduct of those wars on the Eastern frontier that saved the Greek cities from Parthian domination. Another possible tack was biographic treatment of those Greeks whom one might credit with political power. One might see Lucian's works on the Stoic philosopher Demonax and the charlatan Peregrinus (published *c.* 170) partly in this light, but it is not their most obvious or important aspect. It is in Philostratus' *Lives of the Sophists* sixty years later that a substitute for a Greek political and cultural history of the recent past is most clearly found. Emphasis is laid equally on sophists' contributions to Greek culture and benefactions to Greek cities and on their high rank and acceptability in Roman governmental circles. Philostratus is writing the nearest thing to a Greek history of the period that could have fitted into the limitations of ancient genres. A similar presentation of Greek cultural history through the biography of a sophist (this time largely fictional) is to be found in his earlier work on Apollonius of Tyana. One might conjecture that the same substitute for Greek history was to be found in his contemporary Cassius Dio's lost biography of Arrian.[46]

[46] On the range of subject matter eligible for Greek historiography see H. Strasburger, *Die Wesensbestimmung der Geschichte durch die antike Geschichtsschreibung* (Weisbaden, 1966), esp. pp. 20 ff. and 27–8, citing

With only biographic approaches open to the student of the contemporary Greek world it is understandable that archaism should affect historiography. The cause is the same that drives contemporary sophists (in some cases the very men who write history) to declaim on fifth- and fourth-century topics instead of tackling the problems of the present. There were problems enough, as is clear from several of the orations of Dio of Prusa as well as many anecdotes in Philostratus,[47] but to a high proportion of cultured Greeks they seemed ultimately petty because autonomy was gone. Cities could, and did, make a show of quarrelling that recalled ancient wars—witness again Dio's Bithynian speeches, and Philostratus' account of the quarrel between Athens and Megara that reflected fifth-century attitudes and the Megarian decree of Pericles.[48] But the decisive factor which would resolve such disagreements was no longer oratory in the *ecclesia* and hoplite warfare but representations to an emperor, his *legatus* or a *proconsul* and the appearance of Roman officialdom.[49] This was not

Tacitus' complaint in *Annals*, 4. 32 and concluding 'Denn im Sinne der Ereignisgeschichte war selbst eine so eminente Erfüllung der Geschichte wie die pax Romana kein ἀξιόλογον: nicht berichtswürdig, ein sozusagen geschichtsleerer Raum'. This of a historian wishing to deal with Rome: the problem facing those who might think of attempting Greek history was even more acute. Dio's biography of Arrian is attested by the Suda, *s.v.* Δίων ὁ Κάσσιος. There is no good reason to doubt this (as F. Millar, *op. cit.* (n. 28), p. 10) or to think that it concentrated on Arrian's administrative career to the exclusion of his intellectual and Hellenic side: cf. G. Wirth, ' Ἀρριανὸς ὁ φιλόσοφος', *Klio*, xli (1963), pp. 221 ff.

[47] Dio's orations 38–51 are witnesses to his political activity in Prusa and other cities of Bithynia, and together with the tenth book of Pliny's letters offer a vivid picture of its political and economic problems. Cf. H. von Arnim, *Leben und Werke des Dio von Prusa* (Berlin, 1898); C. Vielmetti, *Studi Italiani di Filologia Classica*, xviii (1941), pp. 89–108; B. F. Harris, *Bithynia under Trajan* (Auckland, 1964), pp. 17 ff. Anecdotes in which sophists tackle civil strife and sedition: Philostratus, *Lives of the Sophists*, 1. 23, p. 526 (Lollianus); 25, p. 531 (Polemo). Cf. R. MacMullen, *Enemies of the Roman Order* (Harvard, 1967), pp. 187 ff.

[48] Philostratus, *op. cit.*, 1. 24, p. 529.

[49] The clearest statement of this dependent situation (and the pointlessness of trying to ignore it) is by Plutarch, urging the aspiring city politician to avoid giving cause for Roman intervention and to leave the precedents of Marathon, Eurymedon and Plataea to the sophists' lecture halls: *praecepta gerendae reipublicae*, c. 17. 813C–814C, esp.: 'You rule as a subject, over a city set under the jurisdiction of proconsuls, of

the situation that had produced a Pericles or Demosthenes. For a Greek, the paradeigmatic political animal, the contemporary balance of politics was profoundly unsatisfactory. This is what led orators to declaim on the happier days of Marathon and Salamis and historians to forget the period after Alexander. The terminus chosen by Cephalion and Jason of Argos is easily intelligible, as is the paucity of histories of the Hellenistic or Roman period, the latter only by those who could identify with the Roman point of view.

Local History

One field might have been expected to give more scope for expressing attachment to Hellenic ideals, namely local history. Here there was ample room for a description of the early and politically eventful period of the city or nation (πόλις or ἔθνος), and a briefer treatment of the period since Roman domination might be less obviously a mere shadow of the rest. Nevertheless there is much less local history being written than in the Hellenistic period.[50] It is not, indeed, so neglected a field as suggested by Schmid-Stahlin, who connect a resurgence of local feeling with the breaking down of imperial unity towards the end of the third century. Local feeling is clear enough in the second century too (see sophists' predilection for being known by the name of their native town), and there is *some* local history. But what there is divides largely into two classes, one that dealt only with the early period, terminating with the advent of Roman rule, and the other guide-books, describing monuments secular and religious, in

the procurators of Caesar . . . this is not ancient Sardis or that old power of the Lydians. You must keep your robes in check, and cast your eye from the generals' office to the tribunal . . . observing the Roman senators' shoes above your head' (813 D–E). On the meaning of κάλτιοι here, see C. P. Jones, *Plutarch and Rome* (Oxford, 1971), app. II. Cf. Dio of Prusa, *Or.*, 46. 14, warning a rioting crowd of the risk of proconsular intervention; Tac., *Ann.*, 4. 36, recording Cyzicus' loss of *libertas* (A.D. 25) for offences including violence to Roman citizens.

50 Various reasons for this might be advanced—that in some cases a standard work had already been written, or that local historical material was being served up in different sophistic genres like Aelian's *Variae Historiae*. But for the purpose of this paper the possible reasons are less illuminating than the *type* of history that is actually produced.

some cases, no doubt, also with an antiquarian bias. The evidence is admittedly limited, and there are many writers of whose manner of treatment we have as little idea as of the century in which they wrote.[51] But such evidence as we have points to the categorization I suggest.

For Boeotia Plutarch's work *On the festival of statues at Plataea* falls clearly into the guide-book class (*periegesis*) as does that of Amphion of Thespiae *On the shrine of the Muses on Helicon*, if indeed Amphion belongs to the imperial rather than Hellenistic age.[52]

Criton of Pieria, tentatively ascribed to the second century A.D., whose work *On the empire of the Macedonians* has already been mentioned,[53] also wrote some local history: *On Pallene* (Παλληνιακά) and *On Sicily* (Σικελικά). In neither case do we know how far down he came. But other titles in his list of works, *A Periegesis of Syracuse* and *The Foundation of Syracuse*, suggest that the latter at least is likely to have had antiquarian tendencies.[54]

Ephesus was described in a book *On the city of Ephesus* by the same Xenophon who is credited with the erotic novel *Ephesian Tales*: the title suggests periegetic rather than historical treatment, but certainty is impossible.[55] At least, if the man's identity is sound, he is writing in the sophistic period, probably early second century.

An interesting exception to the rule is found in Timogenes of Miletus, if indeed he belongs to this period, as the Suda's label

[51] Examples: Euphemius of Thespiae, *On my country*, Jacoby, *FGH*, no. 386; a work on Cyrene by the sophist Favorinus, apparently accepted by Jacoby, but thought to be a part of the *omnigena historia* by his two recent editors—see A. Barrigazzi, *Favorino di Arelate: Opere* (Florence, 1966), fragment 54; on Samos, a *Chronicle of the Samians* by Potamon of Mytilene (early first century A.D.), Jacoby, *FGH*, no. 147; works on Caria by Apollonius of Aphrodisias (Jacoby, *FGH*, no. 740) and Leon of Alabanda (*ibid.*, 278), probably early imperial.

[52] Plutarch's περὶ τῶν ἐν ταῖς Πλαταιαῖς δαιδάλων is attested only by Euseb., *Praeparatio evangelica*, Book iii and the Lamprias catalogue no. 201; cf. Jacoby, *FGH*, no. 388; cf. his work on the oracle of Trophonius at Lebadeia, the Lamprias catalogue no. 181. Amphion of Thespiae, Jacoby, *FGH*, no. 387.

[53] Above, p. 179.

[54] For Criton, Jacoby, *FGH*, no. 277 (cf. n. 37).

[55] Xenophon is credited with a work on the city of Ephesus by the Suda *s.v.* Ξενοφῶν Ἐφέσιος: cf. Schmid-Stählin, *op. cit.*, p. 810. But for doubts about this man's acquaintance with the city of Ephesus, B. E. Perry, *The Ancient Romances*, p. 170 (following Lavagnini).

'historian and *rhetor*' and ascription of epistles strongly suggest. Timogenes wrote a work in three books *On Heracleia Pontica and its Great Men*, and since the great men of Heracleia distinguished themselves in the cultural rather than the political arena, we seem here to have a local cultural history.[56]

Only conjecture puts three books of *Corinthian Histories* (Κορινθιακά) by one Theseus in the Roman period. The author's name fits the ascription, and what evidence there is suggests that all three books dealt with the archaic period.[57]

Telephus of Pergamum is fortunately securely dated to the Roman period, even if we do not accept the statement of the *Historia Augusta* that he was tutor to the emperor Verus (and there is no particular reason to reject it). Apart from many philological and literary treatises Telephus wrote a *Periegesis of Pergamum*, *On the temple of Augustus at Pergamum*, and five books *On the Pergamene Kings*. The former two works will have been firmly in the guide-book class. The last was clearly historical, and shares with Arrian's work on Bithynia, to which I shall return, the *terminus* of the transition from independent kingdom to Roman *provincia*.[58]

The other great city of the Asian seaboard, Smyrna, found its historian in the primarily medical writer Hermogenes, son of Charidemus, whose literary fertility has been commemorated for us on stone. To seventy-seven medical works he added *A historical essay on Smyrna* in two volumes; a volume on the *sophia* of Homer and another on his birthplace; two on *Asian Settlements* (κτίσεις), four on *Settlements in Europe* and a similar volume for the *Islands*; two geographical volumes and two of stratagems, and a catalogue of (great?) Romans and Smyrnaeans. The approach is that of a scholar, if not a litterateur, and the works on *Settlements* will naturally have concentrated on, if not been limited to, the archaic period of cities' foundations. The catalogue of Romans and Smyrnaeans again suggests cultural history, but the interpretation of this title is ambiguous. We have no independent means of

---

[56] Timogenes, Jacoby, *FGH*, no. 435.

[57] Theseus, *ibid.*, 453. The name does not exclude his being a Corinthian, cf. *SEG*, xi. 77+Add. p. 216, claiming Attic stock. (I owe this reference to Mrs S. C. Humphreys.)

[58] Telephus, Jacoby, *FGH*, no. 505; the *Historia Augusta*, *Verus* 2.5 includes Telephus in a reputable list of tutors. For the reliability of this notice, T. D. Barnes, 'Hadrian and Lucius Verus', *JRS*, lvii (1967), p. 67.

inferring the content of the work on Smyrna, but the author's other antiquarian tendencies would make a work devoted largely to the distant past more probable than any other.[59] Fortunately he can be dated fairly securely, to the middle of the second century, as his interests might anyway have indicated.

Alexandria was the subject of a work addressed to Hadrian by the scholar Nicanor (his chief work was on punctuation, but he also tackled the Homeric catalogue of ships), and another such by Aelius Dios should belong to the same century. We have no indication how they treated the subject.[60]

Already under Augustus, Tarsus had been written up by its distinguished citizen Athenodorus in a work whose only surviving fragment deals with the time of its foundation. Its rival and neighbour Aegae had to wait for the work *On my country* (περὶ τῆς πατρίδος) of the late second-century sophist P. Anteius Antiochus. We have no direct testimony on the content of this history, but it is perhaps relevant that inscriptional evidence for Antiochus' researches shows him to have been interested in the early period that we would label mythical.[61]

The distant past will also have most probably been the content of Claudius Iolaus's *Phoenician History*—the date should be late first century—as of, in the second century, Philo of Byblos's nine books purporting to translate the Phoenician historian of pre-Trojan vintage, Sanchuniathon. A work of Philo on Hadrian has already been mentioned[62] and it is also worth remarking that he produced a monumental encyclopedia of cultural history *On Cities and their Famous Men* in thirty books. A similar but more limited approach is likely for Aspasius of Tyre's work on his native city entitled *On Tyre and its Citizens*, while the more dis-

---

[59] Hermogenes, Jacoby, *FGH*, no. 579; cf. Schmid-Stählin, *op. cit.*, p. 925.

[60] Nicanor, Jacoby, *FGH*, no. 628; Dios, *ibid.*, no. 629. The existence of a political history of Alexandria in the Roman imperial period *in some form* is a strong possibility: it would provide the context for the many fragments of 'pagan martyr acts' that have turned up on papyrus, professing to relate contumacious encounters of leading Alexandrians with Roman officials and emperors. On the problem, H. Musurillo, *The Acts of the Pagan Martyrs* (Oxford, 1954).

[61] Athenodorus, Jacoby, *FGH*, no. 746. Antiochus, *ibid.*, no. 747; Philostratus, *Lives of the Sophists*, 2. 4, p. 586; epigraphic evidence, *Bulletin de Correspondance Hellénique*, xxviii (1904), pp. 421 ff.

[62] Above, p. 181.

tinguished Aspasius of Byblos wrote *On Byblos*, with no further clue to content. The latter certainly, and the former probably, belongs to the second century.[63]

Although in many cases scanty and uninformative on detail, the evidence here assembled suggests that in local history the same avoidance of the more recent past is to be found as was detected in world histories: the exceptions appear to have been periegetic literature (where, as we shall see in Pausanias, there may also have been opportunity for conscious archaism) and cultural histories where Greece could be seen still to be producing great figures who dominated the intellectual world (Greek and Roman alike). The bias is confirmed if we analyse our only full example of periegetic literature to survive and compare two other by-forms of history, collections of stratagems and collections of myths.

Periegesis, Stratagems and Myths

Pausanias's *Periegesis of Greece* displays archaism in both treatment and content. His language is Atticizing, while his turns of phrase recall Herodotus, and the form of his work can be related to early Ionian periegetic literature. His interest in antique local history and mythology and in classical works of art coheres well with the middle of the second century to which he belongs. He was not an Athenian (Magnesia ad Sipylum seems to be his native place, but the problem is not simple) yet he shared contemporary admiration for Attica and not unnaturally starts his periegesis with it.[64]

It is not surprising, then, that he almost completely neglects monuments and dedications later than *c.* 150 B.C. There are indeed references to the benefactions of contemporary philhellenic emperors, Hadrian and Antoninus Pius, but notable monuments of the intervening period are not mentioned, and his list of dedications by Olympic victors stops at the same point. The traditional explanation of the phenomenon throws the chief blame on his sources: he was using writers of the second century B.C. and did not trouble to supplement them by later information. But this

[63] Iolaus, Jacoby, *FGH*, no. 788; Philon, *ibid.*, no. 790; Aspasii, *ibid.*, nos 792 (Byblos) and 793 (Tyre).
[64] On Pausanias cf. Schmid-Stählin, *op. cit.*, pp. 755 ff. For admiration of Attica cf. Paus., i. 17; i. 24. 3; i. 29. 6.

cannot be the whole truth of the matter. His omission of the later period must have been patent to his readership, and both readers and writers must have acquiesced in the neglect. This acquiescence is only intelligible if it was taken for granted that the intervening years were of no interest to a Greek, and their lack of interest was due to the political (rather than cultural) decline that they represented. It is significant for Greek attitudes that the political decline seems to have been allowed to influence the treatment of what was essentially a cultural history. The political and cultural achievements of classical Greece, and particularly Athens, were very closely woven together in the Greek memory of the past, and this may well have fostered the illusion in some that a cultural resurgence would somehow bring with it a restoration of political power and independence. Monarchist though he is, Pausanias cannot help praising the archaic institution of Athenian democracy.[65]

The eight books of *Stratagems* dedicated in 162 to the Emperors Marcus and Verus by the *rhetor* from Macedon, Polyaenus, show the same archaism of style and content. Polyaenus tries, if not always successfully, to Atticize (using dual and optative forms) and he recognizes Homer as the first war correspondent.[66] He concentrates almost entirely on the classical and Hellenistic world of Greece and devotes only the first twenty-five sections of his eighth book to Roman incidents (the remainder being allotted to stratagems involving women!). The latest reference is to the year 43 B.C. It may be that he omits the ensuing two hundred years because he has no easily accessible handbook to turn to, but as in the case of Pausanias, the omission presumes acquiescence on the part of writer and reader in so glaring a lacuna.[67]

The *Bibliotheca* of Apollodorus is in a somewhat different category. The date of its composition is uncertain, but almost all the evidence points to the late first or the second century A.D.

[65] Democracy, Paus., iv. 35. 3. On Pausanias and his sources, cf. Schmid-Stählin, *loc. cit.*

[66] i. pref. 4 f.

[67] On Polyaenus, Schmid-Stählin, *op. cit.*, p. 754. Polyaenus's work *In defence of the assembly of the Macedonians* should not be classified as local history (as Jacoby, *FGH*, no. 739); it is more probably a speech on behalf of the Macedonian *koinon* (so, independently, J. Deininger, *Die Provinziallandtage der römischen Kaiserzeit* (Munich, 1965), pp. 91 n. 8, 95 n. 8).

The subject-matter, a collection of the Greek myths, allows no room for anything other than archaism, so it cannot be taken as evidence of reluctance to treat contemporary events. What is remarkable, however, is that Roman versions of Greek myths, most notably, for example, the foundation of Rome by Aeneas, are entirely absent. It is instructive to quote the reaction of one scholar to this phenomenon, J. G. Frazer, in his introduction to the Loeb edition, 1921:

> From this remarkable silence we can hardly draw any other inference than that the writer was either unaware of the existence of Rome or deliberately resolved to ignore it. He cannot have been unaware of it if he wrote, as is now generally believed, under the Roman Empire. It remains to suppose that, living with the evidence of Roman power all around him, and familiar as he must have been with the claims which the Romans set up to Trojan descent he carefully abstained from noticing these claims, though the mention of them was naturally invited by the scope and tenor of his work. It must be confessed that such an obstinate refusal to recognise the masters of the world is somewhat puzzling, and that it presents a serious difficulty to the now prevalent view that the author was a citizen of the Roman empire. On the other hand it would be intelligible enough if he wrote in some quiet corner of the Greek world at a time when Rome was still a purely Italian power, when rumours of her wars had hardly begun to trickle across the Adriatic, and when Roman sails had not yet shown themselves in the Aegean (p. xii).

There is no possibility of dating the *Bibliotheca* so early as the last whimsical fantasies of Frazer's paragraph would suggest, nor is there any need. Apollodorus's attitude is not puzzling. It supports rather than conflicts with a second-century date. Like many other cultured Greeks of his time the writer liked to forget from time to time the ubiquitous dominance of Rome, and where better to exercise that amnesia than in a work devoted to the safely antique and established Greek myths?[68]

---

[68] On Apollodorus cf. Schmid-Stählin, *op. cit.*, vol. ii. 1, pp. 428 ff.

Arrian

It has been suggested that a general tendency can be detected in historians of the late first and second centuries to turn to themes from the classical age of Greece and neglect the present, a tendency that is present even in men who held high positions in contemporary society. In the person of Arrian of Nicomedia this type of behaviour can be examined more closely and assessed against our not inconsiderable knowledge of the man's life.[69]

Arrian's cultural background in Bithynian Nicomedia and his education, culminating in attendance at the lectures of Epictetus in the first decade of the second century, were undoubtedly Greek. His name, Flavius Arrianus, lacking any Greek *cognomen*, suggests that his family may have been partly of Italian origin; by the end of the century, however, it will have been absorbed into the life of the Greek *polis*. Arrian's entry into imperial service, in which he rose to a consulate (almost certainly a suffect of the year 129) and then was given the important legateship of the large and strategically vital *provincia* of Cappadocia, points to a realistic appraisal of the contemporary world and proved ability in grappling with its problems. There is nothing to confirm, and certain considerations cast in doubt, the later tradition that he was promoted by reason of his literary prominence (*paideia*), the major monuments to which can be securely dated *after* his consulate.

It is clear, however, that his literary interests dated from his youth,[70] and his approach to literary activity seems already to be

[69] A satisfactory study of Arrian is lacking, and the brief sketch given here is an abbreviation of a paper which will be published elsewhere. A. B. Bosworth, *CQ* 22 (1972), pp. 163–85, offering a different chronology, is now fundamental: I cannot agree with his conclusions. The best treatment remains that of E. Schwartz in *RE*, ii (1896), cc. 1230 ff., *Arrianus* (9). See also H. Pelham, *English Historical Review*, xi (1896), pp. 625 ff.; G. Wirth, *Historia*, xiii (1964), pp. 209 ff.; E. Gabba, *RSI*, lxxi (1959) pp. 361–81. The suggestion that his full name was Q. Eppius Flavius Arrianus (*Prosopographia Imperii Romani²*, F 219, followed in *Past and Present*, 1970) is no longer acceptable. A new fragment of an inscription from Delphi (*Fouilles de Delphes*, III. iv, p. 57 n. 294 last line = inv. no. 4961, illustrated Pl. IX: ed. A. Plassart) shows Q. Eppius and Fl. Arrianus to be different persons, and a new inscription from Athens gives his *praenomen* as Aulus or Lucius (D. Peppa-Delmouzou, *AAA* 3 (1970); J. H. Oliver, *GRBS*, xi (1970), pp. 335 ff.); E. Borzz, *AAA* 5 (1972).

[70] *Anabasis*, I. 12. 5, quoted below n. 75.

fixed by the time of his earliest firmly dated work to survive, the *Circumnavigation of the Black Sea*. This takes the ostensible form of a Greek letter to Hadrian that accompanied and covered the same ground as an official (Latin?) report from the legate of Cappadocia to his emperor. The date is early in Arrian's legateship. It is a literary game, and in it Arrian already plays Xenophon, the Athenian whose generalship led the Ten Thousand back across Anatolia to safety and the sea and whose literary skill recorded that achievement and the ways of Socrates in simple and lucid Attic Greek. Xenophon is already the model for Arrian's style and is constantly referred to for comparison or precedent.[71] The form does not in fact correspond with any of Xenophon's works but rather to the Ionian genre of periegesis.

The same game is also being played in the surviving fragment of the slightly later *Order of battle against the Alans*: here Arrian actually refers to himself as Xenophon.[72] In the *Essay on Tactics*, which proclaims its date as the 20th year of Hadrian (136/7) there is fulsome praise of the emperor and the régime, and the impression is given of an attempt to harmonize a love of the Greek past with an involvement in the Greco-Roman present. So far, at least, Arrian's admiration for the classical past has not excluded application to things contemporary, and if in peregrination of Anatolia he kept a text of Xenophon by his side, it did not prevent him from checking the Alans.

We have no evidence of his imperial career being prolonged after his legateship of Cappadocia, and it is a reasonable inference that his political participation was reduced if not abandoned after the death of his friend Hadrian. As his permanent residence Arrian appears to have chosen not Rome, where he might have attended meetings of the senate and influenced policy through less formal channels, but Athens. The main reason for the choice of Athens rather than his native Nicomedia will doubtless have been that other literary people had settled there. After Hadrian's benefactions to the city it might justly be considered the centre of the Greek world. But the cause of this resurgence of culture in Athens

---

[71] *Chs* 1, 2, 11–14, 16, 25.

[72] Arrian, *Expeditio contra Alanos*, 10. 22. The epigraphic evidence is sufficient (cf. *Prosopographia Imperii Romani*[2] F 219) to exclude the suggestion of P. A. Stadter, *GRBS*, viii (1967), pp. 155 ff. that Xenophon was ever part of Arrian's official nomenclature.

and of Hadrian's trend-setting patronage of the Athenians was the city's association with the classical past: this too, and in particular the fact that it was Xenophon's native city, will have determined Arrian's choice. He may have returned to his native Nicomedia to hold a priesthood, but all the evidence suggests that he did not stay there. He became an Athenian citizen, enrolling, like Hadrianus of Tyre about the same time,[73] in a tribe and deme. In 145/6 he held the archonship, and the *Essay on hunting* (κυνηγετικὸς) makes it clear that he regarded Athens as his home.[74] This work also provides one detail which shows the sentimental extremes to which even an intelligent man like Arrian could take his admiration of the past: he named his dogs after those of Xenophon.

Imitation of Xenophon percolates his literary production. First, probably, he turned to writing up the lectures of Epictetus in a manner that might recall Xenophon's *Memorabilia*. Then (but the chronology cannot be firmly established) he published monographs on Dio of Syracuse and Timoleon, now lost: Xenophon's *Agesilaus* will perhaps have been the model. But the *magnum opus* was the work on Alexander, entitled the *Anabasis* to recall Xenophon's account of the march of the Ten Thousand. He stresses that it has been important to him from his youth, and values it higher than his birth and successful political career: 'But this I wish to record, that to me this work represents my country and my family and my public offices, and has done right from my youth. And on this account I think myself not unworthy of the first rank in Greek letters, just indeed as Alexander was first in military achievement.'[75]

The *Anabasis* was almost certainly published early in the reign of Marcus, in the first half of the 160s, and may have owed some of its inspiration to Trajan's wars in Arrian's youth and to Arrian's own experience on Rome's Eastern frontier. But the primary inspiration is Alexander himself and the absence of a great work on him *in the classical tradition*. This is made clear by the preface. The title, division into seven books and constant stylistic echo remind

[73] Philostratus, *Lives of the Sophists*, 2. 10, p. 588; cf. M. Woloch, *Historia*, xviii (1969), pp. 503 ff.

[74] See especially *ch.* 5.

[75] ἀλλ᾽ ἐκεῖνο ἀναγράφω, ὅτι ἐμοὶ πατρίς τε καὶ γένος καὶ ἀρχαὶ οἵδε οἱ λόγοι εἰσί τε καὶ ἀπὸ νέου ἔτι ἐγένοντο. καὶ ἐπὶ τῷδε οὐκ ἀπαξιῶ ἐμαυτὸν τῶν πρώτων τῶν ἐν τῇ φωνῇ τῇ Ἑλλάδι, εἴπερ οὖν καὶ Ἀλέξανδρος τῶν ἐν τοῖς ὅπλοις; *Anabasis*, 1. 12. 5.

us of Arrian's rôle as the 'new Xenophon'. Arrian did not completely lose interest in the present, as is clear from his publication (probably after the *Anabasis*) of a *Parthian history* which gave considerable space to Trajan's Parthian wars. But he makes little concession to the present in his *Anabasis*[76] and it may be thought characteristic that he gives his dates not in the universally accepted and intelligible system of Olympiads but in Athenian archon years.

His native Bithynia was not entirely neglected, and he dedicated a work on it (*Bithyniaca*) to Nicomedia. Here, as has already been mentioned, we know that he did not come beyond the creation of the Roman *provincia*[77] on Nicomedes' death in 75 B.C. In Arrian's case we know enough of the man to understand why. It is not that he disapproved of the Roman empire, but that he admired the Greek past which could exhibit great men and great deeds. Such could not be exampled when autonomy was lost.

The case of Arrian gives life and body to the skeletal picture of historiographic trends. It is clear that there is an archaism much deeper than that of style which governs the choice of Attic or Ionic dialect, an archaism that influences subject and treatment. It involves an emphasis on the classical period down to Alexander and neglect of the period of Roman dominion that can be paralleled in the preferred topics of the sophists. In the case of the historians it cannot be the product of stylistic considerations alone: writers who wished to Atticize could easily clothe the events of the present in the vocabulary of the past, as did some satirized by Lucian in his essay on the writing of history. To a certain extent the archaistic tendencies must be taken as a flight from the present. With the autonomy of Greek cities only nominal those Greeks who felt that in a different age they might have wielded political power in a Greek context must needs be dissatisfied with the present and attempt to convert it to the past where their ideal world lay. In at least one case, that of Aristides (whose feelings of inadequacy were particularly strong), the escape to the past could take the form of dreaming one was conversing with its great figures. For others the illusion that the past was still with them might be more easily maintained if subscribed to by a sub-

---

[76] There are some few references to Roman things: *Anabasis*, 3. 5. 7; 5. 7. 2; 7. 15. 5.

[77] Photius, *Bibliotheca*, Cod. 93.

stantial group of people in a suitably evocative environment such as that of Athens.

ATHENS AND RE-CREATION OF THE PAST

Admiration of the past went together with admiration of Athens. It was classical Athens that had produced most leading writers, and if Athenians had not been the only great statesmen, at least they had got the best press. When Hellenic culture spread over the Eastern Mediterranean in the wake of Alexander its exponents looked backwards towards Athens, historically as well as geographically. In Athens itself the attitude can be traced at least to fourth-century regret for the loss of the Athenian empire of the fifth century, and Demosthenes is one of the first witnesses to a nostalgia of which he was later to become one of the prime objects. Attic local history had been written up as early as any, but with the Hellenistic interest in Attic literature it took a new turn. Initially to help elucidate Attic writers, then for its own sake, Attic local history (particularly of the antiquarian variety) received more attention, more continuously, than the history of any other Greek city. The same scholars produced Attic lexicography and Attic local history. Istrus, pupil of Callimachus, produced both a work on Athens (Ἀττικά) and a work on Attic phrases (Ἀττικαὶ λέξεις).[78] The grammarian Nicander of Thyateira wrote both on the demes of Attica and *A Guide to the Attic dialect*. Crates, an Athenian, wrote *On sacrifices at Athens* and *On the Attic dialect*. The wide range of Polemon of Ilium covered both literature and antiquities, though markedly biased towards the latter. Not all subjects were as dry and antique as the law tables (*axones*) of Solon. A persistent fascination produced works by at least five scholars *On Athenian courtesans*. For those interested in Athens's past a study of the *Realien* went together with study of the literature and language. Likewise in the second century the local antiquities of Attica are vigorously studied by literary historians. Telephus of Pergamum[79] added to his considerable volume of writings on literary matters a work *On Athenian law courts* and one *On Athenian laws and customs*. Aristomenes, himself an Athenian,

[78] Istrus, Jacoby, *FGH*, no. 334; cf. Pfeiffer, *A History of Classical Scholarship*, pp. 150 ff.
[79] Cf. above, p. 186.

freedman 'of the most cultured monarch Hadrian, called by him Attic-partridge', wrote a work *On rituals* (πρὸς ἱερουργίας).[80] Athens attracted the attention of such antiquarian works to a greater degree than any other city of the Greek world.

The primacy of Athens was clear even to orators from Asia. In the Panathenaic oration Aelius Aristides of Hadrianoutherae and Smyrna praises Athens as the creator and centre of an empire of culture that embraces the whole world. The praise is directed at and delivered to contemporary Athenians, although of course in his catalogue of their political achievements Aristides stops at Chaeronea. There is a similar praise of Athenian culture in Lucian's *Nigrinus*, and it is worth mentioning in this context that many of Lucian's dialogues are explicitly set in Athens, a feature that ought not to be taken as evidence that they were composed or recited there. For Philostratus the Athenian youth is the arbiter of literary elegance, and he regarded Hadrianus of Tyre as sailing very near the wind when in his inaugural lecture after election to the Athenian chair of rhetoric he talked not of the Athenians' accomplishment but his own, beginning 'Once more letters come from Phoenicia'.[81]

There can be no doubt that, intellectually at least, Athens in the second century was swinging. Material prosperity followed, aided by the benefactions of Herodes Atticus and Hadrian. When the temple of Olympian Zeus was finally dedicated in 131 (it had been begun by Peisistratus) and religious processions and festivals were being maintained in archaic splendour, as both Philostratus and inscriptional evidence attest, one might well believe that the glories of the fifth and fourth centuries B.C. were returning and that Athens was once more mistress of the civilized world. One can document the sort of exaggeration that must have been rife in Athens of the second century by reference to Philostratus' remark in the *Lives of the Sophists* that two of Herodes Atticus' buildings in Athens, the stadium and odeon, were without equals in the Roman empire.[82]

---

[80] Nicander, Jacoby, *FGH*, no. 343; Crates, *ibid.*, no. 362; Poseidonius of Olbia, *ibid.*, no. 279, Melito, *ibid.*, no. 345 and Telephanes, *ibid.*, no. 371 also contributed to Attic local history. Hadrian's pun against Aristomenes, Ἀττικοπέρδιξ, does not lend itself to translation (Athenaeus, 115B).
[81] *Lives of the Sophists*, 2. 10, pp. 586–7.
[82] *Ibid.*, 2. 1, p. 551: δύο μὲν δὴ ταῦτα Ἀθήνησιν, α οὐχ ἑτέρωθι τῆς ὑπὸ

One motive for such exaggeration was the real state of affairs, that Athens was of no political importance whatever. Athenians tried to re-live the glorious past by quarrelling with Megara, so that the Megarians refused to admit the Athenians to the lesser Pythian games and the conciliatory activity of the sophist Marcus of Byzantium was required to put matters right.[83] The fantasy of the hyper-educated Athenian must have been to walk out into the countryside of Attica and discover that he was in the fifth century. This is virtually what happened to Herodes Atticus. Herodes held communion with an Attic rustic variously called Heracles, Sostratus and Agathion who claimed Marathon as his father and was suspected of being immortal. He lived on a simple, milk-based diet and, as a result of his habitation of the central plain (*mesogeia*) of Attica, preserved a pure speech uncorrupted by foreign elements that must have been the envy of Herodes' Atticizing rivals.[84] The same sort of fantasy is being elaborated when Philostratus makes Apollonius of Tyana in his Eastward travels find a settlement of Eretrians who had been captured in the Persian wars and resettled in Cissia. They even preserve a four-line epigram which the Anthology[85] ascribes to Plato. Another plunge into the distant past is made in Philostratus's *Heroic Tale*. Here a vintner on the Trojan plain is interviewed by the narrator from the city and tells him of his encounters with the ghosts of Homeric heroes, encounters which contribute valuable additions and corrections to Homer's account of Troy.[86]

Ῥωμαίοις—the contrast between Athens and Roman power is conscious and revealing.

[83] *Ibid.*, 1. 24, p. 529, see above p. 183. Compare Tacitus' description of the Athenians (*Ann* ii. 53) as 'highlighting the ancient deeds and words of their countrymen so that their flattery might carry more weight' (*vetera suorum facta dictaque praeferentes quo plus dignitatis adulatio haberet*).

[84] *Ibid.*, 2. 1, pp. 552 f.

[85] 7. 256.

[86] On Lucian's *Nigrinus*, cf. esp. A. Perètti, *Luciano, un intellettuale greco contro Roma* (Florence, 1946) (but cf. the review of A. Momigliano in *RSI*, lx (1948), pp. 430–2). An English translation and commentary on Aelius Aristides' Panathenaic oration is now available in J. H. Oliver, 'The Civilising Power' *TAPS*, lviii. 1 (1968). Philostratus's Eretrians, *Life of Apollonius*, 1. 31; his *Heroicus*, nn. 5 and 17:— the interest in Troy has been connected with Caracalla's sacrifices commemorating the Trojan wars at Ilium in 214 (themselves recalling Alexander — Cassius Dio, lxxvii. 16. 7 with F. Millar, *op. cit.* (cited n. 28), pp. 214 ff.); cf.

Men who could not so easily arrange such trips into the past through literature might at least emphasize their connections with it in life. A descendant of Themistocles, contemporary and fellow pupil of Plutarch with Ammonius, still received the honours due to Themistocles from Magnesia.[87] The sophist Marcus of Byzantium could trace his family to the founder Byzas, son of Poseidon, Herodes Atticus to the Aeacidae.[88] Nor was it only sophists who dragged up such antique connections. In Parium, once within the Lydian sphere of influence, one Tiberius Claudius Ardys derived his line from the Heraclid royal house of Lydia (the date is A.D. 181). More recent but more respectably Hellenic connections were proclaimed in the commemorative stone put up about this time at Otrous in Phrygia to Alexander of Macedon, laying claim to him as 'founder of the city'. It is in this period, too, that Eumeneia (patently, one would have thought, a foundation of the Attalid Eumenes) took to calling itself the city of 'the Achaean Eumeneians' and Blaundos the city of 'the Macedonian Blaundeians'. The fashion recalls Philostratus's occasional reference to the Greeks as 'Achaeans'.[89] Apamea reverted to the pre-Seleucid

K. Münscher, 'Die Philostrate' *Philologus Supplement*, x (1905–7), pp. 500 ff.

[87] Plut., *Life of Themistocles*, 32; cf. for Athenian families *IG*, ii². 3688 (claiming descent from Callimachus — the polemarch at Marathon — and Conon) and *ibid.*, 3679 (a Iunia Themistocleia, claiming descent from Pericles, Conon and Alexander the Great), both after 200. (I owe this reference to Dr J. K. Davies.) Plutarch also knew of a sole surviving descendant of Brasidas under Augustus who was saved from imprisonment by his ancestry (he referred Augustus to Brasidas's achievements as recorded by Thucydides: *Mor.*, 207F). Cf. also *SEG*, xi. 77 (cited n. 57).

[88] Marcus of Byzantium, Philostratus, *Lives of the Sophists*, 1. 24, p. 538; Herodes, *ibid.*, 2. 1, pp. 545–6.

[89] Ardys, *SEG*, xv. 715; Otrous, W. M. Ramsay, *Cities and Bishoprics of Phrygia*, i (2) (Oxford, 1897), p. 702, n. 638; Eumeneia, *ibid.*, p. 371; Blaundos, *ibid.*, p. 611, n. 514, cf. the appellation of the people of Nacrasa in *IGR*, iv. 1160, 'Macedonian Nacrasites'. Cf. for Pergamum, Suda *s.v.* cited n. 33; Corinth being called by its Homeric name Ephyre *SEG*, xi. 77 (cited n. 57); Ephesus, 'city of Androklos' (its legendary founder), *Anatolian Studies presented to W. H. Buckler* (Manchester, 1939), p. 119. Cf. Cibyra claiming ancestral ties with Athens, *IG*, xiv. 829. 'Achaeans', Philostratus, *Lives of the Sophists*, 1. 21, p. 518. Note also the restoration of its antique name Mantineia to Arcadian Antigoneia, precisely by Hadrian (Paus., viii. 8. 12), and the commemoration of mythical founders on Ionian cities' coinage (*Brit. Mus. Coin. Ionia*,

name by which it was known to readers of Herodotus, Celaenae. Such Hellenism may well have been embarrassing for those cities that had no Hellenic past, and Sebaste in Phrygia was driven to the expedient of commissioning a foundation legend in hexameter verse which attested that Apollo could be credited with the idea of its foundation (normally referred to Augustus).

Whatever one's real claims to be part of the Hellenic past, a good impression could be created by one's name if one had the good fortune to have had archaizing parents. To take Phrygia and adjacent areas of Asia Minor as a sample (and I am aware that without a full statistical survey such a sample may be misleading), here Homeric names become especially popular. It was, after all, the hinterland of Troy. Hence an Achilles from late first-century Hierapolis and another from Traianopolis. There are two instances of Menelaus in Phrygia (about A.D. 200) and one at Asian Ancyra, another at Cyzicus. Idomeneus is also common enough: a group of four in Phrygia and a Sempronius Idomeneus from Mysia. Aeneas is another favourite, attested in Phrygia, Asian Ancyra and Aezani. A Deiphobus appears appropriately at Ilium and elsewhere we have a Troilus and a Bianor. A citizen of Hierapolis names his son and daughter Laomedon and Iphianassa.[90]

The literary record bears out this tendency. We have already encountered a Jason of Argos and a Theseus of Corinth, and Telephus of Pergamum was appropriately named to recall his fellow countryman who was king of Mysia. Nestor of Laranda also belongs to our period. Unfortunately we are not in a position to date securely Amphion of Thespiae,[91] Menelaus of Aegae (writer of a *Thebais*) or the Idomeneus who wrote on Samothrace and the Aeneas who wrote *Samian Histories*. It would be dangerous to assume that they *must* belong to this period, for although it does

---

Ephesus n. 232 Androclos; Miletus n. 197 Meiletos; Magnesia n. 54 Leucophrys; Erythrae n. 228 Erythros).

[90] Sebaste, Ramsay, *op. cit.*, i (2), p. 606, n. 495. Achilles, *ibid.*, i (1), p. 146, n. 33 and *IGR*, iv. 629 — also a gladiator *ibid.*, iv. 511. Menelaus, Ramsay, *op. cit.*, i (1), p. 304, n. 104 and p. 308, n. 117; *IGR*, iv. 555; iv. 154. Idomeneus, Ramsay, *op. cit.*, i (1), p. 155, n. 60; *IGR*, iv. 239. Aeneas, Ramsay, *op. cit.*, i (2), p. 662, n. 622; *IGR*, iv. 555 and 557. Deiphobus, *IGR*, iv. 224. Troilus, Ramsay, *op. cit.*, i (1), p. 156, n. 64. Bianor, *ibid.*, i (2), p. 760, n. 698. Laomedon and Iphianassa, *ibid.*, i (1), p. 146, n. 34.

[91] See above, p. 185.

display an especial penchant for antique names, the phenomenon was present to a certain extent throughout Greek history.

Some people objected to the use of Roman names as inconsistent with evocation of the past, despite the fact that by the late second century the Roman citizenship, and with it Roman nomenclature, had spread throughout the Greek upper classes of the Eastern Mediterranean. Accordingly the historians satirized by Lucian in his essay *How to write history*[92] altered names to give them Greek form, writing Cronios (Κρόνιος) for Saturninus and Phrontis (Φρόντις) for Fronto. Lucian himself does it, introducing himself into his dialogues as Lycinos (Λυκῖνος) instead of Lucianus. It is a feature of Atticism that is hard to dismiss as purely linguistic (like attempts to maintain the dual number) since writers of the classical period had always been ready to admit foreign names. The practice should rather be seen as part of the archaism and Atticism of content. It is part of the same pattern that Philostratus never refers to his sophists by their Roman *nomen*, though in most cases they will have certainly had the Roman citizenship, and in some we can document this from inscriptions which use their formal nomenclature. A positively hostile attitude to Roman names is displayed in the letters ascribed to the wandering sage Apollonius of Tyana: he rebukes Greeks for taking names like Lucullus, Lucretius, Lupercus or Fabricius and condemns this as degeneracy from old Hellenic practice.[93]

We should view in the same light some current attitudes to technical terms firmly embedded in the Roman administration. Here too there is reluctance to use the usually well-attested official Greek vocabulary. Areas of Anatolia are referred to by their old ethnic names—Ionia, Lydia, Caria, Phrygia—although these did not correspond with any contemporary administrative division of *provincia Asia*.[94] Governors become 'satraps' or 'harmosts', and provinces are referred to as 'nations' (ἔθνη) instead of by the technical term *eparcheia* (ἐπαρχεία). Even areas deep in the Latin

---

[92] *Ch.* 21.

[93] Menelaus of Aegae, Jacoby, *FGH*, no. 384; Idomeneus, *ibid.*, no. 547. Hostility to Roman names, *Letters of Apollonius*, 71. 72; cf. *Life of Apollonius*, 4. 5.

[94] E.g. Philostratus, *Lives of the Sophists*, 2. 1, p. 530 and *passim*. There was some substance for referring to Ionia as an entity: cf. J. Deininger, *op. cit.* (cited n. 67), pp. 10 ff., and the term βασιλεὺς τῶν Ἰώνων (cf. *SEG*, xv. 532).

half of the empire keep their Greek names in our literary sources: *Celtica* (Κελτικὴ) for Gallia in Lucian and Appian, and *Iberia* (Ιβηρία) for Hispania; *Eridanos* (Ηριδανὸs) almost universally for the river Po (*Padus*). A whole range of Greek writers (Strabo, Appian, Aelian, Philostratus) perversely refer to Puteoli as Dicaearcheia, although to judge from inscriptions of the period no Greek-speaking trader who called at the port would have known what that name referred to: there the transliteration Ποτίολοι from the Latin *Puteoli* is normal. Likewise Appian refers to Vibo Valentia by its old Greek name Hipponium (Ιππώνιον).[95]

Retention of the old systems of measurement and dating may have contributed to the illusion that the world had not changed since the classical period. *Plethra*, *stadia* and even *parasanges* were preferred to Roman *iugera* and miles, although the latter term in Latin or transliteration (μείλια) must have been familiar to anyone who left his native village and used one of the many roads cut by the Romans through the Greek world.[96] The same bias appears in Atticizing writers over dates. Olympiads were naturally preferred, even if the chronographer Phlegon had synchronized these with Roman consuls. The Athenian bias of Arrian in dating by archons is not typical,[97] but Appian, in giving the equivalences for Roman months, chooses the Attic calendar.[98]

There was much in the paraphernalia of everyday life that must have made this literary behaviour odd. Everywhere Latin inscriptions and Roman coins with Latin legends; Latin spoken in the governors' courts and even in the circle of Fronto, Gellius and Herodes in Athens. Some Greeks did read Latin writers in the original; for others there were translations, among these Vergil

---

[95] Satrap, Philostratus, *Lives of the Sophists*, 1. 22, p. 524; cf. Dio of Prusa, *Or.*, 33. 14; Lucian, *Nigrinus*, 20. Harmost, *ibid.*, *Toxaris*, 17 (cf. for the same words, though not of Roman governors, Dio of Prusa *Or.*, 30. 27; Appian, *Bell. Civ.*, 4. 5). ἔθνη, e.g. Lucian, *Alexander*, 9. Dicaearcheia, Strabo, ii. 3. 4, p. 99C etc.; Appian, *Bell. Civ.*, 5. 50; Aelian, *de nat. animal.*, 2. 56; Philostratus, *Life of Apollonius*, 7. 10. Ποτίολοι, *IG*, xiv. 830, 1102, 1114. Hipponium, Appian, *Bell. Civ.*, 5. 91. On technical terms of Roman administration in Greek writers see now the valuable article of H. J. Mason, 'Roman government in Greek sources', *Phoenix*, xxiv (1970), pp. 150–9.

[96] *Plethra*, Aelian, *Var. Hist.*, 3. 1; *stadia*, Cassius Dio, lii. 21. 2; *parassangae*, Arrian, *Anabasis*, i. 4. 4.

[97] See above, p. 194.

[98] Appian, *Bell. Civ.*, 2. 149.

and Sallust. The architectural style of the period was undeniably a synthesis in which the Roman elements were often as obvious as the Greek. Of Herodes Atticus' great buildings in Athens his odeon was in many respects a Roman building and could not, as the stadium might, have recalled the age of Critias whom his oratory imitated.[99]

There are, however, instances of archaism in architecture in imperial Athens, and in other features of daily life the archaizing spirit will have been more in evidence. The statues that decorated private and public buildings drew their themes and styles more from classical than Hellenistic sculpture or were actually copies of classical masterpieces. The same preference is clear in literary references to sculptors. The Zeus of Pheidias was the focal point of Dio of Prusa's *Olympian Speech* (*Oration* 12) and Pheidias, Myron and Polycletus are frequently taken as examples of sculptors in Lucian. This archaism in sculpture is often argued to start considerably before our period, beginning about the middle of the second century B.C., and has been connected by art historians with Roman preferences as much as Greek. But it is interesting that the mid-second century A.D. is associated with a tendency to imitate the details of classical models with pedantic accuracy. Painting has a similar 'Philhellenic' phase.[100]

There is archaism in the lettering of commemorative inscriptions too. The practice can be documented as far back as Augustan Athens, but the greater number of examples are Hadrianic or shortly after, and can in several cases be associated with Herodes Atticus. It is a superficial sort of archaism, like wearing the beard

---

[99] Still fundamental on the Greeks' attitudes to Latin is L. Hahn, 'Der Sprachenkampf im römischen Reich', *Philologus Supplement*, x (1905–7), pp. 677 ff. The *extent* to which Greek writers were familiar with Latin cannot be discussed here: but most knew at least the technical terms necessary to their subject. Translation of Vergil's *Georgics*, Suda *s.v.* Αρριανὸς ἐποποιός; of Sall., *ibid.*, *s.v.* Ζηνόβιος; Odeon of Herodes, cf. D. S. Robertson, *Greek and Roman Architecture*, 2nd edn (Cambridge, 1959), p. 276; P. Graindor, *Hérode Atticus et sa famille* (Cairo, 1930), p. 218 (bibliog., n. 5).

[100] On classicism in second-century A.D. sculpture, see now A. Carandini, *Vibia Sabina* (Florence, 1969). Against the view that it is manifest in the first centuries B.C. and A.D., G. M. A. Richter, *JRS*, xlviii (1958). For painting cf. F. Wirth's 'Philhellenic style' in *Römische Wandmalerei* (Berlin, 1934).

or the himation, but taken together such fashions give some indication of the range of the period's archaistic tendencies.

It is also, of course, the case that a high proportion of the serious reading matter of a cultivated Greek in the second century was drawn from the great classics. This is no new phenomenon, though to judge from the papyrus finds the second century is the great age of literacy, and more classical authors can be shown to be read in this than in any other period. Comparison of the papyrus finds and quotations in second-century writers also shows that the reading pattern of the people of (for example) Oxyrhyncus and the sophists and essayists like Dio, Plutarch, Lucian was very much the same, and the classical favourites were ranged in very much the same order by both. This is worth emphasizing because it is sometimes suggested that the readers of Oxyrhyncus were abnormal in their preference for (for example) the Greek lyric poets (who were difficult and had to be read with commentaries) or indeed that the second century neglected the reading of poetry. Neither of these suggestions is true.[101]

CONCLUSIONS

The evidence presented has shown that in the sophistic period certain elements in the Greek world showed a marked tendency to adopt the conventions and attitudes of the past over a wide spectrum of activities. Are the Greeks of this period behaving differently from their predecessors in any significant degree or manner? And if so, why?

In the matter of archaism in language and literary style (usually

[101] For archaic letter forms see W. Larfeld, *Handbuch der griechischen Epigraphik* (Leipzig, 1902–7), ii. 487 ff. Note especially the use of the pre-Euclides Attic alphabet in *IG*, xiv. 1390 (Triopeum of Herodes Atticus on Via Appia, c. A.D. 161); i². 865 (has been linked with Atticus); ii². 3380, 5004; *Deltion*, 1885, p. 125, n. 9; *Hesperia*, xxxvii (1968), p. 292, n. 35 and plate 84. For Augustan examples of archaic letter forms (but not of pre-Euclides alphabet), *IG*, ii². 1040, 1070, 3173. There is not space here to present a full analysis of the reading habits of the second sophistic as attested both by papyri and by authors' allusions and quotations. For the papyri see now W. H. Willis, *GRBS*, ix (1968), pp. 205–41; for Plutarch cf. W. C. Helmbold and E. N. O'Neil, *Plutarch's Quotations* (Baltimore, 1959); for Lucian, F. W. Householder, *Literary Allusion and Quotation in Lucian* (Columbia, 1941). For a curious contention that the second century neglected poetry, P. De Lacy, 'Galen and the Greek poets', *GRBS*, vii (1966), pp. 259 ff.

called Atticism) the writers of this period are not breaking any completely new ground. Since Attic writers had first been studied by Alexandrian scholars and then, by the second century B.C., been taken as models for style, linguistic Atticism had been a force of varying intensity in literature and oratory. At all times this literary archaism was more extreme and far-reaching than archaism in other fields. A considerable part of the credit or blame is due to the Greek system of education, which not only prescribed the reading of classical authors but involved imitation of them in the course of training rhetoric. Not all the contributory factors need have been internal: in particular Dionysius of Halicarnassus (in the first century B.C.) indicates that the contemporary interest in the Attic orators was a reflection of Roman taste (though in assessing this assertion due allowance should be made for its being a compliment to his patrons). If we were dealing with evidence of linguistic archaism alone we might argue that the situation in the second century is simply a predictable continuation of a previously detectable tendency, and that the Atticizing writers and Attic lexica of the second century were the intelligible consequence of a cumulative literary orientation to the past: after many generations of education on a fare of Attic classics it had become natural to apply their terminology and conventions to everyday language.

But it is clear from the examination of oratory and historiography that a wider archaism, that of theme, is at work. Although the choice of classical themes in oratory can be associated with the selection of classical orators as models for style, and can be documented before our period,[102] rhetoric cannot alone be the explanation of historians' attraction to classical themes. Some historians were indeed rhetoricians, but others, like Arrian, were not, and showed by their careers that they were practical men fully aware of contemporary realities. A further explanation is required for the archaism of theme in second-century historians and for the archaizing behaviour in other areas, which in its extreme forms seems to be an attempt to pretend that the past is still present. If such an explanation is required, it must be considered whether it does not also explain the intensification of linguistic archaism in literature. Rather than seeing the linguistic archaism as a product of internal literary developments running in parallel

[102] Cf. Seneca's *suasoriae*, above p. 173.

with the other manifestations of archaism, or than the more probable and general view that these manifestations are by-products of the linguistic developments, we ought perhaps to see this literary situation as only a part of the wider pattern of cultural archaism, not causing it but being itself a part of the consequences of other factors.

What are these factors? It would not be enough to adduce the tastes of an individual, for example Herodes Atticus (whom Schmid made responsible for intensification of linguistic Atticism and for a general resurgence of interest in the Hellenic past[103]) or Hadrian (whose archaism and influence on the Greeks were both very marked). One would still have to explain why the individual's tastes were what they were, and why the individual succeeded in communicating them to a large section of the Greek upper classes: in each case the historical background would be relevant. Moreover the particular cases of Hadrian and Herodes are unsatisfactory because the tendency already seems to be in evidence before they can have influenced it.

The political situation of the Greek aristocracies in the period seems to offer an answer. On two related levels their power was constricted by comparison with their memorable forbears. Within the cities they were still dominant—more so, indeed, than under the democratic régimes that had characterized Athens and other Greek cities in the fifth and fourth centuries. But that dominance was, for each individual, precarious and dependent, dependent not on persuading their fellow citizens to elect them to public office or exempt them from compulsory liturgy, but on the ultimate decision of a governor or emperor. A wrong move, and their estates might be confiscated and their persons banished, while a rival, securing his advancement by well-timed delation or prosecution, took over primacy in the *polis*. Such incidents are documented for Dio's Bithynia, and Hipparchus, grandfather of Herodes Atticus, lost his patrimony in this way; and other instances can be inferred.[104] The late first century saw the beginning of ever-increasing interference by the imperial government

---

[103] Schmid, *op. cit.*, i, pp. 192 ff.
[104] For Hipparchus, P. Graindor, *op. cit.*, pp. 11 ff.; J. H. Oliver, 'The ruling power', *TAPS*, xliii. 4 (1953), pp. 960 ff. Cf. Herodes Atticus' own feuds with opponents in Athens, discussed by Bowersock, *op. cit.*, pp. 92–100, concluding: 'There can be no undervaluing the fact that the

in the internal administrative (and particularly financial) affairs of the Greek cities, a process that began with *ad hoc* appointments and ended with a permanent office of *curator*. It is perhaps no accident that the first evidence for these officials appears in the *Life* of Philostratus's earliest imperial sophist, Nicetes of Smyrna.[105]

The same applied on the level of inter-city disputes. Cities, whatever their honorific titles, were no longer free to settle their quarrels in the manner exhorted by their leading politicians. Rivalry was all the more intense for its having no natural outcome of battle that might settle claims of primacy: instead it was directed into channels of competitive munificence, financially ruinous to city and individual aristocrat alike, or into embassies seeking privileges and titles from governors and emperors. In all these areas sophists could exercise their influence and talents, but addresses to a crowd angry with a neighbour and rival city had to be conciliatory, not allowing it to be forgotten that sedition or tumult would simply invite the intervention of Rome, and the more lasting consequence would be a loss of the city's privileges and honours.[106]

It might be objected that these had been the circumstances ever since the Greek cities had passed under Roman dominion. Why then should the situation precipitate nostalgia for the past in the latter part of the first century, and not earlier? Moreover, was not the period under discussion precisely that in which upper-class Greeks began to move closer than ever to the corridors of imperial power, gaining admission to the Roman senate in ever-increasing numbers and advancing to high places in the equestrian service, or often exercising even greater power through the status of emperor's friend?

Athenian disputes of Herodes were ultimately settled on the banks of the Danube by the emperor Marcus'. (For new documentation of this, see now *Hesperia*, supp. xiii.) For attempts to expose Dio to perilous prosecution by his opponents in Prusa, Pliny, *Epist.*, x. 81; for attempts to use the régime against his opponent Archippus (one of which appears to have been successful), *ibid.*, x. 58.

[105] *Lives of the Sophists*, 1. 19, p. 512.

[106] See the evidence cited n. 49. On *curatores* and imperial encroachment on city administration see *CAH*, xi (Cambridge, 1936), pp. 218 ff. and 467 ff. (but the dating of the *logistes* in Philostratus, *Lives of the Sophists*, 1. 19, p. 512 to Nerva is dubious: manuscripts are divided between *Nerva* and *Nero*).

There are, however, significant differences between the situation in, say, the first century B.C. and in the late first century A.D. Roman control of the Eastern Mediterranean was only finally consolidated by the battle of Actium and annexation of Ptolemaic Egypt. Until then there was hope that the invader might be dislodged: early in the century Mithridates could successfully pose as liberator of the Greeks, and the alliance of Antonius with the Ptolemies offered more prospect of a Greek empire than did Augustus. Oracles circulated predicting the fall and punishment of Rome.

By the time, under Augustus, it had become clear that the Roman empire was there to stay, Greece and much of Asia Minor were exhausted by the ravages and exactions of the Mithridatic followed by the Roman civil wars. Mainland Greece was particularly badly off (Strabo's descriptions are full of evidence for an economic nadir) and Athens had still not recovered from Sulla's campaign against Mithridates. It would have required immense delusions to imagine that the Greek cities were eligible for greatness commensurate with that of their past.

In time, however, the security of the *Pax Augusta* had its effect. From exploitation of land and trade wealth poured into the city aristocracies, and from them, by the traditional channels of aristocratic munificence, into the cities. The prosperity was particularly marked in the great cities of Asia Minor, the centres of the sophistic movement, and externally, at least, they possessed all the material constituents of grandeur. Such eminence can only have aggravated the absence of political power that would formerly have gone with it. It was no longer absurd to remember the great days of fifth-century Greece and imagine that they were but a step away from the present. Athens, too, was once more flourishing, and when the emperor Nero toured mainland Greece its cities will have received encouragement to recall their past glories that was, in their case, less justified by their economic situation. Nero's culminating act of declaring the cities of the Greeks free (though it applied only to mainland Greece) not only secured for him vast popularity but must have provided an additional impetus to those who were inclined to meditate on the splendours of the past in preference to the realities of the present, realities that rapidly became all to obvious when Vespasian cancelled the grant of 'freedom'.[107]

[107] For Mithridates and anti-Roman oracles cf. H. Fuchs, *op. cit.* (cited

In some ways, it is true, the admission of Greeks to the senate and equestrian service will have helped the situation. Men of genius like Arrian were able to exercise as much power in the emperor's service as they could have done in an independent Bithynia. But the numbers of Greek aristocrats thus honoured were never large (and many listed as 'oriental senators' turn out to be descended from Italian families settled in the East, as perhaps Arrian himself). It was not possible for all to achieve prominence in this way, and anyway some will have preferred to honour the traditional obligations to their *polis* and put their persons and wealth at its disposal and not the empire's.[108]

Furthermore, the emperor's service was still the service of Rome, however Philhellenic the emperor might be. In the international Greco-Roman aristocracy comparisons between the achievements of Greece and Rome will naturally have arisen, and it will have been fairly maintained that Roman political and administrative skill, attested by its product the empire, was pre-eminent and unexampled. The Greeks could make a counter-claim to an equally far-flung empire of culture, as does Aristides for Athens in his Panathenaic oration.[109] But ancient aristocracies thought primarily in terms of political life. To reassure themselves

n. 39), pp. 7 ff. and 16 ff. (with notes). For the economic state of Greece in the principate, U. Kahrstedt, *Das Wirtschaftliche Gesicht Griechenlands in der Kaiserzeit* (Bern, 1954); for Athens, P. Graindor, *Athènes sous Auguste* (Cairo, 1927); *Athènes de Tibère à Trajan* (Cairo, 1931); *Athènes sous Hadrien* (Cairo, 1934); for Asia, esp. A. Boulanger, *Aelius Aristide* (Paris, 1923); for Bithynia, E. Gren, *Kleinasien und der Ostbalkan in der wirtschaftlichen Entwicklung der römischen Kaiserzeit* (Uppsala, 1941). For the impression made on the Greeks by Nero's grant of freedom cf. esp. Plut., *Mor.*, 567F–568A. Cf. already a restoration of ancient games (τὸ ἀνανεώσασθαι τὴν ἀρχαιότητα τοῦ ἀγῶνος) at Acraephia in the mid-first century A.D. by a benefactor named Epaminondas: *IG*, vii. 2712 esp. l. 56 ff.

108 For Italian families in the East rising to prominence cf. B. M. Levick, *JRS*, xlviii (1958) and *Roman Colonies in Southern Asia Minor* (Oxford, 1967); R. Syme, *Colonial Élites* (Oxford, 1958); F. Millar, *op. cit.* (n. 28), pp. 184–5.

109 Aristides in the Roman Oration (26 Keil: translation and commentary by J. H. Oliver, in *The Ruling Power*, cited n. 104) and the Panathenaic Oration (cf. above, n. 86) puts the case for each empire with equal fluency and (*mutatis mutandis*) the same arguments. Cf. Plutarch's essay *On the fortune of the Romans* (*Mor.*, 316C ff.), c. 13; Livy, ix. 17–19 for comparison between the achievements of Rome and Alexander.

that Greece had a claim comparable to that of Rome, they began to dwell more and more, in their principal cultural activities, on the political greatness of the past. Sometimes the reaction took the extreme form of anti-Roman sentiments, on occasion with Atticist overtones, as in the letter of Apollonius of Tyana objecting to the use of Roman names, more often directly political, as in another letter of his criticizing the régime, or in the *Acts of the Pagan Martyrs* from Alexandria, the Greek city most recently imperial. The tedious present could be compared adversely to the greatness of Greece, as by the philosopher Lucius who criticized the emperor Marcus for attending philosophy lectures into his old age, whereas 'my king Alexander died at thirty-two'.[110] Most often, however, the past was resorted to as an alternative to rather than an explicit reflection on the present, for most Greeks were in no real sense *anti*-Roman, and their absorption in the Greek past *complemented* their acquiescence in the politically defective Roman present. By re-creating the situations of the past the contrast between the immense prosperity and the distressing dependence of the contemporary Greek world was dulled, and a man like Arrian could think of his Athenian archonship and his work on Alexander as of equal importance with his Roman career.[111]

[110] Apollonius on Roman names, *Epist.*, 71, 72; criticizing the administration, *ibid.*, 30. 31. 54. For *Acts of the Pagan Martyrs*, cf. above n. 60. The remark of Lucius, Philostratus, *Lives of the Sophists*, 2. 1, p. 557; cf. Appian, preface, 39 applying the expression 'my kings' to the Ptolemies. On the whole question of anti-Roman sentiments, H. Fuchs, *op. cit.* (cited n. 39); R. MacMullen, *op. cit.* (cited n. 47). That the Greeks in the latter half of the third century were to be called upon to defend their cities against barbarians, providing a *real* context for the traditional oratory echoing the fifth century B.C., could not have been foreseen in the Antonine peace (although the rare occasions when similar situations developed — e.g. Arrian repelling the *Alani* — naturally produced echoes of the past). Accordingly the rôle played by recollection of classical greatness in moulding the resistence of the Greek East to third-century invaders and, ultimately, its survival into the Byzantine empire (on which cf. F. Millar, *op. cit.* (n. 1) pp. 28–9) cannot be used to explain late first- and second-century archaism.

[111] Since the first publication of this paper there has appeared the first thorough study of the literature. B. P. Reardon, *Courants littéraires grecs des IIe et IIIe siècles après J.C.* (Paris, 1971). This is now fundamental to an understanding of the age.

IX

WHY WERE THE EARLY CHRISTIANS PERSECUTED?*[1]

G. E. M. de Ste Croix

The persecution of the Christians in the Roman empire has attracted the attention of scholars of many different kinds. The enormous volume of literature on the subject is partly due to the fact that it can be approached from many different directions: it offers a challenge to historians of the Roman empire (especially of its public administration), to Roman lawyers, to ecclesiastical historians, to Christian theologians, and to students of Roman religion and Greek religion. In fact all these approaches are relevant, and they must all be used together.

The question I have taken as a title needs to be broken down in two quite different ways. One is to distinguish between the general population of the Graeco-Roman world and what I am going to call for convenience 'the government': I mean of course the emperor, the senate, the central officials and the provincial governors, the key figures for our purpose being the emperor and even more the provincial governors. In this case we ask first, 'For what reasons did ordinary pagans demand persecution?', and secondly,

* From no. 26 (1963).
[1] This article is a revised version of a paper read to the Joint Meeting of the Hellenic and Roman Societies and the Classical Association at Oxford on 12 August 1961. As I am engaged upon a book on the persecutions, in which the matters discussed here will be treated in greater detail, I have not attempted to supply complete documentation and bibliographies; but I have added a certain number of references. Except when otherwise stated the Passions of the martyrs to which I have referred here can be found in G. Krüger and G. Ruhbach, *Ausgewählte Märtyrerakten*, 4th edn (Tübingen, 1965).

'Why did the government persecute?'. The second way of dividing up our general question is to distinguish the reasons which brought about persecution from the purely legal basis of persecution—the juridical principles and institutions invoked by those who had already made up their minds to take action.

But let us not look at the persecutions entirely from the top, so to speak—from the point of view of the persecutors. Scholars who have dealt with this subject, Roman historians in particular, have with few exceptions paid too little attention to what I might call the underside of the process: persecution as seen by the Christians—in a word, martyrdom, a concept which played a vitally important part in the life of the early Church.[2]

It is convenient to divide the persecutions into three distinct phases. The first ends just before the great fire at Rome in 64; the second begins with the persecution which followed the fire and continues until 250;[3] and the third opens with the persecution under Decius in 250-1 and lasts until 313—or, if we take account of the anti-Christian activities of Licinius in his later years, until the defeat of Licinius by Constantine in 324. We know of no persecution by the Roman government until 64, and there was no general persecution until that of Decius. Between 64 and 250 there were only isolated, local persecutions; and even if the total number of victims was quite considerable (as I think it probably was), most individual outbreaks must usually have been quite brief. Even the general persecution of Decius lasted little more than a year, and the second general persecution, that of Valerian in 257-9, less than three years. The third and last general persecution, by Diocletian and his colleagues from 303 onwards (the so-called 'Great Persecution'), continued for only about two years in the West, although it went on a good deal longer in the East.[4] In the intervals between these general persecutions the situation, in my opinion, remained very much what it had been earlier, except that on the whole the position of the Church was distinctly

[2] See W. H. C. Frend, 'The failure of the persecutions in the Roman empire', chapter II below. 'The persecutions: some links between Judaism and the Early Church', *JEH*, ix (1958), pp. 141–58; 'The Gnostic sects and the Roman empire', *JEH*, v (1954), pp. 25–37.

[3] In fact the persecuting edict was probably issued before the end of 249, but there are no recorded martyrdoms before January 250.

[4] See my 'Aspects of the "Great" persecution', *HTR*, xlvii (1954), pp. 75 ff., at pp. 95–6.

better: there were several local persecutions, but there were also quite long periods during which the Christians enjoyed something like complete peace over most of the empire;[5] and in addition the capacity of the Christian churches to own property was recognized, at least under some emperors. But I agree with Baynes[6] and many others that complete toleration of Christianity was never officially proclaimed before the edict of Galerius in 311.

The subject is a large one, and I cannot afford to spend time on the first phase of persecution (before 64), during which, in so far as it took place at all, persecution was on a small scale and came about mainly as a result of Jewish hostility, which tended to lead to disturbances.[7] After the execution of Jesus, the organs of government come quite well out of it all: their general attitude is one of impartiality or indifference towards the religious squabbles between Jews and Christians. In consequence of riots provoked by Christian missionary preaching, action was sometimes taken by the officials of local communities. But any Christians who were martyred, like Stephen and James 'the Just' (the brother of Jesus),[8] were victims of purely Jewish enmity, which would count for little outside Judaea itself. The Sanhedrin acted *ultra vires* in executing James—and Stephen, if indeed his death was not really a lynching.

I do not intend to give a narrative, even in outline, of the second and third phases of persecution, which I shall mainly deal with together. The earliest stages of intervention on the part of the government, before about 112, are particularly obscure to us. We cannot be certain how and when the government began to take action; but, like many other people, I believe it was in the persecution by Nero at Rome which followed the great fire in 64. The much discussed passage in Tacitus[9] which is our only informative source leaves many problems unsolved, but I can do no more here

[5] Especially from the reign of Gallienus (260–8) to the beginning of the Great Persecution (303).

[6] N. H. Baynes, *CAH*, xii, p. 655.

[7] See Acts 6:8–7:60; 8:1–4; 9:1–2; 12:1–2, 3–19; 13:45, 50–1; 14:2, 4–6, 19–20; 17:5–9, 13–14; 18:12–17; 20:2–3; 21:27 ff. Cf. I Thessal. 2:14–16. Jewish hostility continued, and Tertullian (*Scorp.*, 10) could call the Jewish synagogues 'fontes persecutionis'.

[8] Acts 6:8–7:60 (Stephen); 12:1–3; Jos., *Ant. Jud.*, xx. 9. 1, §§ 197–203; Euseb., *Eccl. Hist.*, ii. 23 (James).

[9] Tac., *Ann.*, xv. 44. 3–8.

than summarize my own views, which agree closely with those
expressed by Professor Beaujeu in his admirable recent monograph
on this persecution.[10] In order to kill the widely believed rumour
that he himself was responsible for starting the fire, Nero falsely
accused and savagely punished the Christians. First, those who
admitted being Christians[11] were prosecuted, and then, on information provided by them (doubtless under torture), a great
multitude were convicted, not so much (according to Tacitus) of
the crime of incendiarism as because of their hatred of the human
race ('odio humani generis').[12] Tacitus, like his friend Pliny and
their contemporary Suetonius,[13] detested the Christians; and
although he did not believe they caused the fire[14] he does say they
were 'hated for their abominations' ('flagitia') and he calls them
'criminals deserving exemplary punishment'.[15] The Christians
were picked on as scapegoats, then, because they were already
believed by the populace to be capable of horrid crimes, *flagitia*:
that is worth noticing. (Had not the Empress Poppaea Sabina been
particularly sympathetic towards the Jews,[16] they might well have
been chosen as the most appropriate scapegoats.) And once the
first batch of Nero's Christian victims had been condemned,
whether on a charge of organised incendiarism or for a wider
'complex of guilt',[17] there would be nothing to prevent the
magistrate conducting the trials (probably the Praefectus Urbi)
from condemning the rest on the charge familiar to us in the second
century, of simply 'being a Christian'—a status which now neces-

---

[10] J. Beaujeu, *L'Incendie de Rome en 64 et les chrétiens* (*Coll. Latomus*, xlix,
Bruxelles, 1960). The other sources are discussed and quoted by L. H.
Canfield, *The Early Persecutions of the Christians* (*Columbia University
Studies in History, Economics and Public Law*, lv, 1913), pp. 43 ff., 141 ff.
A good selective bibliography up to 1934 will be found in *CAH*, x,
982–3.

[11] The imperfect tense, 'qui fatebantur', shows that the confession was one
of Christianity and not of incendiarism.

[12] Tac., *Ann.*, xv. 44. 5. Cf. *Hist.*, v. 5; Tert., *Apol.*, 37. 8; Cic., *Tusc.
Disp.*, iv. 25, 27; Diod. Sic., xxxiv. 1. 1.

[13] Suet., *Nero*, 16. 2.

[14] His words 'abolendo rumori Nero *subdidit* reos' (44. 3) prove that.

[15] *Ann.*, xv. 44. 4, 8.

[16] Jos., *Ant. Jud.*, xx. 8. 11, § 195; cf. *Vita* 3, § 16. Jos. describes
Poppaea as 'God-fearing' (θεοσεβής). And see Canfield, *op. cit.*, pp. 47–
9, on the implications of *I Clem.*, 4–6.

[17] A. Momigliano, *CAH*, x, pp. 725–6, 887–8.

sarily involved, by definition, membership of an anti-social and potentially criminal conspiracy.

I now want to begin examining the attitude of the government towards the persecution of the Christians. I propose to consider mainly the legal problems first, because although they involve some highly technical questions of Roman public law, the more important ones can, I believe, be completely solved, and we shall then be in a very much better position to understand the reasons which prompted the government to persecute; although before we can finally clarify these, we shall have to consider the other side of our problem: the reasons for the hatred felt towards Christianity by the mass of pagans.

The legal problems,[18] from which a certain number of non-legal issues can hardly be separated, may be grouped under three heads. First, what was the nature of the official charge or charges? Secondly, before whom, and according to what form of legal process, if any, were Christians tried? And thirdly, what was the legal foundation for the charges? (For example, was it a *lex*, or a *senatusconsultum*, or an imperial edict specifically directed against Christianity, or some more general edict, or an imperial rescript or series of rescripts?) I will deal with the first question now, and then the other two together.

First, then, the nature of the charges against the Christians. Here I am going to be dogmatic and say that from at least 112 onwards (perhaps, as we have seen, from 64) the normal charge against Christians was simply 'being Christians': they are punished, that is to say, 'for the Name', the *nomen Christianum*. This is quite certain, from what the Christian Apologists say in the second and early third centuries,[19] from several accounts of martyrdoms,[20]

---

[18] The modern literature is vast and much of it is worthless. All the works that anyone could wish to consult today are given by Krüger and Ruhbach, *op. cit.* (in n. 1 above), pp. vi–xi, 130–44 and the bibliographies for individual Passions; A. N. Sherwin-White, 'The Early Persecutions and Roman Law Again', *JTS*, new ser. iii (1952), pp. 199–213; V. Monachino, *Il fondamento giuridico delle persecuzioni nei primi due secoli* (Rome, 1955, reprinted from *La Scuola Cattolica*, lxxxi, 1953); A. Wlosok, 'Die Rechtsgrundlagen der Christenverfolgungen der ersten zwei Jahrh.', *Gymnasium*, lxvi (1959), pp. 14–32.

[19] E.g. Justin, *I Apol.*, 4; *II Apol.*, 2; Athenag., *Legat.*, 1–2; Tert., *Apol.*, 1–3 etc.; *Ad Nat.*, i. 3; and many similar passages.

[20] Euseb., *Eccl. Hist.*, iv. 15. 25 and *Passio Polyc.*, 12. 1; *Passio SS. Scillitan.*, 10, 14; *Passio Apollon.*, 1 ff.

and from the technical language used by Pliny and Trajan in their celebrated exchange of letters, probably at about the end of 112,[21] concerning the persecution conducted by Pliny in his province of Bithynia et Pontus.[22] Pliny speaks of the Christians he had executed as 'those who were charged before me *with being Christians*' ('qui ad me tamquam Christiani deferebantur'), and the only question he says he asked these confessors was whether they admitted this charge ('interrogavi ipsos, an essent Christiani');[23] and Trajan in his reply speaks of 'those who had been charged before you *as Christians*' ('qui Christiani ad te delati fuerant'), and goes on to say that anyone 'who *denies he is a Christian*' ('qui negaverit se Christianum esse') and proves it 'by offering prayers to our gods' can go free.[24] With the other evidence, that settles the matter. Now the *delatores* who first accused the Christians as such before Pliny could not be sure (as we shall see) that Pliny would consent to take cognizance of the matter at all, let alone inflict the death penalty. Since they thought it was worth 'trying it on', they evidently knew that in the past other officials had been prepared to punish Christians as such. And in fact Pliny now did so,[25] although later on he had second thoughts and consulted the emperor, saying he was doubtful on what charge and to what extent he should investigate and punish, and in particular whether he should take the age of the accused into account, whether he should grant pardon to anyone who was prepared to apostatize, and whether he should punish for the Name alone or for the abominable crimes associated with being a Christian (the 'flagitia cohaerentia nomini'). Trajan explicitly refused to lay down any general or definite rules and was very selective in his answers to Pliny's questions. In two passages which do him great credit he instructs Pliny that Christians must not be sought out ('conquirendi non sunt'), and that anonymous denunciations are to be ignored, 'for they create the worst sort of precedent and are quite out of keeping with the spirit of our age'. Christians who are accused as such, in due form (by a private prosecutor, *delator*), and

[21] But perhaps a year or even two years earlier: see R. Syme, *Tacitus* (Oxford, 1958), i, p. 81; ii, p. 659 (App. 20).

[22] Pliny, *Epist.*, x. 96–97. It is a pleasure to be able to welcome at last a really good English translation of Pliny's *Letters*, by Betty Radice (Penguin Books, 1963; 2 vols, Loeb Classical Library, 1969).

[23] *Idem*, 96. 2–3.

[24] *Idem*, 97. 1, 2.

[25] *Idem*, 96. 3.

are convicted must be punished, but anyone who denies he is a Christian, and proves it 'by offering prayers to our gods', is to receive 'pardon on the score of his repentance' and be set free. In my opinion, Pliny could justifiably take this to mean that punishment was to be for the Name alone.

As I have shown, I believe that persecution 'for the Name' began either in 64 or at some time between 64 and 112. As an alternative, many writers have brought forward certain passages in the New Testament, especially the Apocalypse and I Peter,[26] and have sought to show that under Domitian, if not under Nero, emperor-worship was enforced in Asia Minor, and that the Christian sect was proscribed when Christians refused to take part in it, the charge being really political disloyalty. I would put no weight on such considerations; although on the evidence of the Apocalypse I do not doubt that some Christians may have been put to death in Asia (especially at Pergamum) for refusing to pay cult to the emperor. (Of course, they ought not to have been *compelled* to do anything of the sort, no emperor being officially numbered among the gods of the Roman state until he was dead and had been duly pronounced *divus*, even though in practice he received cult in his lifetime at provincial level and below.) One often hears it said that the Christians were martyred 'for refusing to worship the emperor'.[27] In fact, emperor-worship is a factor of almost no independent importance in the persecution of the Christians.[28] It is true that among our records of martyrdoms emperor-worship does crop up occasionally;[29] but far more often it is a

[26] Especially Rev. 2:10, 13; 6:9–11; 7:13–14; 13:15; 17:6; 18:24; 19:2; 20:4; I Pet. 4:12–19. The dates of both works are still controversial. As regards I Peter, I agree with F. W. Beare, *The First Epistle of Peter*, 2nd edn (Oxford, 1958), pp. 9–19, that it comes from the early second century.

[27] Cf. Syme, *op. cit.*, ii, p. 469: 'an invincible spirit that denied allegiance to Rome when allegiance meant worship of Caesar'.

[28] That this is just as true of the third century as of the second has recently been demonstrated by R. Andreotti, 'Religione ufficiale e culto dell'imperatore nei "Libelli" di Decio', *Studi in onore di A. Calderini e R. Paribeni*, i (Milan, 1956), pp. 369–76. It is particularly significant that Cyprian never mentions the imperial cult. And 'the cult of the emperors plays a very subordinate part in the last great persecution' (Baynes, *CAH*, xii, p. 659).

[29] As in Pliny, *Epist.*, x. 96. 5 (contrast 97. 1: 'dis nostris'); Euseb. *Eccl. Hist.*, vii. 15. 2.

matter of sacrificing *to the gods*[30]—as a rule, not even specifically to 'the gods *of the Romans*'. And when the cult act involved does concern the emperor, it is usually an oath by his Genius (or in the East by his Τύχη)[31] or a sacrifice to the gods on his behalf.[32] Very characteristic is the statement of Vigellius Saturninus, proconsul of Africa in 180, to the Scillitan martyrs: 'We too are religious, and our religion is simple, and we swear by the Genius of our lord the emperor, and we pray for his welfare, as you also ought to do'.[33] This is also the situation which is reflected in the Apologists. Tertullian, addressing himself in 197 to the Roman governing class in the *Apologeticus*, examines at great length the charges against the Christians: he sums them up by making the pagans say to the Christians, 'You don't worship the gods, and you don't offer sacrifice for the emperors'.[34] And there is ample evidence to show that the situation remained substantially the same right through the third and early fourth centuries, even during the general persecutions.[35]

I now turn to the nature of the judicial process against the Christians. (In considering this, I shall go beyond the strictly legal sphere from time to time, and look at some of the reasons why persecution took place.)

The procedure against Christians was in every case that used for the vast majority of criminal trials under the Principate: *cognitio extra ordinem* (or *extraordinaria*), which I shall discuss in a moment. Capital trials under this process in the provinces took place before the provincial governor and no one else. In Rome, the only trials of Christians about which we have good evidence

---

[30] As e.g. in Pliny, *Epist.*, x. 97. 1; *Passio Justini*, v. 8; *Passio Carpi et al.* (Gr.), 4 etc.; *Passio Fructuosi*, ii. 2; *Passio Conon.*, iv. 3–5.

[31] As e.g. in Euseb., *Eccl. Hist.*, iv. 15. 18, 20, 21 and *Passio Polyc.*, 9. 2, 3; 10. 1; *Passio SS. Scillitan.*, 3, 5; *Passio Apollon.*, 3. Contrast Tert., *Apol.*, 32. 2–3.

[32] As e.g. in *Passio SS. Scillitan.*, 3; *Passio Perpet.*, vi. 2; and other sources. See also Tert., *Apol.*, 10. 1; 28. 2 etc.

[33] *Passio SS. Scillitan.*, 3.

[34] Tert., *Apol.*, 10. 1; and see, for discussion of the two charges separately, 10. 2–28. 1 and 28. 2–35. Tert. goes on (10. 1) to sum up the two charges against the Christians as *sacrilegium* and *maiestas*, but he is hardly using either word in its technical sense: his 'sacrilegium' seems to be a rhetorical equivalent for ἀθεότης. (For the technical meaning of *sacrilegium*, see T. Mommsen, *Römisches Strafrecht* (Berlin, 1899), pp. 760 ff.).

[35] See n. 28 above.

were before the Praefectus Urbi[36] or a Praefectus Praetorio;[37] none of the known cases was important enough to come directly before the emperor himself, or the senate,[38] although in the early Principate appeals by Roman citizens first accused elsewhere may have gone to the emperor's court.

Now Roman law was surely the most impressive intellectual achievement of Roman civilization. But what Roman lawyers of today mean when they speak of Roman law is essentially private law, a large part of which is concerned with property rights, their definition and protection. (Did not Cicero in the *De Officiis*, anticipating Marx, say that the main reason for the very existence of political communities was the security of private property— 'ut sua tenerent'?)[39] Large areas of Roman criminal and public law, however, were by contrast very unsatisfactory, and one of the worst of these blemishes was precisely *cognitio extra ordinem*, the procedure by which the large deficiencies of the *quaestio* system (the *ordo iudiciorum publicorum*, regulating the punishment of what may be called 'statutory crimes'), which at least was subject to fairly strict rules, were supplemented by direct governmental intervention. As Mr Sherwin-White pointed out in his Sarum Lectures for 1960–61, the rather few offences dealt with by the *quaestio* system were essentially those of 'high society and the governing personnel'; the 'crimes of the common man'—theft and so forth—had largely to be dealt with *extra ordinem*, even at Rome.[40] In making use of *cognitio extra ordinem* the magistrate concerned had a very wide discretion[41]—even more so, of course,

---

[36] Justin, *II Apol.*, 1–2 (Ptolemaeus, Lucius and another); *Passio Justini*, 1.

[37] Early in the reign of Commodus, Apollonius was tried and sentenced by the Praetorian Prefect Perennis; but the surviving versions of the Passion, and the narrative of Euseb., *Eccl. Hist.*, v. 21, are confused, notably with regard to the rôle played by the senate, which has been much discussed. A confident explanation is hardly possible: the best so far produced seems to me that of E. Griffe, 'Les actes du martyr Apollonius', *Bulletin de littérature ecclésiastique*, liii (1952), pp. 65–76; cf. Monachino, *op. cit.* (in n. 18 above), pp. 33–9.

[38] See the preceding note.

[39] Cic., *De Offic.*, ii. 73.

[40] A. N. Sherwin-White, *Roman Society and Roman Law in the New Testament* (Oxford, 1963), pp. 13–23 and *passim*.

[41] The 'arbitrium iudicantis', on which see F. M. de Robertis, 'Arbitrium Iudicantis e Statuizioni imperiali', *Zeitschrift der Savigny-Stiftung für Rechtsgeschichte*, lix (1939), Rom. Abt., pp. 219–60.

in criminal trials than in civil actions, just because of the relative vagueness of the criminal law. This discretion extended not only to fixing penalties, but even to deciding which cases the magistrate would recognize as criminal and which—like Gallio when appealed to by the Jews of Corinth against St Paul[42]—he would refuse even to consider. The right of judicial *cognitio* (*iurisdictio*) belonged to all provincial governors as part of their *imperium*. In the criminal sphere it was almost unlimited, save in so far as the rights of Roman citizens (under the *Lex Iulia de vi publica*)[43] had to be respected, and in so far as a prosecution might be brought against the governor at Rome after his term of office was over.[44] The sphere in which the judge might exercise his discretion was actually at its widest in the early Principate, before it began to be circumscribed by the imperial constitutions issued more and more frequently from Hadrian's time onwards.[45] Tacitus, in his famous comment on Antonius Felix, governor of Judaea in St Paul's time, can speak of his 'royal prerogatives' ('ius regium');[46] and, in one of the worst cases of provincial misgovernment on record, a proconsul of Asia, towards the end of the reign of Augustus, could congratulate himself proudly and in Greek, over the dead bodies of three hundred provincials he had executed in a single day, on having performed a kingly act.[47]

In a sense, the power to conduct a criminal *cognitio* was part of the power of *coercitio* inherent in *imperium*; but it is quite wrong to conceive the Christians as being punished by pure *coercitio* in the narrower sense, summarily and without the exercise of proper *iurisdictio*: *coercitio* in that sense, exercised (as the lawyers put it) *de plano*, in an informal manner, was limited to minor offences.[48]

[42] Acts 18:12–17.
[43] The principal text is *Dig.*, xlviii. 6. 7; cf. *Sent. Pauli*, v. 26. 1. See esp. A. H. M. Jones, *Studies in Roman Government and Law* (Oxford, 1960), pp. 54 ff.
[44] See P. A. Brunt, 'Charges of provincial maladministration under the early principate', *Historia*, x (1961), pp. 189–227.
[45] See n. 41 above.
[46] Tac., *Hist.*, v. 9.
[47] Seneca, *Dial.*, iv (*De Ira*, ii) 5. 5; cf. Tac., *Ann.*, iii. 68. 1. The proconsul was L. Valerius Messalla Volesus and the date A.D. 11 or 12.
[48] The principal text is *Dig.*, xlviii. 2. 6 ('levia crimina'); cf. i. 16. 9. 3; xlviii. 18. 18. 10. Several passages in the law-books and elsewhere (e.g. Seneca, *De Clem.*, i. 5. 3) distinguish between a decision given 'pro tribunali', as a result of a formal trial, and one given 'de plano',

I cannot help feeling that some of those who have persisted in speaking of the proceedings against the Christians as 'police measures' have not fully realized that the trials in question were in no way summary proceedings by pure *coercitio* but proper legal trials, involving the exercise of *iurisdictio* in the fullest sense.

The arbitrary and irresponsible character of the *cognitio* system was well understood by Mommsen, who says contemptuously in his *Römisches Strafrecht* that it entirely eludes scientific exposition, its very essence being a 'legalised absence of settled form'.[49] 'To Roman criminal law', says Schulz, 'the rule "nullum crimen sine lege, nulla poena sine lege" was and remained for ever unknown'.[50] Jolowicz, discussing the criminal system of the Principate, rightly pointed out that it 'never passed through a stage of strict law', and 'the "rule of law", towards which the *quaestiones* had been a step forward, was never established'.[51] To find that in a very important part of the Roman legal system the rule of law as we know it did not exist will surprise only those who fix their eyes on the splendid system of civil jurisprudence[52] and ignore criminal and administrative law and procedure.

Recalcitrant as it is to precise analysis, the system of *cognitio extra ordinem* has been adequately discussed in the standard textbooks.[53] Through his understanding of the nature of the *cognitio*

informally: the technical terms 'cognitio' and 'decretum' are reserved for the former type (see *Dig.*, xxxvii. 1. 3. 8; xxxviii. 15. 2. 1; xlviii. 16. 1. 8). The position was much the same in civil cases: see R. Düll, *ZS-SR* (n. 41 above), lii (1932), Rom. Abt., pp. 170–94.

49 Mommsen, *Römisches Strafrecht*, p. 340.

50 F. Schulz, *Principles of Roman Law* (Oxford, 1936), p. 173, cf. p. 247 ('No criminal charge except by a law, no punishment except by a law').

51 H. F. Jolowicz, *Historical Introduction to the Study of Roman Law*, 2nd edn (Cambridge, 1952), p. 413.

52 Even in civil jurisdiction the growth of *cognitio extraordinaria* resulted in an 'assimilation to administrative and police action' (W. W. Buckland, *A Text-Book of Roman Law*, 2nd edn (Cambridge, 1932), p. 663).

53 Notably Mommsen, *op. cit.*, pp. 340–1, 346–51; P. F. Girard, *Manuel élémentaire de droit romain*, 6th edn (Paris, 1918), pp. 1084–97; and in more detail U. Brasiello, *La repressione penale in dir. rom.* (Naples, 1937). See also Maxime Lemosse, *Cognitio. Études sur le rôle du juge dans l'instruction du procès civil antique* (Thèse de Droit, Paris, 1944), pp. 129 ff., esp. 211–57. Useful contributions have been made in this country by J. L. Strachan-Davidson, *Problems of the Roman Criminal Law*, ii (Oxford, 1912), pp. 159–75; Jones, *op. cit.* (n. 43 above), pp. 53–98; Sherwin-White, *op. cit.* (n. 40 above), v. Index, *s.v.* 'Cognitio'.

process, Mr Sherwin-White, in an article published in 1952,[54] has been able to cut away a vast amount of dead wood and provide by far the best introduction to the study of the legal aspects of the early persecutions—although I shall argue presently that he is mistaken in one very important point.

Since our information comes almost entirely from Christian sources, interested in recording martyrdoms, the great majority of the trials of Christians we know about in detail end in conviction and a death sentence. But the very wide discretion exercised by the provincial governor might on occasion work in favour of accused Christians. The most significant evidence comes from Tertullian's *Ad Scapulam*, written probably in 212, where we hear that the very first proconsul to shed Christian blood in Africa was Vigellius Saturninus,[55] who was in office as late as 180;[56] and that a whole series of African proconsuls (after Saturninus, it seems) had gone out of their way to be friendly to accused Christians:[57] one of them helped the Christians to conduct their case in such a way as to secure an acquittal (I only wish we had more details of that); another acquitted an accused Christian outright, apparently on the ground that to convict him would cause a riot; yet another, reluctant at having to deal with such a case, released an accused Christian who consented under torture to apostatize, without actually making him sacrifice; and a fourth tore up the vexatious indictment of a Christian when his accuser failed to appear.

That shows how things might work in practice. A governor exercising *cognitio extraordinaria* in a criminal case was bound (for all practical purposes) only by those imperial *constitutiones* and *mandata*[58] which were relevant in his particular area and were still

[54] See n. 18 above.

[55] Tert., *Ad Scap.*, 3. 4.

[56] See *Passio SS. Scillitan.*, 1.

[57] Tert., *Ad Scap.*, 4. 3-4.

[58] *Mandata*, imperial administrative regulations relating mainly to the provinces (some of general application, others not), were technically distinct from *constitutiones*. The most complete definition of *constitutiones* is Ulpian's, in *Dig.*, i. 4. 1. 1 (cf. *Inst. J.*, i. 2. 6; Gaius, i. 5): it can be reduced to *epistulae* and *subscriptiones*, *edicta*, *decreta* (formal legal decisions), and summary decisions *de plano* (see n. 48 above). A technical term often employed, which cuts across the definition just given, is *rescripta*: this includes all *subscriptiones* (dealt with through the emperor's secretary *a libellis*) and most *epistulae* (dealt with through the secretary *ab epistulis*).

in force.[59] Unfortunately, official publication of imperial *constitutiones* seems to have been an extremely inefficient and haphazard process,[60] and a conscientious governor might often find himself in great perplexity as to what the law was. This is nicely illustrated by a letter from Pliny to Trajan dealing with the problem of the status of foundlings (θρεπτοί).[61] He can find nothing to the point, he says, in the *constitutiones* of previous emperors. An edict *said* to have been issued by Augustus had been quoted to him, with letters of Vespasian, Titus and Domitian, addressed to other parts of the empire, but he did not enclose copies of these, as he was not certain of their accuracy or even (in some cases) of their authenticity, and he felt sure there would be proper copies in the offices of the emperor's central administration. One sentence is particularly significant: he did not feel that in a matter which called for the emperor's authoritative decision he ought to be 'content with precedents'.[62]

Once Pliny's correspondence with Trajan had been 'published'

[59] Some modern scholars have held that in strict legal theory imperial *constitutiones* originally remained law only during the reign in which they were issued. Yet by the third quarter of the second century Gaius (i. 5) could say it had never been doubted that such *constitutiones* had 'the force of law'. Cf. Pomponius in *Dig.*, i. 2. 2. 11, 12; Ulpian in *Dig.*, i. 4. 1. 1; also i. 4. 1. 2, explaining that some *constitutiones* are 'personal' and not to be treated as precedents. By the early second century the *constitutiones* of emperors were evidently regarded as holding good until reversed by their successors—and this is true not only of 'good emperors' such as Augustus (Pliny, Epist., x. 79, esp. §§ 2, 4, 5; x. 80 and 84), but even of Domitian (who had suffered a 'damnatio memoriae'): see *Idem*, x. 58 (esp. §§ 3, 10); 60. 1; 65–6 (esp. 65. 3; 66. 2); 72; cf. Papinian in *Dig.*, xlviii. 3. 2. 1 (Domitian) and Gai., i. 33 (Nero). See on the whole question Jolowicz, *op. cit.* (n. 51 above), pp. 374–83.

[60] See F. von Schwind, *Zur Frage der Publikation im röm. Recht (Münchener Beiträge zur Papyrusforschung*, xxxi, 1940); and briefly Jolowicz, *op. cit.*, pp. 381–3; Schulz, *op. cit.* (n. 50 above), pp. 243–7. Cf. also U. Wilcken, 'Zu den Kaiserrescripten', in *Hermes*, lv (1920), pp. 1–42; F. M. de Robertis, 'Sulla efficacia normativa delle costit. imp.', *Annali della fac. di giurispr. della R. Univ. di Bari*, new ser. iv (1941), pp. 1–100, 281–374; G. I. Luzzatto, 'Ricerche sull'applicaz. delle costit. imp. nelle provincie', *Scritti di dir. rom. in onore di C. Ferrini*, ed. G. G. Archi (Pavia, 1946), pp. 265–93.

[61] Pliny, *Epist.*, x. 65.

[62] On precedent in Roman law, see Jolowicz, *op. cit.* (n. 51 above), pp. 363–5, and the works cited on p. 569.

(no doubt by his friends, soon after 117, when he and Trajan were both dead), every educated Roman would be likely to know what instructions Trajan had given regarding the Christians; and thereafter any provincial governor might well feel that until official policy towards the Christians changed he had better follow the same procedure. But other governors, at any rate in other provinces, were not absolutely bound by this precedent; and indeed some ten years later we find a proconsul of Asia consulting Hadrian on the treatment of the Christians, and instructions being sent in return to his successor, C. Minicius Fundanus, the purport of which, unhappily, is not entirely clear from the version which has come down to us through Christian writers[63]—I myself believe this rescript represented no departure from the policy laid down by Trajan. The decisions taken by Nero in 64 and Trajan in 112 did not constitute precedents absolutely binding upon provincial governors generally. Tertullian's notorious reference to an 'institutum Neronianum'[64] does not refer to a general edict: 'institutum' is not a technical legal term, and we must translate 'the practice adopted by Nero'. We are told by Lactantius that Ulpian (in the early third century) collected and published in his treatise *De Officio Proconsulis* the nefarious imperial rescripts laying down the penalties to be inflicted on Christians.[65] I would emphasize that Lactantius speaks of *rescripta*, not *edicta* or *mandata*. Unless he is using the word very loosely, this is another piece of evidence against the existence of a 'general law' specifically proscribing Christianity, a notion which, as far as I am aware, no

---

[63] Justin, *I Apol.*, 68 (our texts give Eusebius's Greek version); Euseb., *Eccl. Hist.*, iv. 9; Rufinus, *Hist. Eccles.*, iv. 9. The traditional date of Fundanus's proconsulate is 124–5, but it is 122–3 according to R. Syme, *Tacitus*, ii, p. 468 n. 5. I believe this rescript has been misunderstood by e.g. H. Grégoire, *Les Persécutions dans L'Empire romain* (*Mémoires de l'Académie royale de Belgique*, lvi, 1964), pp. 55 ff.; contrast W. Schmid, 'The Christian reinterpretation of the Rescript of Hadrian', *Maia*, vii (1955), pp. 5–13; Canfield, *op. cit.* (n. 10 above), pp. 103–18; Wlosok, *op. cit.* (n. 18 above), p. 23 n. 29. The alleged letter of Antoninus Pius, in Euseb., *Eccl. Hist.*, iv. 13, is certainly fictitious (contrast 26. 10).

[64] Tert., *Ad Nat.*, i. 7. See J. W. Ph. Borleffs, 'Institutum Neronianum', *Vig. Christ.*, vi (1952), pp. 129–45, esp. 141–4. Cf. Cic., *In Pis.*, 30; *Ad Att.*, iv. 18. 1; *Brut.*, 269; Tac. *Ann.*, xiv. 43. 1; *Inst. J.*, i. 2. 10; Suet., *Nero*, 16. 2.

[65] Lact., *Div. Inst.*, v. 11. 19.

specialist in Roman public law and administration has ever been willing to entertain, popular as it has been among ecclesiastical historians.[66] It is very possible that these rescripts laid down no more definite rules than those we find in Trajan's letter to Pliny or Hadrian's to Fundanus. A rescript of Marcus Aurelius ordered the penalty of relegation to an island to be applied to anyone who did anything to alarm the fickle minds of men with dread of the supernatural;[67] but this is scarcely relevant for our purposes, especially as we never hear of any Christians suffering under this provision. The *Sententiae Pauli* include a rule of unknown date, threatening punishment to those who 'introduce new sects or religious practices not founded on rational grounds, so as to influence the minds of men';[68] but this too seems to me of little importance for us. Nor does it seem at all likely that a governor would wish to commit himself in his provincial edict on such a minor criminal matter as the prosecution of Christians. And if he was ever in serious doubt about the course he ought to pursue, he could always consult the emperor.

It is important to remember that the standard procedure in punishing Christians was 'accusatory' and not 'inquisitorial': a governor would not normally take action until a formal denunciation (*delatio nominis*) was issued by a *delator*, a man who was prepared not merely to inform but actually to conduct the prosecution in person, and to take the risk of being himself arraigned on a charge of *calumnia*, malicious prosecution, if he failed to make out a sufficient case.[69] Trajan, as we have seen, forbade the seeking out of Christians. This principle, however, could be and sometimes was disregarded. The best attested example comes from the savage persecution at Lyons and Vienne in 177, when the governor did order a search to be made for Christians[70]—and incidentally seems to have punished apostates for what Pliny had called the 'flagitia cohaerentia nomini', the shocking crimes of

---

[66] Against the historicity of the statement in *Scr. Hist. Aug., Sep. Sev.*, 17.1, that Severus forbade conversion to Christianity ('Iudaeos fieri sub gravi poena vetuit. Idem etiam de Christianis sanxit'), see the convincing arguments of K. H. Schwarte, 'Das angebliche Christengesetz des Sep. Sev.', *Historia*, xii (1963), pp. 185–208.

[67] *Dig.*, xlviii. 19. 30. Cf. Marcus Aurel., *Med.*, i. 6.

[68] *Sent. Pauli*, v. 21. 2.

[69] Cf. Euseb., *Eccl. Hist.*, iv. 9. 3.

[70] *Idem*, v. 1. 14.

which Christians were supposed to be guilty, and which had been alleged against them in this case by their pagan slaves.[71] It is wrong to say the governor here was acting 'illegally', because of course he was not absolutely bound to follow Trajan's rescript to Pliny; but it looks as if the great majority of governors did follow it. On this occasion the governor actually condemned to the beasts, as a favour to the enraged populace, a Christian named Attalus, who was a Roman citizen, although the emperor had just given specific instructions to the governor that Christians who were Roman citizens should be beheaded.[72] He was exceeding his instructions, certainly; but he could plead political necessity, and there is no reason to think he was taken to task by the emperor, who was Marcus Aurelius.

This raises another point: the attitude of the emperor. Christian propaganda from at least the middle of the second century onwards tried to make out that it was only the 'bad emperors' who persecuted, and that the 'good emperors' protected the Christians;[73] but there is no truth in this at all. We know, for example, of quite a number of martyrdoms under the first two Antonines in widely separated parts of the empire, and even at Rome itself.[74] In reality, persecution went on automatically, if sporadically, whoever the emperor might be; and until the third century at any rate it is better not to think of persecutions primarily in terms of emperors. It was the provincial governor in each case who played the more significant role—and even his attitude might be less important than what I must call 'public opinion'. If the state of local feeling was such that no one particularly wanted to take upon himself the onus of prosecuting Christians, very few governors would have any desire to instigate a persecution. If, on the other hand, public opinion was inflamed against the Christians (as we shall see it often was, down to the middle of the third century), then delators would

---

[71] *Idem*, 33, cf. 14.

[72] *Idem*, 50–52, cf. 44, 47 (where ἀποτυμπανισθῆναι is explained by ἀπέτεμνε τὰς κεφαλάς). Cf. *Dig.*, xlviii. 19. 31.

[73] The first writer we know to have asserted this is Melito of Sardis: see Euseb., *Eccl. Hist.*, iv. 26. 9. It soon became 'common form': see Tert., *Apol.*, 5, etc.

[74] E.g. those of Polycarp, of the Christians of Lyons, of the Scillitans, and, at Rome, of Ptolemaeus and Lucius, of Justin and his companions, and of Apollonius—to name only a few of whom we possess reasonably reliable records.

not be lacking, and Christians would be put on trial; and few governors would have any motive for resisting strong local feeling demonstrated in this perfectly permissible way, especially if some of the more influential men in the area were leading the agitation, as they often would be. Imperial instructions (*mandata*) given to provincial governors bade them take care to rid their provinces of 'bad men' (*mali homines*);[75] and Ulpian said it was characteristic of a good and serious-minded governor that he keep his province 'settled and orderly' ('pacata atque quieta'), adding that he would have no difficulty in securing this end if he diligently saw to it that the province was cleared of 'mali homines' —and sought them out accordingly.[76] The governor was advised by a first-century jurist to consider not so much what was the practice at Rome as what the circumstances required;[77] and the principle that in the exercise of his criminal jurisdiction the governor should act according to the circumstances existing in his particular province was well recognized.[78] Probably the main reason why some martyrdoms—perhaps many martyrdoms—took place was that they were thought to be necessary if the province were to be kept 'pacata atque quieta'.[79] Most governors were doubtless only too willing to take action against men who were strongly disapproved of by 'all right-thinking people', and who tended to become the centre of disturbances. Everyone will remember how Pilate yielded to the vociferous demands of the local notables and their followers for the crucifixion of Jesus.[80] If a governor, indeed, refused to do what was expected of him in this way, not only would he become unpopular: the general indignation against the Christians would be only too likely to vent itself in riots and lynching, as we have evidence that it did on occasion;[81] and once violence began, anything might happen.

Christians might also be suspect, as *mali homines*, in the eyes of

[75] Paulus, in *Dig.*, i. 18. 3; cf. *Sent. Pauli*, v. 22. 1.
[76] *Dig.*, i. 18. 13. pr.
[77] Proculus, in *Dig.*, i. 18. 12.
[78] See e.g. Ulpian, in *Dig.*, xlvii. 11. 9, 10 (cf. 14. 1. pr.); Saturninus, in *Dig.*, xlviii. 19. 16. 9.
[79] A. Ronconi, 'Tacito, Plinio e i Cristiani', *Studi in onore di U. E. Paoli* (Florence, 1956), pp. 615 ff., at p. 628, gives great emphasis to the need to satisfy 'public opinion' as a cause of persecution.
[80] Mark 15: 1–15 and parallel passages; and esp. John 19: 12, 15.
[81] See e.g. Euseb., *Eccl. Hist.*, v. Praef. 1; 1. 7; vi. 41. 1–9.

some governors, because they worshipped a man who had admittedly been crucified by a governor of Judaea, as a political criminal,[82] who thought of himself as 'king of the Jews'.[83] Their loyalty to the state, whatever they might say, could well appear doubtful, if only because they refused even to swear an oath by the emperor's Genius.[84] They were always talking about the imminent end of the world; and one of their books spoke with bitter hatred of Rome, thinly disguised under the name of Babylon, and prophesied its utter ruin.[85] And furthermore the secrecy of their rites might well seem a cover for political conspiracy, or at any rate anti-social behaviour. A governor who had such considerations in mind when trying Christians might even decide to find them guilty of *maiestas* (treason): this would account for various statements by Tertullian about Christians being accused of that crime[86]—although I would not take these pieces of rhetoric very seriously myself. In any event, the factors I have just been mentioning would have less and less weight as time went on, and it became clear that Christians had no political objectives whatever and few particularly anti-social habits.

Sometimes a Christian who was in danger of being put on trial might be able to escape altogether by bribing the intending delator or the authorities. There is evidence that this was happening in Africa by the early third century at the latest:[87] not merely individuals but whole churches had purchased immunity, to the disgust of Tertullian,[88] who believed that during persecution Christians must stand their ground and neither take to flight nor buy themselves off. This rigorist attitude was only partly shared by the churches of the West, and in the East it seems to have been generally repudiated: flight or concealment during persecution was officially approved everywhere (except in so far as leading clergy might incur disapproval for deserting their flocks); but in the West, though apparently not in the East, the purchase of immunity, at any rate in a form which might give the impression

[82] See Min. Fel., *Octav.*, 9. 4.
[83] Mark 15:2, 9, 12, 26 (and parallel passages); Luke 23:2; John 19:12, 15.
[84] Cf. n. 31 above.
[85] Rev. 14: 8; 16:19; 17–18.
[86] Tert., *Apol.*, 10. 1; 28. 3 ff., etc.
[87] Tert., *De Fuga in Persec.*, 5. 5; 12–14 (written *c.* 212, during Tertullian's Montanist period).
[88] *Idem*, 13. 5.

of apostasy, was regarded as a sin, if not a particularly grave one.[89] Our evidence comes mainly from Africa, Spain and Rome during the Decian persecution, when certificates of compliance with the imperial order to sacrifice to the gods were purchased wholesale by the less steadfast members of the Christian community.[90]

Although we have not yet disposed of all the legal issues, we have at least reached a point from which we can see that the last of my three questions of a legal nature, 'What was the legal foundation for the charges against the Christians?', has answered itself, because under the *cognitio* process no foundation was necessary, other than a prosecutor, a charge of Christianity, and a governor willing to punish on that charge. Theories that the Christian churches could be legally regarded as *collegia illicita*, unlawful associations, either in the sense of being irremediably illegal (so that their members were at all times liable to criminal punishment), or merely because they were unlicensed (and liable to be prosecuted if they failed to obey an order to disband), have been strongly attacked in recent years by specialists in Roman public law;[91] and in spite of some texts which suggest there may have been some technical irregularity,[92] I am convinced that this issue can have had no real importance: we never hear that any Christian was ever prosecuted as a member of a *collegium illicitum*.

I want to deal at this point with a theory produced by Mr Sherwin-White in the admirable article I mentioned earlier[93] and repeated in his Sarum Lectures.[94] According to this theory, once

[89] See my *op. cit.* (n. 4 above), pp. 87–8.

[90] *Ibid.*, n. 58.

[91] See esp. F. M. de Robertis, *Il diritto associativo romano* (Bari, 1938), pp. 289–91, 366–86; G. Bovini, *La proprietà ecclesiastica e la condizione giuridica della chiesa in età precostantiniana* (Milan, 1949); Sherwin-White, *op. cit.* (n. 18 above), pp. 205–6. Contrast P. W. Duff, *Personality in Roman Private Law* (Cambridge, 1938), pp. 169–70: until its recognition by Constantine 'the Church must have appeared to the private law as a collection of unauthorised and therefore illegal colleges'.

[92] Notably Orig., *c. Cels.*, i. 1; cf. Pliny, *Epist.*, x. 96. 7 (with 33. 3; 34. 1); Tert., *Apol.*, 38. 1–2; 39 (esp. §§ 20–1); *De Ieiunio*, 13. But for the third century see *Scr. Hist. Aug., Sev. Alex.*, 49. 6; Euseb., *Eccl. Hist.*, vii. 13; 30. 19.

[93] *Op. cit.* (n. 18 above), pp. 210–12. The essence of the theory (though without actual endorsement of the view that the crime was *called* 'contumacia') seems to have been accepted by H. Last, *Reallex. für Antike und Christentum*, ii (Stuttgart, 1954), col. 1208 ff. (see col. 1213).

[94] *Op. cit.* (n. 40 above), pp. 4, 18, cf. pp. 19–20, 72–3.

Pliny had discovered that the *flagitia* generally attributed to the Christians did not exist, the real foundation for condemning them was their *contumacia*, their refusal to obey the reasonable order of a magistrate; and in the second and early third centuries this *contumacia* was 'the core of the official objection'. Against this theory there are five separate arguments:—

1. In every single case the very word required is stubbornly lacking. Pliny does not use the term *contumacia* at all: employing entirely untechnical language, he says he did not doubt 'whatever sort of thing it was they were confessing to, their pertinacity and inflexible obstinacy ought to be punished';[95] and as far as I know the essential word never appears in any authentic account of a martyrdom or any other reliable ancient source dealing with the persecutions.[96] This alone is enough to put the theory out of court in so far as it depends on attaching a technical meaning to *contumacia*.

2. Pliny's victims, Mr Sherwin-White says, had refused to comply with 'a reasonable order. . . . the test requiring homage to the *di nostri* . . . . The test was reasonable, and its refusal revealed *contumacia*'.[97] In fact Pliny never says he had asked any self-confessed Christians to sacrifice: he makes it quite clear that he had imposed this act only upon those who denied that they were Christians, as a test of their sincerity.[98] This destroys the whole foundation of the theory, an essential presupposition of which is that the Christians were ordered to sacrifice and contumaciously refused.

3. It is true that in many later trials of Christians the accused are actually ordered to sacrifice or to do some other act which their religion did not allow them to perform. But even here *contumacia*

---

[95] *Epist.*, x. 96. 3: 'pertinaciam . . . et inflexibilem obstinationem'.

[96] The other examples given by Sherwin-White, *op. cit.* (n. 18 above), pp. 210–12, show nothing more than what he himself calls 'the remarkable reluctance of Roman officials to condemn Christians'. For the further assertion, 'They are only condemned when their *contumacia* has been proved' (p. 211), there is no evidence at all.

[97] *Op. cit.* (n. 18 above), p. 210. The same mistake has been made by other writers, even A. D. Nock, in his mainly admirable article in *HTR*, xlv (1952), pp. 187 ff., at p. 218.

[98] Pliny, *Epist.*, x. 96. 5, cf. 3. Sherwin-White himself admits elsewhere (p. 205) that Pliny did not require 'the first batch' of Christians to sacrifice to *di nostri*!

could not make its appearance until after the trial had begun. And would it not be absurd to accept as the legal ground of a prosecution an element which could not even arise until after proceedings had begun and the accused was being questioned?

4. The theory we are considering would make *contumacia* the essential element, quite gratuitously, in every persistent crime—as of course it is, in a sense; but would it not be perverse to pick out the mere persistence and hold it up as the essential part of the crime? Only in so far as the act or default originally complained of is itself criminal can the mere persistence in it be a crime. The essential element in the condemnation of Christians is the illegality of Christianity, not the mere behaviour in court of the accused, which, as we have seen, is the only point at which *contumacia* could conceivably come in. We want to know why the government wanted Christians to be brought to trial. The *contumacia* theory distracts attention from this main issue.

5. Close examination of three legal texts to which Mr Sherwin-White appeals in defence of his theory[99] and of the dozens of others in which *contumacia* (and the corresponding adjective and adverb) are used does not at all support his interpretation; but this question is too technical to be discussed in the body of this article.[100]

[99] In the first, *Dig.*, xlviii. 19. 4, *contumacia* merely increases penalties already incurred (cf. Trajan, in Pliny, *Epist.*, x. 57. 2). The second, *Dig.*, xlviii. 19. 5, deals with the condemnation of accused in their absence: here the *contumacia* consists in not appearing at the trial, and may involve sentence *in absentia*. In the third example, the cases described in *Coll.*, xv. 2. 2, no one doubted that *professio* of the magic arts was already illegal: all Ulpian says is that the Magi, 'per contumaciam et temeritatem', went from private *scientia*, which on some earlier views (see *loc. cit., init.*) was not forbidden, to public *professio*. Ulpian does not make the *contumacia* a *ground* for the subsequent suppression, as Mr Sherwin-White represents him as doing when he writes (p. 211), 'This, says Ulpian, was *contumacia*. Hence most emperors imposed a total ban'—Ulpian mentions the *contumacia et temeritas* incidentally.

[100] The words 'contumacia, contumax, contumaciter' occur very frequently in the legal sources—over 40 times in the *Digest* alone. They are often used quite untechnically (as of the behaviour of children to their parents: *Cod. Just.*, viii. 46. 3; 49. 1), and as a rule they simply indicate an attitude of mind, rather than any specific act: in at least 13 of the texts in the *Dig.* the expression used is 'per contumaciam' and merely signifies that the person concerned is acting deliberately, wilfully, defiantly (it will be sufficient to cite *Dig.*, l. 1. 13), and thereby in many

Nor can I accept Mr Sherwin-White's statement that 'the Roman official is indifferent to the religious aspects in the known cases, provided that the Christian sheds his *contumacia*'.[101] This is to ignore a significant part of Pliny's letter: 'It is clear that the temples, recently almost deserted, are beginning to be frequented again, and that the sacred rites, long neglected, are being renewed; also that the flesh of the sacrificial animals, which has been finding very few purchasers, is on sale everywhere'.[102] In view of this it can hardly be denied that Pliny was genuinely concerned—whether for what we should call religious reasons or not!—about the decline of the traditional religion in his province, and regarded its revival as a justification of his policy of repression, tempered by mercy to apostates.

On the face of Pliny's letter the 'obstinacy' of the Christians consisted merely in their threefold confession of Christianity, in face of a warning (after the first confession) that they would be punished for it. Further light is shed upon this 'obstinacy' by some of the Passions of the martyrs, many of whom either repeat the standard formula, 'Christianus sum', in reply to all questions, or make legally irrelevant replies.

> If you will give me a quiet hearing, I will tell you the mystery of simplicity . . . . I do not recognize the empire of this world, but rather I serve that God whom no man sees or can see with these eyes. I have committed no theft; but if I buy anything, I pay the tax, because I recognize my Lord, the King of kings and Emperor of all peoples . . . . It is evil to advocate murder or the bearing of false witness.

These are the answers given to the proconsul of Africa by

cases incurring an added penalty (see e.g. *Dig.*, xlviii. 19. 4). The only texts I have been able to find which use *contumacia* and its cognates in anything approaching a technical sense are those referring to men who deliberately refuse to comply with a summons to appear (or produce documents), whether in criminal or in civil trials: e.g. *Dig.*, xlii. 1. 53. pr., 1, 2, 3; 1. 54; *Cod. Just.*, iii. 1. 13. 2b, 2c, 3, 4, 7 (dealing with civil cases only); vii. 43. 4, 7, 8, 9 etc.; *Cod Theod.*, ii. 18. 2; x. 13. 1; xi. 31. 5. This gave rise to what has been called in modern times a 'Contumacialverfahren': see Mommsen, *Römisches Strafrecht*, pp. 335–6; Kipp in Pauly-Wissowa, *RE*, iv, cols. 1166–70.

[101] *Op. cit.* (n. 18 above), p. 211.
[102] *Epist.*, x. 96. 9–10.

Speratus the Scillitan[103]—edifying, no doubt, but irritating to a judge and certainly giving an impression of other-worldly 'pertinacity and inflexible obstinacy'.

My next point concerns what I call "the sacrifice test", used by Pliny in order to give those who denied being Christians a chance to prove their sincerity.[104] The earliest example we have of the use of such a test in the Roman world, as far as I know, is at Antioch early in the year 67, when it was used during a pogrom by the Greeks of that city, to distinguish between Jews and non-Jews.[105] The character of the sacrifice test changed when judicial torture, which until the second century had been used (except in very special circumstances) only on slaves, came to be regularly applied to all those members of the lower classes (the vast majority of the population of the empire) who became involved in criminal trials, whether they were Roman citizens or not.[106] Once judicial torture had become a standard practice, the sacrifice test naturally tended to lose its original character as a privilege, and to become something which was enforced, usually with the aid of torture. But the essential aim was to make apostates, not martyrs. One could say without exaggeration that a governor who really wanted to execute Christians would be careful to avoid torturing them, lest they should apostatize and go free. For there is no doubt that with few exceptions an accused who was prepared to perform the prescribed cult acts was immediately released without punishment. Tertullian, of course, in his barrister's way, makes much of this as evidence that the authorities did not really regard the Christians as criminals at all. 'Others, who plead not guilty', he cries, 'you torture to make them confess, the Christians alone to make them deny'.[107] This was perfectly true, and it must surely count as a lonely anomaly in the Roman legal system. The

---

[103] *Passio SS. Scillitan.*, 4, 6, 7. Cf. Euseb., *Eccl. Hist.*, v. 1. 20; *Passio Conon.*, iv. 2; etc.

[104] Pliny, *Epist.*, x. 96. 5.

[105] Jos., *Bell. Jud.*, vii. 3. 3, §§ 50–1. For the date, see § 46.

[106] The practice seems to have been well established by the reign of Marcus Aurelius (161–80): see the references in my *op. cit.* (n. 4 above), p. 80 n. 29.

[107] Tert., *Apol.*, 2 (esp. § 10); cf. *Ad Scap.*, 4. 2; Cyprian, *Ad Demetrian.*, 13; Min. Fel., *Octav.*, 28. 3–5.

explanation is that the only punishable offence was *being* a Christian, up to the very moment sentence was pronounced, not *having been* one. I certainly know of no parallel to this in Roman criminal law. Tertullian ridicules the situation. What is the use of a forced and insincere denial, he asks scornfully. What is to prevent a Christian who has given such a denial and been acquitted from 'laughing at your efforts, a Christian once more?'.[108]

I need not spend much time on the question of the supposed abominations (*flagitia*) with which the Christians were charged— Θυέστεια δεῖπνα καὶ Οἰδιπόδειοι μίξεις, as they are called,[109] meaning of course cannibalism and incest. It is hard to say how seriously these charges were taken by the government. The Christian Apologists of the second and early third centuries devote a good deal of attention to rebutting such accusations, which were evidently believed by the populace in both the eastern and the western parts of the empire. After the first half of the third century, however, they seem to have died out, although we know from Eusebius that a Roman military commander in Syria in 312, under the bitterly anti-Christian emperor Maximin, did try to fake charges of immoral behaviour against the Christians of Damascus, in order to inflame public opinion against them.[110] The behaviour of the ordinary pagan during the Great Persecution suggests that he no longer believed such slanders. Moreover, even for the early period, when these accusations were generally credited, one may feel that a more fundamental interpretation is necessary. As Macaulay said over a hundred years ago, 'There never was a religious persecution in which some odious crime was not, justly or unjustly, said to be obviously deducible from the doctrines of the persecuted party'.[111] The reproaches of *flagitia* seem to have been essentially appendages of some more real complaint. Unfortunately, these charges were given some colour by the fact that orthodox Christians and heretics tended to fling them at each other, a fact upon which Gibbon severely remarks, 'A pagan

---

[108] Tert., *Apol.*, 2. 17.
[109] Euseb., *Eccl. Hist.*, v. 1. 14; Athenag., *Legat.*, 3, 31; cf. Euseb., *Eccl. Hist.*, iv. 7. 11; v. 1. 26; ix. 5. 2; Justin, *I Apol.*, 26; *II Apol.*, 12; *Dial. c. Tryph.*, 10; Tert., *Apol.*, 6. 11–7. 2 etc.; Min. Fel., *Octav.*, 8–9, 28, 30–1; Orig., *c. Cels.*, vi. 27, 40.
[110] Euseb., *Eccl. Hist.*, ix. 5. 2.
[111] See H. Last, *JRS*, xxvii (1937), p. 89 n. 63.

magistrate . . . . might easily have imagined that their mutual animosity had extorted the discovery of their common guilt'.[112]

Before I come to the final stage of this investigation, I want to take a brief glance at a long series of events which may have given pagans rather more ground for their active antagonism to Christianity than we tend to suppose: I refer to what I have called 'voluntary martyrdom'.[113] Examination of it will require us to look at persecution, for once, mainly from the receiving end.

It is a significant fact, as yet not generally appreciated, that a very large number of sources (Passions as well as literary texts) show intrepid Christians going far beyond what their churches officially required of them, often indeed offering themselves up to the authorities of their own accord, and occasionally acting in a provocative manner, smashing images and so forth. After making a detailed study of the evidence for these 'voluntary martyrs', I would claim that the part they played in the history of the persecutions was much more important than has yet been realized. It seems to me impossible to doubt that the prevalence of voluntary martyrdom was a factor which, for obvious reasons, both contributed to the outbreak of persecution and tended to intensify it when already in being. Contrary to what is usually said, voluntary martyrdom was by no means confined mainly to heretical or schismatic sects such as Montanists and Donatists, but was a good deal more common among the orthodox than is generally admitted. The heads of the churches, sensibly enough, forbade voluntary martyrdom again and again, and were inclined to refuse to these zealots the very name of martyr—passages to this effect could be cited from a dozen different sources, including Clement of Alexandria, Origen and Lactantius, at least three bishops (Cyprian and Mensurius of Carthage and Peter of Alexandria), the Passion of Polycarp, and the Canons of the Council of Elvira.[114]

---

[112] E. Gibbon, *Decline and Fall of the Roman Empire* (ed. J. B. Bury), ii, ch. xvi, pp. 80–1. For examples, see Justin, *I Apol.*, 26; Iren., *Adv. Haeres.*, i. 6. 3–4; 24. 5; 25. 3–5 (and see Euseb., *Eccl. Hist.*, iv. 7. 9–11); Clem. Alex., *Strom.* iii, esp. 2, 4, 5; Tert., *De Ieiun.*, 17; Philaster, *De Heres.*, 29 (57), ed. F. Marx.

[113] For some remarks on this phenomenon, see my *op. cit.* (n. 4 above), pp. 83, 93, 101–3. I shall give the very considerable body of evidence for voluntary martyrdom in a forthcoming article.

[114] For some of these references, see my *op. cit.*, p. 83 n. 40.

Nevertheless, we do hear of an astonishingly large number of volunteers, most of whom, whatever the bishops might say, were given full honour as martyrs, the general body of the faithful apparently regarding them with great respect.

One of the most fascinating of the Passions of the Great Persecution is that of Euplus, who suffered at Catana in Sicily. It begins

> In the consulship of our lords Diocletian (for the ninth time) and Maximian (for the eighth time) [that is, in 304] on the 29th of April, in the most famous city of Catana, in the court room, in front of the curtain, Euplus shouted out, 'I wish to die, for I am a Christian'. His excellency Calvisianus the *corrector* said, 'Come in, whoever shouted'. And the Blessed Euplus entered the court room, bearing the immaculate Gospels—

and he achieved the end he had sought.[115]

In the next year, 305, while a festival was being celebrated at Caesarea in Palestine, a false rumour began to spread that certain Christians would be given to the beasts as part of the joyful celebrations. While the governor was on his way to the amphitheatre, six young men suddenly presented themselves before him with their hands bound behind them, crying out that they were Christians and demanding to be thrown to the beasts with their brethren. We can well believe Eusebius when he adds that the governor and his entire suite were reduced to a condition of no ordinary amazement. The young men were arrested and imprisoned, but instead of giving them to the beasts as they had demanded, the merciless pagan condemned them to a speedy death by decapitation.[116]

These are but two of a large number of similar examples. Sometimes the fact that certain martyrs were volunteers, and were not sought out by the authorities, may alter our whole picture of a persecution. For example, the many Christians Eusebius says he himself saw condemned to death in a single day in the Thebaid in Upper Egypt during the Great Persecution are described by him in terms which show that they were volunteers, who, after sentence had been pronounced upon one of their brethren, 'leapt up

[115] *Passio Eupli*, 1.
[116] Euseb., *Mart. Pal.*, 3. 2–4 (in both Recensions).

before the judgment seat from this side and from that, confessing themselves to be Christians'.[117] The seeking out of Christians in this area, therefore, need not have been nearly as vigorous as we might otherwise have assumed from the evidently large number of victims.

Now voluntary martyrdom was not just a late phenomenon, which appeared only in the general persecutions: we have examples from the second century too—indeed, from the very earliest period at which we have any detailed records of martyrdoms at all: that is to say, from the 150s onwards, including one on quite a large scale from about the year 185, recorded in Tertullian's *Ad Scapulam*. When Arrius Antoninus, proconsul of Asia, was holding his periodic assize in one of the towns of his province, a whole crowd of Christians presented themselves in a body before him, demanding the privilege of martyrdom—all the Christians of that town, says Tertullian, but we must allow for his customary exaggeration. The astonished proconsul ordered a few off to execution, but contemptuously dismissed the remainder, saying to them, 'If you want to die, you wretches, you can use ropes or precipices'.[118]

The positive evidence for voluntary martyrdom begins in the Antonine period, about 150. Conceivably, I suppose, it could have been a Montanist practice in origin. But I should like to suggest, with all the reserve necessitated by lack of direct evidence, that in fact it is likely to have begun much earlier, and that the reason why we do not hear of it before the middle of the second century is simply that we have too little specific evidence of any sort about persecution or martyrdom before that time. Here the Jewish background of Christianity, above all the Jewish martyr-literature, is a very material factor. As far back as the Maccabaean period, as Professor Baron has put it, there was born 'that great exaltation of religious martyrdom which was to dominate the minds of Jews and Christians for countless generations'.[119] We have examples of voluntary martyrdom on the part of Jews even before the Christian era, notably the incident in 4 B.C., described by Josephus, when two pious rabbis instigated their followers to cut down the golden eagle set up by Herod over the great gate of the Temple:

[117] Euseb., *Eccl. Hist.*, viii. 9. 5.
[118] Tert., *Ad Scap.*, 5. 1, quoting the proconsul's words in the original Greek.
[119] S. W. Baron, *A Social and Religious History of the Jews*, 2nd edn (New York, 1952), i, p. 230.

about forty men were executed, the rabbis and·the actual perpetrators of the deed being burnt alive.[120] Now the two most fervent works of Jewish martyr-literature, the Second and Fourth Books of Maccabees, with their unrestrained sensationalism and gruesome descriptions of tortures, both formed part of the Septuagint, and must therefore have been well known to the early Church. And indeed a detailed linguistic study by Dr Perler has shown it to be very likely that IV Maccabees exerted an important influence on the thought and writings of Ignatius,[121] whose martyrdom must have taken place during the first quarter of the second century. Although there is no evidence of any value that Ignatius himself was actually a voluntary martyr,[122] we may, I think, see him as the precursor of the whole series; for in his letter to the Church of Rome, written while he was being taken from Antioch to the capital for execution, he displays what has often been called a pathological yearning for martyrdom. He describes himself as 'lusting for death' (ἐρῶν τοῦ ἀποθανεῖν),[123] and he admonishes the Roman Christians not to try to do anything to save him. The eager way in which he speaks of the tortures confronting him—'Come fire and cross and encounters with beasts, incisions and dissections, wrenching of bones, hacking of limbs, crushing of the whole body'[124]—shows an abnormal mentality. It is difficult to believe that Ignatius was an isolated case, even in his own day. If even a few Christians of the late first and early second centuries had a similar craving for martyrdom (as so many others certainly did later), and gave practical expression to it, especially if they did so by insulting pagan cults, it would be even easier to understand how persecution quickly became endemic in many parts of the Roman world.

[120] Jos., *Bell. Jud.*, i. 33. 2–4, §§ 648–55 (cf. ii. 1. 2–3); *Ant. Jud.*, xvii. 6. 2–4, §§ 149–67.

[121] O. Perler, 'Das vierte Makkabäerbuch, Ignat. v. Antiochien u. die ältesten Martyrerberichte', *Rivista di archeologia cristiana*, xxv (1949), pp. 47–72.

[122] John Malalas (*Chronogr.*, xi, p. 276, ed. W. Dindorf) speaks of Trajan as 'exasperated against Ignatius because he reviled him', and the 'Antiochene Acts' of Ignat. (§ 2) say he was ἑκουσίως ἤγετο to Trajan at Antioch. But this hardly makes Ignat. a volunteer, and is entirely unreliable anyway: cf. *The Apostolic Fathers*, ed. J. B. Lightfoot, 2nd edn (London, 1889), ii. 2, pp. 363 ff., 383–91, 436 ff., 480–1 ff., 575–6.

[123] Ignat., *Epist. ad Rom.*, 7.2.

[124] *Ibid.*, 4. 1–2; 5. 2–3.

We are in a position at last to attempt to answer the question confronting us, which, it will be remembered, is twofold: 'Why did the government persecute?', and 'Why did the mass of pagans often demand and initiate persecution?'. I propose to take the second question first.

The answer is clear: it is given to us over and over again in the sources. It was not so much the positive beliefs and practices of the Christians which aroused pagan hostility, but above all the negative element in their religion: their total refusal to worship any god but their own. The monotheistic exclusiveness of the Christians was believed to alienate the goodwill of the gods, to endanger what the Romans called the *pax deorum* (the right harmonious relationship between gods and men),[125] and to be responsible for disasters which overtook the community. I shall call this exclusiveness, for convenience, by the name the Greeks gave to it, 'atheism' (ἀθεότης);[126] characteristically, the Latin writers refer to the same phenomenon by more concrete expressions having no philosophical overtones, such as 'deos non colere' (not paying cult to the gods): the word *atheus* first appears in Latin in Christian writers of the early fourth century, Arnobius and Lactantius.[127]

Whatever view we may hold about the mentality of educated, upper-class intellectuals, we must admit that the great mass of the population of the Roman empire, in both East and West, were at least what we should call deeply superstitious; and I see not the least reason why we should deny them genuine religious feeling,

---

[125] This subject has been discussed in innumerable works, of which I will mention here only W. Warde Fowler, *The Religious Experience of the Roman People* (London, 1911), pp. 169 ff., 272 ff.

[126] See A. Harnack, *Der Vorwurf des Atheismus in den drei ersten Jahrh.* (*Texte u. Untersuch.*, xxviii (N.F. xiii). 4, 1905). Among the texts are *Epist. ad Diogn.*, 2. 6; *Passio Polyc.*, iii. 2; ix. 2; cf. xii. 2 (Euseb., *Eccl. Hist.*, iv. 15. 6, 18–19, cf. 26); Euseb., *Eccl. Hist.*, v. 1. 9; Justin, *I Apol.*, 5–6, 13; Athenag., *Legat.*, 3, 4–30; Clem. Alex., *Strom.* vii. 1. 1. 1; Tert., *Apol.*, 6. 10 (note 'in quo principaliter reos transgressionis Christianos destinatis'); 10. 1–28. 2 (esp. 24. 1, 9); Arnob., *Adv. Gentes*, i. 29; iii. 28; v. 30; vi. 27.

[127] Arnob., as cited in the preceding note, each time referring to pagan charges against Christians. Lact. (*Epit.*, 63. 2; *De Ira*, 9. 7) uses the word of pagan philosophers only. Cicero (*De Nat. Deor.*, i. 63) has the Greek word ἄθεος (applied to Diagoras), and Min. Fel. (*Octav.*, 8. 2) transliterates (acc. 'atheon').

provided we remember the essential differences between their kind of religion and that with which we are familiar. By far the most important of these was that pagan religion was a matter of performing cult acts rather than of belief, or ethics. No positive and publicly enforceable obligation, however, rested upon any private individual, whether a Roman citizen or not, or upon a common soldier,[128] to participate in any particular acts of cult,[129] although magistrates and senators of Rome itself,[130] and magistrates (and perhaps senators) of individual Greek and Roman towns,[131] might be legally obliged to do so; and of course great social pressure might be brought to bear upon individuals who refused (on adopting Christianity or Judaism, for instance) to take part in family or other observances. No compulsion was necessary, because until the advent of Christianity no one ever had any reason for refusing to take part in the ceremonies which others observed—except of course the Jews, and they were a special case, a unique exception. Much as the Jews were detested by the bulk of the Roman governing class, as well as by many humbler Romans and Greeks, it was admitted (by the educated, at any rate) that their religious rites were ancestral, and very ancient. All men were expected piously to preserve the religious customs of their ancestors. And so even Tacitus, who strongly disliked Judaism, could say that the religious rites of the Jews 'have the recommendation of being ancient'.[132] The gods would forgive the

[128] See Tert., De Idolol., 19: for a man serving in a '[militia] caligata vel inferior quaeque' there is no 'necessitas immolationum'.

[129] See, briefly, Mommsen, Römisches Strafrecht, p. 568, and on the whole subject Nock, op. cit. (n. 97 above), esp. pp. 189–92, 212–3.

[130] For Roman senators, see e.g. S.C. ap. Edict. Augusti ad Cyren., 135–6 (S. Riccobono, Fontes Iuris Romani Anteiustiniani, i, 2nd edn (Florence, 1941), no. 68); Suet., Div. Aug., 35. 3. If Euseb., Eccl. Hist., viii. 1. 2, is to be believed, some Christian officials in the provinces in the late 3rd century will have been given an imperial dispensation from religious duties. (These men to whom the emperors entrusted τὰς τῶν ἐθνῶν ἡγεμονίας will hardly have been provincial governors: cf. Eccl. Hist., viii. 9. 7; 11. 2).

[131] If only to take oaths when required: see e.g. the Lex Municipalis Salpensana, xxvi (Riccobono, FIRA, i², no. 23). The Severi gave Jews holding municipal honores exemption from religious acts offensive to them: Dig., l. 2. 3. 3.

[132] Tac., Hist., v. 5: 'antiquitate defenduntur'. Cf. Orig., c. Cels., v. 25 ff. And the fact that Jewish cult was aniconic seems to have appealed to some Romans, e.g. Varro (August., De Civ. Dei, iv. 31).

inexplicable monotheism of the Jews, who were, so to speak, licensed atheists.[133] The Jews of course would not sacrifice to the emperor or his gods, but they were quite willing, while the Temple still stood, to sacrifice to their own god for the well-being of the emperor; and Augustus, if we may believe Philo,[134] by a happy compromise not only accepted this but himself paid for the sacrifices. Matters were very different with the Christians, who had *ex hypothesi* abandoned their ancestral religions. Gibbon expressed the contrast perfectly when he wrote, 'The Jews were a people which followed, the Christians a sect which deserted, the religion of their fathers'.[135]

The Christians asserted openly either that the pagan gods did not exist at all or that they were malevolent demons. Not only did they themselves refuse to take part in pagan religious rites: they would not even recognize that others ought to do so. As a result, because a large part of Greek religion and the whole of the Roman state religion was very much a community affair, the mass of pagans were naturally apprehensive that the gods would vent their wrath at this dishonour not upon the Christians alone but upon the whole community; and when disasters did occur, they were only too likely to fasten the blame on to the Christians. That the Christians were indeed hated for precisely this reason above all others appears from many passages in the sources, from the mid-second century right down to the fifth. Tertullian sums it all up in a brilliant and famous sentence in the *Apologeticus*: the pagans, he says, 'suppose that the Christians are the cause of every public disaster, every misfortune that happens to the people. If the Tiber overflows or the Nile doesn't, if there is a drought or an earthquake, a famine or a pestilence, at once the cry goes up, "The Christians to the lion" '.[136]

---

[133] For pagans calling Jews 'atheists', see J. Juster, *Les Juifs dans l'Empire romain* (Paris, 1914), i, p. 45 n. 1, § 2.

[134] Philo, *Leg. ad Gai.*, 157, 317. Contrast Jos., *c. Ap.*, ii. 6, § 77 (and cf. *Bell. Jud.*, ii. 10. 4, § 197). For an attempt to explain the contradiction between Philo and Jos., see E. M. Smallwood's edn of the *Leg. ad Gai.* (Leiden, 1961), pp. 240–1.

[135] Gibbon, *op. cit.* (n. 112 above), ii, ch. xvi, p. 74 (marginal summary).

[136] Tert., *Apol.*, 40. 1–2 (with 37. 2); cf. *Ad. Nat.*, i. 9; also Firmilian, *ap.* Cypr., *Epist.*, lxxv. 10; Cypr., *Ad Demetrian.*, esp. 2–5; Arnob., *Adv. Nat.*, i. 1 ff. (esp. 13, 16, 26) and *passim*; August., *De Civ. Dei*, ii. 3 (proverb: 'No rain, because of the Christians') etc.; Orig., *c. Cels.*, iii.

The essential point I want to make is that this superstitious feeling on the part of the pagans was due above all to the Christians' 'atheism', their refusal to acknowledge the gods and give them their due by paying them cult. The Christian Apologists have much to say in reply to this charge[137]—and, by the way, they are addressing themselves to the educated class, sometimes in theory to the emperors themselves. The earliest surviving Apologists are of the mid-second century, but there is no reason to think the situation was different earlier.

We must not confuse the kind of atheism charged against the Christians with philosophical scepticism. Tertullian pretends to be very indignant because philosophers are permitted openly to attack pagan superstitions, while Christians are not. 'They openly demolish your gods and also attack your superstitions in their writings, and you applaud them for it', he exclaims.[138] The vital difference was, of course, that the philosophers, whatever they might believe, and even write down for circulation among educated folk, would have been perfectly willing to perform any cult act required of them—and that was what mattered.

That the religious misbehaviour of certain individuals should be thought of by pagans as likely to bring unselective divine punishment may seem less strange to us when we remember that similar views were held by Jews and Christians. Orthodox Christians felt towards heretics much as pagans felt towards them. The martyred bishop Polycarp, who (it was said) had actually known the Apostles personally, used to tell how the Apostle John, entering the baths at Ephesus, rushed out again when he saw the heresiarch Cerinthus inside, crying, 'Away, lest the very baths collapse, for within is Cerinthus, the enemy of the truth'.[139]

About the middle of the third century, however, the attitude of the general run of pagans towards the Christians begins to undergo a distinct change. Whereas until then the initiative in persecu-

15; *Comm. ser. in Matt.*, 39; Maximin Daia, in Euseb., *Eccl. Hist.*, ix. 7. 3–14 (esp. 8–9); 8. 3.

137 See n. 126 above.

138 Tert., *Apol.*, 46. 4.

139 Iren., *Adv. Haeres.* (ed. W. W. Harvey), iii. 3. 4; Euseb., *Eccl. Hist.*, iii. 28. 6; iv. 14. 6. The same mentality can be found among the Christian emperors: see e.g. Constantine's letter to Aelafius, of 313–4 (Optatus, *Append.* iii, f. 30b); *Cod. Theod.*, xvi. 5. 40. 1 (A.D. 407); *Nov. Theod.*, iii. pr., and above all 8 (A.D. 438).

tion seems to have come from below, from 250 onwards persecution comes from above, from the government, and is initiated by imperial edict, with little or no sign of persecuting zeal among the mass of pagans. The beginning of the change seems to me to come with the Decian persecution. The last two recorded major outbreaks of popular fury against the Christians which I know of were those in Cappadocia and Pontus in 235[140] and at Alexandria in 249.[141] The change has gone quite far by the time of the Great Persecution, when the majority of pagans (except in a few places, like Gaza)[142] seem to be at least indifferent, some even sympathetic to the Christians,[143] and few provincial governors display any enthusiasm for the task. 'The government had outrun pagan animosity'.[144] The reason for the change, I take it, is that Christianity had by now spread widely and lost its secretive character, and pagans had come to realize that Christians were not so different from themselves, and just as religious.

I have ignored minor reasons for popular dislike of the Christians; but no doubt some people might feel a grudge against them on simple economic grounds: we may remember how these are said to have been responsible for arousing opposition to apostolic preaching at Philippi and Ephesus.[145]

Finally, we can try to analyse the attitude of the government. For once it is of little avail to ransack earlier Roman history for precedents, in the hope of discovering the principles on which Rome treated foreign religions,[146] because the great problem posed by Christianity, its exclusiveness, was something Rome had never encountered before—except under very different conditions, in the Jewish national religion.[147]

[140] Firmilian, as cited in n. 136 above.
[141] Dionys. Alex., *ap.* Euseb., *Eccl. Hist.*, vi. 41. 1–9. The cause of this outbreak is not given.
[142] See Euseb., *Mart. Pal.*, 3. 1 (Long Recension).
[143] See esp. Athanasius, *Hist. Arian.*, 64.
[144] N. H. Baynes, *CAH*, xii, p. 677.
[145] Acts 16:16–24; 19:23–41. (For the trade in images, see Philostratus, *Vita Apollon.*, v. 20.) See also Tert., *Apol.*, 42–3. And cf. Pliny, *Epist.*, x. 96. 10—perhaps in a case such as this the butchers might be aggrieved!
[146] The article by H. Last in *JRS*, xxvii (1937), pp. 80–92, is nevertheless useful for its detailed examination of earlier acts of interference in religious matters by the Romans.
[147] It was perhaps a failure to realize the importance of this factor that led

I do not myself believe that there is a single solution to our problem. I believe that different members of the governing class may have been actuated by different motives, and I think that each one of us must decide for himself how much weight he would attach to each. I have already mentioned some minor factors, which may in some cases have played an important and even a decisive part: the need to pacify public opinion; and suspicion of the Christians as a conspiratorial body, or at least as undesirables, *mali homines*. But for my own part I believe that the main motives of the government, in the long run, were essentially religious in character, according to the ancient conception of religion. These religious motives appear in two rather different forms, which some people might prefer to call 'superstitious' and 'political' respectively, thereby avoiding the term 'religious' altogether. Some of the governing class, in the third century at any rate (and I believe from the first), were undoubtedly inspired by the very motives I have described as characteristic of their subjects. Among the persecuting emperors, we must certainly place Galerius in this category (on the contemporary evidence of Lactantius),[148] and also Diocletian, who seems to have been a thoroughly religious man.[149] About Decius and Valerian I would reserve my opinion. It is true that after the Severan period we find many soldier-emperors of little or no education, whom we might suspect of the grosser forms of superstition; and of course among the higher officials such as provincial governors there will have been a greater proportion of uneducated men. But, as it happens, Decius cannot

Nock, *op. cit.* (n. 97 above), p. 217, to make a generalization about the policy of the Roman government in religious matters which seems to me mistaken in regard to Christianity: 'To sum up, the state interfered not because the Roman gods were failing to get their due but because particular practices or groups were held to be unsuitable or subversive or demoralizing. That is in substance true of official action against the Christians prior to Decius'.

[148] Lact., *De Mort. Persec.*, 9 ff., esp. 10. 6; 11. 1–4, 8. Galerius seems to have been the chief instigator of the Great Persecution: see my *op. cit.* (n. 4 above), p. 109.

[149] See e.g. Euseb., *Vita Const.*, ii. 51, and note the tone of parts of Diocletian's copious legislation, esp. the long edict concerning marriage (*Mos. et Rom. Leg. Coll.*, vi. 4, esp. §§ 1, 2, 6), or that against the Manichees (*Idem*, xv. 3, esp. § 3), or even the opening of the edict on prices (see *Economic Survey of Ancient Rome*, ed. T. Frank (Baltimore, 1940) v, p. 311). See also Lact., *De Mort. Persec.*, 11. 6.

be called a man of that sort, and conspicuously not Valerian. I would concede that even in the third century, and to a far greater extent in the second, especially the early second, there may have been a significant number of members of the governing class who did not share the superstitious horror felt for the Christians by the masses. But even such people, I believe, were impelled to persecute—perhaps as vigorously as their less emancipated brethren—by motives I think we are justified in calling religious,[150] in that their aim also was always primarily to break down the Christian refusal to worship the pagan gods, even if the basis from which they proceeded was different.

I want to stress two vital pieces of evidence which I do not see how we can explain away. First, there is the fact that except to a limited extent in the time of Valerian, and more seriously under Diocletian, what I have called the positive side of Christianity is never officially attacked: persecution did not extend to any aspect of the Christian religion other than its refusal to acknowledge other gods. No attempt was ever made, even in the general persecutions, to prohibit Christians from worshipping their own god in private, although Valerian[151] and Diocletian[152] (but not Decius) forbade them to assemble for common worship, and Diocletian also ordered the destruction of churches and the confiscation of sacred books and church property.[153] As the deputy prefect of Egypt said to Bishop Dionysius of Alexandria in 257, 'Who prevents you from worshipping your own god also, if he is a god, along with the natural gods?'.[154] And of course the sacrifice test continues to be used, and if the Christian complies with it he goes free, even in the general persecutions.

Secondly, there is what I believe to have been the complete immunity from persecution of most of the Gnostic sects. Some of these professed doctrines of a recognizably Christian character

---

[150] In general, I warmly agree with the views expressed by J. Vogt, *Zur Religiosität der Christenverfolger im Röm. Reich* (*Sb. Akad. Heidelberg.*, Phil.-hist. Klasse, 1962).

[151] See *Passio Cypr.*, i. 7; Euseb., *Eccl. Hist.*, vii. 11. 10–11.

[152] See Euseb., *Eccl. Hist.*, ix. 10. 8; *Passio Saturnini et al. Abitin.*, esp. 1, 2, 5–14 (the best text is by P. Franchi de' Cavalieri, *Studi e testi*, lxv (1935), pp. 49–71; see also Th. Ruinart, *Acta Martyrum*, edn of 1859, pp. 414 f.); *Passio Philippi Heracl.*, 4 (Ruinart, *op. cit.*, p. 441).

[153] The references are given in my *op. cit.* (n. 4 above), p. 75 nn. 1–3.

[154] Euseb., *Eccl. Hist.*, vii. 11. 9.

(heretical in varying degrees as they were) and called themselves Christians. Yet in Roman eyes there was evidently a fundamental difference between Gnostics and orthodox Christians, if Gnostics were not persecuted. Why? The reason can only be that the Gnostics did not think it necessary to be exclusive, like the orthodox, and refuse to pay outward respect to the pagan gods when the necessity arose. We are told by orthodox Christian sources that Basilides, perhaps the most important of all the Gnostic heresiarchs, permitted his followers to eat meat which had been offered to idols, and in time of persecution 'casually to deny the faith', doubtless by accepting the sacrifice test.[155] It appears, then, that although the tenets of the Gnostics must have appeared to the Roman governing class to be very similar to those of the orthodox, the Gnostics escaped persecution precisely because they consented to take part in pagan religious ceremonies on demand, when the orthodox refused to do so.

What then was the attitude of the more enlightened pagans among the governing class? Why did they too persecute?

Here I think it may be helpful if I re-tell a story told by Henry Crabb Robinson about the reception by Lord Thurlow, Lord Chancellor of England, of a deputation which waited upon him in 1788 to secure his support in their efforts to bring about the repeal of the Corporation and Test Acts. Lord Thurlow 'heard them very civilly, and then said, "Gentlemen, I'm against you, by God. I am for the Established Church, damme! Not that I have any more regard for the Established Church than for any other church, but because *it is* established. And if you can get your damned religion established, I'll be for that too" '.[156]

Lord Thurlow may not have been exactly what we should call today a religious man, but his attitude may help us to understand that of some members of the Roman governing class of the late Republic and early Principate—though of course I am not saying it is the same. Religion, for such Romans, was above all the *ius divinum*, the body of state law relating to sacred matters, which

---

[155] Agrippa Castor, *ap.* Euseb., *Eccl. Hist.*, iv. 7. 7; cf. Iren., *Adv. Haeres.* (ed. W. W. Harvey), i. 19. 3; iii. 19. 4; iv. 54; Tert., *Scorp.*, esp. 1, 15; Clem. Alex., *Strom.*, iv. 4. 16. 3–17. 3; 9. 71. 1–72. 4; 12. 81–8. And see Frend, *op. cit.* (1954) in n. 2 above.

[156] *Diary, Reminiscences, and Correspondence of Henry Crabb Robinson*, ed. T. Sadler, 3rd edn (London, 1872), i, p. 197 (ch. xv).

preserved the *pax deorum* by means of the appropriate ceremonial.[157] It derived its great value, as Cicero repeatedly affirms,
mainly from the fact that it rested upon the *auctoritas maiorum*,[158]
the force of ancestral tradition. As Dr Weinstock has pointed
out,[159] St Augustine was very much in the Ciceronian tradition
when he declared that he would not believe the very Gospel itself,
did it not rest upon the *auctoritas* of the Catholic Church[160]—a
point of view still held today by some Christian churches. Cicero,
legislating in the *De Legibus* for his ideal commonwealth, begins
with *ius divinum*.[161] In the *De Natura Deorum* he makes his more
sceptical speaker, Cotta, open his case in Book i by proclaiming
that he is himself a *pontifex*, who believes that 'religious rites and
ceremonies ought to be maintained with the utmost reverence',[162]
and much more to the same effect. He makes his Stoic speaker,
Balbus, echo sentiments he had expounded himself in his speech
to the senate, *De Haruspicum Responsis*, to the effect that the Romans
'in religion, that is the cult of the gods, are far superior to other
nations'.[163] Such passages could be multiplied. It seems to me
entirely beside the point (though doubtless true enough) to object
that Cicero rarely if ever shows any unmistakable sign of 'personal religion', as we should call it. And when Professor Latte, in
his great history of Roman religion, says that one finds in Cicero's

---

[157] See the remark by Caecilius, the pagan speaker in Minuc. Fel., *Octav.*,
7. 2: all religious ceremonies were invented 'vel ut remuneraretur divina
indulgentia, vel ut averteretur imminens ira aut iam tumens et saeviens
placaretur'.

[158] Cic., *De Nat. Deor.*, iii. 5–9 is perhaps the most illuminating passage.
See also *De Div.*, ii. 148, etc.

[159] S. Weinstock, *JRS*, li (1961), pp. 206 ff., at p. 210. (I am grateful to Dr
Weinstock for allowing me, before the delivery of the paper on which
this article is based, to read the MS of his very impressive discussion,
then not yet published. I found his para. 3, pp. 208–10, particularly
helpful.)

[160] August., *Contra Epist. Manich.*, 5.

[161] Cic., *De Leg*, ii. 18–22.

[162] Cic., *De Nat. Deor.*, i. 61.

[163] *Ibid.*, ii. 8; cf. *De Har. Resp.*, 19. Among many similar passages in other
authors, see Val. Max., i. 1, esp. §§ 8, 9; Tert., *Apol.*, 25. 2. An
interesting early text is *SIG*³, no. 601 (B.C. 193), and one of the last (and
most important) is Symmachus, *Rel.* iii (ed. O. Seeck, pp. 280–3), of
A.D. 384. Other texts are cited in A. S. Pease's edn of the *De Nat. Deor.*,
ii (Cambridge, Mass., 1958), p. 567.

philosophical works no 'inward participation',[164] I feel as if I were being invited to note the absence of colour in a black-and-white drawing. The Roman state religion contained nothing that was personal to the individual. And as for *rational* belief (or disbelief) in the gods—did it ever figure in the thoughts of Cicero and his kind except when they were playing the Greek game of philosophical disputation? Contrast the *instinctive* belief which Cotta in the *De Natura Deorum*, speaking to Balbus, proclaims in the words, 'From you, a philosopher, I am bound to ask for a rational account of religion. Our ancestors I must *believe*, even in the absence of rational explanation'.[165] These people had a deep emotional feeling for Roman religion, as the *ius divinum*, the 'foundation of our state',[166] an essential part of the whole Roman way of life. One can still hold this to be true, even if, taking perhaps an uncharitable view (as I would myself), one holds that quite a large part of that religion was above all an instrument by which the governing class hoped to keep the reins of power in its own hands.[167] In the *De Legibus*, Cicero, himself an augur, glorifies that office because past augurs have been able to annul laws passed by reforming tribunes, to which Cicero refuses the very name of law.[168] But such deep-seated expressions of his own interests and those of his class are far from making his conception of religion 'insincere' or 'cynical'—indeed, the reverse is true.

I have appealed to Cicero because I suppose most people would agree that the author of the *De Divinatione* may well be considered one of the least superstitious men in an age which was distinctly less superstitious than the age of the persecutions. For Cicero's

---

[164] K. Latte, *Röm. Religionsgesch.*, 2nd edn (Munich, 1960), p. 285.

[165] Cic., *De Nat. Deor.*, iii. 6.

[166] *Ibid.*, iii. 5.

[167] For δεισιδαιμονία (which in this passage is perhaps best translated 'fear of the supernatural') as the very cement of the Roman constitution, see Polyb., vi. 56. 7–12. Varro, the greatest authority on Roman religion, thought it expedient, as did Scaevola before him, that 'states should be deceived in matters of religion': August., *De Civ. Dei*, iv. 27, cf. 31, 32. See in addition Augustine's attack on Seneca (based on his lost work on Superstition), in *CD*, vi. 10; also Livy, i. 19. 4–5; Dio Cass., lii. 36. 1–3.

[168] Cic., *De Leg.*, ii. 14, 31. In the face of conflicting opinions among the experts whether divination really had a supernatural basis or was simply a political expedient ('ad utilitatem . . . reipublicae composita'), Cicero proceeds (*Ibid.*, 32–3) to declare his belief in the divine origin of augury,

spiritual descendants of the early Principate, Roman religion was part of the very stuff of Roman life and Roman greatness; and they were prepared to extend their protection also to the cults of the peoples of their empire, whose devotion to their ancestral religions seemed to their rulers only right and proper. Can we imagine that such men, however intellectually emancipated from the superstitions of the vulgar, would have had any compunction about executing the devotees of a new-fangled sect which threatened almost every element of Roman religion, and indeed of all the traditional cults conducted by the inhabitants of the Roman world? I would be prepared to speak of persecution so motivated as being conducted for religious reasons, though I realize that other people might prefer to use another word—political, perhaps.

I shall end by quoting what seems to me the most illuminating single text in all the ancient sources, for the understanding of the persecutions. Paternus, proconsul of Africa, is speaking to Cyprian at his first trial in 257, and telling him what the emperors have just decreed. This, it is true, is a special edict, making it incumbent upon the Christian clergy, on pain of exile, to perform certain acts which ordinary folk would not normally be obliged to carry out; but what is enjoined is something any accused Christian might be ordered to perform, and this gives the text general significance. The decree is: 'Eos qui Romanam religionem non colunt debere Romanas caerimonias recognoscere'.[169] I think the sense is brought out best by translating the main clause negatively: 'Those who do not profess the Roman religion'—it is admitted that there are such people—'must not refuse to take part in Roman religious ceremonies'.[170]

while lamenting its present decline. In the later *De Div.*, however, he makes it perfectly clear that he had no belief in the reality of divination (ii, esp. 28–150), although in public he would keep up a pretence of taking it seriously, as a useful buttress of the constitution and the state religion (ii. 28, 70–1).

[169] *Passio Cypr.*, i. 1.

[170] By far the most important book on the persecutions published during the past few years is W. H. C. Frend, *Martyrdom and Persecution in the Early Church*; cf. the reviews by F. Millar, *JRS*, lvi (1966), pp. 231–6, and G. E. M. de Ste Croix, *JTS*, xviii (1967), pp. 217–21. *Re* n. 18 and pp. 228–33: Sherwin-White's article of 1952 has been reprinted (with an Addendum) as Appendix V in his *The Letters of Pliny* (Oxford, 1966), pp. 772–87. See further T. D. Barnes, 'Legislation against the Christians', *JRS*, lviii (1968), pp. 32–50. *Re* n. 22: see

the analysis of Pliny, *Epist.*, x. 96 by de Ste Croix in *The Crucible of Christianity*, ed. A. Toynbee (London, 1969), pp. 345–7, and the commentary by Sherwin-White, *Letters to Pliny*, pp. 691–712. Re n. 63: The best account is now E. J. Bickerman, 'Trajan, Hadrian and the Christians', *Rivista di filologia*, xcvi (1968), pp. 296–315.

I agree with F. Millar, *JRS*, lviii (1968), p. 222, that the standard procedure in Roman criminal trials should not (as on pp. 217–18 and 220 of this chapter) be *called* 'cognitio extra ordinem', an expression which is never actually used in the ancient sources.

X

WHY WERE THE EARLY CHRISTIANS PERSECUTED? AN AMENDMENT*

A. N. Sherwin-White

Mr de Ste Croix, in his article in *Past and Present*, No. 26 (Nov. 1963) (chapter IX) has given what will for long rank among the most satisfactory treatments of this theme. But he is primarily concerned with popular opinion and the attitude of the government in the later second and third centuries when the administration had become aware of the nature and extent of the Christian phenomenon. Few will disagree that the central objection was then to the 'godlessness' of the Christians—their refusal to recognize a citizen's duty towards the gods of the local communities, and, in some circumstances, of Rome. But in what concerns motives Ste Croix's method is to begin at the end and to work backwards, and inevitably his treatment of the period before Hadrian is less satisfactory in this respect, although he concedes that other objections were on occasion then invoked against the Christians. Since Ste Croix starts from a criticism of some views expressed by myself, perhaps I may take up the question of the earlier period.

The belief that 'godlessness' was the core of the matter depends entirely upon the evidence of the later period, which is drawn not from Roman or official sources, but from the Christian 'apologies' and the early martyr-acts, composed from a Christian view-point, though sometimes written in the format of a Roman court-record.[1] But for the earliest period of Christian persecution we have

* From no. 27 (1964).

[1] In this discussion it suffices to refer back to Ste Croix's chapter for most references. See pp. 216 f., 234 f. His article and mine on 'The early

the testimony of three highly placed Roman administrators, the consulars Pliny and Tacitus, who had governed oriental provinces, where Christians were most numerous, and the equestrian Suetonius, who had been the chief imperial secretary for provincial affairs at Rome. Their accounts were written within a short span of time, in the last years of Trajan and the early years of Hadrian, approximately between A.D. 110 and at the latest 125. In all three the only ground indicated for the proscription of the cult is its association with crimes and immoralities—*flagitia, scelera, maleficia*.[2] Pliny at the time of the first trials which he reports knew only that the 'name' was punishable, and that this might be connected with certain *flagitia*. Subsequently he became concerned at the reported neglect of civic cults due to the influence of the Christians.[3] But he does not put this forward as the supposed ground of the proscription of the 'name' at that time.

Ste Croix's account makes no serious allowance for change and development in the attitude of the government to the Christians, as it learned more about them in the very long period of over 180 years which the intermittent lesser persecutions covered. He is historically at fault in rejecting any approach to the problem, in the terms of Hardy and Last, through consideration of the well-documented treatment of other *superstitiones pravae* in the earlier Principate, where in each case the ground of action against the cult was the criminal behaviour of its followers.[4] Though the notion that a *Roman citizen* ought only to worship his own civic gods was never entirely forgotten, it plays a very minor role in the treatment of foreign cults in the first century A.D. The evidence of the three officials, Pliny, Tacitus and Suetonius, confirms that in its first dealings with the Christians, the Roman government—and the individual governors—behaved exactly as it did towards

persecutions and Roman law again', *JTS*, new ser., iii (1952), pp. 199–213, provide all relevant bibliography.

[2] Pliny, *Epist.*, x. 96. 2. Tac., *Ann.*, xv. 44. 3–4 and 8. Suet., *Nero*, 16. 2. For the dates cf. R. Syme, *Tacitus* (Oxford, 1948), app. nos. 71–2, 76, 77.

[3] *Loc. cit.*, 10, 'certe satis constat prope iam desolata templa coepisse celebrari', etc. refers to the situation some time after the measures reported by him in 1–6.

[4] Ste Croix, p. 242, notes 146–7. E. G. Hardy, *Christianity and the Roman Government* (London, 1894), ch. i, with H. M. Last, 'The study of the persecutions', *JRS*, xxvii (1937), pp. 80 ff.

other 'superstitions'. How else could they behave when the Christian cult first came to their attention?

The crucial question is—when did the central government perceive that the extensiveness of the Christian following required that their exclusive godlessness was in itself not to be tolerated, apart from other associated offences? Pliny's letter suggests that this did not happen before his time, and the coherence of the three official witnesses suggests that for the earliest period, from Nero to Hadrian, *flagitia* and *scelera* are the key, despite Ste Croix's efforts to pooh-pooh them. No doubt these gradually dropped out of favour as the nature of the Christian communities became better known. Pliny clearly had *flagitia* in mind when he reported that his examination of the apostates and the deaconesses revealed nothing scandalous. But Trajan discounted this in the opening words of his reply, to which, I think, adequate attention has never been given.[5] To all Pliny's queries about the nature of the charges Trajan simply replied: 'You have followed the correct procedure—*actum*'. This word *actus* is technical for judicial procedure, and by this sentence Trajan laid down a much more precise instruction than is generally realized, confirming exactly the system of *accusatio nominis*, triple inquisition, and death sentence followed by Pliny. Hence he had no occasion to explain or justify the grounds of the accusation. But it is apparent that he was satisfied with the previous official line as defined in the three official witnesses, and rejects any suggestion that it should be re-examined.

Surprisingly Ste Croix makes no use of the independent evidence of Lucian, though it supports his account of the later period very satisfactorily. Writing at the end of the second century, in an explicit passage of his *De morte Peregrini* (11–14), and more briefly in his *Alexander* (25), Lucian is quite unaware of any charges of immoral behaviour against Christians, and regards their sole offence as lying in their 'godlessness', though he is acquainted with the official prosecution of Christians. Between the time of Pliny and that of Lucian and the earlier Christian sources the line of development is clear. Stress on *flagitia* has been replaced by stress on 'godlessness'. The charge of *flagitia* recurs for the last time seriously in the events at Lyons under Marcus Aurelius. Thereafter the thesis of Ste Croix prevails. There has been a switch of emphasis.

[5] Pliny, *Epist.*, x. 97. 1.

It was to explain this switch that my theory of *contumacia*—much criticized by Ste Croix—was proposed. Now it is surely beyond dispute that when Pliny affirmed that whatever the underlying nature of the 'name' might be, he was satisfied that it was right to execute the Christians on account of their *pertinaciam . . . et inflexibilem obstinationem*, he was referring to their defiance of his authority as a governor. To what else could he be referring? Though he uses the associated term *perseverantes* of the Christian refusal to change their plea, he does not use the word *contumacia* itself; but it is a prosaic lawyer's word, whereas his report is written in a markedly literary style.[6] Equally, the word does not reappear in later 'persecution' contexts—because there are *no* later official documents, apart from the garbled version of Hadrian's rescript to Minicius Fundanus, in which it might appear. *Contumacia* in some legal contexts may amount merely to a kind of 'contempt of court'. But it frequently means a great deal more than this, as Ste Croix's own citations show.[7] The best illustration is not in the legal texts of the Severan period, but in a document much nearer Pliny's day, neglected by Ste Croix—the decree of a proconsul of Sardinia issued in A.D. 69.[8] Here the persistent failure of a village to observe a decision about boundaries is equated with *contumacia* and *seditio*, and the villagers are warned that a heavy physical punishment awaits them if they persist in their disobedience, which weighs more heavily on the governor's mind than the boundary question itself. The line of thought in Pliny is the same. The point for the general history of the persecutions is that Christian defiance eventually drew attention to the hard core

---

[6] Cf. R. M. Grant, 'Pliny and the Christians', *HTR*, xli (1948), pp. 273 ff., who however overestimates the echoes of Livy in Pliny's letter. Similarly in *Epist.*, 81. 2 and 7–8 Pliny describes charges of *maiestas* without using the technical term, which occurs in Trajan's matter-of-fact reply.

[7] Ste Croix, note 100. He curiously underestimates the importance of 'deliberate wilful defiance' in Roman eyes. The disobedience of a child to a father, which he cites from Justinian as a type of *contumacia*, was far more heinous to a Roman magnate than to an Oxford don, who does not have the notion of *patria potestas*. But Ste Croix rightly criticized me in so far as I limited my evidence to the narrower conception of *contumacia*.

[8] *ILS*, 5947. The text is composite, and quotes decisions of governors from 66 to 69. Cf. my *Roman Society and Roman Law in the New Testament* (Oxford, 1963), pp. 19–20.

of the Christian attitude, their 'godlessness', which was the basis of their defiance. It is clear from Ste Croix's own citations, to which may be added the instance cited from Lucian above, that many governors were reluctant to sentence Christians even in the late second century, when on his view this very 'godlessness' was the principal objection against them.[9] It is arguable that some of these reluctant governors, who nevertheless executed some Christians, reacted as Pliny had done. Though unconvinced by talk of *flagitia* or indifferent to 'godlessness', they still thought that the Christian attitude to themselves, like that of the Sardinians to their Neronian governor, was seditious and hence deserved a capital punishment. It is not just a matter of 'behaviour in court', but of a basic attitude towards authority. The emperor Marcus Aurelius had something to say in a famous passage, the relevance of which Ste Croix does not note. Death should be sought, he wrote, only on rational grounds, not as by the Christians, *out of sheer disobedience*. How else may one translate his Greek but by the Latin *ob meram contumaciam*?[10]

One last refinement. The second century A.D. saw a steady transformation in the attitude of the Roman government to the subject peoples. As the governing class came to be recruited increasingly from outside of Italy the distinction between Roman citizens, subjects and foreigners became blurred politically. Upper class provincials of foreign status, the *honestiores*, tended to acquire particular privileges of Roman citizens even though they lacked the technical condition. The peoples of the empire came to be regarded as 'our people', *cives* or *homines nostri*. This attitude led finally to the amalgamation of all subjects as Roman citizens under the *constitutio Antoniniana*.[11] In this social environment it was inevitable that much more attention should be paid to those who neglected gods who were no longer just the gods of foreign and subject communities, but gods of an increasingly unified world-state. The attitude of the provincially born governors and emperors of the second and third centuries was likely to differ in the end from that of the predominantly Italian aristocracy of the first century A.D.[12]

---

[9] *Art. cit.*, pp. 221, 236.

[10] *Meditations*, xi. 3: κατὰ ψιλὴν παράταξιν.

[11] See e.g. my *Roman Society*, pp. 69, 180, or more fully my *Roman Citizenship*, ch. xiii.

[12] Of the three official witnesses, Pliny came from north Italy, Tacitus

more probably from Narbonensis than north Italy (Syme, *op. cit.*, ch. xlv), and Suetonius more probably from central Italy than from Africa Proconsularis (Syme, *op. cit.*, app. no. 76; the debate continues). But all three were educated from their early teens at the capital.

XI

WHY WERE THE EARLY CHRISTIANS PERSECUTED? A REJOINDER*

G. E. M. de Ste Croix

There are two different questions in dispute between Mr Sherwin-White and myself: (1) whether 'sheer disobedience', as such, was ever a ground for the judicial condemnation of Christians; and (2) whether at first the government behaved to Christianity *'exactly* as it did towards other "superstitions" ' (pp. 251–2 above), and 'the *only* ground indicated for the proscription of the [Christian] cult[1] is its association with crimes and immoralities—*flagitia, scelera, maleficia'* (p. 251, with the next two paragraphs: my italics).

1. On the first question, most of my criticisms of Mr Sherwin-White's article of 1952 still stand (see pp. 228–31 of chapter IX), especially the second, to which he has made no reply; and he now exposes the weakness of his case even more clearly by citing texts which, when correctly interpreted, turn against him.

First, the passage in Marcus Aurelius (xi. 3). Here Mr Sherwin-White takes the phrase κατὰ ψιλὴν παράταξιν, out of its context, as the equivalent of 'ob meram contumaciam' and assumes that Marcus is accusing the Christians of seeking death 'out of sheer disobedience'. In fact Marcus is contrasting the attitude of the Christians to death with the attitude he himself approves, formed by an act of individual judgment (ἀπὸ ἰδικῆς κρίσεως), arrived at 'rationally and with dignity and without theatricality' (λελογισμένως καὶ σεμνῶς καὶ . . . ἀτραγῴδως). There is no room here for any idea of disobedience or defiance of authority ('contumacia').

* From no. 27 (1964).
[1] It is inexact to speak of the Christian 'cult' in this connection: the Christian *cult* was not directly attacked before the Valerianic persecution (see p. 244 of chapter IX).

What Marcus is objecting to is the Christians' *irrational pig-headedness*, and the Latin equivalent of παράταξις here is *obstinatio*[2] —a complaint often levelled against Christians.[3] Mr Sherwin-White, substituting *contumacia* for *obstinatio*, converts 'mere obstinacy' (cf. pp. 230–2 of chapter IX) into 'sheer disobedience'. In exactly the same way he tries to turn the puzzled Pliny's attribution to the Christians of 'pertinacia ... et inflexibilis obstinatio' into something quite different: 'defiance of his authority as governor'. But again, the text speaks of 'obstinacy', not of defiance or disobedience. And Pliny is not giving a formal, technical justification of his actions: that was not necessary. What he is saying is, '*Well anyway*, they were a thoroughly obstinate crew and deserved what they got'. In spite of his 'nescio quid ... puniri soleat', his own actions (see the first two sentences of § 3 of his letter) show that he knew confessors should be executed for the 'Name', for 'being Christians'. Their 'obstinacy' was one of the undesirable manifestations of the Christian *superstitio*.

Secondly, the Sardinian inscription (p. 253 above). I ignored this as irrelevant: it reveals an entirely different situation, and the text actually underlines Mr Sherwin-White's inability to cite any direct evidence. Here the proconsul does indeed accuse the Galillenses of disobedience, to an actual judicial decision ('nec parentes decreto suo'), and of *contumacia* (even *longa contumacia*, defiance of repeated orders to clear out), and he threatens that if the situation continues he will treat them as guilty of *seditio*. How convenient it would be for Mr Sherwin-White if he could quote even a few statements of this sort in relation to the persecution of Christians, as his theory demands that he should! But there is in fact no evidence that Christians were ever executed *because* they were guilty of 'disobedience'. When Mr Sherwin-White says there are 'no later official documents' in which his favourite expression 'contumacia' might appear, he forgets that 'the early martyr-acts, ... written in the format of a Roman court-record' (p. 250 above), sometimes preserve the actual words spoken by the magistrate trying the case. Here the sentence on the Scillitan martyrs is very significant: the proconsul says, 'quoniam oblata sibi facultate ad

---

[2] See F. Martinazzoli, *Parataxeis* (Florence, 1953), pp. 17 ff.
[3] See, e.g., Tert., *Apol.*, 27. 2 (where Tert. goes on in § 3 to call it 'constantia'), 7; 50. 15; *De Spect.*, 1. 1; *Ad Nat.*, i. 17–19; and of course Pliny, *Epist.*, x. 96. 3.

Romanorum morem redeundi obstinanter perseveraverunt'[4]—not that they 'disobeyed an order', but that they *obstinately persevered*, although given an *opportunity* of returning to Roman behaviour'. What I have called 'the sacrifice test' (see pp. 232–3 of chapter IX) was indeed originally a *privilege offered* to those who were prepared to apostatize, or who denied being Christians, to enable them to prove their detachment from the Christian *superstitio*.

2. On the second question, Mr Sherwin-White has not paid attention to what his sources (Suetonius, Tacitus and Pliny) actually *say*.

His 'maleficia' can only refer to Suetonius, *Nero* 16.2, where, however, only the corresponding adjective appears, with a significant difference of emphasis. Suetonius calls Christians a 'genus hominum superstitionis novae ac maleficae'. His attention is concentrated upon *the actual religion*, the *superstitio*: this itself he regards as 'malefica', as a likely *cause* of evil-doing.

In Tacitus (*Ann.*, xv. 44. 3–5, 8, in Furneaux' edition) it is again precisely the *superstitio* which is detestable ('exitiabilis'), an evil ('malum', to be classed with 'atrocia aut pudenda'). Although Tacitus describes the Christians as 'hated for their abominations', and doubtless himself shared the belief in their 'flagitia' which he attributes to the common herd, and although he calls the Christians 'guilty and deserving exemplary punishment', he evidently did not believe the Christians fired Rome (as Mr Sherwin-White admits in his 1952 article, p. 208); and—the essential point—unless Tacitus is misleading us, the government did not believe this either![5] The government, then, was not persecuting the Christians for a crime it believed them to have committed. The evidence of Tacitus here may be recalcitrant to precise analysis; but such as it is it merely shows the government persecuting the Christians (primarily as incendiaries) because *the populace* believed them guilty of abominations and would therefore be the readier to suppose them guilty of starting the fire.

Fortunately, the evidence of Pliny can be pressed, and is conclusive. There is not the least suggestion in Pliny's letter or in Trajan's reply that on this occasion the 'flagitia' were actually the *ground* of persecution, although Pliny was prepared to regard persecution for 'flagitia' as a theoretical possibility (§ 2 of his

---

[4] *Passio SS. Scillitan.*, 14.
[5] See the treatment of the expression 'subdidit reos' by Beaujeu, on pp. 16–17 of the work cited in n. 10 to my article.

letter). Pliny executed the confessors for the 'Name', without any evidence of 'flagitia', or indeed of anything except their confession that they were Christians, and he later discovered (from apostates) that there were *no* 'flagitia'. He nevertheless, *in the acknowledged absence of* 'flagitia', still regarded Christianity as something disgusting; but again, as with Suetonius and Tacitus, it is *the religion itself*, the *superstitio*, which is abhorrent: it is 'prava, immodica' (§ 8 of his letter). Even Last, on p. 91 of the article recommended by Mr Sherwin-White (see his n. 4), had to admit that Pliny is 'far . . . from proving that the denial of the Roman gods was not the essence of the Christian offence'.

At first Pliny had not felt certain what it was customary to do about Christians (note the word 'soleat' in § 1 of his letter). Among other things, he says he did not know whether he ought to punish (1) for the 'Name' alone, even in the absence of 'flagitia', or (2) for the 'flagitia'. The vital difference, which commentators seldom bring out, is that (1) punishment for the 'Name' alone (a) would be inflicted for the mere confession of Christianity, but on the other hand (b) could be avoided by denial or apostasy, demonstrated by sacrificing, whereas (2) punishment for the 'flagitia' (a) would involve an inquisition into their nature, but (b) presumably, if 'flagitia' were discovered (or invented), the guilty could not escape by merely apostatizing from Christianity. We must distinguish between three categories among those accused before Pliny as Christians: some proved to be confessors (§§ 2–4 of his letter), others denied that they had ever been Christians (§ 5), others again had apostatized or were ready to do so (§ 6). After some hesitation, Pliny decided in practice to consider the charges both against confessors and against outright deniers as being in respect of the 'Name' alone; and he clearly hoped that Trajan would allow him to apply exactly the same policy to apostates as to deniers (§§ 6–10). It was to *this* course of conduct, in relation to all three categories (confessors, deniers and apostates), that Trajan, betraying no surprise at the absence of 'flagitia', explicitly gave his official approval. (It looks to me as if Mr Sherwin-White has not fully realized this: cf. p. 252 above.) It is most significant that deniers and (by Trajan's rescript) *even apostates* were allowed to escape by accepting the sacrifice test: this is yet another proof that the 'flagitia' were not nearly as important as Mr Sherwin-White thinks—if you take charges of cannibalism seriously, you do not pardon the cannibals simply because they tear up their membership cards of the Cannibals' Club. Again, it was *having the 'superstitio'* which *made* the Christians dangerous, and *abandoning the 'superstitio'* removed the cause of offence: get them to give up Christianity, and the likelihood of their wanting to go in for 'flagitia' would disappear. This makes excellent sense of the Roman attitude, which on Mr Sherwin-White's version of the facts is unreasonable in the extreme.

In view of the scantiness of the evidence, no one could safely deny that belief in 'flagitia' supposedly committed by Christians *may* have been a factor, on occasion perhaps an important factor, inducing the government to persecute. But the evidence to which Mr Sherwin-White himself appeals affords no basis for taking the 'flagitia' as the only element, or even the main element, in the mind of *the government*, although it still leaves open the possibility that the 'flagitia' may have played an important role in the minds of ordinary folk. Only in so far as the government felt it necessary to give in to popular demands for persecution motivated in this way can we confidently put particular emphasis on the 'flagitia' as a factor influencing the government.[6] But apart from the fact that the Christian *superstitio* was itself the objectionable thing, there is no direct evidence for the ground of persecution in the early days, so far as the government is concerned. I am myself inclined to think that riots—especially with Jews—caused by Christian preaching (see n. 7 to my article) and perhaps provocative acts committed by early enthusiasts (see pp. 234-7 of my article, on 'voluntary martyrdom') may have played an important part. It is when we look at the behaviour of the Roman government over the centuries[7] (undeterred by Mr Sherwin-White's description of this as 'beginning at the end and working backwards') that we find reason to attribute a major role to the Christians' total rejection of the whole of Roman 'religio', summed up in the charge of 'atheism'. The onus is on those who deny the early importance of this long-lasting element to produce reasons why it should have arisen only after Pliny's day, when all that we know of Roman religion would lead us to expect its appearance very soon after Christianity first attracted the attention of the government.

[6] Here, some pertinent remarks have been made by A. Ronconi, in the last paragraph of his paper referred to in n. 79 to my article.
[7] See esp. n. 139 to my article.

I wonder why Mr Sherwin-White interprets § 10 of Pliny's letter to mean that it was only 'subsequently' (some time after his persecution began) that Pliny 'became concerned at the reported neglect of civic cults due to the influence of the Christians'. How can he possibly know this? Pliny says (perhaps with some exaggeration) that the temples, which had been almost empty, were beginning to be frequented again. This, says Mr Sherwin-White (n. 3), 'refers to the situation some time after the measures reported by him in §§ 1–6'. But it is only the *revival* of the cults which we can thus date. And Pliny goes on to say something Mr Sherwin-White fails to repeat: that the sacred rites which had *long* been allowed to lapse ('diu intermissa') were being renewed, and the flesh of the sacred victims was again being sold. We cannot *know* when Pliny 'became concerned', but in view of the words 'diu intermissa' we may well think it likely that the neglect of the traditional observances was something that forced itself on Pliny's notice soon after his arrival in the area. However, my point is not so much that this may have influenced Pliny in deciding whether to persecute (on this we have no information), but that Pliny, in his tactful attempt to get Trajan to approve the policy he had followed, laid great emphasis on the religious revival he had brought about, which he evidently believed would weigh with the emperor.

That anyone can say the government behaved to Christianity 'exactly as it did towards other "superstitions"' is incomprehensible to me. The devotees of what *other* 'superstitio' did the Romans ever execute as such whenever anyone brought a charge against them of holding that superstition? The answer, of course, is: None. Mr Sherwin-White should reflect in particular upon the details of the suppression of the 'Bacchanalia' in B.C. 186.[8] Here, (1) punishment was inflicted *not* for professing adherence to the cult, or even taking part in it, but for committing 'flagitia'; (2) the cult was *not* made altogether illegal but was sanctioned even at the time to devotees already committed to it, in small groups of not more than five members, if they obtained the permission of the senate; and (3) later, the Bacchic cult was *freely tolerated*. Actions taken by Rome against other cults (that of Isis, for example) were equally short-lived and always for specific abuses, and they con-

[8] For which see A. H. McDonald, in *JRS*, xxxiv (1944), at pp. 26–31, with full references.

trast equally strongly with the permanent ban on the mere *profession* of Christianity.

Mr Sherwin-White would do well to re-read a very useful work to which he himself appeals as if it fully supported his theories: that of E. G. Hardy (cited in his n. 4, and more familiar to most people as the first section of Hardy's *Studies in Roman History*, i, London, 1906, 1910). Here he will find a point of view rather different from his own. 'The Christians', says Hardy, 'subsequently to, as *before* [my italics], the rescript of Trajan were punished generally for the name, i.e.... for the inherent disloyalty to the state involved in their ἀθεότης [atheism], and manifested in the *obstinatio* with which they clung to it' (*Studies*, 2nd edn, p. 101, cf. 13). This is much nearer the truth. Christianity, unlike all the various forms of paganism, which enjoyed 'peaceful co-existence' among themselves, would never countenance other religions: this was surely the heart of its unique offence—against the gods and therefore against the state. Toleration of a very ancient idiosyncrasy of the national faith of the Jews (cf. pp. 239–40 of my article) could not be extended to the potentially dangerous innovations of a missionary *superstitio*.

XII

THE FAILURE OF THE PERSECUTIONS IN THE ROMAN EMPIRE*

W. H. C. Frend

The Great Persecution of 303–312 has been often discussed.† The purpose of the present article is to ask contemporary writers what kind of men, in what parts of the Roman Empire, championed the new religion, or looked kindly upon it, and why the government attacked it, both then and in the previous half-century. This was the period that had witnessed the disasters of barbarian invasions, defeat by the Persians, civil war, and economic collapse. But for the innate soundness of the central and provincial administration the Roman Empire might well have been wholly destroyed there and then. The years of restoration, however, culminating in the twenty years' rule of Diocletian, witnessed profound changes in men's traditional opinions. The old gods had not brought the aid expected of them, and men were turning to the new, Christian faith. By 300, Christian and non-Christian were hardening into fixed, opposing loyalties. But within the Christian camp, contemporaries were already noting the presence of deep rifts (Eusebius, *Ecclesiastical History*, VIII. i. 9). And these, in the very hour of the Church's triumph, were to break out in the Donatist and

---

* From no. 16 (1959).

† See in particular, N. H. Baynes, Ch. xix in *CAH*, XII, A. Manaresi, *L'Impero romano e il Cristianesimo* (Turin, 1914), Ch. x, Henri Grégoire, *Les Persécutions dans l'Empire romain* (Mémoires de l'Académie royale de Belgique, tome XLVI. i, 1951), G. E. M. de Ste Croix, 'Aspects of the "great persecution",' *HTR*, xlvii, 2, 1954, 75–113, and J. Moreau, ed., Lact., *De Mort. Pers.*, Sources chrétiennes 39, Paris, 1958, W. Eltester, 'Die Krisis der Alten Welt und das Christentum', *Zeitschrift für die neutestamentliche Wissenschaft*, xiii (1949), 1–19.

Arian controversies which were to dominate its life for the next century.

It was about the year 248 that Origen wrote his famous challenge to the Empire in the *Contra Celsum*. Christ was stronger than Caesar. The Church had survived despite all that its enemies could do against it. 'The Roman Senate, the contemporary emperors, the army, the people and the relatives of believers fought against the Gospel and would have hindered it; and it would have been defeated by the combined force of so many, unless it had overcome and risen above the opposition by divine power, so that it has conquered the whole world that was conspiring against it' (*C. Cels.*, 1. 3, tr. Chadwick).[1] Origen believed in ultimate Christian victory (*ibid.* viii. 70), and his assurance was not disturbed by the onset of the Decian persecution in the following year. More prescient than most, he had come to the conclusion that the era of partial and local pogroms against the Christians was over, and that the next conflict would be on a world scale.[2] So, he was prepared for what happened, and his comment, preserved in the Latin text of his commentary on the *Book of Joshua*, is eloquent. 'Israel's enemies had attacked Joshua. Now Christ's enemies attacked the Church. The prophecy had been fulfilled in his own time. It was in vain that the Emperor and Senate forbade the name of Christ "(ut non sint Christiani)". Every city had condemned the Christians; in vain! Not only would the Christian name spread more widely and swiftly, but the Lord Jesus would crush his enemies beneath the feet of his servants'.[3]

Origen's confidence was well justified. The great efforts made by Decius, Valerian, and, a generation later, the Tetrarchy failed to defeat the Church. The Roman Empire did not possess the means of overthrowing an organisation whose ramifications extended from 'Gaul to Osrhoene' even in the time of Pope Victor (189–198),[4] and whose adherents in 250 already numbered a sizeable proportion of the population in the provinces bordering

[1] See also Orig., *c. Cels.* (ed. and tr. H. Chadwick), ii. 79 and viii. 44.

[2] Orig., *Comm. in Matt.*, 24. 9, Sermo 39 (ed. Klostermann, *Griec. Christ. Schriftsteller*, p. 75). I accept the view that Origen was thinking of his own day as well in terms of eschatology.

[3] Orig., *Homil. in Jesu Nave*, 9. 10 (ed. Baehrens, *Griec. Christ. Schriftsteller*, p. 356–57).

[4] Euseb., *Eccl. Hist.* (ed. Lawlor and Oulton), v. 23. 4.

the Mediterranean. The exile of Christian leaders to remote parts was an unwitting means of spreading the Word. Thus, the natives of the oasis of Kufra were converted by Dionysius of Alexandria and his clergy who had been exiled thither by the Prefect of Egypt, Aemilianus, in 257. As Dionysius wrote, 'Then for the first time was the word sown through our agency among those who had not received it'.[5] Much the same happened a century later when Valens exiled monks to a still-heathen island in the Nile Delta. They cured the local priestess of a malady and converted the inhabitants![6] Christian missionary zeal was one of the obvious reasons why the Persecutions eventually failed. The conversion of Constantine comes as the climax of a long historical process. Origen himself had looked forward to a Christian Empire, and the unification of mankind under the Christian law.[7] To his disciple Eusebius of Caesarea (died 339) this happy state of affairs had come about under the Constantinian monarchy.[8]

Origen's own career is itself a landmark. His personal contribution to the final victory of the Church was no mean one. Although his outlook combined what appear to be two conflicting principles, namely a philosophical approach to religion and life, and zeal for a martyr's death, he was able to make both serve the cause of the Church. As a Christian philosopher he sought to wed the current interpretation of Plato to the traditional teaching of the Church. He could speak with the philosophic aristocracy of the early third century on level terms, and he lifted the Church out of the rut of Judaistic sectarianism in which it had threatened to founder in the second century. His influence among educated Greek-speaking provincials with whom he came into contact in Alexandria and Caesarea was immense. During his exile at Caesarea

[5] *Ibid.*, vii. 11. 13.
[6] Socrates, *Hist. Eccl.*, iv. 24.
[7] Orig., *c. Cels.*, viii. 72.
[8] Euseb., *Tricennial Oration*, 3 (ed. Heikel, p. 201). Compare Constantine's view of his role as minister of a divine order for the human race, Euseb., *Vita Constant.*, ii. 28. The Almighty 'starting from the British sea and the lands where the sun is ordained to set, He repulsed and scattered by His divine might the encompassing powers of evil, to the end that the human race might be recalled to the worship of the supreme law, schooled by my helping hand, and that the most blessed faith might be increased with the Almighty as guide' (Text from A. H. M. Jones, *JEH*, v. 2, 196–200, and Ernest Barker *From Alexander to Constantine* (Oxford 1956), 478–480).

in Palestine, from 232, he met and converted a young Cappadocian
lawyer named Gregory. The latter has left a remarkable account
of his influence on him.

> Like some spark kindled within my soul, there was kindled
> and blazed forth my love towards Him, most desirable of all
> for His beauty unspeakable, the Holy Word, and towards this
> man, His friend and prophet. I was led to neglect all that had
> seemed to concern me, business, study, even my favourite
> law, my home and my kin, no less than those with whom I was
> staying. One thing only was dear to me, philosophy and its
> teacher, this divine man.
>
> *(Address to Origen*, ed. Metcalfe, Ch. 6.)

In the event, Gregory returned to his native Caesarea in Cappadocia in 243. He allowed himself to be consecrated bishop and
remained there till his death in about 272. If it is not strictly true,
as his biographer, Gregory of Nyssa,[9] claimed a century later, that
when he arrived there were 17 Christians and when he died there
were 17 pagans, there is no doubt that he was responsible for a
perceptible movement towards Christianity in Cappadocia. His
missionary methods were as intelligent as anything recorded about
Christian proselytism in the Ancient World. He broke the power
of the traditional local priests by revealing their oracles and cures
as swindles, but he replaced the local festivals with those of the
martyrs, celebrated also with a good deal of jollification.[10] We thus
have an interesting example of the actual transition from the
pagan cult of local divinities to the Christian cult of saints and
martyrs accompanying the conversion of the inhabitants.

In linking Platonism and Christianity, Origen had built on an
Alexandrine tradition whose origins extended beyond the arrival
of Christianity, back to Philo and even to the Jewish apologetic
enshrined in *The Letter of Aristeas*. But in Asia Minor it was to
prove extraordinarily fruitful for the Church. Gradually, Platonism became for the upper classes the bridge between the conflicting philosophies of Hellenism and Christianity. The process begun
by Origen leads directly to the ideas and influence of Basil (his

[9] Gregory of Nyssa, *De Vita Gregorii Thaumaturgi*; ed. Migne, *Pat.
Graec.* 46, col. 909 C and 954 D.
[10] *Ibid.*, col. 954 B and C. See A. Harnack, *Die Mission und Ausbreitung des
Christentums* (Leipzig, 1902), p. 476.

grandmother herself a convert of Gregory) and the great Cappa-docians a century later.

The significance of Origen's success may be judged in the light of other possibilities. In the 240s it was not at all sure that the heir to the Platonic tradition would eventually be Greek Christianity rather than pagan neo-Platonism. As against Origen, Gregory, and Eusebius of Caesarea one can set Plotinus, Longinus, Porphyry, Iamblichos and Hierocles; and if Origen made Chris-tianity acceptable to the court of the Severi,[11] it was Plotinus and his disciples who influenced the ideas of the rulers of the Roman world in the period from 253–300, from Gallienus to the Tet-rarchy. Only gradually did these two systems of thought, similar both in ultimate aim and method but at variance regarding the Incarnation, emerge as rivals. Yet by 275 this development had taken place, and neo-Platonist leaders such as Porphyry and Hierocles, who was successively governor of Bithynia and prefect of Egypt (303–305 and 305–308), were among the most deter-mined of the enemies of Christianity at the time of the Great Persecution.[12]

That victory ultimately went to the Church may be due in part to the other side of Origen's Christianity. Logically, Platonic contemplation of the divine and martyrdom are irreconcilable as ends. Union with God through gradual self-purification is a ladder of ascent. It demands long life, not sudden death. The next cen-tury accepted the taming of the human passions through asceti-cism as a substitute for martyrdom. Even Antony, though he encouraged the Egyptian confessors, did not become one himself. Yet Origen realised truly enough that what had given the Christian Church its power of survival had been its followers' readiness to die for it.

The youth who had to be forcibly restrained from following his father, Leonidas, to execution in 202 was to exhort hearers in season and out of season to activities, including actual defiance of authority, which would lead to martyrdom.[13] He who sought the

[11] Eusb., *Eccl. Hist.*, vi. 21. 3.
[12] Lact., *Div. Inst.* (ed. Brandt), v. 2, and 11. 15. For the view that Hierocles was the author of the heathen objections in the *Apocriticus* of Macarius Magnes, see T. W. Crafer's ed. of Macarius (Translations of Christian Literature, S.P.C.K., 1920) XV. H. Delehaye, 'Hierocles in Egypt', *Analecta Bollandiana*, 40 (1922), p. 28.
[13] *C. Cels.*, i. 1.

spiritual truths hidden beneath the bare words of the Scriptural texts, applied the literal text to himself when he read Matt. 19:12.[14] An intense idealism was never far below the surface. Christianity, he reminded his friend Ambrosios, was a religion of martyrdom, and that singled it out as unique among the religions of mankind. 'But the only people who fight for religion are "the elect race, the royal priesthood, the holy nation, a people for God's possession". (1 Peter 2:9). The rest of mankind do not even try to make it appear that if there is persecution of religious people they intend to die for religion and to prefer death rather than deny their religion and live'.[15]

He would not have disagreed with Tertullian that 'the blood of Christians is seed' (*Apol.*, 50), but he also said that 'true religion was utterly impossible to one who was not a philosopher' (Gregory Thaumaturgus, *Address to Origen*, 6). It was this combination of philosophy and zeal that gave the Church its invincibility in the final conflict with the Empire.

Even so, the Decian persecution (249–251) came near to success. The main weakness of the Church in the first half of the third century was that, except perhaps in parts of Asia Minor, it was almost entirely an urban organisation. In the previous century it had been both the heir and the rival of the Jewish synagogues which were to be found in nearly every centre of any size near the coasts of the Mediterranean. Though the Church had increased its members considerably[16] during the period of practical toleration under Alexander Severus (222–235), Gordian (238–244) and Philip (244–249), the pattern of development had not changed. Penetration of the countryside had been slow. The Church was based on an urban episcopate. The persecutions it had suffered had been urban pogroms, the result of riots, as at Lyons in 177[17] or Alexandria in 248.[18] Its leaders seem to have been drawn mainly from middle-class urban provincial life. Justin, the wandering philosopher from Neapolis (Nablus) in Palestine, Marcion the ship-owner

[14] Euseb., *Eccl. Hist.*, vi. 8. 2.
[15] *Exhortation to Martyrdom* (ed. Oulton and Chadwick), 5. Compare Josephus' assertion of the superiority of Judaism over Hellenism on the same grounds, *Contra Apionem* (ed. Niese) 1. 8. 42.
[16] Euseb., *Eccl. Hist.*, vi. 36. 1, Orig., *Comm. in Matt.*, 15. 26 (Klostermann, p. 426).
[17] Euseb., *Eccl. Hist.*, v. 1. 7.
[18] *Ibid.*, vi. 41. 1 ff.

from Sinope, Theodotus the money-changer in Rome, his name-sake the tanner from Byzantium, Florinus, a member of the governor's staff in the province of Asia, or Tertullian, son of a centurion in the Proconsul's guard at Carthage, these men seem to have been representative of Church or sect life in the period 150–220.

Concentration in the cities had brought stability and sound organisation. By 250 the priesthood was an attractive profession commanding a regular monthly stipend.[19] But it also rendered the Church more vulnerable to attack. When the blow fell about the end of 249, the leaders were marked men[20] who faced the alternatives of flight or arrest and execution; and their flocks, swelled by too many nominal adherents, fell away in droves.

At this stage, the authorities still had the initiative, and acts directed against the Church commanded a large measure of public support. Confessors in Carthage were mishandled by an enraged crowd (*ferociens populus*, Cyprian, *Letter*, 6. 4). Trials were conducted there and in Smyrna to the accompaniment of the shouts of the mob.[21] Loyalty to the Roman Empire, expressed by an outward cult act, had become accepted as a matter of course in the provinces. Tribal and municipal centres had their *fora*, and these were often dominated by a Capitol dedicated to the Roman gods. Such temples had continued to be built in the first decades of the third century. To this was added the view that on the safety and prosperity of the Emperor (the *Salus Augusti*) depended that of his subjects, and this in turn hung on the good-will of the gods.[22] Thus Celsus had told the Christians in 178 'even if someone tells you to take an oath by the emperor among men, that also is nothing dreadful. For earthly things have been given to him, and

---

[19] Cypr., *Letter* (ed. Hartel), 34. 4. See Euseb., *Eccl. Hist.*, v. 28. 10, for the payment of 150 denarii a month to Natalius, schismatic bishop of Rome in 200, by his adherents.

[20] For instance, Dionysius of Alexandria says of himself, 'when the persecution under Decius was publicly proclaimed, that selfsame hour Sabinus sent a *frumentarius* to seek me out'. Euseb., *Eccl. Hist.*, vi. 40. 2. Fabian of Rome was seized and executed on 20 January 250, see Cypr., *Letter* (ed. Hartel), 55. 9.

[21] Cypr., *Letter* 40, and 56. 1–2, *Acta Sancti Pionii* (ed. Krüger and Knopf), 7, 10, 11.

[22] See A. Alföldi's important study of the Decian persecution, 'Zu den Christenverfolgungen in der Mitte des 3. Jahrhunderts', *Klio*, 31 (1938), pp. 323–47.

whatever you receive in this world you receive from him'.[23] The coins in common use, exalting the 'providentia' and 'pax' of the emperor and his titles of 'pius felix', emphasised the point.

Therefore, when in the spring of 250 Decius ordered as a 'dies Imperii', that is a sort of general supplication to the gods for the safety and victory of the emperor and his house in the face of mounting threats to the State, the idea was not unfamiliar. Indeed, something similar may have taken place in 212 on the promulgation of the *Constitutio Antoniniana*.[24] It was complied with by the vast majority of the inhabitants of the Roman world, including the Christians. Their acquiescence may have been made the easier by the arguments used by the authorities both then and in the persecution of Valerian (257–259). The Christians were told that they were not being asked to give up their own religion, but simply to pay respect to the gods on whom the welfare of the Empire depended.[25] Thus, the deputy prefect of Egypt, Aemilianus, told Bishop Dionysius of Alexandria at a hearing in 257. 'And,' he continued, 'who prevents you from worshipping this god (the Christian God) also, if he be a god, along with the natural gods? For ye were bidden to worship gods, and gods whom we all know' (Euseb., *Eccl. Hist.*, vii. 11. 9). In Carthage, numerous Christians sacrificed cheerfully, and then proceeded to offer themselves for the Sacrament.[26]

Contemporaries emphasise the vast numbers of the lapsed. The Church was saved from utter ruin by a few noble examples. In Alexandria, Dionysius has left a vivid description of events (Euseb., *Eccl. Hist.*, vi. 41, 11–13, ed. and tr. Oulton):

> On the arrival of the edict all cowered with fear. And of many of the more eminent persons, some came forward immediately through fear, others in public positions were compelled to do so by their business, and others were dragged by those around them. Called by name they approached the impure and unholy sacrifices, some pale and trembling, as if they were not for sacrificing but rather to be themselves the sacrifices and victims to the idols, so that the large crowd that stood around heaped mockery upon them,

[23] Orig., *c. Cels.*, viii. 67.
[24] A. Alföldi, *op. cit.*, p. 333.
[25] Euseb., *Eccl. Hist.*, vii. 11. 7.
[26] Cypr., *De Lapsis*, 15.

and it was evident that they were by nature cowards in every-thing, cowards both to die and to sacrifice. But others ran eagerly towards the altars, affirming by their forwardness that they had not been Christians even formerly; concerning whom the Lord very truly predicted that they shall hardly be saved. Of the rest, some followed one or other of these, others fled; some were captured, and of these some went as far as bonds and imprisonment, and certain, when they had been shut up for many days, then forswore themselves even before coming into court, while others, who remained firm for a certain time under tortures, subsequently gave in.

The effective staff of this already important see was reduced to four priests who were in hiding and 'secretly visited the brethren'. Two others, Faustinus and Aquila, 'who are better known in the world, are wandering about in Egypt' (Euseb., *Eccl. Hist.*, vii. 11. 24).

In Africa, matters were, if anything, worse. Cyprian admits (*Letter*, 11. 1) that the great majority of his flock had lapsed; few of his clergy stayed at their posts. The treatise *On the Lapsed*, written in 251, recounts in awe-inspiring terms the extent of the disaster. The magistrates at Carthage were so busy that they begged would-be sacrificers to return the next day (*De Lapsis*, 8). In the provincial towns whole congregations apostatised, in one case led by the bishop himself (*Letter*, 59. 10). Nor are we dependent on the word of a single bishop whose own role had not been a heroic one. The whole problem of the *libelli pacis*, that is the pardons given out in quantities by surviving confessors to their friends and relatives at the end of the persecution, arose only because of the enormous numbers of those concerned. Cyprian indeed says that they were given out 'by the thousand' (*Letter*, 20. 3).

In Asia Minor, the hitherto triumphant mission of Gregory in Cappadocia came to an abrupt halt. Gregory himself seems to have accepted the fact that most of his new converts would give way under the threat of persecution, and he himself fled.[27] In Smyrna, bishop Euctemon and other leading Christians sacri-ficed.[28] Here, perhaps for the last time, the pagan magistrates felt really confident of their superiority. They know that the Christians

---

[27] Gregory of Nyssa, *Life*, Migne, *Pat. Graec.* col. 46, 945 D.
[28] *Acta Sancti Pionii* (ed. Knopf and Krüger, 1929), 15. 2 and 16. 1.

'worship the crucified one', and openly laugh at the idea.[29] They also know that the Church was riddled with sects. Pionius was asked at his trial to which one he belonged.[30]

Half a century later the atmosphere has changed. Once more one looks at the contemporary accounts, this time of the Great Persecution (303–312), and the contrast is evident.

The Imperial directives indeed were carried out in the provinces without hesitation. In Africa the magistrates were kindly and fair-minded. Sometimes even, they were friends of the bishop, as is shown by evidence given by Alfius Caecilianus, Duumvir of Aptunga, at the inquiry into the conduct of Bishop Felix in 315.[31] But they were prepared to do what was asked of them. Munatius Felix, the Curator of Cirta, refused to close his enquiry until Bishop Paul and his clergy had surrendered all the Scriptures they possessed.[32] Churches were burnt down, and the general order to sacrifice contained in the Fourth Edict in the spring of 304 was carried out.[33] Panic and apostasy in the ranks of the Christians there was too. Optatus of Milevis records two generations later how 'the devil triumphed in the temples', that grey-beards, infants in arms, and indeed everyone, hastened to sacrifice.[34] An eye-witness of the events of Cirta in 303, Victor the Grammarian, tells how the first reaction of the Christians there to the Imperial edict was flight.[35] In Palestine, Eusebius describes in contrast to the heroes, that many others 'gave way at the first assault',[36] and sacrificed; and at Antioch 'numbers of men, women and children crowded up to the idols and sacrificed'.[37] In Rome, Bishop Marcellinus may have apostatised.[38]

This tale of weakness is not, however, the dominant feature.

[29] *Acta Sancti Pionii*, 16. 5.

[30] *Ibid.*, 9. 2, 19. 4, and 21. 4.

[31] *Acta Purgationis Felicis* (ed. Ziwsa, *C.S.E.L.* XXVI).

[32] *Gesta apud Zenophilum* (ed. Ziwsa), pp. 187–8.

[33] The question whether or not the Fourth Edict was applied in Africa has been ably discussed by G. E. M. de Ste Croix, 'Aspects of the "Great" persecution', *HTR*, lvii. 2, p. 86.

[34] Optatus of Milevis, *De Schismate Donatistarum* (ed. Ziwsa), iii. 8.

[35] *Gesta apud Zenophilum*, p. 186.

[36] Eusebius, *Mart. Pal.*, 1. 3 (Lawlor and Oulton, p. 333).

[37] *Ibid.*, 2. 2, pp. 336–7.

[38] Indicated by mutually independent sources; August., *Contra Litteras Petiliani*, ii. 92. 202 (Migne, *Pat. Lat.* 43), col. 323, and *Acta Synod. Sinuessae*, Mansi, *Concilia*, i. 1250.

Rather, examples of apostasy are used to set off what was the real character of the Christians at that time, namely their constancy and their defiance of the persecuting magistracy. Thus, the passage we have just quoted from the *Palestinian Martyrs* is followed by a description of the confessor Romanus, 'who mingled with the multitude' and appeared on his own initiative before the magistrate to preach Christianity at him.[39] In Egypt defiance was carried to extraordinary lengths. Eusebius was an eyewitness of some of the events of Maximin's reign (306–313) and records as follows (*Eccl. Hist.*, trans. Oulton, viii. 9. 2):

> And we ourselves also beheld, when we were at these places, many all at once in a single day, some of whom suffered decapitation, others the punishment of fire; so that the murderous axe was dulled and, worn out, was broken in pieces, while the executioners themselves grew utterly weary and took it in turns to succeed one another. It was then that we observed a most marvellous eagerness and a truly divine power and zeal in those who had placed their faith in the Christ of God. Thus, as soon as sentence was given against the first, some from one quarter and others from another would leap up to the tribunal before the judge and confess themselves Christians; paying no heed when faced with terrors and the varied forms of tortures, but undismayedly and boldly speaking of the piety towards the God of the universe, and with joy and laughter and gladness receiving the final sentence of death; so that they sung and sent up hymns and thanksgivings to the God of the universe even to the very last breath.

The authorities worked with energy born of desperation. Lactantius alludes to the 'blind and irrational fury' of the persecutors.[40] In the East there was the feeling that this was not persecution but 'war', in which one side or the other would emerge finally victorious.[41]

Once again, the pattern is repeated in North Africa. In Numidia, pagan shrines and even Imperial property were looted by Chris-

---

[39] *Mart. Pal.*, 2. 2 (Lawlor and Oulton, p. 337).
[40] Lact., *Div. Inst.* (ed. Brandt), v. 21. 2, 'caeco et irrationabili furore'.
[41] Euseb., *Eccl. Hist.*, viii, 13. 10.

tians, and those who took part were regarded as popular heroes.[42] Their failings, even their acts of apostasy and simony, were pardoned. The spirit too, of those in prison was that this was either the gateway to Paradise or merely a temporary phase of demonic oppression before victory. Their discussions ran on what would happen after the Persecution and how the lapsed should be treated.[43] Any idea that the Emperors might be successful was evidently far from their thoughts. Their optimism and idealism reflected the spirit of many. Services went on despite the lapse of a bishop. We hear of young Christians in the African cities leaving their houses to 'go and join', as they said, 'the brethren who obeyed the precepts of God'.[44]

Quite clearly, the intervening years had seen a change of public opinion towards the Church. There is some contemporary evidence. Cirta, the capital of Numidia, for instance, had been violently hostile towards the Christians during the persecution under Valerian. The mob hounded the two confessors Marianus and Jacobus before the magistrates.[45] In 305 the same city was the scene of a formidable Christian demonstration, ending in the election of the sub-deacon Silvanus as bishop. His most fervent supporters were described fifteen years later as the lower orders and country folk.[46] Indeed, there is no evidence in 303, except perhaps at Gaza, of people welcoming the persecuting edicts as many of the inhabitants of the Roman world had done in 250.[47] In the largely Jewish city of Dio-Caesarea in Palestine the sympathies of the inhabitants turned in favour of the Christians when the latter were put to torture.[48] Even in Diocletian's and Galerius' capital, Nicomedia, wholehearted support seems to have been

[42] Gesta apud Zenophilum (Ziwsa, p. 193) 'Nundinarius dixit, "de cupis fisci, quis illas tulit"?' These had been housed in a temple of Serapis.

[43] For instance, in the prisons of Alexandria (Epiphanius, Panarion, 68. 3 (ed. Holl. p. 142), and Carthage, Acta Saturnini, 18. (Migne, Pat. Lat. viii, col. 701.)

[44] Acta Saturnini 5 and 14, concerning Victoria. (Pat. Lat., viii, cols 693C and 698D.)

[45] Acta Mariani et Jacobi, ii. 2 (ed. Knopf and Krüger) 'in qua tunc maxime civitate (i.e. Cirta) gentilium caeco furore et officiis militaribus persecutionis impetus quasi fluctus saeculi tumescebant . . .' Cf. N. H. Baynes, CAH, xii, p. 658.

[46] Gesta apud Zenophilum (ed. Ziwsa), p. 194.

[47] Mart. Pal., 3. 1.

[48] Euseb., Mart. Pal., 8. 1.

lacking. Lactantius could write that God had allowed the persecution in order to bring the pagans within the community of the Church.[49]

A number of factors have long been recognised as contributing to this situation. Since 260, the date of Gallienus' restoration of Church property,[50] Christianity had been a *religio licita*. Though little has come down in the way of literature for the next forty years, it is evident that the Church had been gaining vastly in power and authority. The pagans themselves admitted that the Gospel had been preached in every corner of the inhabited world.[51] In Africa alone, the number of bishoprics seems to have doubled in the period 260–300, to a total of about 250.[52] In fact, we know that the Church made a remarkably rapid recovery from the effects of the Decian persecution. Cyprian's letters covering the period 251–258 give an unmistakable picture of vitality and assurance. New converts there were in plenty.[53] Indeed, the question of re-baptising those who had been baptised in the first place by the Novatianists would never have arisen unless this had been the case. The finances of the Church of Carthage were flourishing and were used to ransom prisoners on the outbreak of the Kabyle revolt of 253, while the behaviour of its ministers during the plague of 252–253 gained it lasting respect.[54] The comings and goings of clergy from Carthage to Rome and distant Cappadocia, and the assembly of frequent episcopal councils, culminating in the meeting of no less than 87 African bishops on 1 Sept., 256, leaves no doubt as to the resilience of the Christians, and the strength of their organisation in Africa. Nor does Africa stand alone. It was in these years that Bishop Dionysius of Rome (259–268) sent gifts to the church of Caesarea in Asia Minor, whose munificence was remembered a century later, and was recorded by Basil.[55] What is more, he sent a private embassy to

---

[49] Lact., *Div. Inst.*, v. 21. Other examples are cited by N. H. Baynes in his chapter on the Great Persecution in the *CAH*, xii. pp. 676–7.

[50] Dating, see R. Marichal, 'La date des graffiti de la basilique de Saint-Sébastien à Rome', *La Nouvelle Clio*, v (1958), p. 119.

[51] Macarius Magnes, *Apocritus* (ed. Crafer), iv. iii (Crafer, 124).

[52] A. Harnack, *Mission*, 520.

[53] Cypr., *Letter*, 66. 5 (Hartel, 730) 'Novus credentium populus'.

[54] Cypr., *Letter*, 62. 4. (Hartel, 700) 'Misimus autem sestertia centium milia nummorum'. Cf. N. H. Baynes, *CAH*, xii, p. 658.

[55] Basil, *Letter* 70 (ed. Courtonne, 166.).

negotiate the ransom of prisoners taken by the Gothic invaders.[56]
In Neo-Caesarea, Bishop Gregory's mission was resumed with
even greater success, and in Alexandria, Dionysius restored the
church to its former prosperity despite civil war and plague.

Then, during the period 260–300 all the evidence points to the
growing together of Church and Roman society. Paul of Samosata
(*flor.* 260–270) was only the first of the clerical politicians of the
late Roman Empire. In 303, in Diocletian's court, Eusebius mentions Dorotheus, Peter and Gorgonas as high officials who were
active Christians.[57] There were Christians or their supporters
among the families of the emperors.[58] Christianity was no bar to
advancement; indeed, at times the opposite may have been true.[59]
There were distinguished converts like the Africans, Arnobius and
Lactantius, and the former is probably quite justified in his
assertion that members of the liberal professions could be numbered among those who having once despised the Word now
believed.[60] The Council of Elvira in southern Spain shows that
Christianity had penetrated so deeply there, that the problem was
arising of Christians who held nominal pagan priesthoods, as part
of their recognised obligations as members of the ruling body of
their city.[61]

Lactantius, however, warns us against placing too much emphasis on the influence of prominent individual Christians. Tertullian,
he says roundly, 'found little popularity', and Cyprian was
understood 'by the faithful only'. 'By the learned of this world,
to whom his writings have by chance become known, he is
commonly ridiculed'. He was dubbed 'Koprian' ('dung-head')
and that, so far as his influence went, implies Lactantius, was
that.[62]

The Great Persecution might still have succeeded but for one
important development which took place during these years. In

[56] Basil, *Letter* 70.
[57] Euseb., *Eccl. Hist.*, viii. 1. 4 and 6. 5; cf. B. de Gaiffier, 'Palatins et
Eunuques dans quelques documents hagiographiques', *Analecta
Bollandiana*, 75 (1957), pp. 17 ff.
[58] Lact., *De Mort. Persec.*, 15.
[59] Euseb., *Eccl. Hist.*, viii. 1. 4; cf. *ibid.*, vii. 32. 3.
[60] Arnob., *Adv. Nationes* (ed. Reifferscheid), ii. 5.
[61] Canons 2 and 3 (ed. Hefele-Leclercq, *Histoire des Conciles*, 1907, I. 1
pp. 231–64).
[62] Lact., *Div. Inst.*, v. 1, 22–27.

three great territories of the Empire, Anatolia, Egypt and North Africa, the second half of the third century sees the conversion of large numbers of the country populations to Christianity. From a mainly urban movement, Christianity becomes a universal and popular one, and this decisively altered the balance between Church and paganism. Moreover, Egypt and Africa were the sources of grain and other supplies for the eastern and western halves of the Empire, and in Africa the native population was large.[63] Here, certainly, there was no depopulation in the later Empire. The Roman Empire could not survive the loss of large provinces by invasion or successful agrarian revolt which would cut off supplies from the towns and cities. Constantine faced the spectre of famine in Rome in the first winter after the Milvian Bridge, just as Maxentius had done in 310 during the temporary loss of the African provinces to a usurper.[64] The unexpected surrender of North Africa without a blow was of immense value to his cause, and he realised it.[65]

What evidence is there for these religious changes? The course of events in all three areas is often obscure and difficult to establish, but on the whole, the story is intelligible. One finds, for instance, in each case, evidence for a decline in the popularity of the hitherto all-powerful native cults, coupled with positive indications for the extension of Christianity. For Egypt, Idris Bell has remarked that, 'as we advance into the Roman period, we get the impression that even the traditional temple worship of Egypt was losing some of its vitality'. Outwardly, all was the same. Sacrifices were still offered with due formality. The festivals were observed, the animal deities, such as Petsouchos the Crocodile-god still recruited their priests. But a certain formality and lifelessness was becoming apparent. Mummies were often embalmed in a perfunctory fashion, the symbolism on the mummy-cases shows that the original religious meaning of the signs was becoming lost. Hieroglyphic inscriptions degenerated, until after about 250 no more are to be found.[66] It is not perhaps surprising that one reads

---

[63] Herodian (ed. Stavenhagen), vii. 9. Euseb., *Eccl. Hist.*, x. 5. 18. Cf. the author's *The Donatist Church* (Oxford, 1952), p. 67.

[64] *Chronica minora* (ed. Mommsen, *Mon. Germ. Hist.*, 1. 148), 'Maxentius Imp. ann vi . . . fames magna fuit'.

[65] Euseb., *Eccl. Hist.*, x. v. 18. (letter to Miltiades) on the spontaneous character of the surrender of North Africa.

[66] H. I. Bell, *Cults and Creeds in Greco-Roman Egypt* (1956), p. 64.

of deserted temples of Serapis affording shelter to monastic saints in the late third and early fourth centuries.

In Asia Minor too, the third century sees a decline in the popular religion of the countryside. Ramsay indeed believed that the old Phrygian religion had degenerated into a superstition before the century was out, and that educated men and women were therefore prepared to listen to the new Christian preaching.[67] However, cult organisations such as the Tekmoreian brotherhood flourished on the Imperial estates around Pisidian Antioch in the late third century,[68] and one shrine at least, that of Mén at Colonia Caesarea near the same city retained its worshippers until early in the next century.[69] Indeed, the more obvious signs of collapse, such as the wholesale abandonment of temples, neglect of cults, the transfer of temple lands to the Church, and the absorption of priestly families into Christianity, did not come about until the second quarter of the fourth century.[70] Julian watched the process as a despairing eye-witness (*Letter* 89, ed. Bidez). In Africa, however, the erstwhile national deity of both Carthaginians and Berbers, Saturn (Baal-Hammon), seems to have forfeited his popularity some time before the more Romanised cults which flourished in the cities lost theirs. No dedication to him has been found dated later than A.D. 272, and though in itself this might not be very significant, the next dated religious inscriptions in the same area (A.D. 299 and 324) are Christian.[71] There was no revival of interest in the Tetrarchy, such as the Roman gods experienced in some of the towns. At Cuicul in Mauretania, dedications in Saturn's honour were even being used as paving stones in the fourth century.[72] The cult had died out. When Constantine wrote to Miltiades of Rome in 314 concerning the Donatist schism, he

---

[67] W. M. Ramsay, *Cities and Bishoprics in Phrygia* (London, 1883), p. 137.

[68] W. M. Ramsay, 'The Tekmoreian guest-friends, an anti-Christian society on the imperial estates at Pisidian Antioch', *Studies in the East Roman Provinces* (1923), pp. 305–77.

[69] W. M. Ramsay, 'Studies in the Roman province of Galatia', *JRS*, viii (1918), pp. 107–45.

[70] Julian (ed. Bidez), *Letter* 84 to Arsacius, High-Priest of Galatia.

[71] P. Massiera, 'Inscriptions chrétiennes de Maurétanie Sitifienne', *Revue Africaine*, c (1956), p. 325. See W. H. C. Frend, *The Donatist Church*, pp. 84 ff. Since I wrote this, a dedication of A.D. 323 to Saturn was found in Western Tunisia.

[72] M. Leglay, 'Les stèles à Saturne de Djemila-Cuicul', *Libyca*, i (1953), p. 36.

appears to treat Africa as Christian, but divided between the Catholics and their opponents.[73] Paganism became increasingly isolated as the cult of the traditional ruling groups in some of the African cities, such as Timgad and Calama.[74] It had lost contact with the people.

At the same time, the last half of the third century was not one of universal decay and despair for the native populations of the Empire as it was for the old urban middle-class.[75] In all of these three areas, for instance, new art forms based on traditional pre-Roman motives were beginning to supersede the stereotyped provincial art of the previous two centuries.[76] In Egypt, Coptic was emerging from being an important adjunct for the magician and was becoming a national Egyptian literary language.[77] None of these literary and artistic movements were connected with Christianity initially, indeed, the first example of the elaborate geometric designs typical of Berber art in the fourth century comes from a temple frieze at Timgad,[78] but Christianity provided each with a vigorous means of expression which evidently could not be found in the traditional cults. As the art historian, Gauckler, has stated, 'in the domain of art as well as that of politics the triumph of the Church assures the victory of the native over the foreign'.[79]

Quite apart from the evidence for the decline in the popularity of the main pagan cults, there are certain facts pointing to the actual conversion of the rural areas to Christianity. For Egypt the testimony of Eusebius is impressive. He was, as we have seen, an eyewitness of the final ferocious stages of Maximin's persecution in 311–312. He stresses that Christians formed the majority of the population, and that while the evil spirit of idolatry was striving to keep the Egyptians in a ferment, 'thousands' were deserting

[73] Euseb., *Eccl. Hist.*, x. 6.

[74] *CIL*, viii, 2403; Augustine, *Letter* 90, cf. L. Leschi, *REA*, L., 1948, 71 ff.

[75] For a good example of despair, Cypr., *Ad Demetrian.* (ed. Hartel), 4 and 5.

[76] W. H. C. Frend, 'The revival of Berber art', *Antiquity* (1942), pp. 342–52. On a similar movement in Asia Minor, Miss Ramsay, in *Studies in the East Roman Provinces*, pp. 3–92.

[77] For the part played by magic in the evolution of Coptic, W. E. Crum, *PBA* (1931), pp. 235–87.

[78] Frend, *art. cit.*, Pl. ii.

[79] P. Gauckler, 'Mosaiques tombales d'une chapelle des martyrs à Thabraca', *Monuments Piot*, xiii (1906), p. 225.

paganism—'and anyone who is not wholly lacking in vision can see this'.[80] Fifty years before, Dionysius of Alexandria had stated that though Christianity had made some progress in the country-side there were still places near Alexandria which had not heard of the name of Christ,[81] but now 'His altars were now in every town and village.'[82] We know from another source that at Oxyrhynchos there were two churches in the town about the year 300 and that many of the inhabitants were Christians.[83] But it was from the villages that most resistance to the persecution came. In the Thebaid for a period extending over years, as Eusebius says, 'sometimes more than ten, at other times above twenty persons were put to death: and at others not less than thirty, now nearer sixty, and again at other times a hundred men would be slain in a single day along with quite young children and women, being condemned to manifold punishments which followed one on the other'.[84] That there really were numerous Egyptian confessors is shown by the fact that in 308 parties of more than 100 each were being sent up north to work in the mines of Palestine and Cilicia, as though there were sufficient in those of the Thebaid.[85] All efforts to crush the Church proved vain, but in the mind of the Copt, the 'era of the martyrs' replaced the official 'era of Dio-cletian'.

In all this ferment of religious change, the beginnings of the monastic movement were being born; in its first stages it was en-tirely Coptic and rural in inspiration.[86] Antony's flight from even the primitive surroundings of his village took place about the year 270. There were monks in the prison at Alexandria when Bishop Peter quarrelled with Meletios in 307–308, and they took the latter's side.[87] As a perceptive Egyptian Neo-Platonist, Alexander of Lycopolis, remarked, round about A.D. 300, Chris-

[80] Euseb., *Demonstratio Evangelica*, ix. 2. 4; see also, vi. 20. 9.

[81] Euseb., *Eccl. Hist.*, vii. 11. 15.

[82] Euseb., *Demonstr. Evangelica*, viii. 5. Cf. N. H. Baynes, *CAH*, xii, p. 675.

[83] C. Schmidt. 'Fragmente einer schrift des Märtyrerbischofs des Petrus von Alexandrien', *Texte und Untersuchungen, Neue Folge*, v. 4.

[84] Euseb., *Eccl. Hist.*, viii. 9. 3. Schmidt, *op. cit.* 23.

[85] Euseb., *Mar. Pal.*, 8. 13. cf. H. Delehaye, 'Les martyrs d'Egypte', *Analecta Bollandiana* 40 (1922), pp. 5–154.

[86] Athanasius, *Vita Antonii*, i. cf. Epiphanius, *Panarion*, 67. 1. 3. and 6 (Hieracas and his followers).

[87] Epiphanius, *Panarion*, 67. 3. 4.

tianity had become the religion of the populace, attracted to it by its simplicity and high ethics (in contrast to the complicated dualism of the Manichees).[88] In another part of the Roman East, Edessa, the writer of the *Acta Sancti Habibi*, remarks that under Licinius there were more persecuted than persecutors![89]

For Africa, there seems to be little doubt about the rapid extension of the Church in the rural area in the latter part of the third century. Recorded dated Christian inscriptions begin in 266.[90] The huge popularity of the cult of the martyrs in the next century, and the evil reputation achieved by the 'persecutor', the *Praeses* Florus, who was governor of Numidia Militana 303–304 are relevant facts and there is evidence for the establishment of new bishoprics in the Numidian countryside, such as Tigisis, between 256 and 300. The enthusiasm aroused by Christianity among the common people was real enough. In the next century no village yet investigated has failed to yield one or more churches.[91] In Numidia too, the presbyterate was a post worth having. Victor the fuller was prepared to pay 20 folles (i.e. 20,000 nummi) for his election at Cirta in 305.[92]

Similar events were taking place in Asia Minor in the same period. Here the literary evidence has been supplemented by the archaeological. Both Eusebius and Lactantius mention the total destruction of a small unnamed Phrygian town (perhaps Eumeneia) in which all the inhabitants, including the city magistrates, were Christians.[93] In the same province, the village of Orcistus was able to gain the rank of *civitas* from Constantine about A.D. 325, among other reasons because, as it claimed 'everyone was Christian'.[94] Indeed, a close study of Phrygian religious inscriptions during the third century shows a steady movement towards Christianity in

---

[88] Alexander of Lycopolis, *De Placitis Manichaeorum, Pat. Graec.* 18, col., 411.

[89] Published in *Ante-Nicene Fathers*, XX, f. 91.

[90] *CIL*, viii. 8430. cf. P. Massiera, 'Inscriptions chrétiennes de Maurétanie Sitifienne', 329.

[91] Frend, *The Donatist Church*, p. 84.

[92] *Gesta apud Zenophilum*, p. 194 (top).

[93] Euseb., *Eccl. Hist.*, viii. 11. 1. Lact., *Div. Inst.*, v. 11. 10, cf. W. M. Ramsay, *Cities and Bishoprics*, pp. 505–8.

[94] Re-published with amendments by W. M. Calder, *Monumenta Asiae Minoris Antiqua*, vii, no. 305, with Calder's comments that 'the situation it discloses did not come about in a day', p. xxxviii.

some of the towns, and a more violent one in the countryside. In the northern part of the province, near Dorylaeum (Eski-Sehir) a group of inscriptions dated between 249–279 leaves no doubt about the religion of those whom they commemorated.[95] They contain a ringing message 'from Christians to Christians'. On two, the Cross has been included in the design, and the qualities of the deceased as an ascetic and 'a soldier' of Christ have been recorded.[96]

The term 'soldier' brings us to the problem of theology. The rural Christianity of all three areas had much in common. It was first and foremost a religion of the martyrs and the elect, inspired by the Holy Spirit and the Word of God contained in the Bible. Thus, Athanasius wrote of Antony that he considered 'the Scriptures were enough for instruction' (*Life*, c. 16). They alone sufficed to rout the power of the demons. Antony scorned both pagan philosophers who visited him and urban theologians. To these simple minds acceptance of the Bible implied complete rejection alike of the native pagan past and the classical literary heritage.[97] So far did some of the Egyptian confessors who were converts carry this, that when they were asked their names by the governor of Palestine at Caesarea while en route to the mines of Cilicia, they refused to give them since they recalled the names of idols. Instead, they called themselves Elijah, Jeremiah, Isaiah, Samuel and Daniel (Euseb., *Mart. Pal.*, 8. 1).

A similar outlook may be found in both Africa and Asia Minor. Part of the anger felt against the Betrayers (i.e. the *traditores*) was due to the fact that the Bible itself was the object of their defection. As the martyrs of Abitina asserted in 304, even to alter a single letter of Scripture was a crime, but contemptuously to throw the whole Bible into the flames at the command of heathen magistrates was an act of apostasy which merited eternal punishment. Persecution was the work of anti-Christ, and this itself was a sign that the last days were at hand, when the martyrs would enjoy their reward in Paradise and sit in judgment on their enemies.[98]

In Asia Minor the strength of the Montanist and Novatianist

[95] J. G. C. Anderson, 'Paganism and Christianity in the Upper Tembris valley', *Studies in the East Roman Provinces*, pp. 186 ff.
[96] W. M. Calder, 'Philadelphia and Montanism', *Bulletin of John Rylands Library*, 7 (1923), p. 35 and figs 2 and 3.
[97] For Africa, see *Passio Marculi*, 1, *Pat. Lat.*, viii, 760C.
[98] *Acta Saturnini*, 18. (*Pat. Lat.*, viii, 701C.)

movements in the countryside testifies to the existence of the same puritanical view of Christianity at this period.

But theologically all this was a century out of date. In the East, the failure of the prophetic Succession and the discrediting of Montanism had opened the way for the more liberal Alexandrian tradition, the Logos theology, to become the predominant Christian idea. The conservatives protested from time to time, such as in the *Refutation of the Allegorists* by Bishop Nepos of Arsinoe (circa 260), but in vain.[99] Now however, the Church was confronted, as a result of the conversion of the countryside with a revival of the old Biblical and Millenarist Christianity in a militant and uncompromising form. While in the towns the gulf between Church and Roman society was diminishing, that between Christian and Christian was widening. The Great Persecution was to be the signal not only for conflict over Trinitarian doctrine, but between the representatives of two forms of ecclesiastical order. On the one hand, there were those who thought in terms of a universal Church with its elaborate hierarchy and strict division between layman and cleric; on the other, those who believed that the Church was the Church of the martyrs and the elect, and who regarded the safe-keeping of the sacraments, regardless of geography, as its essential duty. Meletianism in Egypt, Donatism in Africa and Novatianism in Asia Minor, all showed the latter outlook, and all represent the same primarily rural Christianity.

Why were the new Christians inspired by this puritan and apocalyptic form of Christianity?

A clue may be found in the strongly social basis of the new religion's appeal in all three parts of the Roman world. From the outset, monasticism in Egypt had a bias towards righting acknowledged social wrongs. Flight from the world, as Athanasius pointed out, included flight from the tax collector (*Life*, 44). The same term 'anachoresis' was used to describe withdrawal in the face of secular debt and withdrawal to satisfy religious vocation. The great monasteries of the Pachomian rule that grew up in the first half of the fourth century were economic units as well as centres of prayer and ascetic practices. We may perhaps agree with K. Heussi that their very success denoted widespread misery in the countryside whence their recruits were drawn.[100]

[99] Euseb., *Eccl. Hist.*, vii. 24. 3.
[100] K. Heussi, *Der Ursprung des Mönchtums* (Tübingen, 1936), p. 118.

In Africa also, it was a well-attested fact that the ranks of the would-be martyrs included those who found their debts to the Treasury too burdensome.[101] In the next generation the depredations of the 'leaders of the saints' (*duces sanctorum*) who commanded the Circumcellion bands, demonstrated the connections between the social and religious discontents of rural Numidia.[102] The martyr's 'agon' against the persecuting authorities in the first three centuries had by this time become extended to a defence against injustice in the present world.

The question may well be asked, whether the conversion of the countryfolk in the areas of which we have been speaking was in itself influenced by changing conditions in the third century. Grégoire, in his study of the persecutions, has assembled evidence to show the extent of the rise of prices during this period and the repercussions on the life of the provincials as a whole.[103] The harassed town-dwellers, unable to support traditional fixed obligations, attempted to push them on to the countryfolk. A papyrus dated to 251 records an inquiry held by the prefect of Egypt into a complaint by peasants, that they were being forced to undertake forced labour from which an edict of Septimius Severus had exempted them. The lawyer representing the citizens replied, 'Yes, that is true, but the towns were prosperous then'.[104] Half a century later, Lactantius paints a grim, if biased, picture of the effects on the inhabitants of Diocletian's Edict of the Maximum, following the reorganisation of the Roman provinces.[105]

A remark by the emperor Julian suggests that increase in economic hardship and the desertion of the traditional deities was more than a coincidence. Writing to Theodorus, high priest of Asia in 362 he observes that 'It was the sight of their undeserved misery that led the people to despise the gods'. It was not, however, 'the gods who were responsible for their poverty, but rather our own insatiable greed. It was that which gave men a false idea of the gods, and in addition, was an unjust reproach against

---

[101] Augustine, *Breviculus Collationis cum Donatistis*, iii. 13. 25. *Pat. Lat.* 43, 637.

[102] Optatus, *De Schismate Donatistarum* (ed. Ziwsa), iii. 4, p. 82.

[103] H. Grégoire, *Les Persécutions dans l'Empire romain* (Académie Royale de Belgique, Classe des Lettres, xlvi. 1. 1951), pp. 75 ff.

[104] Cited from Grégoire, *op. cit.*, p. 75.

[105] *De Mort. Pers.*, 7 and 23.

them'.[106] In contrast, he points out to Arsacius, Theodorus' colleague in Galatia, how Christian social and ascetic ideals had attracted the mass of the provincials to the faith. 'Why do we not observe', he says, 'that it is their benevolence to strangers, the care for the graves of the dead, and the pretended holiness of their lives that have done most to increase atheism (Christianity)?'[107] The fact was that the Anatolians failed to secure earthly 'σωτήρια' from the traditional gods, and turned to Christianity instead. The same may have been true in Africa and Egypt as well.

Eschatological hopes of the Second Coming heralded by the final destructive efforts of Anti-Christ, bringing to the martyrs the joys of Paradise and a happy release from physical sufferings on earth, provided an inspiration to many. Sanctity, martyrdom and poverty are associated themes which recur in the puritan school of Western theologians from Tertullian to Petilian of Constantine and Commodian. Riches and sin were identified. To preserve one's wealth was to prefer Mammon to Christ. Possession of goods, indeed, implied contempt for the poor.[108] Commodian, whether he wrote in the late third or early fifth century, seems to have been an exact interpreter of a mood of popular desperation which found an outlet in Christianity. In the late third century, economic and social conditions would seem to have justified the acceptance of this theology.[109] And this movement ultimately proved too strong for the emperors.

Such are some of the underlying causes of the failure of the persecutions. Given the limited means available for repression—even in the Decian persecution there was not the prison accommodation to house the recalcitrants[110]—and the dependence of the authorities on the good-will of the peasants for the defence and victualling of the Empire, as well as for the maintenance of communications and other services, it was impossible to destroy the Church when it had ceased to be a purely urban movement. Once the villages had been won over, final victory could not be far away. The spread of Christianity beyond the boundaries of the

[106] Julian, *Letter* 89b (ed. Bidez, p. 157).

[107] *Ibid.*, 84 (ed. Bidez, p. 144).

[108] See J. P. Brisson, *Autonomisme et Christianisme dans l'Afrique romaine* (Paris, 1958), pp. 370–1 (texts from Tertullian and Cyprian).

[109] J. P. Brisson, *op. cit.*, pp. 394 ff.

[110] Gregory of Nyssa, *Life of Gregory Thaumaturgus, Pat. Graec.* 46, col. 945C.

Empire to Armenia, moreover, made persecution absurd from the higher political and military viewpoints. This Maximin found during the winter of 311–312.

By the end of the third century, educated provincials, particularly in the East, had had long contact with Christianity. Many, as the personal stories of Gregory Thaumaturgus and others show, had been attracted to it. The Church combined monotheism, a high ethical ideal and a philosophy of history, which enabled individuals to see their own lives within the setting of God's providence. The cults of paganism could provide some of these elements but not all together. One has only to turn to Eusebius' *Demonstratio Evangelica* or the first chapters of the Ecclesiastical History to sense the force that the Christian philosophy of history exercised on his mind. All the time, too, the cults were moving in the direction of monotheism. Towards the end of paganism all the various gods were represented as powers of the Sun-God. And from the Sun-God to Logos, expressing the creative power of God in the universe, was no great step. Constantine took it. So had others before him. The Christos-Helios mosaic in the vault of Tomb M in the cemetery beneath the Vatican, is visible evidence of the fact.[111]

Among the countryfolk the Church represented two ideas which the old religion had lacked, social justice and freedom from an oppressive world. Christianity gave direction to an otherwise confused mass of economic, social and religious discontents, which had previously found vent in works, such as the Egyptian Apocalypse of the Potter[112] which was circulating in the third century, and other magical and oracle literature. The influence of Antony and his disciples ensured that the movement of protest represented by monasticism in Egypt should have a Christian form. In North Africa the puritan tradition emerges as the Donatist Church, all powerful among the densely peopled villages of Numidia and Mauretania. The successive edicts of toleration issued by Maxentius in Rome, by Galerius, Constantine and Licinius, and finally even by Maximin, set the seal on a process which had already run its course.[113]

---

[111] J. M. Toynbee and J. Ward-Perkins, *The Shrine of St. Peter and the Vatican Excavations* (Longmans, 1956), Pl. 32.

[112] W. Wilcken, *Hermes*, xc (1905), pp. 544 ff. and *Pap. Oxy.* 2332.

[113] The more important recent publications (in addition to de Ste Croix's

article reprinted in this volume) include: T. D. Barnes, 'Legislation against the Christians', *JRS*, lviii (1968), pp. 32–50; Daniel De Decker, 'La politique religieuse de Maxence', *Byzantion* xxxviii, 1968 (1969), pp. 472–562; W. H. C. Frend, *Martyrdom and Persecution in the Early Church* (Oxford, 1965), ch. xiv, xv; J. Moreau, *Die Christenverfolgungen im römischen Reich* (Berlin, 1961); Lactantius, *De la mort des persécuteurs*, ed. J. Moreau, 2 vols (Paris, 1954); J. Molthagen, *Der römishe Staat und die Christen im zweiten und dritten Jahrhundert* (Göttingen, 1970); G. S. R. Thomas, 'Maximin Daia's policy and the edicts of Toleration', *L'Antiquité classique*, xxxvii (1968), pp. 172–85; J. Vogt, *Zur Religiosität der Christenverfolger im römischen Reich* (*Sitz. d. Heidelberger Acad. d. Wiss.*, 1962, no. 1); A. Wlosok, *Rom und die Christen* (Stuttgart, 1970); J. Ziegler, *Zur religiösen Haltung der Gegenkaiser im 4 Jh. n. Chr.* (*FAS Frankfurter Althistorische Studien*, iv, 1970).

XIII

THE ROMAN COLONATE*

A. H. M. Jones

The problem of the late Roman colonate has been debated since the seventeenth century. The debate still goes on, but we do not seem much nearer to answering the questions, when, how, and why the *colonus* of the principate, a voluntary tenant of land, free to move when his lease expired, became the *colonus* of the later empire, a serf tied to the land by a hereditary bond.[1] The position of a *colonus* in the early third century is clearly defined by the lawyers cited in the Digest. He held a lease, normally for five years, which by the tacit consent of both parties became on expiry an annual tenancy.[2] In practice conditions varied very greatly. In Egypt short term leases, from one to four years, were normal.[3] But in many parts farms generally descended from father to son. Under Commodus the tenants of imperial lands in Africa speak of themselves as having been born and bred on the estate.[4] In the early third century other imperial tenants in Lydia threaten 'to

---

* From no. 13 (1958).

[1] The history of the controversy down to 1925 is summarized by
R. Clausing, *The Roman Colonate* (New York, 1925). Later discussions include C. Saumagne, 'Du rôle de l' "origo" et du "census" dans la formation du colonat romain', *Byzantion*, xii (1937), pp. 487–581; F. L. Ganshof, 'Le statut personnel du colon au Bas-Empire', *Antiquité Classique*, xiv (1945), pp. 261–77; A. Segrè, 'The Byzantine colonate', *Traditio*, v (1947), pp. 103–33; M. Pallasse, *Orient et Occident à propos du colonat romain au Bas-empire* (Algiers, 1950).

[2] *Dig.*, xix. 2. 9. 1; 2. 13. 11; 2. 14; 2. 24. 2.

[3] A. C. Johnson, *Roman Egypt* (Baltimore, 1936) = *An Economic Survey of Ancient Rome*, ed. T. Frank, ii, pp. 81 ff.

[4] *CIL*, viii. 10570 = *ILS*, 6870, col. iii, lines 28–9.

leave the hearths of our fathers and the tombs of our ancestors' unless conditions are improved.[5] A *colonus* might, if he were, as he often was, in arrears with his rent,[6] find practical difficulty in leaving; for in such circumstances his landlord would have no hesitation in distraining on his stock. But he could leave with arrears outstanding: a case in the Digest concerns 'the arrears of *coloni* who on the conclusion of their lease, having entered into a bond, had abandoned their tenancy'.[7]

The first clear evidence that *coloni*—or at any rate some *coloni*—were tied to their farms and to their landlords is a law of Constantine dated 332: 'Any person with whom a *colonus* belonging to some other person is found shall not only restore him to his place of origin but be liable for his poll tax for the period. It will furthermore be proper that *coloni* themselves who plan flight should be put in irons like slaves, so that they may be compelled by a servile penalty to perform the duties appropriate to them as free men'.[8] The first explicit reference to the hereditary character of the bond is in a law of 364, which orders that 'slaves and *coloni* and their sons and grandsons' who had deserted imperial estates to join the army or the civil service should be recalled.[9]

Before proceeding further it will be as well to say something of the pattern of land ownership in the later Roman empire. It is too often assumed in discussions of the colonate that the entire area of the empire was divided into large estates, each consisting of a home farm cultivated by slaves, surrounded by smaller farms worked by resident free tenants. There were many large estates, though not all were of this pattern. Many, owned by absentee landlords, were entirely divided into tenancies, the original home farm, if there had ever been one, having been let off.[10] And though

---

[5] J. Keil and A. von Premerstein, 'Bericht über eine dritte Reise in Lydien', *Denkschr. Ak. Wien*, lvii. 1 (1914–15), p. 38, no. 55, line 46.

[6] To judge by the frequent allusions to *reliqua colonorum* in *Dig.*, xxxii. 78. 3; 91 pr. 1; 97; 101. 1; xxxiii. 2. 32. 7; 7. 20 pr., 1 and 3; 7. 27. 1.

[7] *Dig.*, xxxiii. 7. 20. 3.

[8] *Cod. Theod.*, v. 17. 1.

[9] *Cod. Just.*, xi. 68. 3; cf. vii. 38. 1 (367).

[10] In a sixth-century rent roll (J. O. Tjäder, *Die nichtliterarischen lateinischen Papyri Italiens aus der Zeit 445–700* (Lund, 1954), p. 188, no. 3, col. ii) an estate in the territory of Patavium is divided into 'locus qui adpelatur saltus Erudianus', 'colonia suprascripta' and seven other *coloniae* (besides two *paludes*). All pay rent, the first 'per Maximum

in some parts of the empire, particularly in Italy and the western provinces, large estates were numerous and must have occupied a large proportion of the total area, they by no means accounted for the whole of it.

There were in the first place peasant proprietors, usually grouped in villages; in Egypt, they were predominant in the fourth century[11] and survived in substantial numbers in the sixth.[12] Villages of peasant proprietors are mentioned side by side with those owned by one landlord in Syria in the fourth and fifth centuries.[13] In Thrace and Illyricum Justinian's legislation shows that peasant freeholders were still important in the sixth century.[14] In the West less is heard of them, but in Gaul Salvian in the middle of the fifth century still speaks of peasants whose plots are being absorbed by the great landlords,[15] while in Africa the peculiar Mancian tenures, small holdings held on perpetual and alienable leases, survived under the later Vandal kings.[16]

In the second place the estates of non-resident landlords were not always large. There were many humble townsmen who owned two or three acres, and medium landlords seem rarely to have owned a single large estate: they generally held a number of parcels of land of varying size, scattered in different villages. This is the pattern shown by the early fourth century land register of Hermopolis in Egypt.[17] The same pattern is shown in the will of Remigius, bishop of Rheims in the late fifth century.[18] Even the

---

vilicum', the others through *coloni*. It would seem that the original home farm, 'saltus Erudianus', had been divided into two, and half let to a group of tenants, half left in the hands of the bailiff, who leased it for a rent.

[11] A. H. M. Jones, 'Census records of the later Roman Empire', *JRS*, xliii (1953), pp. 58–60, 63–4.

[12] There is a large mass of papyrus documents concerning Aphrodito, a village of small proprietors which was 'autopract', collecting its own taxes. Most are published in *Pap. Cairo Maspero* and *Pap. London* v.

[13] Libanius, *Or.*, xlvii. 11; Theod., *Hist. Rel.*, xiv; xvii.

[14] Just., *Nov.*, xxxii–xxxiv.

[15] Salvian, *de Gub. Dei*, v. 38–44.

[16] C. Courtois, L. Leschi, C. Perrat, C. Saumagne, *Tablettes Albertini: Actes privés de l'époque vandale* (Paris, 1952).

[17] A. H. M. Jones, *JRS*, xliii (1953), pp. 52–3, 60–3.

[18] *Mon. Germ. Hist.*, *Script. rer. Merov.*, ed. B. Krusch (Hanover, 1896), iii, pp. 336–40. The authenticity of the will is upheld and its content analysed by A. H. M. Jones, P. Grierson, J. A. Crook, 'The authenticity

great landlords who owned estates big enough to hold a village, often possessed in addition many detached parcels of land. The accounts of the great Apion family in sixth century Egypt show that they owned holdings in the villages of peasant proprietors as well as entire hamlets.[19]

Many of the smaller parcels of land owned by absentee landlords had no resident tenants but were leased to villagers, either peasant proprietors whose plots were too small to maintain their families, or cottagers, who owned their houses but had no land.[20] The analysis of the rural population is thus complicated. There were the resident *coloni* of the great estates, who lived on their farms or in the estate village. There were also on the great estates persons styled *inquilini*, who are frequently coupled with the *coloni* but distinguished from them.[21] The word *inquilinus* in the legal language of the principate means the tenant of a house, as opposed to *colonus*, the tenant of agricultural land.[22] There is no reason to

---

of the "Testamentum S. Remigii", *Revue Belge de Philologie et d'Histoire*, xxxv (1957), pp. 356–73.

[19] E. R. Hardy, *The Large Estates of Byzantine Egypt* (New York, 1931), pp. 88–9.

[20] See below, note 34.

[21] *Cod. Just.*, xi. 48. 6 (365), 'omnes omnino fugitivos [adscripticios] colonos vel inquilinos'; *Cod. Theod.*, x. 12. 2 (368), 'si quis etiam vel tributarius repperitur vel inquilinus ostenditur'; *Cod. Just.*, xi. 53. 1 (371), 'colonos inquilinosque per Illyricum'; *Cod. Theod.*, xii. 19. 1 (400), 'inquilinas vel colonas vel ancillas'; 19. 2 (400), 'colonatus . . . aut inquilinatus quaestionem'; v. 18. 1 (419), 'colonus originalis vel inquilinus'; *Cod. Just.*, iii. 26. 11 (442), 'domorum nostrarum colonus aut inquilinus aut servus'; Valent., *Nov.*, xxvii (449), 'de originariis et colonis, inquilinis ac servis'; xxxv (452), 'nullus originarius, inquilinus, servus aut colonus'; Severus, *Nov.*, ii (465), 'inquilinus vel colonus'. In *Cod. Just.*, iii. 38. 11, 'vel colonorum adscripticiae condicionis seu inquilinorum', has been interpolated after 'servorum' of the original law (*Cod. Theod.*, ii. 25. 1 (325). In *Cod. Just.*, xi. 48. 12 (396), 'vel tributarios vel inquilinos', is also probably interpolated after 'servos'. For *tributarii, adscripticii, originales*, see below, notes 51, 53, 54.

[22] *Dig.*, xix. 2. 25. 1; xli. 2. 37; xliii. 32. 1. 1. Landlords under the principate were obliged to declare their *coloni* and *inquilini* in their census returns, *Dig.*, i. 15. 4. 8. In *Dig.*, xxx. 112 pr., 'si quis inquilinos sine praediis quibus adhaerent legaverit, inutile est legatum: sed an aestimatio debeatur, ex voluntate defuncti statuendum esse, divi Marcus et Commodus rescripserunt', *inquilinus* is used in a unique and obscure sense. The persons so described must be slaves, or they could not be left by will, but are attached to land and are only alienable with

believe that the word had changed its meaning, and these *inquilini* will therefore have been cottagers on an estate, who earned their livings as craftsmen or labourers.[23] Then there were the peasant proprietors and cottagers of the independent villages, some of whom were at the same time *coloni* of detached parcels of land belonging to absentee landlords. Finally there were agricultural slaves. A few were labourers owned by more prosperous peasant freeholders or *coloni*. More were the property of absentee land-lords. Some worked small parcels of land single-handed: the half-dozen vineyards owned by Remigius each had its slave vinedresser.[24] On larger estates the census registers sometimes show in addition to the *coloni* a few slaves, who perhaps worked a home farm and acted as bailiffs of the whole estate.[25] Other estates seem to have been run entirely by slave labour; we do not know if these slaves worked in gangs, or, by a practice already known to the third century lawyers, leased farms as *quasi coloni*.[26]

Between 392 and 395 Theodosius I issued the following con-stitution:[27] 'Throughout the entire diocese of Thrace the census of the poll tax is abolished for ever and only the land tax will be paid. And in case it may seem that permission has been given to *coloni*, freed from the ties of their taxable condition, to wander and

it. It has been suggested that they are barbarian prisoners of war allotted by the imperial government to landowners as agricultural labourers.

23 They are perhaps identical with the cottagers, *casarii*, of *Cod. Theod.*, ix. 42. 7 (369), 'quotve mancipia in praediis . . . quot sint casarii vel coloni'. Their status was very similar to that of *coloni*; *Cod. Just.*, xi. 48. 13 (400), 'inter inquilinos colonosve, quorum quantum ad originem pertinet vindicandum, indiscreta eademque paene videtur esse condicio, licet sit discrimen in nomine'.

24 *Mon. Germ. Hist.*, *Script. rer. Merov.*, iii, p. 337, lines 13–16, 22–3; p. 338, lines 10–11, 20–1; p. 339, lines 1–2.

25 A. H. M. Jones, *JRS*, xliii (1953), pp. 56–7: bailiffs, *vilici* or *actores*, were commonly, as under the principate, slaves.

26 A. H. M. Jones, *loc. cit.* Two Spanish landowners are said to have raised a small army in the early fifth century, 'servulos tantum suos ex propriis praediis colligentes', Orosius, vii. 40. 6, and one of Melania's Italian estates is said to have had 'sexaginta villulas circa se, habentes quadringentos servos agricultores', *Vita Sanctae Melaniae Iunioris*, Latin version, ch. 18, in *Analecta Bollandiana*, viii (1889), pp. 16–63. For *servi quasi coloni* see *Dig.*, xv. 3. 16; xxxiii. 7. 12. 3; 7. 20. 1.

27 *Cod. Just.*, xi. 52. 1.

go off where they will, they are themselves to be bound by right of origin, and though they appear to be free born by condition are nevertheless to be held to be slaves of the land itself to which they were born, and are not to have the right to go off where they will or change their domicile. The landowners are to control them with the care of patrons and the power of masters.' An earlier law of Valentinian I,[28] dated 371, evidently alludes to a similar situation: 'We declare that *coloni* and *inquilini* throughout Illyricum and the neighbouring regions cannot have the liberty of leaving the land on which they are found to reside by virtue of their origin and descent. Let them be slaves of the land, not by tie of the tax, but under the name and title of *coloni*.'

From these two laws it is evident that *coloni* had hitherto been tied to their farms by virtue of the poll tax, or *capitatio*, which they paid, since its abolition in Thrace and Illyricum would have resulted, but for special provisions enacted, in giving freedom of movement to the *coloni* of these areas. The *capitatio* was based on censuses conducted by Diocletian and his colleagues and immediate successors in the various parts of the empire, and the tax itself under that name—there had been earlier poll taxes in many provinces—seems to have been instituted by him. The census included all the working rural population (between minimum and maximum ages) whether slaves or free, whether proprietors, tenants, or landless, and the *capitatio* was levied on all alike.[29]

From these facts two conclusions follow. The measure which tied the *coloni* to the soil cannot be earlier than Diocletian's time, and is probably to be connected with his reorganization of the poll tax. And secondly it was primarily a fiscal measure, designed to facilitate and ensure the collection of the new poll tax, and not specifically aimed at tying tenants to their farms.

There are two facts which support the second conclusion. In the first place not only *coloni* but peasant proprietors were tied to their place of registration. In 332 the three surviving proprietors of the Egyptian village of Theadelphia complained that all their fellow villagers (the registered population of the village was twenty-five) had fled: they had tried to get them back by their own efforts

[28] *Ibid.*, xi. 53. 1.
[29] See A. Déléage, *La Capitation du Bas-Empire* (Nancy, 1945) and A. H. M. Jones, '*Capitatio* and *iugatio*', *JRS*, xlvii (1957), pp. 88–94.

but without success, and they now appealed to the prefect of Egypt to use his official powers.[30]

In the second place the rule binding the rural population to their places of registration did not in all provinces have the effect of tying *coloni* to their farms. It is expressly stated in a law of Theodosius I that in Palestine *coloni* had not hitherto been tied to their lands.[31] In Egypt there is no trace of tied tenancies until the fifth century; short term leases remain the rule as under the principate.[32] In a law addressed to the praetorian prefect of the Gauls in 399[33] a distinction is drawn between the various provinces under his jurisdiction. It is ruled that anyone who buys 'an estate on which a certain number of the humble population is registered' is to take on their fiscal obligations; but this rule is applicable only to those provinces 'in which this system of tying the humble population and this method of registration is observed'.

The explanation of this anomaly probably lies, as the last law suggests, in the different systems of registration adopted in various provinces. The census registers from western Asia Minor, which record both land and population, are drawn up under the headings of the landowner and his estates. In most lists the landowner's name comes first, followed by his several farms, each assessed at so many fiscal units (*iuga*) of land, and so many units of population (*capita*), if there was any population resident on the farm. This form of registration implies that the landowner was responsible for the *capitatio* of the population registered on his farms, and would, if the population were tied to their place of registration, have the effect of tying resident *coloni* to their farms. From the very fragmentary records surviving it would appear that peasant proprietors and landless men who owned houses were registered in their villages, and would be tied to these.[34]

In Egypt on the other hand the land register of Hermopolis gives a list of townsmen who own land, recording the size and location of their holdings but making no mention of their tenants. There are similar village lists of peasant proprietors.[35] In the sur-

[30] *Pap. Thead.*, 16 and 17.
[31] *Cod. Just.*, xi. 51. 1.
[32] A. C. Johnson and L. C. West, *Byzantine Egypt: Economic Studies* (Princeton, 1949), p. 76; cf. note 50 below.
[33] *Cod. Theod.*, xi. 1. 26.
[34] A. H. M. Jones, *JRS*, xliii (1953), pp. 49–55.
[35] A. H. M. Jones, *loc. cit.*, pp. 58–64.

viving personal census returns villagers record details of their families, but register themselves under their village only.[36] It would seem then that in Egypt the rural population was registered by villages, without reference to whose land they cultivated, and that they were tied to their village and not to their farm or landlord. Presumably the registration system in Palestine and some provinces of the Gallic prefecture was similar and led to the same result.

It would seem, then, that the tying of the *colonus* to his farm was the by-product of a fiscal and administrative measure of wider scope. For such a measure there were partial and local precedents from the principate. In A.D. 104 C. Vibius Maximus, prefect of Egypt, issued the following edict.[37] 'Since the house to house registration is imminent it is necessary to instruct all persons who are for any reason whatsoever residing away from their district to return to their hearths in order that they may both carry out the usual procedure of the registration and may devote themselves to the agricultural work incumbent upon them.' Diocletian's more sweeping measure (if he was its author) was doubtless also primarily fiscal in motive, but may likewise have been intended to secure that the agricultural population, on whose labour the land tax depended, was kept to its task.

But if the tying of the agricultural population was in origin a measure dictated by public policy, it proved a great boon to landlords. It is evident that there was in the fourth century a general shortage of agricultural labour. The population had doubtless in many areas been reduced by the constant wars, devastations, famines and plagues of the third century, and the conscription for the greatly enlarged army further depleted it. At any rate many references in contemporary laws show that tenants were hard to find, and that any who were dissatisfied with their position could readily find another landlord, willing and eager to take them on. In these circumstances landlords found the law useful in holding their tenants and reclaiming them if they left.

Since the landowning classes were predominant in governmental circles it is not surprising that the imperial government, when it abolished the *capitatio* in Illyricum and then in Thrace, specially enacted that the *coloni* of these areas should not be thereby

[36] U. Wilcken, *Chrestomathie*, 210; F. Preisigke, *Sammelbuch*, 7673.
[37] U. Wilcken, *Chrestomathie*, 202; cf. Luke 2:1.

given liberty of movement. It soon went further and introduced the tied colonate in provinces where it had not hitherto existed. Theodosius I explicitly states in whose interests he did so in Palestine: 'Whereas in other provinces which are subject to our serenity's rule a law instituted by our ancestors holds *coloni* by a sort of perpetual right, so that they may not leave the places by whose crops they are fed nor desert the fields which they have once received to cultivate: but the landowners of Palestine do not enjoy this advantage . . .'[38]

The dependence of tied *coloni* on their landlords was increased by successive laws. Constantine, as we have seen, authorized landlords to put their tenants in chains if they suspected them of planning flight.[39] In 365 Valens enacted that they might not alienate their own property without their landlord's consent.[40] Some years later he enacted that landlords should collect the taxes due from their registered tenants.[41] In 396 Arcadius ruled that *coloni* registered in the census, since they were virtually slaves of their landlords, should have no right of bringing civil actions against them except for raising their rent.[42] By later laws they were forbidden to join the army or the civil service,[43] or to take holy orders without their landlord's consent.[44]

While tied *coloni* were thus reduced to a quasi-servile status, agricultural slaves were converted into serfs. At first owners had been permitted to sell their agricultural slaves apart from the land, though they were registered on it. Constantine only prohibited sales beyond the boundary of the province, and warned purchasers that their census would be subject to revision.[45] Valentinian I assimilated registered agricultural slaves to tied tenants, and forbade their sale apart from the land.[46]

---

[38] *Cod. Just.*, xi. 51. 1.

[39] *Cod. Theod.*, v. 17. 1.

[40] *Cod. Theod.*, v. 19. 1.

[41] *Cod. Theod.*, xi. 1. 14.

[42] *Cod. Just.*, xi. 50. 2.

[43] *Cod. Just.*, xi. 48. 18; xii. 33. 3.

[44] *Cod. Just.*, i. 3. 16 (409); Valent., *Nov.* xxxv (452); *Cod. Just.*, i. 3. 36 (484).

[45] *Cod. Theod.*, xi. 3. 2 (327).

[46] *Cod. Just.*, xi. 48. 7 (371); this rule was revoked by King Theoderic in Italy, *Edictum Theoderici*, cxlii, in *Fontes Iuris Romani Anteiustiniani*, ed. G. Baviera (Florence, 1940), ii, p. 707.

On the other hand the law, in so far as it affected peasant proprietors, seems to have been generally allowed to fall into desuetude. When the *capitatio* was abolished in Illyricum and Thrace no measures were taken to restrict the movement of the peasant freeholders, in those areas an important and numerous class, but only that of *coloni*. As against scores of laws which deal with restitution of absconding *coloni* to their masters there are only two in the Codes under which freeholders are returned to their villages. A law of Valentinian I[47] rules that if anyone petitioned the crown for the grant of a man alleged to be a vagrant and ownerless slave, an investigation should be held, and if the man were proved to be a *colonus* he should be returned to his master, if a free commoner be sent back to his place of origin. A law of 415,[48] which deals comprehensively with the problem of patronage in Egypt and aims at restoring the villages of peasant proprietors, orders that those who had left the village in which they were registered and gone to other villages or landlords should be compelled to return.

There was probably less need to enforce the law against freeholders. As a rule peasants would not wish to abandon their holdings—the case of Theadelphia was abnormal; the village lay at the end of an irrigation canal and intervening villages had intercepted the water. Normally it was to no one's interest to enforce the law: his fellow villagers or a neighbouring landlord would generally be glad to buy the holding of any peasant who wanted to leave, and would raise no complaint. It was only in the case of mass desertion, as at Theadelphia, that the surviving villagers would wish to recall the runaways, and one may doubt whether their complaints were often successful. Landlords had influence and could get a hearing for their grievances, and the provincial governor, being probably a landlord himself, would be sympathetic. Villagers could exercise no effective pressure, and were unlikely to obtain a hearing, especially if, as at Theadelphia, the runaways had taken refuge on the estates of neighbouring landlords.

The tied colonate was as we have seen introduced into Palestine by Theodosius I. It appears to have been extended to Egypt before 415, for the law of that year alludes to a class called locally *homologi coloni* who were tied to their landlords. But though the

[47] *Cod. Theod.*, x. 12. 2 (368).
[48] *Cod. Theod.*, xi. 24. 6 (415).

institution thus spread to the greater part, if not the whole, of the empire, it does not follow that all *coloni* were tied. Since *coloni* were initially bound by their census registration, only those tenants who were entered on the census under the name of a landlord and registered on one of his estates were tied to the soil. The census registers from western Asia Minor show many, mainly smaller, estates without any *capita* or units of population and these estates were presumably leased to neighbouring peasant freeholders or cottagers in the villages. The distinction is made explicit in a law of Valens,[49] which enacts that owners of estates should collect the taxes of '*coloni originales* who are registered in the same places', but that *coloni* 'who possess any piece of land however small and are registered in their own names' should pay their taxes through the public collector. In effect only the resident tenants of the larger estates were tied. This appears to have been the case on the estate of the Apion family in Egypt in the sixth century. Tied tenants (γεωργοὶ ἐναπόγραφοι) appear only on the hamlets (ἐποίκια) and estates (κτήματα) wholly owned by the family: parcels of land in the villages are let to ordinary tenants.[50]

In the third quarter of the fourth century the laws begin to make a distinction between ordinary tenants and tied tenants. The latter are sometimes called *tributarii*, since their landlord was responsible for their tax (*tributum, i.e. capitatio*).[51] In the Eastern parts they are generally distinguished by some such phrase as 'registered in the census' (*censibus adscripti*),[52] and eventually the technical term *adscripticius* was coined; it is first recorded officially in a law of 460, but the emperor Marcian used the Greek equivalent (ἐναπό-γραφος) in addressing the council of Chalcedon in 451.[53] This term

---

[49] *Cod. Theod.*, xi. 1. 14 (371).

[50] *Pap. Oxy.*, 135, 137, 1979, 1982–3, 1985, 1988–91; *Pap. London*, iii. 774–5, 777–8; *Pap. Soc. It.*, 59, 61–2; *Pap. Amherst*, 149; cf. *Pap. Oxy.*, 1900, 2238 for ἐναπόγραφοι γεωργοί on estates of the church.

[51] *Cod. Theod.*, x. 12. 2 (368); *Cod. Just.*, xi. 48. 12 (396, but the word is probably a Justinianic interpolation, see note 21); xi. 48. 20. 3 (Justinian) In *Cod. Theod.*, xi. 7. 2 (319) *tributarius* appears to be distinguished from *colonus*, and may mean a taxpaying (i.e. rural) slave.

[52] *Cod. Just.*, xi. 50. 2 (396); i. 3. 16 (409); *Cod. Theod.*, v. 6. 3 (409); x. 20. 17 (427); v. 3. 1 (434); *Theod., Nov.*, vii. 4 (441). The phrase is applied to agricultural slaves in *Cod. Theod.*, xi. 3. 2 (327); vii. 1. 3 (349) and *Cod. Just.*, xi. 48. 7 (371).

[53] *Cod. Just.*, i. 12. 6 (466); *Acta Conciliorum Oecumenicorum*, ed. E. Schwartz, (Berlin and Leipzig, 1933), ii. 1, p. 353, para. 17. *Adscripticius* has been

was never used by the Western chancellery, which preferred the words *originales* or *originarii*,[54] belonging by birth or descent to the land. The two expressions came to the same thing in fact, for the census registered a man in the place where he belonged by birth. Both conceptions are sometimes combined in a single sentence. The law of Valens cited above[55] speaks of '*coloni originales* who are registered in the same places', and in a law of Valentinian I[56] *coloni* and *inquilini* are ordered to return 'to their old homes where they are registered and were born and bred'.

The Western terminology emphasizes the hereditary nature of the tie. It is evident from the census documents from western Asia Minor that from the outset registration had been conceived as hereditary. For although adults alone paid *capitatio* and were counted in the total of the village or estate, the detailed returns record children, even infants, with their ages.[57] It was evidently assumed that as they came of age they would come on to the register, filling the places of their elders as they died or reached the age of exemption. These young persons, from whom the number of the registered population was kept up, are alluded to in some laws as *adcrescentes*.[58]

The status of an *adscripticius* or *originalis* was thus hereditary: it was inherited from either parent.[59] The tie was legally unbreakable, until in 419 the rule of thirty years' prescription was applied to it, so that if a landlord made no claim on a *colonus* for that period, he forfeited his rights over him.[60] This rule was extended

interpolated by the Justinianic redactors in *Cod. Just.*, iii. 38. 11 (= *Cod. Theod.*, ii. 25. 1) and xi. 48. 6, and even in viii. 51. 1, of A.D. 224.

[54] *Cod. Just.*, xi. 68. 1 (325); 48, 7 (371); *Cod. Theod.*, x. 20. 10 (380); *Cod. Just.*, xi. 48. 11 (396); *Cod. Theod.*, v. 18. 1 (419); Valent., *Nov.*, xxvii (449), xxxi (451); xxxv (452); Majorian, *Nov.*, vii (458); *Edictum Theoderici*, xxi, xlviii, lvi, lxiii–lxviii, lxxx.

[55] *Cod. Theod.*, xi. 1. 14.

[56] *Cod. Just.*, xi. 48. 6.

[57] A. H. M. Jones, *JRS*, xliii (1953), pp. 53, 55–6, cf. 51, note 12.

[58] *Cod. Theod.*, vii. 13. 6. 1 (370), 'vel adfixos censibus vel [de] adcrescentibus suis obtulerint iuniores'; 13. 7. 3 (375), 'ex incensitis atque adcrescentibus in eorum locum, qui defensi militia fuerint, alios praecipimus subrogari'.

[59] *Cod. Just.*, xi. 48. 16 (419), 21 (Justinian), for maternal descent. In law 24 Justinian altered the rule for paternal descent; Just., *Nov.*, liv, records the old rule.

[60] *Cod. Theod.*, v. 18. 1. The rule had been applied earlier in special cases, *Cod. Theod.*, xii. 19. 2 and 3.

by Valentinian III in 449 even to *coloni* of the crown, whose rights were normally imprescriptable. The reason he gives is interesting: high ranking civil servants were being exposed to vexatious claims that their parents or more distant forbears had been *originales*.[61] Two years later Valentinian III found the rule of thirty years' prescription was being abused by *originales* who fled from their masters to become the free tenants of other landlords. He accordingly ruled that an *originalis* who freed himself from his old landlord by thirty years' absence should become the *originalis* of his new landlord, or if he cunningly moved from farm to farm, of the landlord whom he had served for the longest period, or for the last part of the thirty years.[62] Valentinian III's legislation applied only to the Western empire. In the East the rule of thirty years' prescription survived until Justinian first restricted and then abolished it.[63] Henceforth an *adscripticius* could legally free himself only by becoming a bishop.[64]

While the hereditary character of the status meant that the descendants of an *adscripticius* or *originalis colonus* could never legally (except in so far as prescription operated) free himself, it also meant that no one not of that status by birth could be made an *adscripticius* or *originalis*. The exceptions are negligible. Sometimes barbarian prisoners of war, like the Scirae, were given to landlords as tied *coloni*:[65] sturdy beggars could be claimed as such by those who denounced them.[66] In these circumstances it is probable that the number of *adscripticii* tended to dwindle. The constant repetition of the laws against receiving runaway *coloni* shows that in fact many did leave their farms and establish themselves as free tenants elsewhere. This might well happen with the tacit consent of their landlords. It was not to the interest of a landlord to have more *coloni* than were needed to cultivate his estate, and he would not mind if younger sons went elsewhere to seek their fortunes. Justinian envisages the case where a landlord, satisfied that one of his farms is duly cultivated by a *colonus*, allows his son to leave, and when the *colonus* dies or gets past work, finds

[61] Valent., *Nov.*, xxvii.
[62] Valent., *Nov.*, xxxi.
[63] *Cod. Just.*, xi. 48. 22. 3–5 and 23 pr.
[64] Just., *Nov.*, cxxiii. 4.
[65] *Cod. Theod.*, v. 6. 3 (409).
[66] *Cod. Theod.*, xiv. 18. 1 (382).

that his claim upon the son is barred by thirty years' prescription.[67] *Adscripticii* surplus to the needs of an estate thus tended to join the ranks of free tenants. On the other hand when the number of *adscripticii* for any reason fell below the number required, unless the landlord could fill the gaps from *adscripticii* from other estates which he owned,[68] he had to take on free tenants.

It was presumably in the interests of landlords who had such tenants that Anastasius applied the rule of thirty years' prescription in the opposite direction, enacting that a free tenant who stayed for thirty years should be tied to his farm;[69] Justinian interpreted this rule as tying his children even if they had not lived the full period on the estate.[70] Such tenants were not, however, *adscripticii*, being able to dispose of their own property freely and bring actions against their landlords and in general free from all the disabilities of adscript status except the prohibition to move.[71] Under a law of Justinian they were even entitled to move if they acquired a farm of their own sufficient to support them and requiring their full-time attention.[72]

Justinian, arguing that *adscripticii* were virtually slaves, applied to mixed marriages between them and free persons the rules of law which governed the status of the offspring of free persons and slaves. The principal innovation which followed was that the children of an *adscripticius* and a free woman were no longer *adscripticii*: for it was a basic maxim of Roman law that the offspring of a 'free womb' was free, and the status of an *adscripticius* was now reckoned as servile.[73] Justinian appears to have made this

---

[67] *Cod. Just.*, xi. 48. 22. 3.

[68] *Cod. Just.*, xi. 48. 13 (400).

[69] *Cod. Just.*, xi. 48. 19. Salvian, *de Gub. Dei*, v. 43–7, declares that, in his day (the mid-fifth century) in the West, vagrants who settled on the estates of the rich lost their liberty and became *inquilini*, either it would seem by declaring themselves such (44, 'iugo se inquilinae abiectionis addicunt') or by prescription (45, 'fiunt praeiudicio habitationis indigenae'). They even, he declares, became slaves (45–6). These processes were probably illegal (the second certainly was). Valent., *Nov.*, xxxi. 5, shows clearly that a stranger who settled on an estate (unless he were by birth a *colonus originalis* from elsewhere) could move on when he liked.

[70] *Cod. Just.*, xi. 48. 23. 1.

[71] *Cod. Just.*, xi. 48. 19 and 23. 1–3; Just., *Nov.*, clxii. 2.

[72] Just., *Nov.*, clxii. 2.

[73] *Cod. Just.*, xi. 48. 24.

ruling from mere legal purism. It was greeted by storms of protest from landlords, who complained that their estates were being deserted wholesale by tenants who claimed under the new law to be free. Justinian had hastily to enact that the rule was not retrospective, applying only to children born after the law,[74] and to enact furthermore that children who benefited from the law, though not *adscripticii*, were bound by Anastasius' law (as interpreted by himself) to remain on their farms as free persons:[75] the second of these laws was directed to the praetorian prefect of Illyricum, where protests had been most vehement. Despite these laws unrest continued, and the landowners of Africa on Justinian's death anxiously petitioned his successor Justin II for their confirmation, and on his death again petitioned his successor Tiberius Constantine to the same effect.[76]

The story shows that mixed marriages between *adscripticii* and free women, the daughters of free *coloni* or of peasant proprietors must have been very common. It follows that peasant proprietors must still have survived in substantial numbers, or that free tenants must have become numerous on the great estates.

The tied colonate was then, I would argue, originally the by-product of a measure, probably enacted by Diocletian, and mainly dictated by fiscal motives, binding all the rural population to their places of registration in the census. This measure was, owing to the general shortage of agricultural labour, found very useful by landowners who wished to hold their tenants, and was in their interest maintained by the imperial government for *coloni*, though allowed to lapse in so far as it affected freeholders, and extended to *coloni* in provinces where for technical reasons it had not hitherto tied them to their farms. The status of tied *coloni* was gradually degraded, until they were scarcely distinguishable from agricultural slaves. Not all *coloni*, however, were tied, but only those descended from resident tenants originally registered on their farms. These tended with the passage of time to diminish in

---

[74] Just., *Nov.*, liv pr. and 1 (537).

[75] Just., *Nov.*, clxii. 2 (539). Six months later, in another law (Just., *Nov. App.*, i) addressed to the prefect of Illyricum, Justinian reversed his ruling altogether, but this measure must have been soon revoked, for the rule of *Nov.*, clxii. 2 is cited as a precedent in later African laws (see next note).

[76] Just. II, *Nov.*, vi; Tib. Const., *Nov.* xiii, both in C. E. Zachariae von Lingenthal, *Ius Graeco-Romanum* (Leipzig, 1857), iii.

number and to be replaced by free tenants. These, too, if they remained on one farm for over thirty years, were tied to it by a law of Anastasius, but did not incur the other disabilities of tied *coloni*. This measure was according to its author designed for the benefit both of landlords and tenants, but was clearly more in the interests of the former, who still feared that their estates would be drained of agricultural labour unless they had a better hold on their tenants. Their fears were justified, as the reaction to Justinian's legislation proved. Shortage of agricultural manpower evidently still remained acute in the sixth century, and was the basic cause for maintaining the tied colonate.

XIV
PEASANT REVOLTS IN LATE ROMAN GAUL AND SPAIN*

E. A. Thompson

Many theories have been put forward to account for the fall of the Western Roman Empire, but not all of them have allowed sufficient importance to the prolonged series of revolts which broke out in late Roman times in the countryside of Gaul and Spain, as well as in other regions of the Empire. Our sources seem to suggest that these revolts were due primarily to the agricultural slaves, or at any rate that slaves played a prominent part in them.[1] But the slaves certainly did not fight alone. They won allies from other sections of society including the middle classes—we even hear of a physician joining in their movement—so that if we refer to these risings as 'peasant' revolts we must recognize that we are using the word 'peasant' only for want of a better term.[2] The rebels themselves in Gaul and Spain took on the name of *Bacaudae*—there is little MS. evidence for the form *Bagaudae*—which first makes its appearance in connection with one of their risings late in

* From no. 2 (1952).

[1] *Chron. Min.*, I, p. 660, 'Gallia ulterior Tibattonem principem rebellionis secuta a Romana societate discessit, a quo tracto initio omnia paene Galliarum servitia in Bacaudam conspiravere,' Rutilius Namatianus, quoted below, n. 51. From the third century A.D. onwards it is increasingly difficult to distinguish between rural slaves and rural serfs; both tended to be included in words like 'servus,' 'servitia,' in contrast to 'ingenuus,' free born, while 'rusticus' and related words included poor 'servi' and 'ingenui' in contrast either to well to do 'nobles' or to town dwellers, or both.

[2] For non-servile support see Salvian, v. 21, *Chron. Min.*, I, p. 662 'Eudoxius, arte medicus, pravi sed exercitati ingenii, in Bacauda id temporis mota delatus ad Chunos confugit.'

the third century and which soon came to be used by those against whom the peasants revolted.[3]

I am not competent to discuss the precise methods of exploitation or to say exactly what turn of precisely which screw drove the peasant at last to throw down his plough in despair and run to the greenwood. But it may be worth while to collect the evidence relating to (a) the extent both in time and in space of the peasant movements of Gaul and Spain, (b) the organization and tactics of the Bacaudae, and (c) the aims of their movement.

The exploits, to say nothing of the aims and organization, of the Bacaudae are passed over almost in silence by writers of the time when they were active. All our authorities belonged to a greater or lesser extent to the propertied classes of the Empire, and therefore to a greater or lesser degree had reason to dread the Bacaudae. When it is dangerously threatened, a propertied class will often conceal (if it can), and even deny, the very existence of those who seek to overthrow it. That is why a panegyrist of the Emperor Maximian, whose victory over the Bacaudae in 286 he could not omit to mention altogether—for it was the first and in some ways the most striking of that Emperor's victories—contents himself with hinting briefly at the character of the Emperor's foes, and then hastens to add: 'I pass this by hurriedly, for I see that such is your *pietas* you would prefer that that victory were forgotten rather than glorified.' And a few moments later he does not venture even thus far, but dismisses the whole topic in a brief sentence which is innocent of any explicit mention of the hated Bacaudae: 'I omit your innumerable battles and victories throughout the whole of Gaul' in which his enemies had been Roman

[3] Eutropius, ix. 20 'ita rerum Romanarum potitus [sc. Diocletianus], cum tumultum rusticani in Gallia concitassent et factioni suae Bacaudarum nomen imponerent, duces autem haberent Amandum et Aelianum, ad subigendos eos Maximianum Herculium Caesarem misit, qui levibus proeliis agrestes domuit et pacem Galliae reformavit,' Aurelius Victor, *Caes.*, xxxix. 17 'namque ubi comperit [Diocletianus] Carini discessu Helianum Amandumque per Galliam excita manu agrestium ac latronum, quos Bagaudas incolae vocant, populatis late agris plerasque urbium tentare' etc., Jerome, *Chronica*, a. 2303, Orosius, vii. 25. 2 'dehinc cum in Gallia Amandus et Aelianus collecta rusticanorum manu, quos Bacaudas vocabant, perniciosos tumultus excitavissent,' etc. In *Chron. Min.* loc. cit. *Bacauda* means not a peasant who took part in the movement but the movement itself. There is no agreement on the etymology of the word.

peasants.[4] This practice of suppressing mention of the Bacaudae is repeated by an otherwise scrupulous fourth-century historian who never tires of assuring his readers that to falsify history is no more criminal than to omit mention of important events.[5] As for the rebels' aims it is an exasperating but a far from unexpected fact that in the literature of western Europe in the third, fourth, and fifth centuries only a single sentence, a line of unpoetical poetry, a mere pentameter tells us of these.[6] It seems fair to conclude then that the revolts of the peasantry were considerably more frequent and extensive than our authorities' explicit references to them would suggest. And although the word Bacaudae was not used until late in the third century the phenomenon which it denoted had forced itself upon the attention of historians a century earlier.

The first great Gallic and Spanish revolt of the type that interests us occurred late in the second century A.D., when the calamitous wars of Marcus Aurelius and the interminable plague were followed by the civil wars of Septimius Severus and his rivals. It is likely that the great landowners did what they could to pass the colossal burdens created by these disasters on to the shoulders of the poorer classes. And the massive reaction of the oppressed began in the eighties of the second century. The revolt of Maternus is in its magnitude and doubtless in its purpose, too, without a parallel in the earlier history of the Empire.[7]

Maternus was a soldier with many brave deeds to his name who deserted the army about the year 186 and persuaded some of his fellow-soldiers to do the same. 'In a short time,' writes our main authority for his career, 'he gathered together a numerous band of rascals, and at first he overran villages and estates, and plundered them; but when he was master of great wealth he collected a more numerous throng of rascals with promises of large gifts and a

---

[4] *Paneg. Lat.*, x (ii). 4. 4 'quod ego cursim praetereo: video enim te, qua pietate es, oblivionem illius victoriae malle quam gloriam', 6. 1 'transeo innumerabiles tuas tota Gallia pugnas atque victorias.'

[5] Amm. Marc. cited p. 315 below. Sidonius does not use the word *Bacauda* at all.

[6] Rutilius cited below n. 51.

[7] On Maternus see Herodian, i. 10. 3, cf. 11. 5, SHA, *Pesc. Nig.*, iii. 3 f. For the view that Thermae near Yonne may have been destroyed by his men see *REA*, xli (1939), p. 1943.

share of what was taken, so that they no longer had the status of brigands but of enemies. For they now proceeded to attack the largest cities, and forcing open the prisons they set free those who had been confined in them, no matter what they had been charged with, promised them impunity, and by good treatment won them over to join them. They overran the whole land of the Gauls and the Spaniards, attacking the largest cities, burning parts of them and plundering the rest before retiring.'

Maternus had only to raise the standard of revolt to be joined by 'a numerous band of rascals.' There were evidently oppressed and expropriated men willing to resort to violence in many parts of the West—Marcus Aurelius himself had been reduced to enrolling 'the bandits of Dalmatia and Dardania'[8] into his armies in a period of desperate crisis in his struggle with the barbarians—and when Maternus had put his operations under way he could draw upon a vast supply of (as we must suppose) runaway slaves, coloni, ruined farmers, deserters from the army, and so on. Another authority reports that during Maternus' revolt 'innumerable deserters were harassing the Gallic provinces'; and he calls Maternus' revolt 'the War of the Deserters,' to herald which 'the heavens burst into flame.'[9]

But the movement was clearly much more than an affair of army deserters, though these no doubt provided the leadership. Quite apart from Herodian's description of those who took part in it, its very scale indicates that it was a dangerous uprising of the submerged classes of Gaul and Spain: it was the overture to the Bacaudae.[10] Such a movement cannot be explained merely by the desire of a group of poor and desolate soldiers to enrich themselves by thieving and highway robbery; and Herodian does not try to explain it so. This was an organization which operated from Gallia Lugdunensis down to Spain for a number of years; and, as an eminent Roman jurist points out, 'brigands' cannot escape destruction for long unless they have support from the population among which they are active.[11] Moreover, they were so powerful

[8] SHA, *Marcus*, xxi. 7.

[9] *Ibid.*, *Pesc. Nig.*, iii. 4, *Commod.*, xvi. 2.

[10] A. D. Dmitrev, 'Dvizhenie Bagaudov', *Vestnik Drevnei Istorii*, 1940, iii–iv, pp. 101–14, first showed the significance of Maternus and his followers.

[11] Ulpian, *Dig.*, i. 18. 13 *pr.*

that they could attack 'the largest cities' with success. Even the efficient and ruthless Septimius Severus, who was then Governor of Gallia Lugdunensis, was unable to suppress them. The central government had to be called in, and it found itself obliged to send an army into central and southern Gaul.

The great areas of the provinces which came under the control of Maternus' men can scarcely be regarded simply as areas of mass brigandage. Many estates must have fallen into Maternus' power, and it is difficult to believe that the estate owners were left in undisturbed possession of their lands and that they continued in tranquillity to exploit the labour of such slaves and other workers as had not already joined Maternus' bands. We have no direct evidence of what happened to the landowners, but it may be that they were expropriated of their land and possibly themselves enslaved: at any rate, that is what seems to have happened to them during the Bacaudic revolts of a later time.

However that may be, when the central government's army was sent to Lugdunensis, Maternus' men, or some of them, retired from the scene of their activities, but only to carry out what was at once their most dramatic enterprise and the immediate cause of their downfall. In small groups they began to infiltrate into Italy and Rome, like Romulus and his shepherds long ago, determined to assassinate the Emperor Commodus as he took part in a festival to the Mother of the Gods and to make Maternus Emperor in his place. The programme itself suggests that Maternus and his followers were not themselves the representatives or forerunners of any future form of society: their ideas included no new mode of social existence. Their purpose was merely to replace one Emperor by another, albeit one of their own. 'Anarchistic' methods of personal terrorism together with strong personal ambitions emerged, and, as has happened frequently under similar circumstances, the disintegration of the band was not far away. Maternus' successes and ambitions had caused him to lose touch with the feelings of his followers, and he was betrayed by some of his companions who were content to be led by a brigand but not by a 'master and an Emperor.' Maternus was caught and beheaded; but the movement which he had led was by no means at an end. Nearly twenty years later a general was obliged to operate in Gaul with detachments of no less than four legions against 'dissidents and rebels,' doubtless much the same types of person as had been active under Maternus himself; and it is not claimed that the government forces won shattering victories.[12]

For Herodian, Maternus was a mere deserter, though a troublesome one, and his followers a band of thugs and terrorists. In fact, however, they look more like a powerful army, a combination of soldiers, peasants, and others, whose history was the first act in the long tale of the Bacaudae. The character of their movement must be sharply distinguished from the mere routine brigandage which could be found in all corners of the Empire at that time, and the suppression of which was part of the day-to-day duties of the armed forces of the government;[13] for the ordinary brigands were scarcely concerned to win control of large tracts of the provinces and to expropriate the landowners. It will be convenient for purposes of contrast with Maternus to linger over one of these bands of brigands, the only one of which some detailed information has survived: it caught the attention of an historian because it operated successfully outside the very gates of Rome and in the heart of Italy itself. This is the company of Bulla, *alias* Felix.[14]

Bulla was an Italian who with some 600 companions 'plundered Italy' for a couple of years at the beginning of the third century, and nothing that the Emperor and his armies could do would bring him to a halt. He had a magnificent intelligence system centred outside Rome and Brundisium, and he was supported by members of the local population (either because he bribed them astutely, as our authority suggests, or because they sympathized with his practices). In the case of most of his victims he took only a part of their property and then let them go at once. But when he caught artisans or craftsmen he took nothing at all, but made use of their skill for a time and paid them fairly before setting them free. His exploits, as related by a Roman senator, who speaks of him with a tolerance which he would never have shown to the Bacaudae, were nothing if not audacious. Septimius Severus, when

---

[12] Dessau, 1153. Presumably they were reinforced by the remnants of Clodius Albinus' army. For a usurper's army taking to brigandage after his defeat, see Libanius, *Or.*, xviii. 104 (Magnentius).

[13] S. N. Miller, *CAH*, xii, pp. 21 f., gives some references to brigandage at this date. A noteworthy success of the brigands of the Julian Alps is recorded in Dessau, 2646.

[14] On Bulla see Dio Cassius, lxxvi. 10, cf. Zonaras, xii. 10 (iii, pp. 104 f., Dindorf).

he was told of Bulla's *coups*, complained that while his generals could win wars in Britain he was himself no match for a brigand in Italy—ominous words for the Roman propertied classes if the brigand should rise above mere brigandage. But Bulla's successes are insignificant in comparison with his remark to a centurion whom he captured and later set free, a remark in which he explained the basic cause of brigandage in all times and places: 'Tell your masters that if they would put a stop to brigandage *they must feed their slaves.*'

In the end Bulla was betrayed by his mistress, and after his arrest the City Prefect interviewed him and asked: 'Why did you become a robber?' To which Bulla *alias* Felix replied: 'Why are you Prefect?' He was promptly thrown to the wild animals in the arena, and these satisfactorily completed the task of restoring law and order.

If it is agreed that Maternus had expropriated the great estate owners—and it would be strange indeed if the estates were left entirely untouched by such men as his—then it would seem to follow that Bulla's movement was different in kind from that of Maternus. It certainly differed in scale, for at one period a centurion with a company of soldiers was considered sufficient to hunt Bulla down, whereas an entire army was concentrated against Maternus. And while Bulla was a mere kindly robber, a homely Robin Hood, Maternus appears so to have caught the spirit of the Gallic and Spanish peasantry that he could attack cities and estates alike. The difference between Bulla and Maternus, it seems, is the difference between robbery and something like revolution.

What is of the greatest importance for us to notice is that in this 'Golden Age,' this 'Indian Summer' of the Empire, when some Romans were escaping from the oppression of Roman life by joining Maternus, others were doing so in another way—by deserting to the barbarians. And again and again in their treaties with the northern barbarians, we find the late second-century Emperors demanding the return of these 'deserters.' This, too, indicates the shape of that which was to come.[15]

To conclude this sketch of the pre-history, as we might call it, of the Bacaudae, it may be pointed out that not all 'brigands' remained poor and honest men throughout their days. It is said of

[15] Dio Cassius, lxxi. 11. 2, 4, 20. 1, lxxii. 2. 2, cf. for Trajan's time, Dio Cassius, lxviii. 9. 5, 10. 3, Peter the Patrician, *frag.* 5.

a late third-century usurper that, starting life as a brigand, he was none the less a nobleman in his homeland (the Maritime Alps) but sprung from ancestors who had been brigands like himself; and *consequently* he was very rich in cattle, slaves, and whatever else they had carried off. As a result, at the time when he seized the Imperial power, he was able to arm no less than 2,000 slaves of his own to help him in his venture.[16]

It was *circa* 283–4 that the Bacaudae made their first appearance under that name. The calamities of the mid-third century had fallen most heavily upon the poorest classes; and our authorities hint as briefly and as reluctantly as can be at the ferocity of the Gallic peasants' reply to their oppressors.[17] The Emperor Carinus, hotly engaged with the barbarians elsewhere, could do nothing against them; and it was not until 286 that the new Emperor Diocletian found himself obliged to appoint Maximian as co-ruler in the West with the specific task of crushing the Bacaudae.[18] In this task Maximian was successful, at any rate for a time, although it seems that he drew upon Eastern troops before he completed his victory; and there is a famous tradition that these troops mutinied sooner than fight the Bacaudae, and had to be slaughtered by Maximian.[19] Indeed, at a later time some persons appear to have had even more ambiguous relations with the 'brigands.' It was not at all uncommon in late Roman times for officers in the Imperial armies to reach a compact with the barbarians beyond the frontier: for example, they would allow plundering parties to enter and leave Roman territory in return for a share in the booty

[16] SHA, *Proculus*, xii. 1–2, 5. Sources for peasant movements (as for nearly everything else) in the middle of the third-century are, of course, wanting; but that such movements in fact existed is proved by the increasingly repressive measures taken by the government: see M. Rostovtzeff, *Social and Economic History of the Roman Empire* (Oxford, 1926), p. 620.

[17] *Paneg. Lat.*, vii (vi). 8. 3 'Gallias priorum temporum iniuriis efferatas,' xi (iii). 5. 3 'exacerbatas saeculi prioris iniuriis . . . provincias.'

[18] See the passages of Eutropius, Victor, and Orosius partly quoted in n. 3 above.

[19] See a judicious discussion of the story of the Theban legion by C. Jullian, 'Notes Gallo-romaines,' *REA*, xxii (1920), pp. 41–7; but his view (p. 45, n. 1) that the troops may have refused to fight 'par amour propre de métier', because the Bacaudae were considered 'non comme des ennemis honorables, mais un ramas de brigands', is singularly improbable.

taken from the unfortunate provincials.[20] There was no reason in the world why such men should not work hand in glove with the Bacaudae as eagerly as they did with the barbarians, if it suited their interests to do so; and some lines of the poet Ausonius suggest that they did not let their opportunities slip by unused.[21]

The chief scene of the activities of the Bacaudae in Gaul was the *tractus Armoricanus*,[22] an area which seems to have extended from at least the mouth of the Loire to that of the Seine. It was in this area that the great revolt of 407 broke out—the largest and most successful Bacaudic revolt known to us, for it was not crushed until 417. It was here, too, that Tibatto led the rebellion of 435-7 and again that of 442.[23] But Bacaudae were also active among the Alps early in the fifth century,[24] and doubtless if our sources were more forthcoming we should find them at least locally throughout much of Gaul.[25] In Spain in the mid-fifth century Bacaudae were in arms in Tarraconensis, where they were so strong that no less a personage than the Master of Both Services, Flavius Asturius, had to travel to Spain to take the field against them in 441. He slew 'a multitude of the Bacaudae of Tarraconensis,' we are told,[26] but evidently he did not slay enough (from his own point of view), for his successor and son-in-law had to continue the work of 'main-

[20] *CTh.*, vii. 1. 1, cf. Amm. Marc., xxviii. 3. 8, xxx. 5. 3, etc.

[21] Auson., *Epist.*, xiv. 22–7, speculates on the improbable but not impossible activities of Theon at Médoc: 'An maiora gerens tota regione vagantes Persequeris fures, qui te postrema timentes In partem praedamque vocent? tu mitis et osor Sanguinis humani condonas crimina nummis Erroremque vocas pretiumque inponis abactis Bubus et in partem scelerum de iudice transis?'

[22] Zosimus, vi. 5. 3, Rutilius, i. 213, Sidonius, *carm.*, vii. 247, Merobaudes, *Paneg.*, ii. 8, John of Antioch, *frag.* 201. 3.

[23] For that of 407–17 see Zosimus, vi. 5. 3, Rutilius, *loc. cit.*, and for those of Tibatto see *Chron. Min.*, p. 660, s. a. 435 (quoted in n. 1 above), and s. a. 437 'capto Tibattone et ceteris seditionis partim principibus vinctis, partim necatis Bacaudarum commotio conquiescit', Constantius, *Vita Germani*, xxviii, xl, John of Antioch, *loc cit.*

[24] Zosimus, vi. 2. 5, cf. Sulpicius Severus, *Vit. Martin.* v. 4–6. At Noyon in Germania Superior there was a municipal officer called *praefectus arcendis latrociniis*, *CIL*, xiii. 5010, where another example is cited from Dhaun: cf. the Greek ληστοδιώκτης, 'brigand-chaser.'

[25] Amm. Marc., quoted p. 315 below, Ausonius, *loc. cit.*

[26] Hydatius, s. a. 441 (*Chron. Min.*, ii, p. 24) 'Asturius dux utriusque militiae ad Hispanias missus Tarraconensium caedit multitudinem Bacaudarum.'

taining order'. This was the poet Merobaudes 'who in the short time of his command broke the insolence of the Bacaudae of Aracelli' in 443.[27] But even then they were as active as ever about half-a-dozen years later, if not before. For in 449 one Basilius collected the Bacaudae of the neighbourhood, entered Turiasso, and killed the bishop Leo in his church;[28] and in 454 the Romans set some Visigoths upon the Bacaudae of Tarraconensis.[29] The two places with which they are specifically associated, Turiasso and Aracelli, lie in the uplands near the head of the Ebro valley; but *circa* 456 they are also found far away in the distant north-west of the peninsula in the neighbourhood of Bracara, where they were sufficiently active to find a mention in one of our meagre chronicles.[30] Bearing in mind how scanty are our authorities for fifth-century history and how reluctant they are to record the struggles of the oppressed classes, we need have little doubt that Spain and Gaul swarmed with peasants in open revolt as Western Imperial history drew towards its close.

The great bulk of the Bacaudae being 'yokels,' 'rustics,' 'ignorant farmers,' as our authorities call them,[31] their armies were peasant armies in which ploughmen made up the infantry and shepherds the cavalry.[32] As for their strategy, it closely resembled, if it was not actually modelled upon, the strategy of the barbarian invaders of the Empire:[33] and the Roman army reforms of the later

27 *Idem*, s. a. 443 '. . . brevi tempore potestatis suae Aracellitanorum frangit insolentiam Bacaudarum.'

28 *Idem*, s. a. 449 'Basilius ob testimonium egregii ausus sui congregatis Bacaudis in ecclesia Tyriassone foederatos occidit. ubi et Leo eiusdem ecclesiae episcopus ab isdem, qui cum Basilio aderant, in eo loco obiit vulneratus.'

29 *Idem*, s. a. 454 'per Fredericum Theuderici regis fratrem Bacaudae Tarraconenses caeduntur ex auctoritate Romana.'

30 *Idem*, s. a. 456 ? (p. 29) 'in conventus parte Bracarensis latrocinantum deopraedatio perpetratur.' Salvian says (*de Gub. Dei*, v. 23): 'hi qui ad barbaros non confugiunt barbari tamen esse coguntur, scilicet ut est pars magna Hispanorum et non minima Gallorum, omnes denique quos per universum Romanum orbem fecit Romana iniquitas iam non esse Romanos.'

31 Eutropius, ix. 25. 3 *agrestes*, Victor, *Caes.*, xxxix. 17 *agrestium ac latronum*, Orosius, vii. 25. 2 *rusticanorum*, *Paneg. Lat.*, x (ii). 4. 3 *ignari agricolae*.

32 *Paneg. Lat.*, *loc. cit.* 'cum militaris habitus ignari agricolae appetiverunt, cum arator peditem, cum pastor equitem, cum hostem barbarum suorum cultorum rusticus vastator imitatus est.'

33 *Ibid.*, C. Jullian, *Histoire de la Gaule*, vii, p. 54.

Empire must have been no less effective against the rebellious peasants of the provinces than they were against the barbarians— they may well have been brought into operation in the first place to deal with the former as much as with the latter. At any rate, the character of this strategy, which was common to Bacauda and barbarian alike, is revealed by the history of many a barbarian raid: the raiders would split up into a number of small bands, which were more easily fed than one large host, and would carry on a war of ambuscades, surprises, feints, diversions, and skirmishes rather than of set battles. Maximian's campaign of 286 was of precisely the same kind: we hear of skirmishes and 'innumerable engagements and victories,' which led to the destruction of some of the Bacaudae and to the surrender of others.[34] It is no mean tribute to the generalship of Maximian that he was able to 'restore order' in Gaul in the course of a single summer. Perhaps he divided up the area into military sectors, separated the various groups of the Bacaudae from one another, isolated them, and dealt with them one by one;[35] and in comparison with Maximian's experience and skill the 'rustics' are said to have been confused and clumsy.[36] After his victory he was constrained to show a mercifulness which he cannot have greatly relished:[37] for to kill a Bacauda was to deprive an estate owner of one of his scanty force of labourers. Perhaps the peace which Maximian restored to Gaul in 286 could well be described in the words with which a seventh-century bishop concludes his account of the crushing of a revolt in Egypt by the forces of the Emperor Maurice: 'And great fear prevailed over all the land of Egypt, and its inhabitants dwelt in the enjoyment of tranquillity and peace.'[38]

[34] *Paneg. Lat.*, x (ii). 6. 1, cited in n. 4 above, Eutropius, ix. 20. 3, quoted in n. 3 above, cf. Victor, *Caes.*, xxxix. 19 'sed Herculius [i.e. Maximian] in Galliam profectus fusis hostibus aut acceptis quieta omnia brevi patraverat.' But the extensive and mobile character of the operations of the Bacaudae availed them little against the Huns of Litorius in 437, for Huns were even more mobile than they. In Constantius, *Vita Germani*, xxvii, the 'eques ferratus' of the Alans, another nomadic pastoral people, was about to engage the Bacaudae in 448 when St Germanus intervened.

[35] So Jullian, *loc. cit.*

[36] Orosius, vii. 25. 2 'qui [= Maximian] facile agrestium hominum imperitiam et confusam manum militari virtute conposuit.'

[37] *Paneg. Lat.*, x (ii). 4. 3, xi (iii). 5. 3.

[38] John of Nikiu, xcvii. 29 (p. 160, ed. R. H. Charles).

A similar strategy seems to have been employed against Valentinian I (364–75) in the early years of his reign, when, according to Ammianus, 'many other battles (i.e. other than those fought against the barbarians) less worthy of description were fought throughout various regions of Gaul, which it is superfluous to narrate both because their outcome resulted in nothing worth speaking of (would he have said that if Valentinian had in fact succeeded in crushing the peasants?) and because it is unbecoming to prolong a History with ignoble details.'[39] In addition, the planting of ambushes along the roads of Spain and Gaul could be highly profitable, and on one occasion a brother-in-law of Valentinian was caught and killed in one of their ambuscades.[40] But this sort of activity could scarcely impair the position of the landowning class as a whole; and the main activity of the Bacaudae doubtless lay in their attacks on the great estates and even on the cities, though the mere destruction of Gallic cities interested them less than has been supposed.[41] Probably as a rule they tended simply to raid the cities in search of such commodities as they could not produce themselves in the countryside. After such an exploit they would retire to the forests with the booty they had taken,[42] and resume their life there under their 'woodland laws,' to which we shall now turn.

When Maximian arrived in Gaul in 286 he found that the Bacaudae had set up two commanders of their own named Aelianus and Amandus, who may have had successors in the fourth century.[43] There is no reason for calling these men 'Em-

---

[39] Amm. Marc., xxvii. 2. 11, cf. xxviii. 2. 11 ff., Anon, *de rebus bellicis* ii. 3 'nam saepe gravissimis damnis affedit [sc. afflicta paupertas] imperia populando agros, quietem latrociniis persequendo, inflammando odia, et per gradus criminum fovit tyrannos quos ad gloriam virtutis tuae [probably Valens or Valentinian] produxit magis quam succendit audacia.'

[40] Amm. Marc., xxviii. 2. 10.

[41] Victor, quoted in n. 3 above. It is significant that for some hundreds of years editors have foisted on to the Bacaudae the senseless destruction of Autun in 269–70, although the MSS. of Eumenius, iv. 1, give *Batavicae* and not *Bagaudicae*, which is a conjecture of Lipsius: see P. le Gentilhomme, 'Le désastre d'Autun en 269', *REA*, xlv (1943), pp. 233–40.

[42] Merobaudes, *Paneg.*, ii. 9 f. 'adsuetaque saevo Crimine quaesitas silvis celare rapinas', etc.

[43] Eutropius and Victor quoted in n. 3 above, Zonaras, xii. 31, E. A.

perors': our authorities simply say that the Bacaudae were 'led' by them or that it was they who 'stirred up' the trouble, and they supply no reason for supposing that the organization of the Bacaudae was in this respect a mere replica of the Empire from which they proposed to liberate themselves. In the thirties and forties of the fifth century, when a certain Tibatto led them, no title is given to him in our scanty sources; and his subordinate commanders are termed *principes*, a word that tells us little.[44] What is certain is that the Bacaudae intended to detach themselves altogether from the Roman Empire and set up an independent State of their own.[45]

The only extant passage dealing with the peace-time life of the Bacaudae is very difficult to elucidate, for the writer of it assumes that his readers are already familiar with the Bacaudae. It occurs in a comedy called *Querolus*,[46] which has survived, as it seems, from the early fifth century. Querolus is asking the Lar of his household to give him a place in life which will make him happy, but he cannot decide what that place ought to be. The Lar puts forward various proposals, and one of them, suggested to him by the word *latrocinium*, 'brigandage,' is this:—

LAR: Now I've got it: you as good as have what you are praying for. Go and live beside the Loire.
QUEROLUS: What then?

Thompson, *A Roman Reformer and Inventor* (Oxford, 1952), pp. 33 f., on *de rebus bellicis, loc. cit.*

[44] *Chron. Min.*, i, p. 660. quoted in nn. 1 and 23 above, cf. Constantius, *Vita Germani* xl.

[45] *Chron. Min.*, i, p. 660, quoted in n. 1 above, John of Antioch, *loc. cit.*

[46] Pp. 16 f., ed. R. Peiper (Teubner series). That the passage refers to the Bacaudae is the general and in my opinion the correct view: see e.g. L. Havet, edition (Paris, 1880), pp. 2, 4 n. 1, P. Thomas, 'Le *Querolus* et les justices de villages', *Mélanges Louis Havet* (Paris, 1909), pp. 531–5, Jullian, *Histoire*, viii, p. 176 n. 3, F. Lot, *La Gaule* (Paris, 1947), pp. 472 f., etc. But F. L. Ganshof, 'Note sur le sens de *Ligeris* au titre xlvii de la loi salique et dans le *Querolus*', *Historical Essays in Honour of James Tait* (Manchester, 1933), pp. 111–20, would make it refer to the Alans settled on the Loire by Aetius, while others make it refer to a Germanic people: but these views seem unconvincing and do not explain why the Germans or Alans should be described as *rustici*: see Thomas, art. cit. p. 534, n. 4. In his edition (Paris, 1937), L. Herrmann, p. xix, though seeing in the passage a reference to the Bacaudae, gratuitously assumes that they renounced Roman law only to copy Barbarian law.

LAR: Men live there under the natural law.[47] There's no trickery there. Capital sentences are pronounced there under an oak tree and are recorded on bones.[48] There even rustics perorate, and private individuals pronounce judgement. You can do anything you like there. If you were rich you will be called *patus*—that is how our Greece talks! O woods, O solitudes, who said that you were free? There are much more important things that I say nothing about; but this will be enough to be going on with.

QUEROLUS: I'm not a rich man, and I have no use for an oak. I don't want these woodland laws.

LAR: Well then, look for something milder and more honourable if you can't brawl.

Life along the Loire among the Bacaudae then is sometimes believed to be free in a sense in which Roman life is not free— '*ibi totum licet*'—and Salvian and others repeatedly speak of men escaping to freedom among the Bacaudae or the barbarians,[49] just as they had done in Maternus' day, but this belief the Lar wishes to laugh off as nonsensical: life is regimented on the Loire, too, and there the regimentation is imposed not by responsible judges and policemen but by 'rustics' and 'private persons,' who administer justice under the oak trees. There appears to be little trace of a State apparatus along the banks of the Loire. The word *patus*, at which the Lar sneers, is presumably Celtic;[50] but since its meaning is unknown it is difficult to guess what would have happened to you if you had been rich before coming among the Bacaudae. The point may be that a wealthy landowner, if he fell into the hands of the Bacaudae, would become the slave of his own slaves. For Rutilius Namatianus, to whom the *Querolus* is sometimes believed to be dedicated, says that this was the fate of the territorial magnates of Armorica in 407–17. Exuperantius, he says, was in

---

[47] *Iure gentium*, so translated by Havet, ed. p. 217, and Herrmann, ed. p. 12; *contra*, Ganshof, art. cit. p. 114.

[48] On the interpretation of this passage see P. Thomas, 'Observationes ad scriptores latinos', *Mnemosyne*, xlix (1921), pp. 1–75, at p. 65.

[49] Salvian, v. 22, 26 f., Orosius, vii. 41. 7, Zosimus, vi. 5. 3.

[50] If the reference is to the Bacaudae I do not see how this conclusion can well be avoided. For the suggestion that it is Greek (= *pachys*, 'rich') see Havet, p. 218 n. 1, Herrmann, pp. xxii, 93 n. 42. But who spoke Greek in the Armorican countryside?

417 teaching Armorica to love the recovery of peace—he had crushed the great rising which had broken out in 407—and had 'restored the laws and brought back liberty and does not allow the inhabitants to be slaves of their own slaves.'[51]

Those words are practically the sole evidence for the social aims of the Bacaudae, and they appear to mean that the Bacaudae had expropriated the landlords, and had made them toil in the fields which they had once owned. The laws and the liberty which Exuperantius brought back were the laws and liberty of the former landowning class which he restored for the time being to something like its old position. Rutilius' evidence is in some slight measure supported by the words of a somewhat later poet, Merobaudes by name, whom we have already met defeating the Bacaudae of Spain in 443. He says that after the suppression of the Bacaudic leader Tibatto in 437 'laws' were restored in Armorica, and the tillers of the soil no longer hid their criminal plunder in the woods. At any rate, the passage of the *Querolus* looks like a characteristic piece of distortion of a landlord-less society, with only a rudimentary State apparatus, written by a hostile writer. And although the Lar dismisses it as neither mild nor honourable we may suspect that justice was more equitable and mankind more merciful under the oaks of the Loire than in the Governor's dungeon and torture-chamber.

Whatever the frequency of peasant revolts during the third and fourth centuries, they reached such a climax in the first half of the fifth century as to be almost continuous. It would be strange indeed if this fact were considered to be of slight importance in the study of the fall of the Western Empire: Empires only fall because a sufficient number of people are sufficiently determined to make them fall, whether those people live inside or outside the frontier. But, on the other hand, the various revolts of the Gallic and Spanish peasantry, even when they were successful for years on end, released no new productive forces. If Aelianus and Amandus had been able to win permanent independence for Armorica, they would not have been able to introduce any fundamental change into the class structure of their society. They

---

[51] Rutilius, i. 213–6 'cuius Aremoricas pater Exuperantius oras Nunc postliminium pacis amare docet; Leges restituit libertatemque reducit Et servos famulis non sinit esse suis.' The landlords also claimed that their society was 'free'.

would merely have started afresh that process which had caused the ownership of vast areas of land to concentrate into a few hands and which had brought about in Roman society the very state of affairs against which they themselves had revolted in the first place. Indeed, even in the middle of the fifth century, an event is said to have occurred which, if it is a fact, would seem to suggest that a significant change had come over the relationship of the Armoricans with the outside world. In 451, when Aetius, the champion of the great landowners of Gaul, engaged Attila and the Huns in the battle of the Catalaunian Plains, he is said to have been assisted by the Armoricans. That these should have fought for their enemy is so surprising that some historians have been inclined to throw doubt on the authority who records it. But even if the story is false—and this is far indeed from being certain—the very fact that it could circulate at all is revealing.[52]

Aelianus and Amandus, then, if they had been successful, could have changed the personnel of the ruling classes in Armorica, but they could not have changed the nature of those classes themselves. But the significance of the rebellions should not on that account be underestimated. Although at the end of the process the class-structure of Armorican society might well have been the same as it had been at the beginning, the human beings who formed the various classes would have been very different. And that is precisely the result which the barbarian invaders of the West were able to bring about: they changed the personnel of the ruling classes. Now we have seen that so early as the time of Maternus many Romans of the poorer classes identified the rebels and the barbarians to the extent that they believed a freedom to exist among both which could not be found under the rule of the Imperial government. In Salvian's day men were going off indiscriminately to Goths or Bacaudae or 'other' barbarians: in respect of 'freedom,' at any rate, there was no difference between them.[53] Indeed, it is difficult to resist the impression that the barbarian invasions could scarcely have been carried out so successfully in

---

[52] Jordanes, *Get.*, xxxvi. 191. That the Armoricans fought for Aetius in 451 has been doubted e.g. by F. Lot, *Les invasions germaniques* (Paris, 1945), p. 108.

[53] Salvian, v. 22 'itaque passim vel ad Gothos vel ad Bacaudas vel ad alios ubique dominantes barbaros migrant, et commigrasse non paenitet', etc.

the fourth and fifth centuries had it not been for the help which the Roman peasantry and other oppressed classes among the Romans were able to give directly or indirectly to the newcomers. The significance of the peasant movements will only become fully apparent when they are studied in conjunction with the barbarian invasions.